YALE STUDIES IN POLITICAL SCIENCE, 24

THE BELIEFS OF POLITICIANS

Ideology, Conflict, and Democracy

in Britain and Italy

ROBERT D. PUTNAM

New Haven and London
Yale University Press
1973

Copyright © 1973 by Yale University.
All rights reserved. This book may not be
reproduced, in whole or in part, in any form
(except by reviewers for the public press),
without written permission from the publishers.
Library of Congress catalog card number: 72–75207
International standard book number: 0–300–01498–8

Designed by Sally Sullivan
and set in Times Roman type.
Printed in the United States of America by
The Murray Printing Co., Forge Village, Mass.

Published in Great Britain, Europe, and Africa by
Yale University Press, Ltd., London.
Distributed in Canada by McGill-Queen's University
Press, Montreal; in Latin America by Kaiman & Polon,
Inc., New York City; in Australasia and Southeast
Asia by John Wiley & Sons Australasia Pty. Ltd.,
Sydney; in India by UBS Publishers' Distributors Pvt.,
Ltd., Delhi; in Japan by John Weatherhill, Inc., Tokyo.

To the memory of

F. L. P.

who would have enjoyed listening with me

Contents

Tables

Figures

Acknowledgments

Although the title page does not say so, this book is a collaborative effort. For in a very real sense I have aimed to serve as scribe for the 176 "political philosophers" who spoke with me in London and Rome. These British and Italian politicians are no mere supporting cast—if proof be needed, their "lines" totaled more than six thousand transcript pages—and they deserve warm thanks and star billing.

In grappling with the perils of cross-national research I was exceedingly fortunate to have the guidance and assistance of two wise friends and outstanding scholars. David Butler of Nuffield College, Oxford, and Professor Alberto Spreafico, then Secretary-General of the Comitato per le Scienze Politiche e Sociali in Rome, were more patient and obliging than a brash young American deserved, and I am deeply grateful to them.

Dott. Antonio Maccanico, Dott. Andrea Manzella, and Professor Guglielmo Negri offered particularly important support and cordial hospitality in introducing me to the Chamber of Deputies. To each of them my special thanks. I must make special mention, too, of the sensitive advice and generous aid of Professor Giovanni Sartori.

For special encouragement and thoughtful counsel on two-and-a-half continents I am also grateful to: Robert Axelrod, Samuel H. Barnes, Dott. Franco Cazzola, Robert A. Dahl, On. Luciano De Pascalis, Robert E. Lane, Sir Harry Legge-Bourke, MP, Michael Lessnoff, Warren Miller, J. Roland Pennock, Richard Rose, Donald Searing, Donald Stokes, Sidney Verba, Brian Walden, MP, and On. Amos Zanibelli.

At various stages of this research I have had the skilled and indefatigable assistance of Sig.ra Iride Amadio, Dott. Alfio Mastropaolo, Pamela Poulter, and Sig.ra Carla Venditti. Hugh Grambau has spent several years working with me on this study, and his intellectual contribution has been proportionately great. Marian Neal Ash and her colleagues at Yale University Press provided sensitive editorial advice.

Financial assistance for various stages of this project was provided by the Foreign Area Fellowship Program, the Yale University Council on Comparative and European Studies, and the University of Michigan. Though these organi-

xi

zations share none of the responsibility for the conclusions I have reached, their help was indispensable.

Joseph LaPalombara's contributions to this research have been primarily three: he got it going, he kept it going, and (eventually) he got it stopped. Without the benefit of his deep familiarity with the wonderful complexities of European politics and his remarkable insight into the practical problems of cross-national research, this study would not have been possible, and my debt to him is profound.

Portions of part I of this book have already appeared in the *American Political Science Review* (September 1971) whose permission to reprint is gratefully acknowledged.

Rosemary, Jonathan, and Lara have lived with this study for longer than any of us would have thought possible. Rosemary shared the work, and all three shared the incidental fun.

The responsibility for what we have produced is mine.

                                                                          R.D.P.

Ann Arbor
August 1972

1 The Beliefs of Politicians

Most men are not political animals. The world of public affairs is not their world. It is alien to them—possibly benevolent, more probably threatening, but nearly always alien. Most men are not interested in politics. Most do not participate in politics. And few have much power or influence.

But some men are different. They find public affairs and political life irresistibly alluring. They become deeply involved in politics, perhaps even dedicating their lives to it. And, inevitably, these men win power and influence—often not a great deal but always more than most of us have. They are, in a once noble but now sadly devalued word, politicians. And they are the subject of this study.

Political leaders have always fascinated other people. They have inspired novelists and dramatists and occasionally poets and composers. Their fascination comes, first, from their power, for, in an optical paradox, their power makes them seem both larger than most people and more distant. They are also often personally interesting—not always estimable, but uncommonly interesting. These attractions are not unimportant, but political scientists have another motive, too, for studying politicians, for even in a democratic age, or perhaps especially in a democratic age, the character of a country's leadership touches deeply the patterns of its politics.

What do politicians think politics is all about? How do they think politics works? How do they think politics ought to work? And how do they work in politics? The answers to these questions are, I believe, fundamentally important for understanding the functioning of political systems. If labels are useful—and sometimes they are—we can call the set of politically relevant beliefs, values, and habits of the leaders of a political system, "elite political culture." This, then, is a comparative study of the elite political cultures of Britain and Italy.

Our inquiry lies at the juncture of two important approaches to the study of politics. On the one hand, "elite theorists" and others have pointed to the crucial importance in any political system of what Robert A. Dahl has termed "the political stratum"— "a small stratum of individuals . . . much more highly involved in political thought, discussion, and action than the rest of the population."[1] On the other hand, students of "political culture" and "political ideo-

1. Dahl, *Who Governs?* (New Haven: Yale University Press, 1961), p. 90. For brief introductions to the enormous literature on elite theories of politics, see T. B. Bottomore, *Elites and*

1

logy" have directed our attention to the significance of the belief systems of political actors.[2] I want to say a word about each of these approaches.

Roughly speaking, elite theories of politics have offered two related, but distinct, propositions. The first and more general is that in any political system some actors are more important than others and deserve closer scrutiny from students of politics. The second (and more dubious) is that there is a specifiable, unified, self-conscious, and autonomous group in control of any political system. The distinction between these two propositions is, paradoxically, both trite and important. If, as Dahl and others have pointed out, the truth of the second does not follow from the truth of the first, neither does the falsity of the first follow from the evident falsity of the second. The significant theoretical kernel contained in elite theories of politics (a kernel recognized by the most perceptive critics of these theories) is the notion that political systems can usefully be conceived as stratified—that some people are much more interested, much more involved, and much more influential in public affairs than their fellows.

Numerous well-known theoretical and practical problems complicate the various elite theories: What criteria should be used for ranking individuals? How sharp and discontinuous are the observable gradations in political status? How much autonomy do the various strata have? How unified are members of a given stratum? Here, however, I will simply sidestep these difficulties, and define "political elite" very loosely as those who in any society rank toward the top of the (presumably closely intercorrelated) dimensions of interest, involvement, and influence in politics. In modern societies professional politicians are among the most important members of the political elite in this sense. Therefore, as a practical matter I will concentrate on them, without intending to imply that they are the only significant members of the elite.

The second approach to the study of politics that is relevant to our inquiry focuses on "political culture." The major premise of this approach is that the character and development of a political system is conditioned by "the system of empirical beliefs, expressive symbols, and values which defines the situation in which political action takes place,"[3] or less formally, that attitudes matter. They matter because, as Fred Greenstein puts it,

> behavior . . . is a function of both the *environmental situations* in which actors find themselves and the *psychological predispositions* they bring to those situations. . . . It is also sometimes instructive to think of attitude and situation as being in a kind of push-pull relationship: the stronger the attitu-

Society (New York: Basic Books, 1965) and Geraint Parry, *Political Elites* (New York: Frederick A. Praeger, 1969).

2. See Robert E. Lane, *Political Ideology* (New York: Free Press, 1962); Gabriel Almond and Sidney Verba, *The Civic Culture* (Princeton: Princeton University Press, 1963); and Lucian Pye and Sidney Verba, eds., *Political Culture and Political Development* (Princeton: Princeton University Press, 1965).

3. The quoted definition of political culture is from Sidney Verba's discussion in Pye and Verba, *Political Culture and Political Development*, p. 513.

dinal press for a course of action, the less the need for situational stimuli, and vice versa.[4]

This interplay of the "pulling" environment and the "pushing" attitude will be a recurrent theme in this study, and though I will usually stress the role of attitude, I do not mean to depreciate the importance of environment. Most studies of the activities of political leaders, however, have focused on the pull of environmental factors: on parties and pressure groups, on constituents and courtiers, on statutes and social structure. Relatively fewer inquiries have been directed at understanding the other element in the behavioral equation.[5]

The attitudes of elites have not, of course, been wholly disregarded. At one level, there have been some investigations of the opinions of political leaders on current topics in foreign policy and domestic affairs.[6] Do leaders in Bonn and Paris favor arms control? How do elites in emerging nations like Israel or Jamaica view the problems and prospects for political development? At another level, there have been studies of the personalities and psychodynamic motivations of political leaders.[7] Individual studies, for example, explore the personal drives and private incentives of legislators in Connecticut, revolutionaries in Russia, or party notables in Colombia.

But between these most fundamental needs and psychic compulsions, on the one hand, and fairly specific, perhaps transient opinions, on the other, lies a set of orientations toward society and politics that has been less intensively examined.[8] Here we find the beliefs and values and habits of thought that guide and inform a politician's more ephemeral responses to his environment and that are dependent in ways yet unknown on his deeper personality structure. It is these intermediate orientations (for which I use the rubric "political culture") that will concern us in this study.

4. Fred Greenstein, *Personality and Politics* (Chicago: Markham Publishing Company, 1969), pp. 7, 29. (Emphasis in the original.) This volume is an outstanding discussion of the issues that I treat more briefly in this chapter.

5. There is, of course, an interactive relationship between environment and attitude, for each affects the other through enormously complex "feedback loops." This fact will not be neglected in the analysis that follows.

6. For examples of this approach to the study of elites, see Karl W. Deutsch et al., *France, Germany, and the Western Alliance* (New York: Charles Scribner's Sons, 1967); Daniel Lerner and Morton Gorden, *Euratlantica: Changing Perspectives of the European Elites* (Cambridge, Mass.: M.I.T. Press, 1969); Lester G. Seligman, *Leadership in a New Nation* (New York: Atherton Press, 1964); and Wendell Bell, *Jamaican Leaders: Political Attitudes in a New Nation* (Berkeley: University of California Press, 1964).

7. For examples of this approach to the study of elites, see James David Barber, *The Lawmakers* (New Haven: Yale University Press, 1965); E. Victor Wolfenstein, *The Revolutionary Personality* (Princeton: Princeton University Press, 1967); James L. Payne, *Patterns of Conflict in Colombia* (New Haven: Yale University Press, 1968); and Lewis J. Edinger, *Kurt Schumacher: A Study in Personality and Political Behavior* (Stanford, Calif.: Stanford University Press, 1965).

8. There have been several other scholars whose interests have led them toward the topic of elite political culture. Nathan Leites drew on intensive (but impressionistic) interviews with deputies in Fourth Republic France to speculate *On the Game of Politics in France* (Stanford,

A political culture, in this sense, provides answers to the questions, What is human nature like? Is it basically good or evil? What is society like? Is it harmonious or conflictful? What kinds of social and political differences are important and how are these differences to be dealt with? What is politics all about? What does the political system look like? How do decisions get taken and who is important in the decision-making process? What counts as a political issue and what kinds of solutions are conceivable and preferable? What criteria are relevant in judging alternative solutions? To what extent are political conflicts irreconcilable or "zero-sum"? How does one go about solving public problems or resolving political conflicts? What political tactics are useful and acceptable? Who are my opponents and who are my allies, and what, for me, is the appropriate orientation toward each? What is the nature of political leadership? What is my own role in politics? What are my political ideals and how are these to be interpreted and applied? What is the good society? What is the good polity?

But lists do not make theories, and it will be helpful to classify some of the main themes that compose a political culture. There are, it seems to me, three broad categories worth looking at, for which I will use the terms *political style, cognitive predispositions,* and *operative ideals.*

Sidney Verba defines political style this way:

> By political style I refer to two aspects of political belief systems. The first, which is strictly cultural, involves the structure or formal properties of political belief systems, that is, not the substance of the beliefs, but the way in which the beliefs are held. The second aspect lies on the border between the system of political culture and the system of political interaction, and involves those informal norms of political interaction that regulate the way in which fundamental political beliefs are applied in politics.[9]

In this study we will find it quite important to keep separate the two topics that Verba links in his statement: the way men hold their beliefs and the way they relate personally to other political actors. For clarity's sake, I will use the term

Calif.: Stanford University Press, 1959). Lucian Pye described the political culture of Burmese political and administrative elites, although his intriguing findings, too, are painted with an impressionist's brush. See his *Politics, Personality, and Nation Building* (New Haven: Yale University Press, 1962). Dahl has discussed "the beliefs of political activists" in his recent *Polyarchy: Participation and Opposition* (New Haven: Yale University Press, 1971), pp. 124–88. Some recent research on politics in developing nations has stressed elite political culture. See, especially, John Waterbury, *The Commander of the Faithful: The Moroccan Political Elite* (New York: Columbia University Press, 1970); James A. Scott, *Political Ideology in Malaysia* (New Haven: Yale University Press, 1968); and the briefer discussion in William B. Quandt, *Revolution and Political Leadership: Algeria, 1954–1968* (Cambridge, Mass.: M.I.T. Press, 1969). A similar focus under a different alias has been suggested by Alexander George, "The 'Operational Code': A Neglected Approach to the Study of Political Leaders and Decision-Making," *International Studies Quarterly* 13 (1969): 190–222.

9. Sidney Verba, in Pye and Verba, *Political Culture and Political Development,* p. 545.

"political style" to refer only to the former category, reserving for the latter the more heterogenous labels of "attitudes toward other political actors" or "attitudes toward political opponents." These latter terms are self-explanatory, but what of "political style"?

A full explanation must await the clarifying examples given in chapter 3, but roughly speaking, "political style," as I use it, refers to the "how" of political thinking and policy analysis. People manifestly differ in the way they attack problems. Two individuals who share identical beliefs and values about a specific task will nonetheless handle it rather differently. This is no less true of political leaders facing public problems than of ordinary men grappling with private concerns. Some political commentators, for example, have discussed differences between "ideological" and "pragmatic" politicians. This, in fact, will be the central dimension of political style examined in the present study. There are, of course, other possible dimensions; indeed, a few will be glimpsed in the course of later discussion. Therefore, I want to stress at the outset that this investigation is illustrative rather than comprehensive. Ideology is not all there is to political style. But it is a particularly intriguing part.

Explaining our second category—cognitive predispositions—requires a word about cognitions, or beliefs. Men believe things about their world. Some of their beliefs are quite specific: for example, that this room is painted green, or that I am cold, or that Britain has a parliamentary form of government. These beliefs are specific in that they are directed at individual objects, whether in the physical environment, or in the social environment, or in one's self. They may be quite stable. Occasionally, they are even resistant in the face of contradictory information. But by and large they are susceptible to change if the environment (or the self) changes. Milton Rokeach offers a useful spatial metaphor, terming these kinds of beliefs "peripheral."[10]

But "peripheral" with respect to what? Rokeach argues that "underneath" these ordinary beliefs lie more basic, more "central" beliefs that guide and inform the more peripheral beliefs. These more basic orientations, which Rokeach terms "primitive beliefs," structure man's understanding of his environment, "the nature of the physical world he lives in, the nature of the 'self,' and of the 'generalized other.' "[11] Because I find the term "primitive belief" unhappily ambiguous, I will use the more descriptive (though perhaps clumsier) term, "cognitive predisposition." Not all of a man's cognitive predispositions are relevant to his political behavior, of course. For example, primitive beliefs about the physical environment rarely affect the actions of political leaders.[12] But even if we restrict our attention to cognitive predispositions concerning so-

10. Milton Rokeach, *The Open and Closed Mind* (New York: Basic Books, 1960), pp. 39–51.
11. Ibid., p. 40.
12. One can conceive that a leader's primitive geographical beliefs—his sense of distances and locations on the globe—could affect his foreign policy, however. Something of the sort is said to have distinguished the attitudes toward Europe of Presidents Kennedy and Johnson.

cial and political relations, there are many possible targets for investigation, several of them suggested in the list of questions I offered earlier.

In this study I choose to focus on a single set of cognitive predispositions—beliefs in the essentially conflictful or harmonious nature of society. These beliefs are particularly important, for we will see that they influence many features of a politician's outlook and behavior. Again, however, our inquiry is illustrative rather than exhaustive. Attitudes about social conflict and harmony will exemplify the sorts of cognitive predispositions that merit attention.

The third broad category of political culture consists in the values and norms that guide political action. We must distinguish among different sorts of evaluative orientations. Robin Williams has emphasized the distinction between "the specific *evaluation* of any object" (for example, government regulation is wrong) and "the *criteria* or standards in terms of which evaluations are made" (for example, government regulation is wrong because it interferes with liberty).[13] When Alexander Pope wrote, "For forms of government let fools contest / Whate'er is best administered is best," he was taking issue not with the fools' evaluations of government, but with their criteria. Our emphasis in this study will be on values-as-criteria, though inevitably, we will consider specific evaluations as well. Of course, fundamental values or ideals may be formulated abstractly and remain unapplied as criteria in actual political situations. To underline my intention to restrict this inquiry to values that do affect political judgments, I have borrowed from an older tradition the term "operative ideals."[14]

A large number of operative ideals guide and regulate men's political activities. For example, much of the texture of politics in any age is provided by the interplay among conflicting operative ideals about the business of government, conflicting visions of the good society. But I have elected to focus instead on "procedural" operative ideals, notions about how the business of politics and government should be conducted. In particular, we will examine at some length differing conceptions of democracy, political equality, and political liberty.

The distinction I have implicitly drawn between style, cognition, and evaluation must be interpreted carefully. I do not mean that there are no connections between these three aspects of an orientation, or that a single belief can be discussed in terms of only one category. A passionate belief in the desirability and practicality of a socialized economy has, clearly, cognitive and evaluative and stylistic aspects all at once. A frequent motif in the discussion that follows will be the interaction among political styles, cognitive predispositions, and operative ideals.

I have referred recurringly to the need to get at "basic" or "underlying" predispositions. We want to know not merely how a politician reacts to the

13. Robin Williams, "The Concept of Values," in the *International Encyclopedia of the Social Sciences* (New York: Crowell Collier and Macmillan, 1968), 16:283.
14. As far as I can determine, this term originated with A. D. Lindsay, *The Modern Democratic State* (New York: Oxford University Press, 1943).

most recent proposal for economic planning, but how he habitually analyzes policy issues. We want to know not merely what he believes about the rising crime rate, but what he believes about the nature of man-in-society. We want to know not merely how he evaluates specialist legislative committees, but what his central standards of political evaluation are.

The first priority in our inquiry, then, is to establish the (measurable) existence of these basic orientations. This done, we will place them in a causal context, seeking their effects and their origins. What difference does it make that a politician has a given orientation? And how did he come to have that orientation in the first place? The following diagram, borrowed from Dahl, captures the logical structure of our inquiry.[15]

I		II		III		IV
Factors determining beliefs	$\longrightarrow$	Political beliefs	$\longrightarrow$	Political actions	$\longrightarrow$	Regimes

Our inquiry will focus initially on element II, but we will also want to look backward along the causal chain toward the sources of differing beliefs and forward toward the consequences, to illuminate both the individual politician's behavior and the wider political system in which he participates. As we look in each direction, we will be guided by the light cast by the data gathered in this study. Inevitably, as we peer toward more remote sources and more distant consequences, the light will become dimmer. However, these less accessible causal links are likely to be the most critical in understanding how the attitudes of politicians fit into the flow of history and politics, and it is, I think, important to speculate, to suggest, to hint, even when one cannot demonstrate or prove.

We are going to talk about politicians and their basic attitudes. With a bit of poetic license, we can summarize our interests as *what politicians believe* (cognitive predispositions), *what they believe in* (operative ideals), and *how they believe* (political style). Chapter 2 sets out the tools and techniques that we will use to trace these attitudes and their interconnections. Parts I, II, and III focus in turn on each of the three central themes of this study: political style, cognitive predispositions, and operative ideals. The epilogue provides a brief glance back over our discoveries, summarizing a few of the broader implications for the study of politics.

15. Dahl, *Polyarchy: Participation and Opposition,* p. 124.

2 Studying Elite Political Culture

The fundamental methodological premise of this inquiry is that the best way to study the beliefs of political leaders is to talk with them and listen carefully. From February 1967 through February 1968 I talked with 93 Members of the British House of Commons and 83 *deputati* from the Italian Chamber of Deputies in semistructured interviews lasting somewhat more than an hour each. The analysis of these interviews provides the basis for this volume. Let me say a bit about the four important elements in this research: (1) the national and temporal contexts, (2) the samples, (3) the interviews, and (4) the subsequent analysis.

The Contexts

THE COUNTRIES

Nowhere is the logic of comparative inquiry more important than in the description and analysis of political culture, yet nowhere has it been more ignored. The literature on national character as well as more orthodox political and historical studies have, by and large, been so concerned with the axiomatic "uniqueness" of national cultures that there have been relatively few attempts to place these cultures along common dimensions so that we could see *how* they were unique (and how unique they really were). To take an example to which we will return in part III, both British and Italian attitudes toward authority are typically described as "hierarchical." But does this mean that attitudes toward authority are identical in the two countries, and if not, how do they differ? Such questions cannot be answered without carefully constructed comparisons. A comparative study like the present one runs risks, of course, because certain methodological difficulties rise geometrically with the number of countries studied. Not the least troublesome of these difficulties is the need for constant sensitivity to the genuine peculiarities of each nation. In certain respects the present study does not do perfect justice to the idiosyncracies of British and Italian politics. But if we are to understand the full complexity of political culture, the promises of explicit cross-national comparison far outweigh the perils.

If we are to compare, what should we compare? The choice of Britain and

Italy requires little defense, since both are important examples of modern, pluralist polities. Several useful features of this particular comparison, however, are worth noting.[1] In this comparison certain parameters are held constant. Both countries are parliamentary democracies, in form and in fact. Both have reached levels of socioeconomic development that are quite advanced, seen in world perspective. Both share the vague, but quite real heritage of "Western civilization." On the other hand, they differ in ways that make cultural comparison particularly fruitful. Britain has a celebrated tradition of consensual evolution, while Italy's political history is fractured by disunity, instability, and authoritarian adventures. Italy's socioeconomic development is more recent and less advanced than Britain's. Patterns of party politics in the two countries are obviously quite different. And most important, British government has a justified reputation for effectiveness, stability, and responsiveness that Italian government, alas, has not.[2] One of the opportunities that comparison of this particular pair of countries provides is the chance to look for links between characteristics of elite political culture and the prospects for genuinely democratic stability in modern societies.

THE PERIOD

In November 1964, after thirteen years of Conservative rule, the Labour Party returned to power under the firm leadership of Harold Wilson. Labour's initially thin majority in Parliament was substantially increased in the March 1966 General Election, and at the time of this research Britain and British politicians faced the prospect of at least four more years of Labour rule. One result of these two elections was to bring a wave of new Members into Parliament. Approximately one-third of the House of Commons in the spring of 1967 had entered within the previous sixteen months.

During its long period out of office the Labour Party had moved de facto, if not de jure, from a fairly conventional socialist platform that placed heavy emphasis on nationalization of major industry to a still radical, but less doctrinaire, stance emphasizing economic planning and government encouragement of technologically based economic growth. Deep commitment to social justice

1. For a useful discussion of how to choose countries for cross-national comparison, see Erwin Scheuch, "Society as Context in Cross-National Comparison," *Social Science Information* 6 (October 1967). See also Adam Przeworski and Henry Teune, *The Logic of Comparative Social Inquiry* (New York: John Wiley & Sons, 1970).

2. This list of traits is borrowed from Harry Eckstein's definition of "stable democracy." See his *Division and Cohesion in Democracy* (Princeton: Princeton University Press, 1966), pp. 228–30. Clearly one could overstate the differences in levels of performance between the two countries, but what systematic evidence there is confirms that Italy ranks near the bottom among Western European countries; Britain, near the top. See, for example, Leon Hurwitz, "An Index of Democratic Political Stability," *Comparative Political Studies* 4 (April 1971): 41–68; and Ted Robert Gurr and Muriel McClelland, *Political Performance: A Twelve-Nation Study* (Beverly Hills, Calif.: Sage Professional Papers in Comparative Politics) vol. 2, no. 01–018 (1971).

continued to inform Labour thinking. Within the first few weeks of the new Labour Government, however, an international economic crisis of disastrous proportions struck Britain. The Wilson Government was forced to take a series of drastic measures of retrenchment, not notably different from those adopted by their Conservative predecessors in the face of similar crises. Though the Government continued to hope for the opportunity to implement their radical intentions, their deliberations were overshadowed by the economic crisis and efforts to "save the pound." In the spring of 1967 there was some (premature) hope of "light at the end of the tunnel," but frustration festered among the more radical backbenchers, discontented as well over the Government's European and Far Eastern policies.

On the other side of the House of Commons the Conservatives were recovering from the electoral setbacks of the previous two years. Having gone through two Leaders during this period, the party was uneasily supporting its "new style" (i.e. non-Etonian) Leader, Edward Heath, in his efforts to devise a "new style" program. The party was in a period of self-conscious reevaluation of its policies, and more diversity was apparent in Conservative thinking on major public issues than had existed for more than a decade. From these deliberations would emerge the emphatically "conservative" program of the later Heath Government. Toward the end of the period of interviews a series of unprecedented Conservative victories in local elections gave a new note of optimism to Conservative thinking, but did not immediately change the harmonies and disharmonies characteristic of the party during this period.

In most respects the period of interviewing seemed quite typical of postwar British politics. Daily parliamentary confrontation induced partisan dispute on a number of issues, from the development of a prices-and-incomes policy to the *Torrey Canyon* tanker disaster, but the clashes were not noticeably more or less heated than usual. The topics of political conversation ranged from the overriding problem of "getting the economy right," to the decision to reapply for admission to the Common Market, to the system of social welfare payments, to decimalization of the currency. There was also continuing talk of reform of Parliament, and midway through the research period a sharp controversy arose within the Parliamentary Labour Party about the extent of backbench influence on Government policy. Though the public duration of this controversy was relatively short, interviews both before and after the blow-up indicated that it reflected continuing tensions within the PLP.

In Italy, meanwhile, the bloom was off the once-fair rose of the Center-Left government. Nearly a decade had been spent constructing this alliance of Socialists and Christian Democrats, culminating in the formation of a coalition government in 1963. All sides in Italian politics had taken seriously this *svolta storica,* or historic turning-point, as it was advertised: social reformers had hoped for radical change, conservative and business interests had feared radical change, and the Communists, deprived of their traditional ties to the Italian

Socialist Party, had been forced to reconsider their basic political strategy. Considerable realignment had occurred within the Socialist ranks, as a left-wing group hostile to the new coalition broke away to form the Socialist Party of Proletarian Unity (PSIUP), and the right-wing Social Democratic Party merged with the main body of the Socialist Party.[3] But both hopes and fears about the Center-Left experiment had proved exaggerated.

After years of discussion and debate, in the summer of 1967 the coalition finally passed a bill setting out a five-year program for national economic and social development. But by that fall, when my interviewing began, most of the long-overdue social reforms called for by this plan (and dear to the hearts of the coalition's progressives) remained unaccomplished. Bills for reform of health services, fiscal reform, and urban planning were pending, and a major controversy developed over the Government's plan for introducing regional governments. Opposition to regionalism from the Right, supported covertly by conservative Christian Democrats, led to the first major (and ultimately unsuccessful) filibuster in Italian history. By early spring proposals for reform of the Italian university system were at the focus of public attention, and the debate was warmed by widespread student demonstrations and rioting.

These controversies were all intensified by the approaching general elections, due in May 1968. Reformers within the government coalition were eager to accomplish as much of their original program as possible before the dissolution of Parliament in March, but their efforts were offset by the desires of others within the alliance to avoid conflict and maintain unity in the face of the electoral campaign. The approaching elections seemed to have less effect on the bitterness of partisan confrontation than might have been expected. The explanation lay in the widely shared expectation that the elections would probably show no great shifts in party strength and that politics after the elections would therefore continue much as before. Electoral strategy on all sides thus called for a battle of position rather than a battle of movement. Hostility and tension among the parties was, by Anglo-American standards, quite high, but this was only marginally a function of preelection fervor.

The backdrop for daily politicking was a tapestry woven from the contradictory social trends of postwar Italy. Economic growth continued unabated. Concern about Mafia lawlessness in Sicily was replaced temporarily by concern about an outbreak of banditry and kidnapping in Sardinia. A dark thread of intrigue was provided by half-substantiated rumors of military plots and of intervention in political affairs by a branch of the counterintelligence services. The spring student riots were accompanied by scattered strikes and demon-

3. This union of Socialists and Social Democrats was to fall apart again in the wake of their joint losses in the elections of May 1968. At the time of our interviewing most Socialists and Social Democrats were optimistic about the prospects for the unified party. We will see some evidence later in this study, however, that the basic divergence between the two groups persisted throughout this period. See n. 4, chap. 15.

strations for pension and salary improvements, though on nothing like the scale of the later disturbances in 1969 and 1970.

Thus, despite the shadow cast by the impending national elections, this period displayed all the essential traits of Italian politics. Parties feuding, both internally and with their opponents; many reforms pending, but few passing; the economy growing, but hardly faster than social tensions—these were the main features of Italian politics in 1967 and 1968, as they had been throughout the previous two decades.

Politicians, like most of us, live in a world of foreshortened time perspective, and when talking about politics, talk about today's, or yesterday's, or (more rarely) tomorrow's. It is doubtful that the style of their thought or the pattern of their ideals changes markedly from day to day, but the events to which they apply their thought and ideals do. It is, therefore, important and reassuring that the events of these periods were not radically abnormal in any important respect. It was by and large a period of "politics as usual."

The Samples

Parliamentarians are not the only members of the political elites of Britain and Italy. Indeed, there may be some question that they belong in that category at all. As institutions, the parliaments of these countries are no longer, if ever they were, the hub of governmental power and initiative. Of course, in an era of popular sovereignty the fact that the parliaments are the only national popularly elected bodies in each country means that legitimate decision-making authority lies ultimately with these men and women. In each country the attention of public opinion and the mass media continues to be directed at Parliament as the focus of national policy making. But increasingly the spotlight has had to be shared with other institutions: the Government, the national bureaucracy, and the party organizations.

Parliamentarians in these countries are politically sophisticated, and their own judgments about the patterns of power in national politics confirm these generalizations. Figure 2.1 presents in schematic form composite "profiles of power" drawn from their responses to a series of questions about "what groups or institutions generally have the most influence over the outcome of issues like these we have been discussing [earlier in the interview]?" (The specific questions and codes for this analysis—as will be the case throughout this volume—can be found in appendix B, the codebook.) A number of interesting propositions might be teased out of this diagram, but the one relevant at this point is that in each country parliamentarians rate the power of their own institution quite modestly. From an institutional point of view, their place among the national decision-makers is fairly humble.

From another perspective, however, these parliaments are considerably more significant. To an extent that has not typically been true of the American Con-

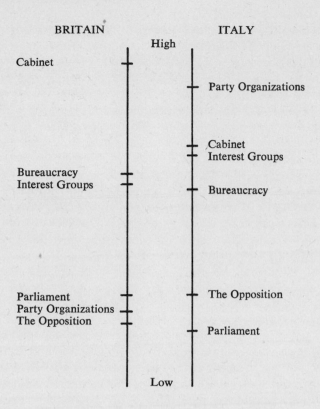

Figure 2.1: Profiles of Power in Britain and Italy

gress, for example, the House of Commons and the Chamber of Deputies serve as reservoirs from which are drawn virtually all the more powerful political leaders of each country.

Take first the case of Britain. Members of the cabinet at the time of the interviews had had an average of eighteen years' service in the Commons; indeed, only one had served less than a decade. Joseph A. Schlesinger has shown that this pattern has characterized British cabinets throughout most of this century. He concludes that "the picture is of full parliamentary apprenticeship before major advancement."[4] Looked at the other way around, a substantial number of Members at any given time either have served or are presently serving in some executive post. Of the random sample drawn for this research 30 percent had been members of some Government, and another 10 percent were to reach the front benches within the next four years.[5] At any point in time a high pro-

4. Joseph A. Schlesinger, "Political Careers and Party Leadership," in *Political Leadership in Industrialized Societies,* ed. Lewis J. Edinger (New York: John Wiley & Sons, 1967), p. 286.

5. Philip W. Buck estimates that about a quarter of all MPs from 1918 to 1955 held some leadership post. See his *Amateurs and Professionals in British Politics, 1918–1959* (Chicago:

portion of the membership of the House of Commons is either on the road up
to higher office or on the road back down. And for virtually all who reach the
top, the road there has passed through the Commons. Westminster's role as the
incubator for British leadership is, of course, widely recognized in the House
itself, though it is less prominent in academic accounts of "the functions of
Parliament." It implies that in sampling the House of Commons we are sampling
a sizable (and not terribly diluted) share of the British political elite.

The Italian case is complicated, first of all, by Italy's genuinely bicameral
legislature. Nevertheless, most (though not all) of the major national political
figures are in the Chamber of Deputies, with the Senate serving often as a sine-
cure for elder statesmen. Even if we count only years in the lower house, the
members of the Italian Government at the time of my interviews had spent an
average of sixteen years in Parliament. Long service in Montecitorio, the seat of
the Chamber of Deputies, is virtually a prerequisite for high executive office.
Conversely, 20 percent of the random sample of deputies drawn for this study—
35 percent of those from the parties that have perennially formed Italian
Governments—had at some point served in at least one Government.

Most observers of Italian politics believe that the real power of decision lies
with the central party organizations, even more than with the Government
itself, and figure 2.1 showed that our sample of deputies share this image.
National party leaders form a central part of the Italian political elite. However,
most of these men and women turn out to be members of Parliament, too.

Fifty-one percent of all members of the central committee of the Communist
Party since 1945 have been members of one house of Parliament or the other,
in most cases, of the Chamber of Deputies. Fully 88 percent of the members of
the still more select *Direzione* have been members of Parliament. For the
Christian Democratic Party the comparable figures are 56 percent and 85
percent.[6] Data are not available for the smaller parties, but the proportions
of parliamentarians among their national party leaders is surely even greater.
Conversely, 51 percent of the deputies in our random sample had held a major
national or regional position in their party.

Not all Italian deputies are in the very top stratum of the political hierarchy;
the Chamber of Deputies is probably slightly more "diluted" than is the House
of Commons. But nearly every important political figure in Italy either is in the
Chamber now or has spent a good deal of time there. And most, if not all, of
those who are there rank quite high in the national political stratification
system. In Italy, as in Britain, Parliament may not be what the Italians call the

University of Chicago Press, 1963). The proportion has probably risen over the last two decades.
See Richard Rose, "The Making of Cabinet Ministers," *British Journal of Political Science* 1
(1971): 393–414.

6. These data have been recalculated from data presented in F. Cervellati Cantelli et al.,
L'Organizzazione Partitica del PCI e della DC (Bologna: Società Editrice Il Mulino, 1968),
p. 516. Cf. Giovanni Sartori, *Il Parlamento Italiano* (Naples: Edizioni Scientifiche Italiane,
1963), p. 132.

stanza dei bottoni, the room where the "push-buttons" of power are kept. But it is the anteroom, and if we talk with those waiting there to enter or those who have just come out, we will have a rather good idea of what kind of men are actually pushing the buttons.

There is another strategy for analyzing the power and influence of our respondents. In each country I asked six experienced parliamentary correspondents independently to rate each parliamentarian in my sample on a four-point scale of "political importance." This is, of course, a purely reputational measure, but these journalists are immersed in the parliamentary climate of opinion, and they probably reflect fairly accurately the "sense of the House" on the political "weight" of various members.[7]

This measure, of course, compares parliamentarians only against each other, not against other members of the political elite. Nevertheless, it is particularly useful. Systematically, every variable discussed in this study has been cross-tabulated with this measure of "political importance," as well as with other measures of stature based on formal positions held. Thus, we can see whether within our sample of political leaders the perspectives of the more important differ from the perspectives of the less important in any significant ways. In fact, among the highly select group we are studying, political importance is rarely correlated with fundamental orientations to politics. There are some interesting exceptions, as we will see; but by and large, we can draw the comforting conclusion that our findings can safely be generalized to the national partisan political elite in these two countries.[8]

Random samples of the House of Commons and of the Chamber of Deputies are thus remarkably good samples of the political elites of Britain and Italy. In turn, those respondents actually interviewed fairly represent the characteristics of their fellow parliamentarians. Of an initial randomly drawn sample of 110 MPs in Britain, 93 (85 percent) were interviewed, and of the initial random sample of 106 Italian *deputati* (stratified by party), 83 (78 percent) were interviewed. Table 2.1 compares our respondents with the random samples as a whole, over a range of personal and political characteristics. In terms of party affiliation, age, education, social class, parliamentary seniority, and political importance

7. In each country my six informants achieved a fairly high level of concordance: the mean intercorrelation among their judgments was tau-beta = .45 in Britain and tau-beta = .38 in Italy.

8. Of course, other groups in the national elites of these countries are not at all represented in our samples: civil servants, prominent businessmen, figures in the Church, interest group leaders, and so on. It would obviously be quite wrong to extend our conclusions to these other groups; hence my references to "politicians" and "national partisan political elite." Two useful studies of the Italian and British parliamentary elites are Sartori, *Il Parlamento Italiano,* and W. L. Guttsman, *The British Political Elite* (New York: Basic Books, 1963). An abbreviated version of Sartori's work appears in his "Parliamentarians in Italy," *International Social Science Journal* 13, no. 4 (1961), reprinted in *Decisions and Decision-Makers in the Modern State* (Paris: UNESCO, 1967). For further discussion of elite theories and their problems, see my *Comparative Political Elites* (Englewood Cliffs, N. J.: Prentice-Hall, 1974, forthcoming).

Table 2.1: Composition of National Samples, by Personal and Political Characteristics (in percentages)

	Britain		Italy	
	Sample inter-viewed (N = 93)	Random sample (N = 110)	Sample inter-viewed (N = 83)	Random sample (N = 106)
British Political Party				
Labour	58	58	–	–
Conservative	40	40	–	–
Liberal	2	2	–	–
Italian Political Party				
Communist	–	–	24	25
PSIUP (Left Socialist)	–	–	5	4
PSI (Center Socialist)	–	–	12	11
PSDI (Right Socialist)	–	–	5	4
Christian Democratic	–	–	40	42
Liberal	–	--	6	6
MSI (neo-Fascist)	–	–	5	6
Other	–	–	4	3
Seniority				
Less than 5 years	39	34	39	38
5-15 years	30	33	41	39
More than 15 years	31	34	20	24
Age				
Less than 45	33	31	23	20
45–55	31	33	49	53
More than 55	35	36	28	26
Education				
Elementary or less	15	13	7	8
Secondary	19	19	19	20
University	67	68	74	72
Parental social class*				
Upper & upper-middle	51	50	37	36
Middle	19	19	37	35
Lower (working)	30	31	26	29
Political importance				
High	15	20	10	14
Medium	37	37	18	16
Low	48	43	72	70
Governmental position				
Minister	3	8	1	5
Junior minister	5	5	5	6
None	91	87	94	90

*Parental social class is unknown for 19 percent of the British sample and for 32 percent of the Italian sample.

those Members actually interviewed faithfully reflect the composition of each parliament as a whole.[9]

9. In this analysis I use the characteristics of the total random sample rather than the whole Parliament as the basis of comparison, because the more detailed information that is available for the sample allows more specific comparison. The laws of statistics ensure that the random samples themselves accurately represent the total population of parliamentarians, within speci-

The only significant exception is that the response rates were markedly lower for those deputies or MPs who were also members of the Government. However, in neither country did I encounter similar difficulties in reaching highly influential respondents who were not ministers at the time; in Britain, for example, I interviewed 90 percent of the Conservative frontbenchers in the random list, but only 50 percent of the Labour ministers in that list. Hence, I conclude that the relevant factor was not political importance per se, but rather the pressures of office. Each final national sample slightly underrepresents ministerial incumbents, but this problem is kept in perspective by noting that the short-fall is of only four or five respondents in each country, or roughly 5 percent of the total sample.

This evidence on the social and political characteristics of our respondents does not, of course, ensure that the samples are not biased in terms of psychological or cultural traits. Particularly in Italy those not interviewed may have been somewhat more suspicious and hostile toward American researchers in particular and toward political antagonists in general. On the other hand, some of those contacted refused for purely idiosyncratic reasons, such as ill health or overwork. Since about four-fifths of each sample were actually interviewed, it would be reasonable to suppose that not more than a tenth of the total random samples declined to talk for reasons that might be relevant to the purposes of the study. This figure can, therefore, be used as an upper limit for the bias that might have been introduced by self-selection. By and large, we can trust these samples.

In social science samples are always too small. With 80 to 90 respondents in each country, we will be able to use moderately sophisticated statistical tools, and the main findings of the study are sufficiently clear that the size of the samples is not a major handicap. But as we strive to understand in more detail the patterns we discover, the problem of "vanishing respondents" will become more severe. Since I believe that hints and suggestions are important at this stage in our understanding of the beliefs of politicians, I will occasionally "squeeze" the

---

fiably narrow limits. In fact, in the British case where data on the characteristics of the total membership of the Commons are available, there are simply no differences worth reporting. In addition to the analysis reported in table 2.1, I carried out a more extensive investigation covering a wider variety of background characteristics, such as type of schooling, experience in local government or party organizations, type of constituency, region of birth, and so on. Apart from the underrepresentation of ministerial incumbents, there are no significant biases to our samples. Sources used for the British background data include the *Times House of Commons 1966* (London: The Times Office, 1966); *Dod's Parliamentary Companion 1966* (Epsom, England: Business Dictionaries, 1966); Andrew Roth, *The MP's Chart* (London: Parliamentary Profile Services, 1967); Andrew Roth, *The Business Background of M.P.s* (London: Parliamentary Profile Services, 1965); and the British *Who's Who*. The primary sources for the Italian background data were *I Deputati e Senatori del Quarto Parlamento Repubblicano* (Rome: La Navicella, 1965) and *Elenco Alfabetico dei Deputati* (Rome: Servizio Prerogative e Immunità della Camera dei Deputati, 1967). In addition, Professor Giovanni Sartori graciously allowed me to use some of the background data he has gathered on Italian deputies; naturally, I remain responsible for the uses to which I have put these data. See Sartori, *Il Parlamento Italiano*.

data quite hard, but always with a warning to the reader about the necessarily lower precision of these detailed results.

The Interviews

THE SETTING

Each of the 110 MPs and 106 *deputati* in the original samples was sent an introductory letter, explaining the study in general terms, stressing its scholarly and confidential character, and asking for an appointment. In Italy more direct methods were necessary as well, and I was helped by personal introductions from staff members of the Chamber of Deputies and by letters of endorsement from the various party organizations. The danger of "contaminating" the respondent's answers by appearing to be "sponsored" by the party in this way is markedly less than the converse danger of appearing *not* to have the approval of the party leaders.

About three-quarters of the interviews in each country were held in the precincts of Parliament, ordinarily in a private interview room, sometimes in a respondent's office (when he was lucky enough to have one), infrequently in some corner of a larger public room. The remainder were held in the respondent's home or hotel room. I conducted virtually all of the Italian interviews myself. In Britain, about half were conducted by an assistant. This latter procedure allowed a check on what psychologists call "interviewer effect."[10] The two interviewers—one a male American graduate student professionally trained in political science, the other an attractive British housewife with long experience in elite interviewing but no training in political science—differed in a number of ways that might have affected respondents' expressed attitudes. But an exhaustive analysis of the responses given to the two interviewers revealed virtually no consistent differences.[11]

THE QUESTIONS

Interviewing elites requires a strategy quite different from that familiar in most survey research. Closed-ended questions are efficient for researchers and allow respondents the convenient option of not taking the exercise seriously. But they are fatally flawed as instruments for understanding basic beliefs and values. Although the bulk of this research relied on open-ended questions, I did ask respondents at the end of each interview to complete a brief questionnaire containing a series of "agree-disagree" items. One British respondent returned his

10. On this problem, see Raymond L. Gorden, *Interviewing: Strategy, Techniques, and Tactics* (Homewood, Ill.: Dorsey Press, 1969), pp. 124–37.
11. One partial exception is a slight hint in the data that more hostility toward political opponents was expressed to my assistant; I interpret this as evidence that she was sometimes seen as a potential elector to be won over. But the differences in the data are so minor that the point has no substantive impact on our study.

questionnaire with a covering letter that admirably sums up the case against that technique and in favor of a more conversational strategy.

Dear Mr. Putnam,

I greatly enjoyed our conversation.

As to the questionnaire, I have assumed that you want, if it is humanly possible, to get an expression of agreement or disagreement with this extraordinary series of statements, and I have done my best to oblige. If, as a result of feeding it into a computer, you come up with the result that I am an elderly Fijian with one leg and strong views on social credit, you will know that something has gone wrong. There were, however, some questions which seem to me to pass any reasonable bounds of the kinds of statements with which one can agree or disagree. . . .

I'm sorry about that.

Yours sincerely,

The strategy of the interview itself was to suggest certain topics for discussion, striving for a formulation as constant as possible across interviews, but striving also to maintain the tone of a genuine conversation. The interview opened with questions close to the personal experience of the respondent—his career path, his likes and dislikes of political life, and his general view of current problems facing his country. After an extended discussion of a pair of policy issues, he was asked to describe and then to assess the policy-making process. Topics subsequently discussed included the "essential characteristics" of democracy, the differences among the major political parties, the nature of social and political conflicts, the nature of political leadership, the need to control potentially subversive organizations, and the kind of society that the respondent wanted for his children and grandchildren. Time constraints made it impossible to cover all questions in every interview, and therefore certain questions were asked only of random subsamples. This strategy allowed us to tap a wider variety of beliefs, at the cost of reducing our effective sample size for certain questions.[12] All questions in the interview schedule are reproduced (in somewhat abbreviated form) as part of the codebook that appears as appendix B. The interviews lasted an average of about 75 minutes, but there was considerable variation. The minimum time available in the case of the busiest respondents (usually ministers) was half an hour, while one loquacious MP stopped reluctantly only after four hours.

As I have already mentioned, respondents were asked at the conclusion of each interview to complete a short written list of agree-disagree items, taken from a variety of earlier attitude scales.[13] (This questionnaire appears as deck

12. This reduced sample size will raise no major difficulties, except in our discussion of the Social Conflict Index in chapter 7.

13. Both the interview schedule and the questionnaire were translated into Italian using the "double-blind" technique: one bilingual assistant translated them into Italian, a second trans-

5 in the codebook.) Ninety-one percent of the MPs and 64 percent of the deputies complied. This means that 78 percent of the original British random sample and 50 percent of the original Italian sample completed the questionnaire. In Britain there is probably no significant self-selection in the "questionnaire sample." In the Italian case deputies from the extreme Left were most reluctant to respond to these items. Therefore, the responses to the questionnaire in Italy are slightly less alienated and slightly less hostile toward political opponents than a purely random sample would have revealed. Although the differences are not great, the net effect is some attenuation of cross-national differences in response to these items. I have already indicated my reservations about such items, and I will use evidence from the questionnaire sparingly, primarily to provide independent confirmation for judgments based on responses in the interview itself.

THE ANSWERS

To eliminate error in the recording of answers, to make the interviews more conversational, and to allow intensive subsequent analysis of modes of expression and styles of thought, we asked each respondent for permission to tape-record the interview. Only 4 of the 93 British respondents and 2 of the 83 Italians refused this request. The benefits of taping are quite considerable. The absence of note taking (plus the design of the interview schedule) succeeded in most cases in creating an atmosphere of conversation rather than cross-examination. We will see later the utility of having at the analysis stage a verbatim record of the interview.

Obviously, one must consider whether the use of a tape recorder affects the quality and veracity of the interview. Raymond L. Gorden has pointed out that studies of this technique have tended to discount earlier fears about the inhibiting effects of the recorder.[14] In the present case our introduction of the technique as "standard operating procedure" and the physical inconspicuousness of the equipment led in most cases to an almost audible "forgetting" of the recorder several minutes into the interview. The conversational style that a tape recorder allows an interviewer to maintain tends to lead the respondent into an "engaged" discussion, which lowers the probability that he will precensor his responses. Most of our respondents seemed genuinely to enjoy this rare opportunity to reflect on their daily experience. But the most convincing argument in favor of this technique is that few respondents would reveal in an interview of this sort *without* a tape recorder beliefs that they conceal in the presence of a recorder. At least on the kinds of topics covered in this study, respondents who hesitate to express a certain view with the recorder on would in all likelihood hesitate to express that view to the interviewer without the recorder. In other

_____

lated that version back into English, and the process was repeated until agreement on equivalent wording was reached. Each respondent was interviewed in his native language.

14. Gorden, *Interviewing*, p. 177.

words, the effect of the recorder on validity and veracity is simply part of the broader problem of frankness in elite interviews.

It is helpful to imagine a continuum of frankness along which respondents' utterances might be ranged, for this is not a black-and-white matter. Frankness depends on at least two factors: the question and the questioner. At one extreme would be instances in which a respondent was asked a personally sensitive question by someone with a clear potential interest in harming him. At the opposite end would be instances in which a respondent was asked a clearly innocuous question by someone thoroughly trusted. From the point of view of the respondent, few, if any, of the questions in our interviews were potentially sensitive. Asked about economic planning or social conflict or "democracy," few respondents would be likely to fear that their responses, even if made public, would jeopardize their personal interests. The questioners had, from the point of view of the respondent, two important characteristics: remoteness from his daily world and professional qualifications that tended to substantiate assurances of anonymity. My general impression, confirmed by explicit discussions with several respondents, is that although a visiting American researcher might occasionally seem boring, he was seldom seen as malevolent. Indeed, often a respondent prefaced some comment by "I will say this in confidence" and proceeded to a remark that would have been indiscreet if made to a listener not trusted. Neither questions nor questioners in this study seem likely to have engendered special prudence.

Moreover, it would have been difficult for even the most paranoid respondent to disguise his attitude on many of the dimensions of interest to us. He might have disguised his attitude to national economic planning, for example, though it is hard to see why he would have wanted to. It would have been much harder, however, to disguise his ordinary pattern of thinking about such questions, that is, his political style. In answer to questions about party leadership, he might well have disguised his view of the current party leader, though few bothered to do so. It would have been harder to be misleading about the qualities he thought important for political leadership. In summary, then, it seems likely that in most cases both the motivation and the opportunity for deception were lacking.

Of course, not all those interviewed were equally open. A few Italians were quite reserved, apparently doubting the stated purpose of my inquiry. The coders who analyzed each interview were asked at the end to judge the respondent's

Table 2. 2: Coders' Ratings of Frankness, by Country
(in percentages)

Rating	Britain (N = 93)	Italy (N = 83)
Very frank and open	91	64
Basically frank	5	28
Pro-con	3	5
Basically reserved	–	1
Very reserved and closed	–	2

relative frankness.[15] Table 2.2 shows how the two national samples were distributed along this dimension. This evidence does not "prove" the veracity or reliability of the responses, of course, but it does indicate the overall impressions of two independent observers. On balance, we can, I think, trust these interviews.[16]

The Analysis

CODING

Having elicited reliable responses from representative samples of national politicians in Britain and Italy, how do we extract from those responses an understanding of elite political culture? Lucian Pye, a pioneer in this field, has described the problem in the following terms:

> Quite different methods of research are called for in the study of [elite and mass] cultures. Work on the elite political culture involves skill in interpreting ideologies, in characterizing operational codes, and in defining the spirit and calculations that lie behind high-risk political behavior. The study of mass political cultures depends, on the other hand, upon the advanced techniques of survey research and modern methods of measuring public opinion.[17]

As will become clear in a moment, I am not convinced that the appropriate method for studying elite culture is quite so different, but Pye has clearly put the accent in the proper place. Political leaders have, by and large, quite sophisticated and complex political belief systems—one can justifiably say "philosophies"—and the cruder techniques of survey research cannot do justice to the nuances that are critical in understanding these philosophies. In another discussion Pye reflects on the consequent methodological difficulties, linking the problem to psychoanalytic techniques.

> As Erikson has noted, "Psychoanalysis for historical reasons often occupies a position on the borderline of what is demonstrably true, and of what demonstrably *feels* true." What "feels true" is a highly relative matter. Those insights that seem convincing to one person may seem strained, implausible, and even foolish to another; just as a metaphor or simile that seems forceful and illuminating to one reader may appear absurd or trite to another.[18]

15. As explained in the following section, two independent coders rated each interview. There was a fairly high concordance between their judgments of the relative "frankness" of the interviews; the tau-beta intercorrelation was .41. This means that the two coders tended to agree which respondents were relatively open and which seemed more reserved.

16. An alternative way of phrasing this issue is in terms of the extent to which the role adopted by a respondent in the interview situation overlaps with the role he ordinarily plays in politics. This conceptualization of the problem leads to a consideration of the probable predictability of actual behavior from our attitudinal measures, a subject that is treated briefly in the last section of this chapter.

17. Pye in *Political Culture and Political Development*, ed. Lucian W. Pye and Sidney Verba (Princeton: Princeton University Press, 1965), p. 16.

18. Pye, "Personal Identity and Political Ideology," in *Political Decision-makers*, ed. Dwaine

The dilemma is clear: we need a method of inquiry that is capable of reaching for these kinds of insights, yet one that also reaches beyond esthetic appreciation toward acceptable scientific canons of intersubjective validity. How can we do justice to the elusive features of elite political culture without doing violence to our normal standards of verification?

The strategy I have elected is to use trained, sensitive coders as a type of special measuring instrument, asking them to assess the responses of these politicians in terms of a set of fairly subtle categories designed to capture certain central features of a personal political philosophy. This measuring instrument, like any scientific tool, must be calibrated and tetsed for reliability. Therefore, a verbatim transcript of each interview was assessed independently by two different coders. By comparing their independent judgments, we can estimate how well these judgments seem to be measuring "objectively" or "intersubjectively" verifiable features of the respondents' belief systems.[19] This technique—not novel in social science, but rarely applied to the study of political culture and political ideology—offers real promise for reconciling our competing demands for both insight and evidence.

STATISTICAL ANALYSIS

Truth, as Karl Deutsch has said, is the confluence of independent streams of evidence. This notion has been applied to the statistical analysis of the present study. In each chapter we will build up in a sedimentary fashion evidence from various parts of the interview and different kinds of indicators. For each of our primary concerns—political style, cognitive predispositions, and operative ideals—I will offer data from questionnaire items, from open-ended interview questions, and from various types of judgments by the coders. Rather than a single indicator of "political egalitarianism," for example, I will rely on three indicators drawn from different parts of the interview and different modes of response and coding.

There are two related reasons for adopting this technique of analysis. First of all, our interests, as described in the opening chapter, are in *basic* orientations, the fundamental features of a politician's belief system. Theoretically, these orientations should inform his responses to diverse queries and probes. Thus, if responses to a range of independent measures tend to cohere, we have good reason for postulating a common underlying orientation. Second, since certain

Marvick (New York: Free Press, 1961), p. 297. The imbedded quotation is from Erik H. Erikson, *Young Man Luther* (New York: W. W. Norton, 1958), p. 21.

19. Throughout this volume I systematically report the intercoder reliability coefficients for all judgments about which there might reasonably be some doubt. The statistic used is tau-beta, a measure of ordinal correlation between the two independent judgments. In the coding process the independent judgments of the two coders were confronted, and the coders arrived at an agreed final judgment; the statistical analyses reported in this volume are based on these consensual judgments of each interview. For additional discussion of this method of coding, see appendix A.

features of our methodology are novel in the study of political culture, concordance among different kinds of evidence will be particularly reassuring.[20]

But the technique of intercorrelating multiple indicators also raises a nasty problem that I shall term "inter-item assimilation." Naturally, if the correlation between two measures is artifactual, then the inference from that correlation to the validity of the measures is ungrounded. One kind of inter-item assimilation can occur among questionnaire items. For example, the well-known phenomenon of "acquiescence response set" means that the correlation between two items may be artificially inflated by the tendency of some respondents to agree with any statement regardless of their attitude to its content.

A less familiar type of inter-item assimilation can occur in the interview itself. If two related questions are asked in close conjunction, the respondent may tend to reply in a falsely consistent way. If he has just said in response to one question that he does not trust members of the opposing party, he is less likely to say that he cooperates frequently with them than had he not been asked the first question.

A third type of inter-item assimilation menaces the accuracy of the kind of coding employed in this study. A coder's judgment on one variable may spuriously influence his judgment on a later variable. The psychologists' term for this is "halo effect."

If more than one characteristic of a person is to be judged, raters frequently carry over a generalized impression of the person from one rating to the next, or they try to make their ratings consistent. . . . It is apparent that the halo effect reduces the validity of the ratings of some traits and introduces a spurious degree of positive correlation among the traits that are rated.[21]

A final kind of inter-item assimilation is of particular concern in a cross-cultural study. If the coders "expect" to find respondents of one nationality higher on a certain trait, then cross-national differences on the coders' ratings of that trait may be artificially inflated.[22] The obvious solution to this problem would be to disguise the nationality of each respondent, but as a practical matter this is impossible.

20. Statisticians have demonstrated more formally that the use of multiple indicators can considerably increase confidence in the reliability and validity of one's findings. See D. T. Campbell and D. W. Fiske, "Convergent and Discriminant Validation by the Multitrait-Multimethod Matrix," *Psychological Bulletin* 56 (1959): 81–105; and Stuart W. Cook and Claire Selltiz, "A Multiple-Indicator Approach to Attitude Measurement," *Psychological Bulletin* 62 (1964): 36–55. Both these articles are reprinted in *Readings in Attitude Theory and Measurement,* ed. Martin Fishbein (New York: John Wiley & Sons, 1967).

21. Claire Selltiz et al., *Research Methods in Social Relations,* rev. ed. (New York: Holt, Rinehart, and Winston, 1959), pp. 351–52.

22. An analogous kind of "inter-item assimilation" flawed the classic study by T. W. Adorno et al., *The Authoritarian Personality* (New York: Harper & Bros., 1950). For an outstanding discussion of these problems, see Richard Christie and Marie Jahoda, *Studies in the Scope and Method of "The Authoritarian Personality"* (Glencoe, Ill.: Free Press, 1954), esp. pp. 79–89, 184–88.

This is a formidable list of perils. In this study several strategies were used to lessen these dangers. First of all, special attention was devoted to the sequencing of the questions and (subsequently) of the coding. Both respondents and coders were less likely to strive for false consistency between items that were widely separated by other topics. Second, coders and interviewers took special precautions to minimize inter-item assimilation. Interviewers, for example, "legitimated" inconsistent responses in the way they phrased questions. Coders self-consciously attempted to keep their judgments on separate variables distinct and to use equal yardsticks for the different national samples. One simple technique used here to minimize cross-national bias is for coders to work alternately on interviews from one country and then the other.

The strategies mentioned so far are aimed at eliminating inter-item assimilation at its source. Other tactics can help detect and correct for inter-item assimilation after it has occurred. One used in this research was the "cross-coder correlation" technique. If we fear that a coder's judgment on variable A has falsely influenced his judgment on variable B, we can compute the correlation between the two variables using one coder's judgment on variable A and the second coder's judgment on variable B. If the correlation between A and B persists, we can be more confident that the correlation is genuine.

A second technique is based on the closed questionnaire items, for it is impossible for the coder to "bias" his judgments about the interview to accord with responses to a questionnaire that he has not seen, and it is highly unlikely that the respondent would strive for "false" consistency in two such segregated modes of interrogation. Therefore, I will frequently buttress my argument by demonstrating that responses to certain questionnaire items are correlated plausibly with judgments based on the interviews. In the end, there are no easy answers to the methodological predicament we have been discussing. I invite the reader to join me in exercising reasonable caution as we examine the evidence.

Beliefs and Behavior

Any study of beliefs must confront the problematic link between attitudes expressed in an interview and actual behavior. This is a problem far from unique to students of political behavior. A recent survey of psychological studies of attitudes opens with the judgment that

> after more than seventy-five years of attitude research, there is still little, if any consistent evidence supporting the hypothesis that knowledge of an individual's attitude toward some object will allow one to predict the way he will behave with respect to the object.[23]

23. Martin Fishbein, "Attitude and the Prediction of Behavior," in Fishbein, *Attitude Theory and Measurement*, p. 477. This article includes an interesting discussion of the logic and psychologic of the attitude-behavior relationship.

And yet psychologists, like other social scientists, continue to study attitudes, no doubt because the contrary hypothesis that behavior is unrelated to attitude is still less plausible.

Milton Rokeach has pointed out that part of the problem is conceptual, rather than empirical. We must distinguish, he suggests, between attitudes toward objects (Tories, urban planning, free speech) and attitudes toward situations (taking a tea break, voting in Parliament, cooperating in committees). Since "an attitude-object is always encountered within some situation about which we also have an organized attitude," it is misguided to hope to predict behavior on the basis of attitude-toward-object alone.[24]

A way of understanding this problem in our own case is provided by the Greenstein paradigm quoted in chapter 1. Behavior is a joint function of the pulling environment and the pushing attitude. Whether a person's attitude will affect his behavior depends on the pull of the situation. Knowing parliamentarians' attitudes toward economic planning is almost totally irrelevant to predicting legislative voting behavior in Britain or Italy, because the pull of party ties in that situation is overpowering. But knowledge of the parliamentarians' attitudes toward economic planning is probably *not* so irrelevant to predicting their behavior in other circumstances, for example, in private, suasive conversation.

Of course, it is difficult to specify, and even more difficult to operationalize, the precise circumstances under which we would expect a given attitude to make a difference. This practical problem is particularly acute when we want to predict the behavior of a whole set of political actors in common circumstances. Roll-call voting or other public legislative activity is thus attractively simple as a behavioral criterion: in such activities all the actors are faced with a common situation. What is less often recognized is that that situation may be so constraining that no reasonable man would ever predict that attitudes would make much difference.[25]

One feature of the behavior of politicians deserves special notice in this context. Most of their relevant behavior is not physical behavior at all, but verbal behavior; parliaments are, after all, "talking shops." When we listen to politicians talk about politics and policy we are in fact watching them behave. The relevant question, then, is how much overlap there is likely to be between their verbal behavior in the interview situation and their verbal behavior elsewhere. On some topics and in some contexts this overlap is likely to be great. It is un-

24. Milton Rokeach, "Attitude Change and Behavioral Change," *Public Opinion Quarterly* 30 (Winter, 1966–67): 529–50.
25. Cf. William B. Quandt's statement: "In general, it seems that those types of behavior over which one does not exercise conscious control are most likely to be related to enduring character traits or personality formation. Acts such as voting may well be strongly affected by circumstantial considerations of costs and benefits so that the impact of earlier experiences is weakened" (*Revolution and Political Leadership: Algeria, 1954–1968* [Cambridge, Mass.: M.I.T. Press, 1969], p. 198).

likely that the way a politician discusses the issue of urban transport in an interview differs dramatically from the way he would discuss it with a colleague.

There are other issues for which the question of behavioral overlap between interview and "real world" is more problematic. Consider, for example, a question about restrictions on the political activities of "subversive" organizations. We certainly cannot predict behavior directly from responses to this question, for the politician's decision to repress such organizations would depend on what other values and attitudes happened to be engaged by a particular situation. We can, however, talk about the relative propensity of different politicians to urge or support political repression. A politician who in an interview expresses willingness to consider repression is probably more likely to advocate repression in real situations than a politician who in the interview argues against repression.

Rokeach argues (on the basis of some experimental evidence) that the relative primacy of "attitude-toward-object" and "attitude-toward-situation" as determinants of behavior will be a function of the "centrality" of each attitude to the actor, that is, of the depth to which each is embedded in his personal belief system. The evidence we will present linking the orientations discussed in this volume to a wide variety of other beliefs and values will, therefore, be prima facie evidence of their "centrality." But political scientists, long mesmerized by the peculiarly American behavioral criterion of roll-call votes, need to devote more attention to discovering appropriate operational criteria for elite behavior in other institutional settings, need to examine attitudes-toward-situations as well as the attitudes-toward-objects that will be the focus of our inquiry here.

In sum, my argument is for a careful balance between the competing claims of rigor and precision, on the one hand, and common sense and sensitivity, on the other. I take my text from an earlier student of comparative politics:

> We must be content, then, in speaking of such subjects and with such premisses to indicate the truth roughly and in outline, and in speaking about things which are only for the most part true and with premisses of the same kind to reach conclusions that are no better. In that same spirit, therefore, should each type of statement be *received;* for it is the mark of an educated man to look for precision in each class of things just so far as the nature of the subject admits.[26]

In this study we will use caution and counting to discipline our imagination. But we must begin with imagination—and with careful listening. Come listen with me.

26. Aristotle, *Nicomachean Ethics,* Book I, Chapter 3, lines 20–27 (emphasis in the original). *Introduction to Aristotle,* ed. Richard McKeon (New York: Modern Library, 1947), p. 310.

PART I
IDEOLOGY AND POLITICS:
AN ESSAY ON POLITICAL STYLE

3 Ideological Politics:
A Style of Political Analysis

Preliminary Problems

Few concepts in social analysis have inspired such a flood of commentary as has "ideology." Yet few have stimulated the production of so little cumulative knowledge about society and politics. The lack of cumulation is the result, above all, of recurrent confusion of empirical with definitional issues and of both with normative concerns. Moreover, most of the speculation has been pervasively culture-bound. The absence of conceptual clarity has been matched only by the nearly total lack of "hard" (i.e. replicable) empirical evidence.

A number of exhaustive classifications of definitions of ideology have been proferred,[1] and there is probably no great gain to be made by compiling yet another. Yet as many commentators have noted, uncertainties about the meaning of ideology lie at the heart of much of the confusion, and the way to progress must cross the arid plain of definitional clarification.

Giovanni Sartori has pointed to one elemental distinction.

> Discussions about ideology generally fall into two broad domains, namely *ideology in knowledge* and/or *ideology in politics*. With respect to the first area of inquiry the question is whether, and to what extent, man's knowledge is ideologically conditioned or distorted. With respect to the second area of [i]nquiry the question is whether ideology is an essential feature of politics and if so, what does it explain. In the first case "ideology" is contrasted with "truth," science, and valid knowledge in general; whereas in the second case we are not concerned with the truth-value, but with the functional value, so to speak, of ideology.[2]

Sartori goes on to recognize that this distinction is not always neat. Like him, however, I shall here be concerned exclusively with the question "What does

1. See David W. Minar, "Ideology and Political Behavior," *Midwest Journal of Political Science* 5 (1961): 317–31; Arne Naess, *Democracy, Ideology, and Objectivity* (Oslo: University Press, 1956); and Samuel H. Barnes, "Ideology and the Organization of Conflict," *Journal of Politics* 28 (1966): 513–30.

2. Giovanni Sartori, "Politics, Ideology, and Belief Systems," *American Political Science Review* 63 (1969): 398.

ideology explain about the nature of politics?" Ideology will not, therefore, be taken to mean "irrationality" or intellectual dishonesty.[3]

A second stipulation is necessary. Ideology has often been used to refer to some sort of disembodied "presence" hovering over the political process.[4] Such a notion may be useful to historians of ideas. Here, however, I assume that if the term is to be useful to social scientists, there must be some identifiable characteristic of individual political actors that justifies describing their attitudes and behavior as ideological.

One final stipulation: The terms "ideology" and "ideological" must refer to characteristics that, at least in principle, are variables rather than constants. I reject, in other words, conceptions of ideology that assume that everyone (or at least everyone in modern society) is equally ideological.[5]

Some political actors are, then, ideological in their attitudes and behavior, while others are less so. What could this assertion mean? Even within the limits already set out the range of interpretations that have been offered is enormous. Perhaps the simplest way to make some sense of this range is to consider a hypothetical "menu" of components. Table 3.1 presents in schematic form a list

Table 3.1: Possible Elements in the Definition of Ideology or Ideological

"A political actor may be said to be ideological when he is . . . " *(Choose one or more.)*

1. Guided by a comprehensive, consistent, deductively organized belief system
2. Guided by an explicit, consciously held belief system
3. Guided by a belief system that is closed, rigid, resistant to new information
4. Guided by a belief system that is affectively or emotionally charged
5. Guided by a belief system that distorts or oversimplifies reality, that is biased or irrational
6. Guided by a philosophy of history and/or a social theory that is applied to everyday questions and issues
7. Concerned with abstract principles, not concrete interests
8. Future-oriented, utopian
9. Hostile and intolerant toward political opponents; prone to dichotomous, "black-white" thinking; paranoid
10. Opposed to compromise, bargaining, incrementalism, and other aspects of pluralist politics
11. Alienated from established social and political institutions
12. Extremist
13. Oriented to conflict and opposed to consensus
14. Authoritarian; a moral absolutist; prone to value ends, not means

---

3. A number of scholars use such a definition, even though they appear to be discussing what Sartori terms "ideology in politics." See, for example, Joseph J. Spengler, "Theory, Ideology, Non-economic Values, and Politico-Economic Development" in *Tradition, Values, and Socio-Economic Development,* ed. Ralph Braibanti and Joseph J. Spengler (Durham, N. C.: Duke University Press, 1961), pp. 3–56; Harry Johnson, "Ideology and the Social System," in *International Encyclopedia of the Social Sciences* (New York: Crowell Collier and Macmillan, 1968), 7: 76–84; Gustav Bergmann, *The Metaphysics of Logical Positivism* (New York: Longmans Green, 1954), pp. 300–25.

4. See R. V. Burks, "A Conception of Ideology for Historians," *Journal of the History of Ideas* 10 (1949):183–98; and Feliks Gross, ed., *European Ideologies* (New York: Philosophical Library, 1948).

5. For such a conception see, for example, Robert E. Lane, *Political Ideology* (New York:

of 14 characteristics, each of which has appeared with some frequency as one element in a definition of ideology or ideological.[6]

Most, if not all characterizations of ideological political actors can be interpreted as different combinations of the elements in table 3.1. Thus, for example, Edward Shils' classic description of "ideological politics" centers on "the assumption that politics should be conducted from the standpoint of a coherent, comprehensive set of beliefs which must override every other consideration"[7] (basically element 1, plus a bit of 14). To this central characteristic he adds element 6 ("ideological politicians must see their actions in the context of the totality of history"), element 7 (he contrasts ideological politics with the politics of "interests"), element 8 ("[ideological politics] have been obsessed with futurity"), element 9 ("ideological politics are the politics of 'friend-foe,' 'we-they,' 'who-whom' "), element 10 (to ideological politics he counterposes "the politics of civility," which relies on "compromise and reasonableness"), element 11 ("ideological politics are alienative politics"), and element 12 ("ideological politicians" are said to believe that all virtue lies at one pole or the other of the left-right spectrum). Using this definition, Shils argues that "the age of ideological politics is passing" and that this is a desirable trend. Here, of course, is the essence of the much disputed "end of ideology" thesis. (Shils is not the only student of politics to make this argument, but his discussion is the most comprehensive and provocatively phrased and will be used here to represent a long list of contributions by equally distinguished scholars.)[8]

Before turning to Shils' empirical and normative assertions, it may be well to pause briefly over his definitional exercise. For although all good logicians know as Humpty Dumpty did that words can mean anything we want them to, it is not true that any definition is as good (or scientifically useful) as any other. Shils' definition (and others like it) in fact embodies a quite complex set of empirical assertions. His argument can be interpreted as follows:

Proposition 1. Certain politicians have characteristic A. (They "conduct politics from the standpoint of a coherent, comprehensive set of beliefs.") Such politicians are "ideological."

Free Press, 1962); and Clifford Geertz, "Ideology as a Cultural System," in *Ideology and Discontent,* ed. David E. Apter (New York: Free Press, 1964), pp. 47–73.

6. The literature is gargantuan. A brief, but representative bibliography is given in Apter, *Ideology and Discontent,* pp. 329–34.

7. Edward Shils, "Ideology and Civility: On the Politics of the Intellectual," *Sewanee Review* 66 (1958): 450–80. All later references to Shils in the text are to this article. For a later version of his views, see his "The Concept and Function of Ideology," in *International Encyclopedia of the Social Sciences* (New York: Crowell Collier and Macmillan, 1968) 7:66–75.

8. Notable examples include S. M. Lipset (for example, *Political Man* [London: Mercury Books, 1960], pp. 403–17); Raymond Aron (for example, *The Opium of the Intellectuals,* trans. Terence Kilmartin [New York: W. W. Norton, 1962]), and Daniel Bell (for example, *The End of Ideology* [Glencoe: Free Press, 1960]). The list is potentially endless. See, for example, the references in *The End of Ideology Debate,* ed. Chaim Waxman (New York: Funk and Wagnalls, 1968).

Proposition 2.   Politicians who have characteristic A also have characteristics
                  B_1-B_n, where B_1-B_n refer to characteristics such as elements
                  6–14 in table 3.1.
Proposition 3.   The frequency of the empirical syndrome composed of A and
                  B_1-B_n among politicians is diminishing.
Proposition 4.   Because B_1-B_n are undesirable traits for politicians to have, the
                  trend stated in proposition 3 is praiseworthy.

In all the debate about "the end of ideology," discussions of proposition 2
have been very rare, probably because in most cases, as in Shils', it appears to
be a definitional (hence, nondebatable) issue. As stated here, however, it is
clearly an empirical assertion about a presumed causal link between A and B_1-
B_n. Naturally, Humpty Dumpty was right; Shils can define "ideological" however he pleases. But it is scientifically counterproductive to close off empirical
questions "by definition." Moreover, if Shils chooses to include B_1-B_n in his
definition, he is then faced with the task of showing that such creatures exist.
As Arne Naess has argued in a similar context, "if 'ideology' is defined so as to
include sweeping causal relations, it is far from being a 'fact' that any ideology
has ever existed."[9]

In this chapter and the next I will investigate propositions 1 and 2 in the light
of some empirical evidence. I will examine, in my two samples of politicians,
the occurrence of some, if not all, of the elements listed in table 3.1. But more
than their occurrence, I want to investigate their *co*occurrence, that is, the extent
to which these traits are empirically intercorrelated. Chapter 5 contains an
analysis of proposition 3 about trends in the frequency with which these traits
occur; chapter 6 discusses the cross-national differences highlighted by this study.
None of this analysis will be conclusive. But the way to progress not only crosses
the arid plain of definitional analysis; it also winds through the murky swamp
of empirical investigation.

Styles of Political Analysis

Politicians manifestly differ in the way they analyze policy. Some concentrate
on broad social and moral principles, while others emphasize specific situations
and details. Some argue deductively from general political or social or economic
theories, while others rely on induction from their own experience. Some refer
to benefits or losses to particular groups in society, while others refer to technical
or financial practicality, or administrative efficiency. Some refer to past or future utopias, that is, more or less ideal states of society. Some consider political
feasibility. Some even refer explicitly to particular doctrines such as capitalism
or socialism. Some place an issue in a historical context. Some attribute blame
for a problem, while others phrase their analysis in "neutral" terms.

I shall use the term "political style" to refer to the complex of attributes listed

9. Naess, *Democracy, Ideology, and Objectivity,* p. 196.

in the previous paragraph. Not *what* men think about politics and policy, but *how* they do so—this is the essence of political style. And political style provides one way of interpreting the notion of "ideological politics."[10] An ideological politician is, according to this interpretation, a politician who analyzes policy in a particular way. It is reasonable to argue (assuming we can find the appropriate empirical clustering of traits) that such a politician is one who focuses on general principles rather than specific details, who reasons deductively rather than inductively, who stresses the role of "ideas" in politics. This is the *core* of what is usually meant by ideological politics. To speak of "ideological conflict," if it is not pleonastic, must be to speak of conflict about ideas or sets of ideas (ideologies). To speak of a "fanatic ideologue," or a "dogmatic ideologue," if it is not pleonastic, must be to speak of a political actor who is fanatic or dogmatic *and* who stresses the importance of political ideas or ideals. Ideological thinking need not, of course, be embedded in one of the familiar "isms"; an idiosyncratic ideologue, who analyzes politics and policy in terms of a grand, but unusual theory, is no less ideological in his style of thought because he lacks allegiance to one of the more commonly recognized doctrines. It is, to repeat, not the what, but the how of political thought that makes it ideological. This investigation of the role of ideology in politics thus begins by asking how politicians think and talk about particular policy problems.

Each British and Italian politician interviewed in this study was asked to discuss several policy issues facing his country. One of the issues was proposed by the respondent himself, in answer to the question "What are the three or four most important [domestic] problems facing this country today?" The second issue was drawn randomly from a list of four that was designed to reflect the diversity of public problems. These four were national economic planning, poverty, crime, and urban transportation. Roughly equal numbers of respondents in each country were asked about each of these four topics. In the case of both "his" issue and the "suggested" issue, each respondent was asked to analyze the causes or origins of the problem and to offer his suggestions for solutions.

One of the stylistic characteristics most relevant to the problem of ideology and politics concerns *the focus of the politician's discussion.* Sometimes a respondent would take a technical issue and deal with it in terms of sweeping principles. Others would take potentially grand issues and move immediately to specific details. Still others offered mixes of both principles and specifics. Each discussion of each respondent was rated by the coders on a five-point scale, from "extreme generalizer, focusing on the general, philosophical principles involved, with little or no attention to the specific details of the problem" to

10. Others who have proposed this interpretation include Herbert Spiro, *Government by Constitution* (New York: Random House, 1959), pp. 178–210; Sidney Verba, "Comparative Political Culture," in *Political Culture and Political Development,* ed. Lucian W. Pye and Sidney Verba (Princeton: Princeton University Press, 1965), pp. 512–60; and Harvey Waterman, *Political Change in Contemporary France* (Columbus, Ohio: Charles E. Merrill, 1969), esp. pp. 113–38.

"extreme particularizer, focusing on the details of the problem, with little or no discussion of general principles."

One example of an "extreme generalizer" was provided by a Conservative MP who found in a passing and apparently technical administrative issue an occasion for a general ethical disquisition.

A Bill has been published today which makes it obligatory for any person selling a radio or television set to give official information so that the G.P.O. can make sure that a licence is taken out for it. Now I regard this as a very dubious step. . . . What seems to me wrong is that one should use for the purposes of government a private transaction. You are really making the private citizen who is a radio dealer, you're bringing him into the scope of law enforcement. . . . It is the duty of the collecting authority—the G.P.O. in this case—to take such steps as are open to it to minimize evasion. But you cross what seems to be a very important line when you say to a third party, "You shall report anybody you know to have a set." . . . It is essentially an informer state. (B 68)[11]

It is characteristic of a "generalizer" that he sees such "very important lines" where others see merely technical questions, that he moves easily and quickly from a specific policy problem to general principles of political philosophy.

The other end of the spectrum can be represented by a leading Scots Labourite and former minister, discussing the issue of poverty.

Well, it's very difficult to explain. First, let me say right away there's probably a certain amount which results from people's own silly activities and stupidities, this sort of thing. But on the other hand, there is a certain amount which arises out of sheer misfortune, if you like. Say a couple get married, and the fellow's a lower-paid worker, say he's only getting about ten pounds a week. And he's not been married about three or four months before his wife is seriously ill, and whilst he gets national insurance benefits, he's involved in expenditures. . . . He then dies and his wife is left a widow. Things of this kind. Well, it's simply through, if you like, a series of events, the fellow is really up against it. . . . There are a number of circumstances like that . . . one can give examples, but it's very difficult to classify them. . . . And we've spent a lot of time in the last two years trying to find out the facts about this, and trying to see what ways this can be tackled. (B110)

Naturally, most discussions fell between the extreme categories and included some reference both to principles and to details. But even in these intermediate cases, differences were often marked. Consider the discussions by two Italian deputies of the problem of crime.

11. References after each quotation indicate the country ("I" or "B") and respondent number for the interview cited.

This has become a problem because all the powers of defense of the State, beginning with the first political nucleus, the family, have been diminished and weakened. When the family is no longer the family, when the father no longer exercises the power over his children which he should exercise . . . society begins to lose that structure . . . . In the name of a pseudo-liberty society has undergone excesses—in other sectors, we've come to the exaltation of the conscientious objector. You know very well that all the moral powers of this people have become slack. In our opinion moral principles must not and cannot undergo evolution. Morality is permanent. It's stupid to argue that in the name of changing times, morality must change. Morality is immanent; it is permanent. [*What can the government do about this problem?*] For the problems of crime, you must always go back to the origin: more powers to the State and give back authority to the executive powers and to the organs of the police, too. (I95)

There doesn't exist a criminality which has a single character in all the Italian provinces. Different forms of criminality exist. Crime in Turin or Milan isn't the same as crime in Sardinia or Sicily or as other forms of crime which exist in the rest of Italy. Crime is profoundly tied to social change—for example, the most recent incidents of bankrobbing in Lombardy. . . . In Sardinia the *banditismo*—there is a certain tradition there. To say, as we used to, that crime has exclusively economic origins, doesn't seem right to me. [*How can this problem be dealt with?*] Well, let's say the criminality of the metropolis you must handle with a new kind of police organization. . . . I don't know, say the creation of specialized teams. (I47)

The first of these discussions, by a neo-Fascist, is not without reference to specifics, but certainly stresses general principles. The second, by a member of the left-wing Socialist Party of Proletarian Unity (PSIUP), mentions some broad generalizations, but emphasizes the particularities of the problem. The first was coded a "moderate generalizer"; the second, a "moderate particularizer."

A second and related stylistic characteristic concerned *the extent to which the respondent appeared to reason synoptically,* deducing his analysis from a general, abstract political or social or economic theory. The coding instructions included the following queries. "Is a chain of reasoning, including certain theoretical premises, given for reply to the (implied) question 'Why do what you propose?' How distant is the solution from the problem? A solution that gets at 'the roots' of the problem implies some theory about what those roots are; a solution that treats symptoms implies no such theory." Once again a five-point scale was used to rate each respondent's discussion of each of the two issues.

One example of the use of theoretical analysis to illuminate a problem is provided by a leading Italian Christian Democrat.

The fundamental problem which we must confront is the problem of modern-
izing the State. . . . I think it won't be possible to deal with it in the traditional ways, revising the career paths, reviewing the organization charts, the
numbers and so on, but really discussing if the functions which the modern
State must have are the same as in the past. [We must] ask ourselves if the
State should stop at the legislative and directive part and then remove all
direct authority for management. . . . If you don't go right to the root in
political philosophy, right to the very concept of the State itself, I don't think
you will be able to really modernize the State. (I38)

Another example of deductive thinking in policy analysis comes from a discussion by a prominent Communist intellectual of the problem of regional
poverty in Italy.

We want a society greatly developed economically, and we argue that Italy
has a type of capitalist structure born late, after the American or British, born
already subject to foreign capitalisms, and a capitalism which isn't able to do
that which has been done in other modern capitalist countries. . . . There
are some islands of capitalist development, which have used the rest of the
country as you use a colony—a place where you get cheap labor and keep
down the level of the labor market. . . . All this happens in all countries
where there is a retarded capitalism. You'll see that any country which has
this type of history has this nature. We maintain that if you want economic
development, you must break up this type of capitalist development. As long
as the great capital remains in the hands of private monopolistic groups, we
won't have the homogeneous development that we need, because it isn't in the
logic of capitalism. . . . The one sure thing is that in Italy we have had all the
forms, right from the handbook—a classic case of retarded capitalism. (I87)

It would, of course, be wrong to take too seriously the half-joking reference to
"the handbook," but implicit throughout this discussion is an image of policy
analysis based on socioeconomic theory.

On the other hand, many respondents discussed policy with little or no theoretical analysis. A British Conservative, for example, was typical of many of his
fellow countrymen in seeing poverty almost exclusively in phenomenological
terms and in reasoning inductively from personal experience.

Well, quite honestly, I don't see very much poverty any more. My constituency is going along fairly well, we've had no unemployment virtually for a
long time. Even the lower-paid workers are really, comparatively speaking,
say compared to fifteen years ago, are quite well off. [*Would you in fact say
there was poverty in Britain today?*] If you go down to the East End [of Lon-
don] you may find some there, or even the sort of Rachmann [an infamous
London slumlord] area in Paddington, but I just don't know. [*What can be
done about this?*] I would say just by getting rid of this wage freeze and getting

expansion going again. I mean, I'm quite sure there wasn't much poverty in the thirteen years of Tory rule. We were gradually overcoming it and standards were going up as is shown by the number of TV aerials outside Council houses [public housing]. (B31)

Rating discussions on these dimensions is not always easy, and there are, of course, many mixed cases. But the coders were fairly consistent in their judgments. Only about 10 percent of all discussions were rated more than one point apart on the five-point "generalizer-particularizer" scale, and only 20 percent were rated more than one point apart on the "inductive-deductive" scale.[12] These two scales are logically distinct, since it would be possible for a respondent to reason deductively from some theory, and yet concentrate most of his attention on relevant details; conversely he could mouth abstractions without building his analysis around any single theoretical framework. Yet we expect intuitively to find a relationship between "generalizing" and "deductive thinking," and later evidence will confirm this.

The remaining stylistic characteristics are more straightforward, and thus illustrations are less necessary. One concerns *the extent to which the respondent placed his analysis of the problem in a historical context.*[13] A respondent, for example, who began his discussion of the problem of economic development in Italy by noting that "the Italian South had its periods of refulgence during the Greek domination and then during the period of the Roman Empire" (I92) was rated "high" on this three-point scale, as were many others in both countries whose historical references were less grand. Another three-point scale rated *the extent to which the respondent "moralized" the issue* "by assigning blame for the problem to someone."[14] Here, for example, a high rating was assigned to a Communist who explained Italy's housing problem by referring to "capitalists and landowners [who want] not a reasonable profit, but 'super-profit.'" (I42)

Other stylistic characteristics involved the presence or absence of a series of criteria for judging policy. These codes all took the following form: "In discussing this issue, does the respondent refer to ——— as a relevant criterion for proposing or opposing policies?" For example, one such characteristic rated the use of *benefits or losses to (named) social groups* as such a criterion; here were noted references to "helping the farmers of this country," "solving the problems of the South," or "increasing the power of the proletariat." Other characteristics rated included references to *political acceptability* ("In this prices-and-incomes thing, a government will find it extremely difficult to operate a

12. The tau-beta reliability coefficient was between .43 and .51 for "generalizer-particularizer" and between .37 and .43 for the "inductive-deductive" scale.

13. Note that this characteristic concerns not mere passing references to historical events, but rather the use of a historical context in explicating the problem. The reliability coefficient for "historical context" ranged between .46 and .60 (between 2 and 5 percent were placed at opposite ends of the three-point scale).

14. The reliability coefficient for "moralizer" ranged between .48 and .58 (5 percent were placed at opposite ends of the three-point scale).

compulsory policy if it was not acquiesced in by the vast majority of people"—
B24); *technical practicality or administrative efficiency* ("We need to rationalize
and simplify our administrative procedures, make them more functional and
economical"—I57); *tradition* ("If you're going to preserve the whole crown of
our Anglo-Christian-Judaic civilization, then the less macrogovernment, the
better"—B32); and *cost* ("We have to cut our cloth according to our requirements; people have to learn the value of money"—B46).[15]

Finally, two kinds of arguments especially relevant to the notion of ideology
were rated. First of all, the presence was noted of *arguments based explicitly on a
named ideology or doctrine,* such as a demand for "socialist planning" or an
attack on "free enterprise in urban transport." (In Britain the most commonly
mentioned ideologies were socialism, capitalism, and free enterprise. In Italy,
in addition to those just listed, Marxism, communism, fascism, and liberalism
were mentioned with some frequency.)

Table 3.2: Stylistic Characteristics of Issue-Discussions, by Country
(in percentages)

| | Country | |
Stylistic characteristics	Britain (N = 177)*	Italy (N = 161)*
1. Generalizer-particularizer		
Extreme generalizer	3	5
Moderate generalizer	16	37
Mixed	25	35
Moderate particularizer	44	20
Extreme particularizer	12	3
2. Inductive-deductive thinking		
Extreme deductive	3	10
Moderate deductive	17	35
Mixed	35	31
Moderate inductive	27	16
Extreme inductive	18	8
3. Historical context given		
Explicitly and centrally	24	38
Vaguely or in passing	42	37
Not at all	34	25
4. Discussion moralized		
Explicitly and centrally	14	29
Vaguely or in passing	29	32
Not at all	57	39
5. Group benefits as criterion		
Explicitly and centrally	14	25
Vaguely or in passing	19	20
Not at all	67	55

15. The reliability coefficients for the stylistic characteristics listed in this paragraph are as
follows: for "reference to group benefits," tau-beta = .68 (15 percent rated at opposite ends of
the three-point scale); for "reference to acceptability," .37 (8 percent); for "reference to practicality," .32 (11 percent). Reliability coefficients have not been calculated for "reference to tradition" and "reference to cost," but they no doubt fall in the same range as those given above.

6. Political acceptability as criterion		
Explicitly and centrally	20	6
Vaguely or in passing	28	14
Not all at	52	80
7. Practicality as criterion		
Explicitly and centrally	37	30
Vaguely or in passing	44	33
Not at all	19	37
8. Tradition as criterion		
Explicitly and centrally	2	1
Vaguely or in passing	8	11
Not at all	90	88
9. Cost as criterion		
Explicitly and centrally	19	4
Vaguely or in passing	18	12
Not at all	63	84
10. Reference to named ideology		
Explicitly and centrally	5	12
Vaguely or in passing	18	19
Not at all	77	69
11. Reference to future utopia		
Explicitly and centrally	1	3
Vaguely or in passing	12	31
Not at all	87	66
12. Reference to past utopia		
Explicitly and centrally	0	0
Vaguely or in passing	5	4
Not at all	95	96

*The unit of enumeration here is a single discussion of a given issue. Nearly every respondent was asked to discuss two separate issues; therefore, the NS shown are approximately twice the total number of respondents in each national sample.

Secondly, *the use of utopias* as standards for judging policy was noted. The instruction to coders was "Does the respondent act politically with respect to this issue by moving toward some pre-defined ideal future or past society, rather than by reacting to existing problems?" The best example of this kind of thinking came from an Italian rightist who, to the amazement of his listener, unfolded an incredibly detailed plan for remolding Italian society along corporativist lines (I52). More typical, if less dramatic, was the Italian Socialist who envisaged a solution to the urban transport problem through the restructuring of city maps, placing both residences and places of work in a ring around the city and then closing the centers to all private transport (I13). Even this pallid utopia was enough to justify a moderate rating on this dimension.[16] As this example indicates, the threshold for a utopian rating was very low. Even so, only a small number of respondents qualified.

These, then, are the main themes of political style investigated in this research. Table 3.2 presents the marginal distributions for each national sample, lumping together both issue-discussions from each interview, for each of the twelve

16. Reliability coefficients have not been calculated for "reference to [named] ideology" and "reference to [past or future] utopias," but they are fairly high, probably in the range of tau-beta = .50–.60.

stylistic dimensions. I will discuss some of the marked cross-national differences later, but first there is a prior pair of questions: Do these characteristics cluster in any intelligible pattern? And if so, what are the main dimensions of political style?

One way of proceeding with this problem is to examine the intercorrelations among the several stylistic themes across different respondents. If respondents who are high on characteristic 1 tend to be high on characteristics 2 and 3, we can say that these characteristics tend to form a "stylistic syndrome." The most efficient way of discovering such syndromes is factor analysis. By adding together his scores on the two separate issue-discussions, each respondent was assigned a summary score on each stylistic characteristic. These summary scores were intercorrelated and the resultant matrix of intercorrelations was factor analyzed, using the varimax rotation procedure.[17]

Because there is often a tendency to treat this methodology as a kind of hocus-pocus, let me clarify what the results mean and what they do not mean. The factors extracted reflect the empirical clusters of stylistic characteristics that tend to "go together." But these factors can be no better than the data from which they are generated. Because most of the correlations among these items are fairly low, the first conclusion must be that, as operationalized in this research, stylistic characteristics tend to be fairly independent of one another.[18] Another restriction lies in the selection of items included in the list of stylistic characteristics. Every attempt was made to construct an exhaustive list. Nevertheless, every reader will no doubt have a candidate that has been ignored, and some may feel that certain aspects are overrepresented. Since the study of political style is in its infancy, there is no generally agreed "laundry list," and adding or deleting a number of items from my list would to some extent change the factor structure. However, subject to these important reservations, the factor structures presented here do reflect the main dimensions of political style.

Table 3.3 identifies the first three factors when data from both countries are pooled for one factor analysis. Each factor can be interpreted in terms of the most closely related stylistic characteristics—in technical terms, those that "load" most heavily on it. Factor 1 represents the clustering of four primary characteristics—generalizer-particularizer, deductive-inductive thinking, refer-

17. In order to employ complex multivariate techniques, I have at this point in the analysis treated the basic data as if they were measured at the interval level rather than merely the ordinal level. For a further discussion of this type of compromise with the realities of data analysis, see Sidney Verba, Norman H. Nie, and Jae-On Kim, *The Modes of Democratic Participation: A Cross-National Comparison,* Sage Professional Papers in Comparative Politics, vol. 2, no. 01–013 (Beverly Hills, Calif.: Sage, 1971), pp. 67–68. A standard treatment of the technique of factor analysis can be found in R. J. Rummel, *Applied Factor Analysis* (Evanston, Ill.: Northwestern University Press, 1970).

18. The mean communality is about .40; that is, about 40 percent of the total variance is common to the set of characteristics and 60 percent represents purely idiosyncratic or random variation in each trait. Of course, the total communality is attenuated as a function of the unreliability of the individual coding judgments.

Table 3.3: Dimensions of Political Style: A Factor Analysis of Stylistic Characteristics,
Both Countries Grouped

Factor 1: Ideological Style	
Generalizer-particularizer	.80
Inductive-deductive thinking	.80
Reference to named ideology	.47
Reference to future utopia	.45
Factor 2: Traditionalism	
Tradition as criterion	.86
Reference to past utopia	.72
Historical context given	.32
Factor 3: Partisanship	
Discussion moralized	.75
Group benefits as criterion	.32
[Practicality as criterion	−.29]

NOTE: Entries are loadings of stylistic characteristics on factors. Except for bracketed entry, cut-off point was loadings $\geq$ .30. Varimax rotation used.

ence to a named ideology, and reference to a *future* utopia. This factor reflects a tendency for some politicians consistently to generalize, to use an abstract deductive theory, to use specifically ideological terms, and to refer to more ideal future states of society. On the other hand, other politicians tend consistently to talk of specific details, to reason without the benefit of general theories, and to avoid the use of ideological or utopian terminology. The clustering of these four variables indicates the importance of a dimension that it is natural to call "ideological style."[19]

While our primary attention will be devoted to this first dimension, the next two factors that emerge from the analysis are also of interest. Factor 2 brings out the mutual linking among three other variables: reference to tradition, reference to a *past* utopia, and provision of a historical context for the discussion of an issue. It seems plausible to call this dimension "traditionalism." Note that the use of a historical framework for analyzing an issue is related not to ideological style as operationalized in factor 1, but rather to traditionalism. Apparently, it is not the ideologues, but the traditionalists who think in historical terms.

Finally, factor 3 indicates that the next clustering of stylistic characteristics includes "moralization" of the issue, reference to group benefits, and the

19. The extent to which this factor dominates this set of stylistic characteristics is revealed by three facts. First, about 44 percent of the total common variance in these variables is accounted for by this factor. Second, essentially the same factor is the first to emerge when we factor analyze subsamples of the data separately. Each national sample was divided into four groups according to which "suggested" issue was discussed, giving a total of eight subsamples. In each case the first factor was virtually identical to the "ideological style" factor. Third, essentially the same factor structure through the first three factors emerges in both the rotated and unrotated versions of the factor analysis. Because of the close apparent relationship between generalizer-particularizer and inductive-deductive thinking and the consequent possibility that inclusion of both had biased the original factor analysis, a seocnd analysis was carried out, omitting inductive-deductive thinking entirely. The resultant factor structure was in all respects virtually identical to that presented in table 3.3.

absence of references to technical practicality or administrative efficiency. This dimension should probably be termed "partisanship," since those who score high on it discuss issues in terms of blame and distributive justice, while those who score low refer instead to more "objective" criteria.

The significance of these three factors is highlighted by the fact that, with only one important modification, separate analyses for Britain and Italy (table 3.4) bring out essentially the same dimensions. The first three factors from the British analysis are virtually the same as those from the analysis based on both samples. (One minor emendation is that in Britain reference to tradition is included in both the first and second factors.) The Italian analysis is best interpreted as showing that within the Italian sample, "ideological style" and "partisanship" (factors 1 and 3 from the joint analysis) are themselves intercorrelated. Factor 1 in the Italian analysis represents both "ideological style" and "partisanship," while factor 2 is virtually identical to factor 2 from the joint analysis. (A minor qualification involves the fairly high loading for "reference to political acceptability.")

The primary conclusion to be drawn from this excursion into a fairly recondite methodology is a simple one.[20] Politicians analyze policy in systematically dif-

Table 3.4: Dimensions of Political Style: A Factor Analysis of Stylistic Characteristics, by Country

BRITAIN		ITALY	
Factor 1		*Factor 1*	
Generalizer-particularizer	.86	Generalizer-particularizer	.82
Inductive-deductive thinking	.76	Inductive-deductive thinking	.79
Reference to named ideology	.41	Practicality as criterion	−.42
Tradition as criterion	.35	Reference to future utopia	.42
Reference to future utopia	.32	Reference to named ideology	.41
		Discussion moralized	.38
Factor 2		*Factor 2*	
Tradition as criterion	.79	Tradition as criterion	.91
Reference to past utopia	.60	Reference to past utopia	.73
Historical context given	.47	Political acceptability as criterion	.43
		[Historical context given	.25]
Factor 3			
Practicality as criterion	.78		
Discussion moralized	−.48		
Group benefits as criterion	−.34		

NOTE: Entries are loadings of stylistic characteristics on factors. Except for bracketed entry, cut-off point was loadings ≧ .30. Varimax rotation used.

20. A final reservation must be noted. The factor structure that has been discovered is, of course, based ultimately on the coders' judgments. It is possible that this structure reflects not the basic dimensions of political style in some objective sense, but rather the basic dimensions along which coders analyze political style. There is no final way of refuting this possibility, except by repeating the study with separate coders independently rating each stylistic dimension. In this study coders were instructed to judge each item independently, and the double-coding procedure provides some protection against such biasing. Moreover, there are a few features

ferent ways, and their modes of analysis differ most notably along a dimension it is reasonable to call ideological style. This dimension certainly does not encompass all the characteristics often ascribed to ideological politics, but it does include the most central ones. We can use each respondent's score on factor 1 as an Ideological Style Index (ISI).[21] A number of correlates of this index justify this identification.

The Ideological Style Index:
Some Validating Correlates

One common approach to the study of ideology and politics focuses on "ideological sensitivity," the extent to which men organize their information about politics in terms of systematic, abstract conceptual dimensions.[22] A similar measure of the ideological sensitivity of our respondents was derived independently of the assessments summarized in the Ideological Style Index, and we must now examine the concordance between these two standards. Our respondents were asked to describe "the most important differences between the major political parties." Each discussion of these party differences was rated on a five-point scale according to the abstractness of the respondent's system of classification. One respondent, for example, clearly used a scheme that fit each party into a more general theory of politics, philosophy, and history.

> Look, as far as I'm concerned *ideologies* don't exist. There is only one ideology, which is derived from certain postulates of the French Revolution. . . .
> The first attack was [made by] liberalism, which contested and attacked the conservative world [of prerevolutionary France] on the basis of certain presuppositions. . . . Then what happened? After this first series of theorems

of the factor structure—like the presence of "historical context" in the second rather than the first factor—that run counter to our expectations (and therefore counter to the presumptive direction of biasing). In any event, even if the possibility discussed here were wholly correct, it would affect only the dimensional analysis in the present section. The Ideological Style Index would still reflect significant and reliable differences in the way politicians discuss issues.

21. Operationally, the Ideological Style Index is the sum of a respondent's ratings on each of the four component variables, standardized and weighted according to the factor loading of each on Factor 1. Of course, the ISI is dependent in part on the nature of the issue being discussed. Discussions of economic planning tended to be more ideological than average, discussions of urban transport somewhat less than average. Because time constraints meant that only two issues were discussed in any given interview, each respondent's precise ISI rating for this study was a function to some extent of the random choice of issues. But there is a high correlation between a respondent's ISI score on "his" issue and his score on the "suggested" issue; about two-thirds of those rated "high" on one issue were also rated "high" on the other, regardless of what those issues were. The ISI, in other words, measures a relatively stable feature of an individual politician's style of policy analysis.

22. The measure was introduced in Angus Campbell, Philip E. Converse, Warren E. Miller, and Donald E. Stokes, *The American Voter* (New York: John Wiley & Sons, 1960), pp. 216–65. Similar measures have been used in Samuel J. Eldersveld, *Political Parties* (Chicago: Rand McNally, 1964); Samuel H. Barnes, *Party Democracy* (New Haven: Yale University Press, 1967); and Everett Carll Ladd, Jr, *Ideology in America: Change and Response in a City, a Suburb, and a Small Town* (Ithaca, N.Y.: Cornell University Press, 1969).

had been derived from the axioms of the ideology, some sharper mathematicians came along and said, "But if that is true, then ergo this is true, too." Socialism doesn't deny liberalism; instead it proceeds from liberalism to demonstrate that if liberalism is true, then it follows you should be a socialist. And then Karl Marx didn't dispute socialism. He only said, "If socialism is true, then socialism must become communism." This is the same reasoning of Mao, who says, "If communism is true, then Maoism must be true." Now then, all the parties are in this line of dialectical reasoning in which the last term, the most evolved, is always right, if you accept the geometry. (I6)

Equally comprehensive and abstract conceptual frameworks for describing the party system were offered by respondents who used the classical Marxist model, linking specific parties to specific economic classes.

At the other extreme came those respondents whose descriptions of the political parties were nearly devoid of abstractions. One working class Labour MP, for example, defined the most important difference between the British parties in these terms:

Well, of course, the Labour Party is the avenue through which the man without advantages, without education, without money, can get to the fore in helping to arrange his country's affairs. The other party, of course, caters less for that type of man, and predominantly for the person who is already blessed with the means to education and economic sufficiency. To put it bluntly, the Conservative Party is the home of the wealthier section of our community and the Labour Party is the place where people who have more brains than money tend to congregate. (B95)

Naturally, even the lowest scorers on this variable have certain basic organizing concepts, unlike many individuals in the mass public. But relatively speaking, some politicians are much more theoretical than others in the way they structure the relations between parties.[23] And as table 3.5 shows, the more abstract the framework for explaining party differences, the higher the average score

Table 3.5: The Ideological Style Index and Frameworks for Explaining Party Differences

	Abstractness of Framework for Explaining Party Differences				
	High				*Low*
Britain	7.0	4.0	4.0	2.9	2.8
	(N = 1)	(N = 22)	(N = 43)	(N = 22)	(N = 5)
Italy	6.4	5.2	5.0	5.0	–
	(N = 16)	(N = 53)	(N = 11)	(N = 2)	(N = 0)

NOTE: Entry is mean score on Ideological Style Index for respondents in each category.

23. The intercoder reliability of this measure was tau-beta = .57. Only 8 percent of all respondents were rated more than one point apart by the separate coders. This measure is based on a section of the interview quite separated from the discussions of policy. Thus, the risk is slight that either the respondent's discussion of party differences or the coder's judgment of that discussion was directly influenced by the "style" of the earlier policy analysis.

on the Ideological Style Index, providing independent confirmation that those who rate high on this index tend to think theoretically. "Stylistic ideologues" are also "conceptual ideologues."

Politics has a wide range of attractions for its practitioners, at least to judge by the responses to an opening question about "what is most appealing to you about being in politics and government." Among the most often mentioned satisfactions were being "in the center of things," serving as an ombudsman for constituents, working in the convivial atmosphere of Parliament, and helping to solve urgent national problems. In addition to these, however, many politicians in both countries mentioned what might be termed "ideological satisfactions." "What would you miss most if you left politics?" I asked a British Labourite.

> The thing I would miss most is the sense of being involved in trying to transform society. The thing which attracts me in politics, and the thing which militates against all the most irksome and difficult aspects of the job, is the sense that—because I believe, you know, that the society in which one's children are going to live should be a different one than the one in which I grew up—that I am doing something towards making it like that. (B8)

An Italian Communist expressed the same point more succinctly. "I believe that the most attractive aspect of politics lies precisely in considering it not a career, but a mission." (I17)

Fifteen percent of the British respondents and 35 percent of the Italians mentioned this kind of satisfaction. Of the ideologically motivated Englishmen, 43 percent were rated "high" on the Ideological Style Index, as contrasted with 24 percent of the rest of the British sample. Of the ideologically motivated Italians, 79 percent were rated "high" on the Ideological Style Index while only 61 percent of the remaining Italians were so rated.[24] Since these two variables are methodologically quite independent, the pattern of relations between them helps to confirm that the Ideological Style Index does indeed measure what its name suggests. "Motivational ideologues" tend to be "stylistic ideologues."

One final bit of evidence will complete the case. On the written questionnaire given respondents at the end of each interview the following item appeared: "Politics is the 'art of the possible' and political leaders should not worry about grand plans and distant ideals." To a number of respondents this question seemed to pose a false dilemma, since the first half concerns tactics and the second, goals. Logic is on their side, but the item does seem to separate the "idealists," for whom goals are paramount, from the "realists," for whom politics consists in doing "what can be done." Table 3.6 shows that the idealists rate significantly higher on the Ideological Style Index than do the realists.

24. To simplify the presentation of results in this and the following chapters, I will often contrast "high" and "low" scorers on the Ideological Style Index and several other indices to be presented later. In all cases "high" and "low" refer to respondents above or below the mean score for both national samples combined.

Table 3.6: The Ideological Style Index and Political Idealism

STATEMENT: "Politics is the 'art of the possible' and political leaders should not worry about grand plans and distant ideals."

	Agree strongly	Agree	Disagree	Disagree strongly
Britain	3.0	3.4	3.9	4.1
	(N = 2)	(N = 17)	(N = 45)	(N = 14)
Italy	4.7	4.5	5.4	6.9
	(N = 4)	(N = 17)	(N = 21)	(N = 8)

NOTE: Entry is mean score on Ideological Style Index for respondents in each category.

There are a number of other differences between the high and low scorers on the Ideological Style Index, but enough evidence has been presented to clarify the empirical meaning of this index. To recapitulate: Some respondents tend to discuss issues in abstract and theoretical terms, referring with some frequency to specific ideologies and to more or less coherent social goals. Those who rank high on the Ideological Style Index also tend to interpret political phenomena such as parties in terms of more abstract schema, to be more frequently motivated by ideological satisfactions, and to reject a merely "possibilist" approach to politics. These men are ideological politicians. Figure 3.1 presents the distribution of each national sample along the Ideological Style Index. The material in this chapter has, then, validated empirically proposition 1: *Certain politicians have characteristic A—they conduct politics from the standpoint of a coherent, comprehensive set of beliefs. Such politicians are "ideological."* In chapter 4 I will turn to proposition 2, linking this central trait to a number of other characteristics of political behavior.

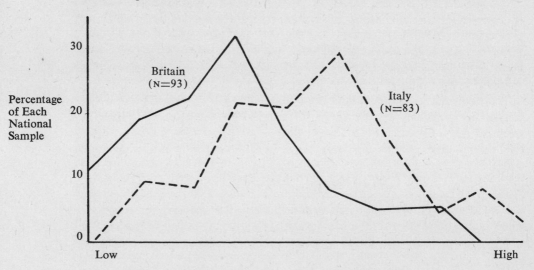

Figure 3.1: The Ideological Style Index in Britain and Italy

4 The Attitudes and Behavior
of Ideological Politicians

Everyone knows that ideological politicians are extremist, alienated, dogmatic, hostile toward opponents, and generally antagonistic to the give-and-take of pluralist politics. The task of social science, of course, is to determine how much of what "everyone knows" is really true. On the basis of the present evidence from Britain and Italy what *are* ideological politicians really like?

Extremism and Alienation

The first point to investigate is whether extremism and an ideological style of political discourse go together. Of course, extremism itself is a problematic concept, but here I use it in a quite literal sense. By extremist I mean respondents who stand at the extremes of a simple left-right continuum. Each respondent was rated on a five-point scale according to his overall view of the proper role of the state in society, from a stress on much more state involvement and social provision to a stress on much more free enterprise and individual initiative.[1] Naturally, there is nothing universally applicable about this criterion; political life is not always unidimensional. But in the case of Britain and Italy this dimension dominates political controversy. Among our respondents, for example, there is a very high correlation between this variable and party affiliation, reflecting the obvious fact that the party systems in both countries are based essentially, if not exclusively, on this dimension.[2]

There is some independent evidence that respondents at the ends of this continuum are genuinely extremists. In the written questionnaire the politicians were asked to respond to the following statement: "Generally speaking, in political controversies extreme positions should be avoided, for the proper approach

1. The intercoder reliability of this placement was quite high: the tau-beta was .76; only 3 percent of all respondents were placed more than one point apart by the independent coders and 63 percent were coded identically.

2. The correlation between party affiliation and position on the left-right continuum is gamma = 1.00 in Britain and gamma = .96 in Italy. For evidence that this left-right dimension dominates perceptions of politics among Italian voters and leaders, see Samuel H. Barnes, "Left, Right, and the Italian Voter," *Comparative Political Studies* 4 (July 1971): 157–75.

usually lies somewhere in the middle." Respondents placed by the coders at the extremes of the left-right continuum were much more likely than those toward the center to disagree with this repudiation of extremism. Table 4.1 presents the data for both countries together; the same pattern appears in each national sample taken separately.

Table 4.1: Extremism and the Left-Right Continuum, Both Countries Grouped

STATEMENT: "Generally speaking, in political controversies extreme positions should be avoided, for the proper approach usually lies somewhere in the middle."

Extreme Left	Moderate Left	Center	Moderate Right	Extreme Right
65%	22%	4%	36%	40%
(N = 20)	(N = 49)	(N = 24)	(N = 25)	(N = 10)

NOTE: Entry is percentage of respondents in each category disagreeing with this statement.

Using this linear definition of extremist, then, figure 4.1 shows that ideologues are indeed concentrated at the political extremes. In both countries the average score on the Ideological Style Index (ISI) rises regularly as we move outward from the center. (The one exception to the regularity of the graphs—the Far Right in Italy—is based on only two cases.) One possible explanation for this relationship lies in the psychological and political demands of extremism. To uphold positions that do not conform to the mainstream of political thought in a given time and place probably requires one to be more "thoughtful" in a literal sense, to develop a more explicit rationale for one's unorthodox opinions. Perhaps those at the extremes of the ideological spectrum are forced more often than those at the center to defend the fundamental tenets of their position, using fairly abstract and theoretical propositions. It would be reasonable to expect this style of political discourse to carry over into more mundane discussions, especially since the style itself implies a tendency to move from particular issues to broader concerns, a tendency to see the "general" in the "specific."

This argument assumes that extremism is the cause; an ideological style, the effect. We can just as easily imagine the reverse relationship. Perhaps those who come to think about politics and society in a theoretical way are drawn irresistibly to strictly logical (and extreme) conclusions, whereas those whose reasoning is more inductive and implicit are content with "the muddled middle." This is a causal conundrum for which the present data offer no solution.[3] For whatever reason, those at the extremes of the left-right spectrum tend to have a more ideological style of thought.

Ideological politics are alienative politics, Shils tells us. "Alienation" rivals "ideology" in its ambiguity, but in the present context a fairly simple meaning is intended. "Alienated" politicians, according to Shils, "shun the central institutional system of the prevailing society"; they oppose, sometimes violently,

3. See the last section of this chapter for further discussion of this point.

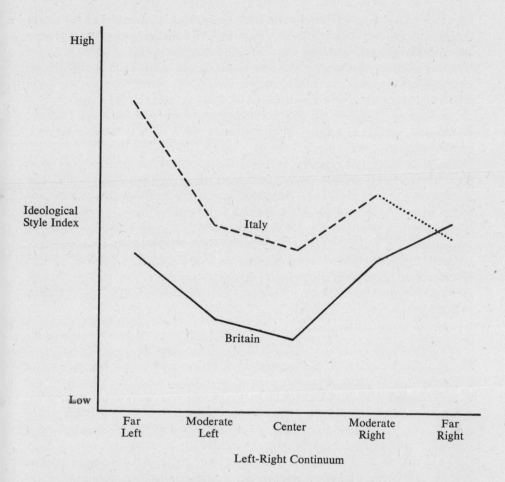

Figure 4.1: The Ideological Style Index and the Left-Right Continuum
Dotted line indicates data point based on subsample of only two respondents.
Ns for Britain (left to right): 12; 38; 8; 23; 12.
Ns for Italy (left to right): 24; 23; 23; 11; 2.

established political and social arrangements. The more alienated the politician, the more radical the social and political reforms he proposes. Because attitudes toward existing institutions are highly correlated with party affiliation and with the left-right continuum, the preceding analysis has prepared us to expect a correlation between the Ideological Style Index and measures of "alienation" in the sense I am using here, and such a correlation does indeed exist. More significantly, even when party affiliation is held constant, this correlation persists. Alienated Communists have a more ideological style than their less disaffected comrades. At the other end of the spectrum, Tories who find the welfare state oppressive and wish to return to an earlier social system have higher ISI scores than those satisfied with things as they are. This same relationship applies to attitudes toward both political and socioeconomic institutions.[4]

One important qualification must be added to this confirmation of Shils' assertion, for he goes on to say that "for the ideological politician, membership in a parliamentary body or the acceptance of office involves only an opportunity to overthrow and destroy the system rather than to work within it and improve it."[5] If this is meant as a definitional statement, there are few "ideological politicians" indeed in our sample. If, on the other hand, it is meant as an empirical proposition, then it is false, for most of those rated high on our Ideological Style Index are, for all their opposition to the status quo, reformers rather than revolutionaries. Evidence to be presented in chapter 15 suggests that only one of the Italians in our sample is a genuine revolutionary, that is, favors destruction rather than amelioration of the existing political system. Not a single British respondent fell in this category. This finding is not surprising, but unless Shils means to argue that there are no ideologues in the British Parliament, it does cast doubt on the quoted proposition. With this reservation we can say that an ideological style is linked to political and social alienation, just as it is linked to extremism.

The Practices of Pluralism

So far in our examination of the propositions linking ideological style to other characteristics of political behavior we are batting 1.000. The connections between ideological style and orientations to conflict will be discussed in chapter 8. I now want to examine the propositions that characterize ideological politicians as dogmatic, hostile, and opposed to the norms of pluralist politics. As it happens, our batting average is about to tumble.

Let us first of all consider the suggestion that ideological politicians are less open to the bargaining and compromise of pluralist politics. A variety of independent indicators of propensity to compromise are available in our data. The most direct came in response to a question asked in the context of a discussion of "the most important political conflict" the respondent could recall facing. "In a situation of controversy where it seems to you that one side is

4. One measure of "alienation" is based on a summary judgment of the respondent's attitude toward the socioeconomic system of his country. The intercoder reliability of this judgment is tau-beta $= .54$; only 3 percent of all respondents were placed more than one point apart. A second measure is based on a similar judgment of the respondent's attitude toward the existing political institutions of his country. The intercoder reliability of this judgment is tau-beta $= .68$; not a single respondent was placed more than one point apart by the independent coders. Detailed statistical evidence of the correlation between the ISI and these two measures is given in my "Studying Elite Political Culture: The Case of 'Ideology,'" *American Political Science Review* 65 (1971): 667–8.

5. Edward Shils, "Ideology and Civility: On the Politics of the Intellectual," *Sewanee Review* 66 (1958): 452.

clearly right and the other clearly wrong," I asked, "would you be inclined to stick to your guns or to try to find a compromise acceptable to all concerned?" I touched much the same problem indirectly earlier in each interview when, following the discussion of specific policy issues, I asked, "How do you feel about situations in which what's politically feasible has to take precedence over what's ideally desirable?" Nearly all our respondents agreed that there were times when the feasible must take precedence over the desirable, but some expressed serious qualms about this necessity, while others accepted it with equanimity as a fact of life in a pluralistic society.

Another measure of attitudes to compromise came from the written questionnaire in which the respondent was asked whether or not he agreed with this statement: "To compromise with our political opponents is dangerous because it usually leads to the betrayal of our own side." Finally, based on the interview transcript as a whole, coders judged each respondent's propensity to play a conflict-resolving role in politics.[6] The consistency of these four largely independent measures of attitudes toward compromise is quite high. Politicians who agree with the statement that "compromising is dangerous . . ." are also apt to deplore giving precedence to political feasibility, to prefer "sticking to one's guns" in situations of controversy, and to be judged to have little or no tendency to define their political role in terms of conflict-resolution.[7]

How do ideologues measure up by these standards? The evidence given in table 4.2 is unequivocal. There is *no* difference between high scorers and low scorers on the Ideological Style Index in terms of willingness to compromise. As measured by the written questionnaire item, for example, there is no difference between high and low scorers in Britain, and in Italy the more ideological politicians seem less —not more—fearful of compromise. The standard description of the ideological politician leads one to suppose that he would be the first to object to considerations of political feasibility, for he is supposed to be a practitioner of the politics of principle, rather than the politics of interests. Yet in each country our ideo-

6. The reliability of this judgment is fairly high, given the diffuse character of the criteria employed. The tau-beta correlation between separate coders' judgments of the same interview was .34; 7 percent of all interviews were rated by the coders at opposite ends of the three-point scale.

7. The matrices of intercorrelations among these four measures are as follows:

		I	II	III	IV
I = "Compromising Dangerous"	I	x	.54	.12	.08
II = Disdain for Political Feasibility	II	.40	x	.31	.67
III = "Stick to Guns"	III	.43	.44	x	.64
IV = Conflict-Resolver	IV	.36	.69	.68	x

The upper right-hand matrix refers to the British respondents; the lower left-hand matrix to the Italians. The entries are gammas. Strictly speaking, variable IV, the summary judgment, is not wholly independent of variables II and III, the responses to interview questions; this apart, the four measures are methodologically independent. For an explication of the gamma measure of ordinal association, see L. A. Goodman and W. H. Kruskal, "Measures of Association for Cross-Classification," *Journal of the American Statistical Association* 49 (1954): 732–64.

Table 4.2: The Ideological Style Index and Measures of Orientation toward Compromise

	Britain		Italy	
	High ISI	Low ISI	High ISI	Low ISI
Percentage of respondents who *agree* that "to compromise with our political opponents leads to the betrayal of our own side."	37 N = 24)	35 (N = 60)	45 (N = 31)	67 (N = 21)
Percentage of respondents who stress *negative* aspects of giving precedence to the politically feasible over the ideally desirable.	16 (N = 19)	22 (N = 54)	12 (N = 51)	22 (N = 27)
Percentage of respondents who "in a situation where one side seems clearly right and the other side clearly wrong," would "stick to [their] guns."	20 (N = 15)	39 (N = 36)	31 (N = 26)	36 (N = 11)
Percentage of respondents judged by the coders to show *very little* tendency to focus on "resolving social and political conflicts."	28 (N = 25)	35 (N = 68)	36 (N = 56)	37 (N = 27)

NOTES: "High ISI" and "Low ISI" refer to respondents with scores on the Ideological Style Index above or below the two-nation mean score, respectively. Reduced NS reflect the fact that not all respondents were asked all of these questions.

logues are marginally *less* disdainful of political expediency. Asked directly about compromising controversies, ideologues in the two countries are, if anything, slightly *less* inclined to reject an acceptable accommodation. Finally, consider the coders' summary judgment. Once again, ideologues are no less disposed to resolve political conflicts than are non-ideologues. The conclusion is obvious: in neither country is there any support for the proposition linking an ideological style of politics to opposition to political give-and-take. There are, of course, politicians ill-disposed to such bargaining, but they are not found disproportionately among the ideologues.

When we turn to other indicators of hostility toward the procedures of pluralist politics, this conclusion is substantiated. Take, for example, responses to a questionnaire item that probed for opposition to interest group politics: "Pressure groups and special interests, like trade unions, commercial associations, and professional organizations, and so on, hamper the proper working of government." Of the ideologues in Britain, 5 percent agreed with this indictment of the politics of pluralism; 11 percent of the low scorers on the ISI agreed with it. Of the Italian ideologues, 20 percent agreed; of their less ideological compatriots, 33 percent agreed. Ideological politicians are *not, pace* Shils, hostile to the usages and practices of pluralism.

Nor is there any evidence that those whose style is ideological tend to value ends at the expense of means. Three of the questionnaire items were directed at this belief: "The ends and objectives of political ideology are much more important than the manner and methods used to attain them"; "To bring about great changes for the benefit of mankind often requires cruelty and even ruthlessness"; and "I don't mind a politician's methods if he manages to get the right things done." Responses to these three items were combined to form a single index, measuring the extent to which the respondent believes that "the end justifies the means." Of the British respondents whose score on the ISI was relatively high, 29 percent were also relatively high on the "end justifies the means" index. Of those low on the ISI, 40 percent were high on the second measure. For the Italian respondents, the comparable figures were 44 percent for the high ISI scorers, and 52 percent for the low ISI scorers. In simpler terms,

Table 4.3: The Ideological Style Index and Measures of Moral Absolutism, Authoritarianism, and Political and Social Distrust

Moral Absolutism Index
1. Of all the different philosophies which exist in the world, there is only one which is true.
2. Unless there is freedom for many points of view to be presented, there is little chance that the truth can ever be known. (This item is reversed for inclusion in the Index.)

	Britain	Italy
Spearman-Brown reliability coefficient:	.50	.39
Correlation (gamma) with ISI:	−.07	.02
	(N = 86)	(N = 55)

Authoritarianism Index
1. A few strong leaders would do more for this country than all the laws and talk.
2. Few people really know what is in their own best interest in the long run.
3. In this complicated world the only way we can know what is going on is to rely on leaders or experts who can be trusted.
4. It will always be necessary to have a few strong, able people actually running everything.
5. A group which tolerates too much difference of opinion among its own members cannot exist for very long.

	Britain	Italy
Spearman-Brown reliability coefficient:	.62	.68
Correlation (gamma) with ISI:	−.04	−.17
	(N = 86)	(N = 56)

Political Distrust Index
1. Most politicians can be trusted to do what they think is best for the country. (This item is reversed in the Index.)
2. People who go into public office usually think of the good of the people more than of their own. (This item reversed.)

	Britain	Italy
Spearman-Brown reliability coefficient:	.39	.67
Correlation (gamma) with ISI:	−.16	.10
	(N = 85)	(N = 53)

Social Distrust Index
1. No one is going to care much what happens to you when you get right down to it.
2. If you don't watch yourself, people will take advantage of you.

	Britain	Italy
Spearman-Brown reliability coefficient:	.30	.44
Correlation (gamma) with ISI:	−.06	−.20
	(N = 81)	(N = 55)

ideologues in both countries were slightly *less* likely to endorse the principle that methods do not matter.

Students of dogmatism and authoritarianism have compiled a large number of questionnaire items to measure these traits. One cannot always have confidence that these items measure what they are supposed to. On the other hand, a consistent pattern of findings is often more convincing than the results from individual items. Since commentators on ideological politicians have long described them variously as "fanatical," "dogmatic," "paranoid," "morally absolutist," and "authoritarian," it is significant that on a series of indices designed to measure these traits, respondents who scored high on the ISI *never* differ systematically from low scorers. Table 4.3 summarizes the evidence, giving the components and internal reliability of each index and the rank-order correlation of each with the Ideological Style Index.[8] The series of negative coefficients implies a series of negative verdicts on the hypotheses referred to above. Some people are more dogmatic than others, but ideologues as a group are not.[9]

Partisan Hostility

For some politicians politics is essentially a morality play, a continual struggle between good and evil. Such politicians are found in all countries and along the entire length of the political spectrum. One Tory, for example, discussed the differences between the British parties:

> They are two entirely different ways of life. They're miles apart. We believe in free enterprise and the capitalist system and the country in which all can get on and everybody can make money and make a fortune, if they're good, but the socialist conception is that they should nationalize all the means of production, distribution, and exchange, and they've also said that they do not believe in the capitalist system. . . . The only difference between socialism and communism is that communism is the imposition of 100 percent socialism all at once by brute force, and you march toward your communist state by degrees in the Socialist party. (B10)

8. The internal reliability of each index is calculated from the Spearman-Brown split-half reliability formula. See Claire Selltiz et al., *Research Methods in Social Relations,* rev. ed. (New York: Holt, Rinehart, and Winston, 1959), pp. 183–4.

9. Some psychological research suggests the possibility of a reversed relation, linking dogmatic and authoritarian attitudes to *low* scores on the ISI. Robert E. Lane reminds us that "as readers of *The Authoritarian Personality* and of *The Open and Closed Mind* will recognize, the dimension of concreteness-abstraction has political and social implications: concreteness is related to authoritarianism and to dogmatic, rigid, and opinionated thinking." Of course, abstraction is one prerequisite for ideological thinking, as here operationalized. This raises the possibility of different kinds of abstract thinking, an issue that will be discussed in chapter 5. See Lane's "The Decline of Politics and Ideology in a Knowledgeable Society," *American Sociological Review* 31 (October 1966): 655.

One of his opponents across the aisle returned the compliment.

The Tories represent those who are best off in society and the Labor Party those who suffer, who are less well off and who suffer the injustices. That's the basic difference. The Tories are there to protect privilege, to protect the big boys, and the Labour Party is there to protect the people against the big boys. (B24)

Such "black-white" perspectives on politics are found in Italy, too. One Communist activist responded to my question about party differences this way:

What difference is there between the class of the exploited and the class of the exploiters? . . . Between the Communists and the Christian Democrats, between the Communists and the Liberals, between the Communists and the neo-Fascists, it's the same difference between the class which has the power in its hands, which dominates the class which instead is dominated. (I32)

A Christian Democrat interpreted politics in equally dichotomous terms. "The greatest difference lies in this: Between those who want to defend liberty, all the liberties of the individual, and those who would like to exchange these liberties for something else which you don't know what it would be." (I99) One of his party colleagues put it more concisely when I asked about his personal relations with members of the largest of the opposition parties: "As far as the Communists are concerned, I simply can't conceive that I would ever be able to believe anything that they could say." (I 106)

But not all politicians see such a clear alignment of good against evil. One young British Conservative suggested that "the main difference between the parties today is simply which party is the best manager of the country's affairs. There aren't really very many important policy differences between us." (B 12) Another of his colleagues expressed more discontent with the policies of the Labour Government, but went on to say that "I think the fear of losing an election would help to correct the most violent excesses. . . . I don't mistrust their intentions. I don't regard Mr. Wilson and his Cabinet as people who are wicked, dishonorable people." (B 44) On the opposite benches one Labour MP, after pointing out the issues on which he disagreed with the Tories, came to my question about interparty relations in the House itself. "One of the things that would, I think, interest the ordinary outsider is that there's often, rather curiously, more comradeship between Members of different parties than between Members of the same party." (B 53)

For each respondent in our sample there are a number of measures of hostility toward political opponents. Some of them are based on explicit questions from the interview schedule. For example, respondents were asked "To what extent can you trust and rely on members of the [opposing party or parties]?" Others were based instead on the coders' assessment of the repondent's partisan stance. For example, each respondent's discussion of party differences was rated on the extent to which he "attributed evil or insidious motives to opposing parties or politicians."[10] Two judgments of the interview as a whole concerned the extent to which the respondent engaged in dichotomous thinking and the extent of his tolerance of opinions contrary to his own.[11]

Not surprisingly, all these measures of antagonism toward political opponents were strongly correlated with each other.[12] To simplify the analysis, therefore, a single summary measure, the Index of Partisan Hostility (IPH), was constructed from them. The distribution of each national sample along this dimension is shown in figure 4.2.[13]

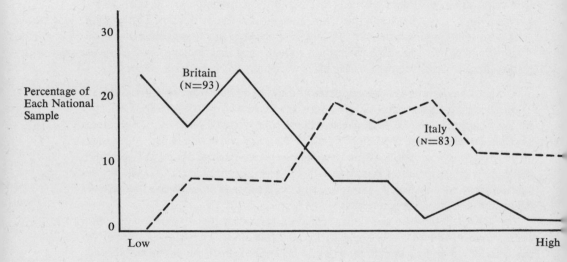

Figure 4.2: The Index of Partisan Hostility in Britain and Italy

---

10. The intercoder reliability of this four-point scale was tau-beta = .53, with 9 percent rated more than one point apart.

11. The reliability of the code for "dichotomous thinking" was tau-beta = .62 (1 percent rated at opposite ends of the three-point scale). The reliability of the code for "tolerance" was tau-beta = .49 (again 1 percent rated at opposite ends of the three-point scale).

12. The matrices of intercorrelations among these four measures are as follows:

		I	II	III	IV
I = Distrusts Opponents	I	x	.87	.76	.73
II = Attributes Evil Motives	II	.88	x	.82	.69
III = Dichotomous Thinking	III	.64	.84	x	.86
IV = Intolerance	IV	.65	.79	.77	x

The upper right-hand matrix refers to the British respondents; the lower left-hand matrix to the Italians. The entries are gammas, measures of ordinal association. In computing the Index of Partisan Hostility, the variables were treated as interval-level data; see n. 17, chap. 3.

13. Methodologically, this Index is simply the factor score for each respondent on the dominant factor that emerges from an orthogonal factor analysis of the matrix of intercorrelations among the four components of the Index. Sixty-four percent of the total common variance is accounted for by this factor.

Attitudes toward political opponents are closely related to one's willingness to compromise and resolve disputes. Table 4.4 shows that high scorers on the Index of Partisan Hostility are, across a range of indicators, much less likely to seek to conciliate political disputes. Differences as marked and as consistent as those shown in table 4.4 are rarely found in research such as this, and they testify to the power and centrality of these attitudes toward political opponents. Analogous, though less dramatic, correlations are found between the IPH and the questionnaire indices measuring authoritarianism and moral absolutism. The moral is clear. Partisan hostility, dogmatism, and resistance to compromise form a single syndrome.

Table 4.4: The Index of Partisan Hostility and Measures of
Orientation toward Compromise

	Britain		Italy	
	Most hostile	Least hostile	Most hostile	Least hostile
Percentage of respondents who *agree* that "to compromise with our political opponents is dangerous because it usually leads to the betrayal of our own side."	62 (N = 16)	29 (N = 68)	64 (N = 39)	23 (N = 13)
Percentage of respondents who "in a situation where one side seems clearly right and the other side clearly wrong," would "stick to [their] guns."	50 (N = 10)	29 (N = 41)	39 (N = 28)	11 (N = 9)
Percentage of respondents judged by the coders to show *very little* tendency to focus on "resolving social and political conflicts."	58 (N = 19)	27 (N = 74)	41 (N = 64)	21 (N = 19)

NOTES: "Most hostile" and "Least hostile" refer to respondents with scores on the Index of Partisan Hostility above or below the two-nation mean score, respectively. Reduced Ns reflect the fact that not all respondents were asked all of these questions.

Like the Ideological Style Index, the Index of Partisan Hostility is related in a systematic way to the left-right continuum. Figure 4.3 shows that those at the extremes of the political spectrum are much more likely than those toward the center to display hostility toward their opponents. The spatial metaphor is apt here, for there is a real psychological sense in which the extremists are "distant" from the other actors in the political system. Those at the ends of the ideological spectrum find considerably less common ground—in policy terms and probably in personal terms—with their opponents than do centrists. Conceivably, political extremism and partisan hostility may have a common origin in some deeper personality trait, a possibility we will explore briefly later. But the relationship shown in figure 4.3 is probably explicable without resort to complicated psychodynamic interpretations. From a vantage point fairly far

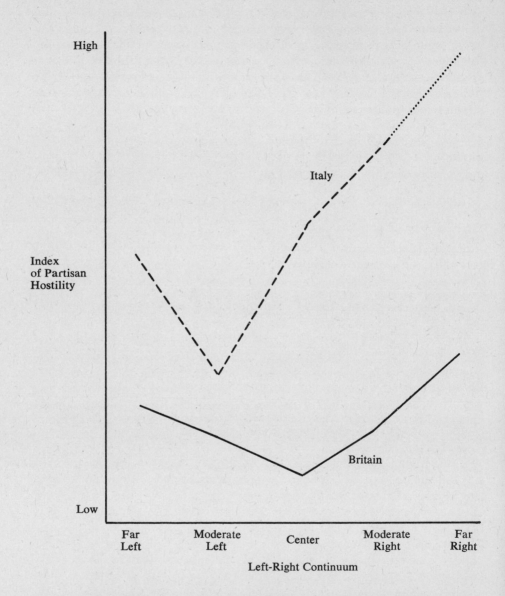

Figure 4.3: The Index of Partisan Hostility and the Left-Right Continuum
Dotted line indicates data point based on subsample of only two respondents.
Ns for Britain (left to right): 12; 38; 8; 23; 12.
Ns for Italy (left to right): 24; 23; 23; 11; 2.

ATTITUDES AND BEHAVIOR OF IDEOLOGICAL POLITICIANS 61

out on the left-right continuum the notion of a dichotomous, "we-they" world is probably more plausible than from a point more toward the center.[14]

Unlike the comparable relationship between extremism and political style, this relationship between extremism and partisanship is, at least in Italy, noticeably asymmetrical. The least hostile politicians are those at the moderate Left, and even those at the far Left are considerably more open in their partisanship than those at the Right. There is also a tendency, detectable in each country but especially marked in Italy, for politicians of the Left to be more favorable to the principle of compromise. Indeed, among Italian Communists the acceptability of compromise solutions to political problems has become almost dogma. For some the dogma is probably only verbal, but for others it is deeply felt. For example, one PCI deputy, a shipyard worker, had spoken at length about the bitterness of class conflict. But when talking about compromise, a different aspect of his outlook became apparent.

> Conflicts always end up with a compromise. You certainly can't always make war. Even with a strike it's that way. . . . I remember once when we were striking, we resisted for seventy days. But afterwards we arrived at a compromise. An agreement is a compromise between the two sides. It doesn't satisfy anyone, doesn't satisfy either the one side or the other side, it's a compromise. It's like husband and wife. Either one dominates or the other dominates, or by compromising you live together. Are you married? [my bachelor assistant: *No!*] Beh, you'll learn. (I48)

Statistical evidence that the Left maintains greater support for compromise comes from the questionnaire item: "To compromise with our political opponents is dangerous because it usually leads to the betrayal of our own side." Seven of eight Communists and nine of thirteen Socialists disagreed with this item. Sixteen of twenty-three Christian Democrats and all six other rightists agreed with it. Nearly all the other indicators of orientations toward compromise that were built into the interview confirm this finding.

The explanation of the greater inclination of the Left in both countries to favor compromise is far from obvious. Possibly, decades of experience in demanding changes in the status quo have left a widely shared conviction that half a loaf or half a nationalization program is better than none at all. Perhaps experience with industrial bargaining, much more common among members of the Left, breeds a respect for the bargaining process itself. Trust and tolerance toward political opponents may also reflect, at least in part, general optimism

14. One might reasonably wonder whether the correlation between the IPH and the left-right continuum has been inflated by a tendency for coders to rate more extreme precisely those respondents who exhibit more antipathy toward their opponents. This fear is eased by the fact that ranging the Italian political parties along the left-right spectrum gives an identical result, and a respondent's party affiliation is not subject to coder bias. The two-party system in Britain precludes a similar test there.

about the trustworthiness of others in society, for as we shall see in chapter 7, politicians of the Left in both Britain and Italy rank significantly lower on an index of misanthropy.

I would not want to argue that all leftist parties are "naturally" more tolerant and open to compromise. In the case of the PCI the general endorsement of compromise seems to be at least in part the result of a systematic attempt to remove "sectarian," hard-line elements from the Party cadres and the Party image. This campaign has succeeded, perhaps more than some Party leaders recognize, and it is, I suspect, virtually irreversible. It is indeed difficult to know whether this left-right asymmetry is very common or not. But our evidence from Britain and Italy shows consistently that the partisanship of the Left is less closed-minded than the partisanship of the Right.

Ideology and Hostility

What is the relationship between partisan hostility and ideological politics? The received wisdom is unambiguous. James B. Christoph argues that among "the conditions associated with the politics of total ideology" are "distrust of and hostility to opposing views."[15] Shils is more dramatic: "Ideological politics are the politics of 'friend-foe,' 'we-they,' 'who-whom.' Those who are not on the side of the ideological politician are, according to the ideologist, against him."[16]

As an empirical generalization, this widely held view is simply false. Certain ideologues in specific historical situations may have been particularly prone to intolerance and hostility. It may be that adherents to ideologies at the *mass* level often engage in such dichotomous thinking. (Recent research has not been kind to the notion that full-fledged ideologies flourish in mass publics, however, and although rank-and-file adherents to ideologies may be intolerant, it is open to question whether they are "ideological" in any other sense.) But as a description of contemporary politicians in Italy and Britain, Shils' generalization is quite inaccurate, as the evidence in table 4.5 shows. In neither country—in fact, in none of the individual parties—is there a significant positive correlation between the Index of Partisan Hostility and the Ideological Style Index. In both countries there are some remarkably hostile politicians; in both countries there are politicians whose view of the world is dichotomous. But such politicians are not found disproportionately among the ideologues.[17]

We have found, in other words, two quite distinct syndromes. One is based on an ideological style of political thought and is linked to ideological motivations and the use of comprehensive conceptual schemes. The other is based on

15. James B. Christoph, "Consensus and Cleavage in British Political Ideology," *American Political Science Review* 59 (1965) 633.

16. Shils, "Ideology and Civility," p. 452.

17. Gary T. Marx has found that among American blacks civil rights militancy is negatively correlated with antiwhite prejudice. See his *Protest and Prejudice: A Study of Belief in the Black Community* (New York: Harper & Row, 1967), pp. 198–213.

Table 4.5: The Index of Partisan Hostility and the Ideological Style Index

British Parties		Italian Parties			
Labour	Conservative	Communist	Socialist	Christian Democratic	Rightist
.18	−.13	−.08	.05	.02	−.33
(N = 54)	(N = 37)	(N = 20)	(N = 18)	(N = 33)	(N = 10)

NOTE: Entry is gamma, positive when high hostility and high ideological style are linked.

hostility and intolerance toward political opposition and is linked to resistance to compromise. Each syndrome is found disproportionately at the extremes of the political spectrum. But the two syndromes are themselves unrelated. In fact, if we look only at the extremists, the two syndromes are *negatively* related. Among British politicians who fall at either the extreme left or the extreme right, the correlation between the Ideological Style Index and the Index of Partisan Hostility is gamma = −.22. Among extremists in Italy the comparable correlation is gamma = −.37. Some extremists are ideological and some extremists are hostile, but they are rarely the same extremists.

To pull apart the mesh of causal connections among these three variables is a task beyond the strength of the present data. If, however, we take for a moment extremism as the dependent variable, the other two variables would fall into place as alternative sources for extremist positions, representing two quite different types of motivation. In this version of the causal script, some extremists are driven to their posture by the violence of their hatred for their political opponents, while others are led by the relentless logic of social theory. There is a certain verisimilitude about this script, but the main lesson is that when considering the political extremes, as when considering the rest of the political spectrum, the two dimensions here discovered—ideological style and partisan hostility—must be kept distinct.

One would, of course, be cautious about generalizing these findings to politicians in systems other than the (relatively moderate) liberal democracies of the West. The point here is not that ideologues are *never* dogmatic and hostile—some are and some are not. Indeed, it may be that certain ideologies are disproportionately held by particularly intolerant people. I am, however, concerned to dispute the contention that ideological thinking per se is alien to openmindedness. This basic distinction may have wide applicability.

To conclude, some of the hypotheses implied in proposition 2 (stated at the outset of chapter 3) are true, but some are empirically false. Ideologues as measured here *are* extremist and alienated. On the other hand, our ideologues *are not* ruthless, dogmatic, authoritarian, paranoid, intolerant, opposed to compromise and pluralism, or hostile toward their opponents. It is, therefore, quite misleading to build these assumptions into the definition of ideological. Just how misleading it can be we will see in chapter 5, as we turn to an examination of proposition 3 and the decline of ideology.

5   Ideology, Hostility, and Change

Age, ISI, and IPH

Whether or not ideological politicians are disappearing depends, of course, both on what you mean by "ideological" and on how you measure the disappearance. Because the interest of social scientists in this topic is fairly recent and because the methods of social research have not yet been adequately adapted for dealing with historical problems, we have no good time-series evidence to cast light on this problem. The dilemma is particularly acute when "ideological" is defined in terms of the characteristics of individual political actors, for survey research at the elite level was virtually nonexistent at the time when ideological politics were presumably at flood tide. We do not really know, in a rigorous way, what politicians forty years ago were like.

There is, however, one possible solution to this methodological dilemma. We can compare different age groups among contemporary politicians, looking for changes across successive "political generations." Differences across age cohorts in data gathered at a single point in time are, of course, notoriously ambiguous. Broadly speaking, three alternative explanations are possible. The first, which may be termed the "life cycle" explanation, proposes that the differences in the dependent variable are a function of age, pure and simple. As people (in this case, politicians) become older and more experienced, their attitudes and perspectives change.

The second explanation is applicable to populations from which one's departure might plausibly be related to the dependent variable. If those who have characteristic X tend disproportionately to leave the population early (by failure to be reelected, for example), then obviously we would expect older cohorts to show a lower frequency of characteristic X. This explanation can be termed the "natural selection" hypothesis.

The third proposal, which may be termed the "generational" explanation, suggests that a person's attitudes do not change with age or experience, but instead are throughout his lifetime a function of his place in the historical sequence of generations. As a result, viewed at any point in time, particular historical generations continue to show distinctive characteristics. This alone among the three types of explanations for cohort differences implies the existence of genuine historical change.

Our evidence, then, is inevitably inconclusive. But in the absence of genuine time-series data it can be quite useful, particularly when independent evidence and inference can help us distinguish among the life cycle, natural selection, and generational alternatives.[1] Our discovery in chapter 4 that partisan hostility and ideological style are distinct syndromes suggests that we should examine changes across age groups in both the Index of Partisan Hostility and the Ideological Style Index. The results of this procedure are given in figures 5.1 and 5.2[2]

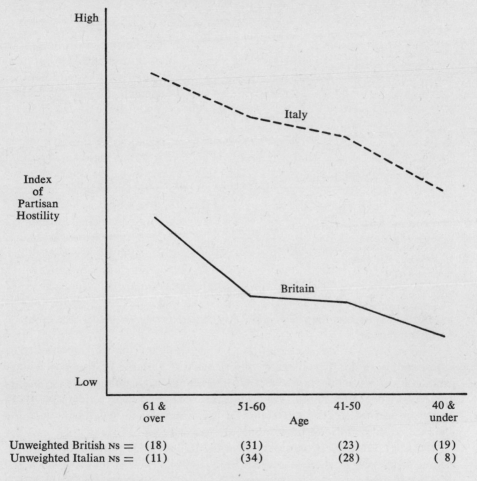

	61 & over	51-60	Age	41-50	40 & under
Unweighted British Ns =	(18)	(31)		(23)	(19)
Unweighted Italian Ns =	(11)	(34)		(28)	(8)

Figure 5.1: Age and the Index of Partisan Hostility
In constructing this figure, weights were used to hold constant the partisan proportions of the cohorts; two members of minor parties had to be excluded from the calculations in each country.

1. For a discussion of alternative interpretations of age-cohort differences, see Donald Stokes and David Butler, *Political Change in Britain* (New York: St. Martin's Press, 1969), pp. 62–4, 248–74.
2. In order to hold constant the effect of the partisan composition of different age cohorts,

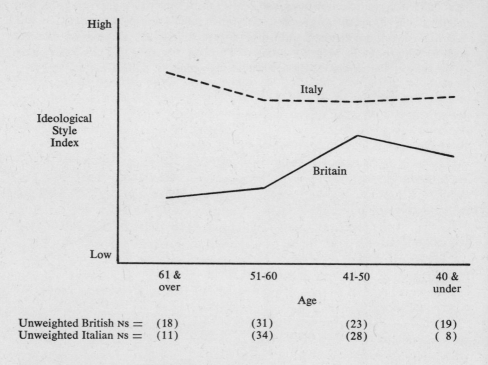

	61 & over	51-60	41-50	40 & under
Unweighted British Ns =	(18)	(31)	(23)	(19)
Unweighted Italian Ns =	(11)	(34)	(28)	(8)

Figure 5.2: Age and the Ideological Style Index
   In constructing this figure, weights were used to hold constant the partisan proportions of the cohorts; two members of minor parties had to be excluded from the calculations in each country.

   Figure 5.1 shows that in each country there is a marked and fairly regular decline in partisan hostility from the older to the younger politicians. Figure 5.2, on the other hand, shows that in neither country is there any decline in the extent of ideological political style. On the contrary, in Britain there is, on balance, a slight increase in the Ideological Style Index among the younger politicians. Correlational procedures confirm this analysis. The product-moment correlation (r) between age and the IPH is $+.23$ in Britain and $+.22$ in Italy. The correlation between age and the ISI is $-.20$ in Britain and $.02$ in Italy.[3] There has been, in other words, some lessening of hostility in Western politics,

the views of each party's members in a given cohort were weighted by that party's share of the total sample, rather than by the party's share of the particular cohort.
   3. Positive signs indicate a decline in the indices among younger groups. The correlations between age and the IPH in each country and the correlation between age and the ISI in Britain are all statistically significant at the .05 level or better.

but there is no evidence of a comparable decline in ideology; no decline, that is, in the tendency to "conduct politics from the standpoint of a coherent, comprehensive set of beliefs."

But what of the possibility these findings result from life cycle change or natural selection? Let us consider each of the graphs, beginning with figure 5.2. In the case of Italy there is virtually no difference in the Ideological Style Index for various age groups, and thus there is no need to choose among the three competing explanations. In the British case younger politicians all along the left-right spectrum have a relatively more ideological style of political analysis than do their elders. ("Younger" is used here in a relative sense, of course; our "younger" politicians are nearly all in their forties.) On the face of it, either the life cycle or the natural selection explanation is plausible. Perhaps age alone has brought a less abstract, more inductive perspective to British elder statesmen and will in time have the same effect on today's younger politicians. Or perhaps theoretically inclined would-be politicos find it relatively difficult to remain in the British Parliament, although when age is held constant, there is no correlation at all between parliamentary seniority and the Ideological Style Index.[4] We will see later that there are some theoretical grounds for entertaining the generational hypothesis here, for regarding the trend as a genuinely historical change in British elite political culture. However, the data themselves do not rule out the life cycle alternative.

As for the curves for the Index of Partisan Hostility in figure 5.1, the life cycle and natural selection hypotheses are again quite reasonable, at least in the Italian case. It is plausible that as Italian politicians grow older and wiser they become more suspicious and intolerant toward political opponents, especially since, as the evidence of this study shows, the pervasive atmosphere of Italian politics is one of fear and mutual antipathy. In such a climate the process of political socialization could easily generate increasing partisan hostility. Similarly, it is not wholly implausible that a kind of natural selection might operate to eliminate relatively more open-minded parliamentarians earlier in their careers, although in fact there is virtually no correlation between seniority and the IPH if age is held constant.

In the case of Britain, however, these two hypotheses are less plausible. The general climate of British politics is one of trust and mutual acceptance. As noted in figure 4.2, the bulk of the British sample falls at the bottom of the Index of Partisan Hostility. Other evidence to be presented in chapter 6 confirms the warmth of the personal relations among British MPs. As a working class

4. One possibility can be ruled out statistically: the age-ISI correlation is *not* simply a function of the large intake of new members onto Labour benches in the 1966 General Election. Assessments of the partial correlations between seniority and other variables, controlling for age, must be interpreted cautiously because of the technical problem of "multicollinearity." Age and seniority are themselves so closely related ($r = .73$ in Britain and $r = .58$ in Italy) that it is difficult to separate their individual effects.

Socialist said, "One of the things I would miss [if I left Parliament] is the camaraderie that there is in this House. Despite your politics, democracy really works inside here. We can miscall each other in committee or on the floor of the House, and then join each other for a cup of tea." (B64) Naturally, it would be quite misleading to describe the atmosphere of the Commons as all sympathy and tea, but most British politicians seem to share this sense of fellowship, even though political battles are often quite bitter.

Given this climate of opinion, it is hard to believe that the life cycle explanation of the trend shown in figure 5.1 is accurate in the case of Britain. It seems unlikely that experience in British parliamentary politics breeds partisan hostility. Nor is the natural selection hypothesis any more enticing, for it would violate all the evidence of this study as well as most common interpretations of British politics to assume that intolerance and hostility toward opponents would be an advantage for political survival. In the case of Italy probably both the life cycle and the generational explanations apply, although evidence presented below supports the notion that the latter accounts for a good share of the decline. Final proof can come only from genuine time-series data, but the most plausible and parsimonious assumption would be that the IPH data depicted in figure 5.1 represent the secular trend that some have referred to as the "decline of ideology."

In chapter 4 we discovered two syndromes, one centered on partisan hostility and the other on ideology. The available evidence indicates that in Britain hostility is decreasing, while ideology is increasing, and that in Italy hostility is decreasing, while ideology remains constant. These generalizations apply to other elements in each syndrome as well. Thus, for example, there is no difference at all between younger and older Italians in terms of the abstractness and comprehensiveness of their frameworks for explaining party differences, and in Britain the younger politicians are, if anything, slightly more "ideologically sensitive" in this sense. On the other hand, antipathy to compromise—part of the partisan hostility syndrome—*is* lower among the younger politicans than among their elders, although this trend is much sharper among the Italians. Thus, in British and Italian politics hostility between opponents is declining, antipathy to compromise is declining, and (as we will see in Chapter 11) so are perceptions of partisan controversy and conflict models of society. In short, everything is declining, except ideology. What are we to make of these findings?

Ideology, Politics, and Change: A Reformulation

Politics in Western Europe is changing, that much is certain. The task of social science is to make sense of things, and a good bit of ink has been spilt in attempts to reduce the complex variety of changes to one simple pattern. Some observers have seen the decline of class cleavage and partisan conflict. Some have noted increased "commitment to the politics of pragmatism, to the rules of the game of collective bargaining."[5] Some have glimpsed signs of increasing political tolerance. Some have seen the growth of widespread consensus on social and economic policy. Some have found evidence of a withdrawal from politics by elites and masses alike, a "depoliticization." Some have even hailed or bewailed the "end of politics." Some, of course, have seen changes in the style of politics that seemed to deserve the label of "the end of ideology." All have acknowledged social and economic changes of historic dimensions. And most have argued that all these changes form a single syndrome, bound together by complex but coherent causal connections. One of the most eminent proponents of this argument has quite correctly stressed, however, that this package of propositions should be tested like any other set of scientific generalizations. "There are many researchable questions. . . . What is needed is hard research."[6]

In this study, I have tried to bring the results of some "hard research" to bear on a few aspects of this broader question of change in contemporary Western politics. Let us begin with patterns of partisanship, one of the two syndromes that have occupied most of our attention thus far. The basic facts are clear: some politicians are relatively tolerant, trustful, open-minded, and flexible in their attitudes toward political opponents, while others are dogmatic, hostile, fearful, and rigidly antagonistic. The former, more open stance is typical of British politicians; the latter, of Italians. However, in both countries there is a consistent decline in intolerance and partisan antipathy among younger politicians. We have examined a number of possible explanations for these patterns in the data, and have concluded that a secular decline in the temperature of politics in both Britain and Italy is under way. Why should this be so?

Part of the answer can be found in the social and economic progress of the last quarter-century. Increased economic productivity, greater consumer affluence, more widespread educational opportunities, increased social and geographical mobility, the creation of a new mass culture—all these changes in the environment of politics have provided the context in which attitudes toward partisan opponents could soften. But though there is a link between these changes and the decline in hostility within the political elite, the link is not immediate or infallible. America in the 1960s demonstrated that affluence and antagonism can increase together. Another, more direct link in the causal chain lies in the lowered levels of political conflict that our respondents in both countries report, when asked to compare the early 1950s and the late 1960s. But still more relevant, I believe, has been the increase in simple contact and then in de facto cooperation between politicians from different camps.[7]

5. S. M. Lipset, "The Changing Class Structure and Contemporary European Politics," *Daedalus* 93 (1964): 296.
6. S. M. Lipset, "Some Further Comments on 'The End of Ideology,' " *American Political Science Review* 60 (1966): 17–18.
7. That contact and cooperation can lead to increased trust and tolerance is a common finding in social psychology. See the studies cited in William J. McGuire, "The Nature of Attitudes and Attitude Change," in *The Handbook of Social Psychology*, ed. Gardner Lindzey and

One particularly sharp hint of this effect is the fact that the biggest difference in hostility in the British sample is found within the Conservative Party between those who reached political maturity before the wartime coalition Government and the postwar Labour Government and those whose entrance into politics came later. Indeed, so dramatic is this difference that it alone accounts for most of the total correlation between age and hostility in Britain.[8] The implication seems clear. For the older Tories, the Labour Party remains a slightly sinister intruder. Their younger colleagues, by contrast, entered a political world in which Labour was simply "the other side."

In the case of Italy the decline in partisan hostility is found all along the ideological spectrum, although it is most marked in the two parties that have dominated postwar politics, the Communists and the Christian Democrats. In this instance the changes in interparty contact and cooperation are ever clearer. Many older politicians formed their basic impressions of their opponents during the Fascist era, when ordinary political interchange was impossible. During our conversations a few of these older and more suspicious respondents themselves acknowledged the impact their life experiences have had on their views. On nearly all sides of the Italian Parliament there is a sense that partisan barriers have been lowered in the course of the last two decades of pluralist politics. This trend is acknowledged even by some older partisans who view it with alarm and see the seeds of apostasy and betrayal in increased personal contacts and cooperation between opposing parties in the Parliament. Their insight into social and psychological dynamics is, I believe, quite sound. It is simply more difficult to hate a political opponent if one meets him daily in the smoking lounge, or sits with him around a committee table discussing Common Market milk price supports, or shares a compartment on the *rapido* for the weekly trip home. It is not impossible, but it *is* more difficult, especially for the younger men on both sides who often find the ideas and outlook of their younger counterparts in the opposition more congenial than those of their older party colleagues.

It is also possible that "market forces" in the democratic competition for votes have moderated partisan hostility in Italy over the years since the "holy wars" of the late 1940s between the forces of the Pope and the forces of Stalin. I asked one older Christian Democrat whether he thought the differences between the parties were greater or smaller than fifteen years earlier.

No, the differences have been attenuated, but attenuated in practice, not in doctrine. The doctrine has remained always the same . . . I'm not afraid to declare that often we men individually attenuate the differences . . . well, I'll say it: simply to save one's own seat. Sometimes if I am in the midst of

Elliot Aronson, 2nd ed. (Reading, Mass.: Addison-Wesley, 1969), 3:191.
    8. The correlation between age and the IPH is gamma = .36 for the Conservative Party and gamma = .06 for the Labour Party.

those who believe in Christian Democracy, I don't concede anything to Communism. But if I emerge from that mass and become a deputy, I reach an accommodation with my antagonist [*transigo,* the verb used, has pejorative overtones], perhaps in order to save my seat as deputy or not to lose those who, in doubt, could vote for me rather than my antagonist. I arrive at a position of transition or transitivity [*sic*]. I am no longer completely, decisively contrary to his ideological position. (I37)

The "transitivity" of which this man disapproves simply is the other face of the growing interparty tolerance we have discovered in this study.

One cannot be certain that these trends will persist. It would not be absurd to argue that mutual antagonism is already about as low in Britain as it is likely to get in a genuinely competitive party system. But the level of partisan hostility in any country deeply affects political behavior, and the declines we have noted will have a definite impact on the nature of politics in these countries. We saw, for example, that openness to compromise and a readiness to resolve conflicts are closely linked to partisan hostility. Conflict resolution is not all there is to politics, but it is quite a bit. Higher levels of mutual trust among the leaders of a country are virtually certain to lubricate the processes of government and politics. Moreover, lower levels of suspicion will facilitate a flexible response to the changing demands that society will place on its political institutions. Recall, for example, that politicians who rate higher on the Index of Partisan Hostility also rate higher on the authoritarianism and moral absolutism indices described in chapter 4.

These trends, I must stress, do not portend the growth of an apolitical utopia of mutual love and concord. Even the most tolerant of our respondents still feels that his own party provides more appropriate, more capable, more just solutions to the problems of his nation. The crucial variable, rather, is the acceptance of one's opponents as legitimate and trustworthy competitors in a common game. The standard is provided by the British politician who said of his opponents, "Well, they're different men with different policies, and some of them I quite like. They seem decent chaps, but I don't know, . . . I don't agree with their policies." (B75)

My conclusions about the decline of partisan hostility in Western Europe are consistent with the speculations of most other observers. My finding that there is no similar decline in the frequency of an ideological style of politics is less orthodox, however, and I want now to examine it a bit further.

First of all, there is a preliminary distinction. I am not arguing that all the individual ideologies or *Weltanschauungen* that have animated politicians in the past are surviving unchanged. It is perfectly clear that certain brands of ideology are dying out; virtually no one supports classical liberalism these days, for example. Some of the persisting ideologies are clearly changing, as their adherents respond to changes in the social, economic, and political environment. Nationalization no longer plays the role in British Socialist thought that it once did, and the corporativist theme in Christian Democracy is no longer expressed so paternalistically as it once was.

But change in the specific content of an ideology is not equivalent to a decline in the importance of ideology as a tool of political analysis, any more than changing hemlines mean a decline in the importance of fashion. This point is nicely illustrated by one of the leaders of the postwar Italian Left, who happened to appear in my sample. He was quite sarcastic in his castigation of the "out-dated ideological schemes" and the "old-fashioned language" of the other parties, and he went on to argue that "all the parties need ideological revision if they are to understand the needs of a modern society." (I57) But then he proceeded to outline the more "modern" doctrine of his own party, to analyze the concrete problems of Italian society in terms of the principles and values of this new theory of "advanced industrial societies," and to itemize the philosophical differences between this new conception of society and the older ideologies of the other parties. Though his substantive position on the issues facing Italy differed in important ways from the positions of his opponents, it would be very misleading indeed to describe his *style* of politics as less ideological.

If we consider, therefore, the *style* of political analysis practiced by politicians, ideology continues to be important in Italy and may in fact be increasingly significant in Britain. In a paradoxical way there may indeed be a kind of convergence going on in national political styles, but if so, it is a convergence toward an increasingly ideological style.[9]

Some acute observers of European politics have argued that increased affluence has set the stage for an increase in the political relevance of ideas. "Man does not live by bread alone—especially if he has plenty of bread."[10] To assume that all political conflicts are about to be abolished, simply because the older bases of cleavage are changing, is to misunderstand the nature of man and society. And as Robert Dahl has argued,

> if we agree with James Madison that "the latent causes of faction are sown in the nature of man," then democracies will not and cannot eliminate all causes of political conflict. If democracies cannot eliminate all the causes of conflict, is it not reasonable to expect that with the passage of time the clash of govern-

9. For evidence that in the case of Germany, too, the "decline of ideology" may have been exaggerated, see Jeff Fishel, "On the Transformation of Ideology in European Political Systems: Candidates for the West German Bundestag," *Comparative Political Studies* 4 (January 1972): 406–37.

10. Ronald Inglehart, "Post-Bourgeois Radicalism in France," (unpublished manuscript, University of Michigan, 1969) p. 51. This article offers an appealing theory of changing patterns of political cleavage in Western societies, based on the assumption that as basic physiological and economic needs are satisfied with increasing ease and regularity, drives for belongingness and self-fulfillment will become dominant. See also his "The Silent Revolution in Europe: Intergenerational Change in Post-Industrial Societies," *American Political Science Review* 65 (1971): 991–1017.

ments and oppositions, indeed of one opposition with another, will generate—
and will be generated by—new political perspectives that we cannot now accurately foresee?[11]

It is, of course, difficult to peer into the distant future, but the behavior of
political activists throughout Europe and America in recent years would certainly not comfort one who believed the time has passed when men strive to "conduct politics from the standpoint of a coherent, comprehensive set of beliefs."[12]
Our knowledge about the effect of rising levels of education on political sophis-
tication would, of itself, lead us to predict an increase in the importance of
abstract principles and explicit values in political discourse. As one student of
ideology in French politics has put it:

> As men become more adept at conceptualization and more universal in their
> values, they become more, rather than less, likely to adopt some overview
> of their political world and some more or less consistent set of values to guide
> them therein.[13]

There is, perhaps, less reason for surprise that I find no decline in ideological
style than if I had found the opposite.[14]

But we must return at this point to the definitional problems that we faced
at the outset of chapter 3. For some scholars offer perspectives closely parallel
to that proposed here, and then conclude that therefore ideology is dying.
Robert E. Lane, for example, argues that we are witnessing the birth of a new
kind of society, a "knowledgeable society," characterized by

> the development of more fruitful categories of thought, increased differentia-
> tion of ego from inner and outer worlds, an imagination of situations contrary
> to fact, reflective abstraction, changing truth criteria, and a changed philosophy
> of knowledge. This increase in knowledge and change in thoughtways lead to
> changes in policy-making procedures. There is increased application of

11. Robert Dahl, "Epilogue," in *Political Oppositions in Western Democracies,* ed. Robert
Dahl (New Haven: Yale University Press, 1966), p. 401.

12. Edward Shils, "Ideology and Civility: On the Politics of the Intellectual," *Sewanee Review*
66 (1958): 450. The argument I am making here received interesting confirmation from the behavior of the new Conservative Government elected in Britain in 1970. The consensus of British
commentators during its first years in office was that it had been the most "ideological" British
Government since the immediate postwar period, ideological not merely in the sense of partisan, but in the ideational sense used in this study. It is tempting to suggest that this movement
away from traditional Tory political style might have been predicted from the evidence and
analysis of this study, completed more than a year before the Heath Government took office.

13. Harvey Waterman, *Political Change in Contemporary France* (Columbus, Ohio: Charles
E. Merrill, 1969), p. 215.

14. Independent confirmation of the thesis here argued may be found in Ladd's study of the
increasingly "ideological' nature of local politics in America. His discussion of the causes of
this phenomenon parallels mine to a large extent, although he also stresses the "metropolitani-
zation" of American community life. See Everett Carll Ladd, Jr., *Ideology in America* (New
York: W. W. Norton, 1969), pp. 146–150.

scientific criteria for policy determination at the expense of the usual short-term political criteria and ideological thinking as well.[15]

Much of Lane's argument parallels my own. Both assert the growing importance of abstract theorizing about policy problems; both assert the increased emphasis placed on explicit principles and carefully analyzed values. The arguments diverge because Lane wishes to place the realm of knowledge in opposition to the realm of politics and ideology. That thought and knowledge can affect politics is a central tenet of this study; that they can *replace* politics seems to me a misunderstanding. Lane wants to distinguish between science and ideology, between veridical abstraction and dogmatic abstraction, but as Harvey Waterman has drily noted, "no measures are available that would distinguish 'bad' abstractions (ideology) from 'good' abstraction (science)."[16] However, if it is simply stipulated that when ideological abstractions are dissociated from dogmatism, they lose their status as ideology, then my conclusions about trends in Western politics are very close to those of Lane, quibble though I might about definitions. One more bit of evidence will help to clarify the point.

I have described the fact that in both Britain and Italy the Index of Partisan Hostility is lower among younger politicians and the fact that the Ideological Style Index among the younger groups is as high as or higher than among the older groups. One corollary is that the basic correlation between the ISI and the IPH is markedly higher among the older.[17] In other words, the original equation of an ideological style with intolerance ánd hostility may have been more accurate in the past.

Should this nest of empirical relationships be described as "the decline of ideology?" We have come to an almost purely verbal issue. For those whose concept of ideological behavior includes by definition the feature of intolerance, the answer will be "yes."[18] For those who wish to save the term "ideological" to refer to a certain style of political analysis, without regard to partisan attitudes, the answer will be "no."[19] I have chosen the latter course, but the facts of the matter do not depend on this terminological choice.

15. Robert E. Lane, "The Decline of Politics and Ideology in a Knowledgeable Society," *American Sociological Review* (October 1966), 31:649.

16. Waterman, *Political Change in Contemporary France,* p. 123.

17. Among respondents over 50 years old, the correlation (gamma) between the ISI and the IPH is $+.28$ in Britain and $+.20$ in Italy; among those 50 and younger, the correlation is $-.00$ in Britain and $-.21$ in Italy.

18. S. M. Lipset, for example, has said of "*Weltanschauung* politics" that "*by definition,* such political views do not include the concept of tolerance" ("Some Social Requisites of Democracy: Economic Development and Political Legitimacy," reprinted in *Empirical Democratic Theory,* ed. Charles F. Cnudde and Deane E. Neubauer [Chicago: Markham, 1969], p. 173). Emphasis added.

19. See, for example, Duncan MacRae, Jr.: "Ideology as a reasoned view of the world is not inconsistent with tolerance for alternative ideologies in the same political system" (*Parliament, Parties, and Society in France, 1946–1958* [New York: St. Martin's Press, 1967], pp. 329–30).

There is, however, one important issue yet to be disposed of. Some have argued that the persistence of an ideological style of political analysis, if it is divorced from hostility and intolerance, is essentially insignificant.

The fact that party leaders (and/or followers) may continue to think in ideological terms . . . does not seem nearly as important as the proposition that there has been a decline in the intensity and divisiveness of ideology in the Italian political system.[20]

The challenge here is clear: If, as I claim, everything is declining except ideology, why worry about ideology?

The answer is plain, however. The manner in which politicians structure and analyze issues of public policy will affect their behavior and ultimately, therefore, will affect the political process by which decisions on those issues are reached. The thesis that differing strategies of policy analysis constitute a variable of some importance for comparative politics is strongly supported by the fact that students of the policy-making process have disagreed vehemently about what the proper strategy *ought* to be.

Charles E. Lindblom has furnished the most extensive consideration of this topic, and his two models of policy analysis provide a helpful framework for our discussion. "Synoptic problem-solving," in Lindblom's terms, assumes that the decision-maker:

1. identifies, scrutinizes, and puts into consistent order those objectives and other values that he believes should govern the choice of a solution to the problem;
2. comprehensively surveys all possible means of achieving those values;
3. exhaustively examines the probable consequences of employing each of the possible means;
4. chooses a means—that is, a particular policy or combination of policies—that will probably achieve a maximum of the values or reach some acceptable level of achievement.[21]

This image of problem solving is remarkably similar to my description of the "ideological style." Lindblom argues that this method is not sufficiently adapted to the limits on man's intellectual capacities, to the inevitable inadequacies of information, to the ambiguities of our value systems, and in general, to the actual situation within which a policy-maker operates. Therefore, he proposes an alternative model, which he terms "disjointed incrementalism." This strategy is characterized by such features as:

20. M. Rejai, W. L. Mason, and D. C. Beller, "Political Ideology: Empirical Relevance of the Hypothesis of Decline," *Ethics* 78 (July 1968): 309.
21. Charles E. Lindblom, *The Intelligence of Democracy* (New York: Free Press, 1965), pp. 137–38.

1. the comparison and evaluation of marginal changes only
2. the consideration of only a restricted number of policy alternatives and of only a restricted number of important consequences for any given alternative
3. the adjustment of objectives to available policy alternatives
4. a serial and remedial orientation to analysis and evaluation rather than a comprehensive orientation[22]

This strategy is, Lindblom argues, more likely to be successful in coping with policy problems, because it is better adapted to the context of decision making.

Lindblom's argument against what I have called an "ideological style" is that it is ineffective. Others have added that this style is more apt to foster irreconcilable political conflicts than a pragmatic outlook. Ideologues operating with a comprehensive and detailed theory of society are more likely to have relatively fixed ideas about how a given problem should be handled. Italian Marxists are apt to have more precise notions of how to engage in economic planning than do the more pragmatic British Fabians. Even if the Italians are not in principle more opposed to compromise, in practice they will be less open to give-and-take, because they have a more detailed notion of what is being given and taken.[23] Moreover, the sense that one's policy proposals are linked to a grander theory may itself encourage more intense conflict. "Ideological struggles that transcend merely individual ones allow the participants a 'good conscience' in the choice of their means of struggle."[24]

Finally, an ideological style is often said to lead directly to government paralysis. Robert de Jouvenel put it simply: "Stagnation is perhaps the only practical form of fidelity to principles . . . . Ideas are eternal and men are pressed for time."[25] This conclusion is supported by a recent study of Swedish metropolitan reform, which traces the effectiveness of the Stockholm reformers precisely to the "pragmatism" and "particularization" of the Swedish style of policy analysis.[26]

This critique of a synoptic or ideological style of politics is powerful, but there

22. This summary is drawn from Lindblom, *The Intelligence of Democracy*, pp. 143–51 and Charles E. Lindblom and David Braybrooke, *A Strategy of Decision* (New York: Free Press, 1963), pp. 81–110.

23. Cf. Ladd's insight that, "As you come to see politics ideologically, you become aware of divisions you never knew were there" (Ladd, *Ideology in America*, p. 151). Of course, the content of the ideology is relevant here, too, since the divisions highlighted by some ideologies are more "bargainable" than those stressed by other ideologies. A plausible assumption might be that ideologies focused on religious or ethnic issues may be more conflict producing than ideologies focused on economic issues. On the connection between political style and propensities to detect conflicting interests, see chapter 8.

24. Lewis A. Coser, "Conflict: Social Aspects" in the *International Encyclopedia of the Social Sciences* (New York: Crowell Collier and Macmillan, 1968), 3:234

25. Robert de Jouvenel, *Le République des camarades* (Paris: Bernard Grasset, 1914), pp. 58, 62, as quoted in Waterman, *Political Change in Contemporary France*, p. 120.

26. Thomas J. Anton, "Incrementalism in Utopia: The Political Integration of Metropolitan Stockholm," *Urban Affairs Quarterly* 5 (September 1969): 75–6.

are some powerful opposing arguments. First of all, an ideological style may encourage consistency, coherence, and comprehensiveness in policy.[27]

> Compromise cannot be an end in itself; it is at best a means to some desirable end. And without rational examination of the end, we can never be truly assured that we are in fact approaching it. . . . A principled view of the world is conducive not merely to disagreement, but also to coherent policy; to viewing politics in terms of its central issues rather than its peripheral bargains. It may enable statesmen to see beyond the necessities of the moment and pursue policies that will be viable in the long run.[28]

A comprehensive, reasoned approach to policy issues may highlight neglected public values and reveal undiscovered trade-offs among competing values. This sort of approach may be more effective than an incremental and atheoretical style in achieving breakthroughs in the solution of persistent problems.

Some concerned observers of British policy making in recent years have questioned the effectiveness of the British style of problem solving. Andrew Shonfield, in particular, has attributed Britain's celebrated economic failures to "the pragmatic illusion."[29] A deep-seated national reluctance to think systematically and theoretically about policy, a reliance on intuition rather than ratiocination, a distaste for explicit statement of principles and values and alternatives—these are the traits Shonfield attributes to British policy-makers, and they are precisely the characteristics of British political style documented by the present study. They constitute, according to Shonfield, "the British formula for muffling public purpose." Instead, he argues, a "consistently high standard of intellectual rigour in the conduct of public affairs [is] the necessary condition for accelerating the pace of reform in Britain. . . . It is as if the British political genius were entirely devoted to the business of make-do and mend."[30]

This controversy about the most effective style of policy analysis is, ultimately, an empirical question—although an immensely complicated one—for Shonfield and Lindblom disagree not over moral issues, but rather over how one makes effective policy. I will not try to resolve this dispute here, but its very existence makes the point. How politicians think about policy is a matter of some significance, and students of comparative politics may find it fruitful to examine systematically the impact that differing strategies of policy analysis can have on the operation of political systems.

27. Note that this is not a logically necessary link. Consistency, coherence, and comprehensiveness in thinking about policy are by definition characteristic of an ideological style, but the resultant policy outcomes will not necessarily have these traits, for the gap twixt thought and deed is great, particularly in a decision-making system involving many actors and influences.

28. Duncan MacRae, Jr., *Parliament, Parties, and Society in France*, p. 329.

29. Andrew Shonfield, "The Pragmatic Illusion," *Encounter* 28 (June 1967): 3–12.

30. Ibid., pp. 10–11.

6 Britain and Italy:
Contrasts in Style and Partisanship

Explaining Ideological Style

No fact stands out more sharply from this investigation than the contrast between politicians from the two nations.[1] On nearly all the various components of the several dimensions of "ideological" we have examined, the Italians score markedly higher than the British. Italians treat problems of public policy more theoretically and deductively than the British, making more frequent reference to future utopias and to explicit ideologies. Italians more frequently find ideological satisfactions in their political activity. Italians use more comprehensive and articulated social theories to account for party politics. An indirect indicator of the greater "structuredness" of Italian ideologies is that in Italy, much more than in Britain, nearly the whole range of variables considered in this study is closely related to our simple measure of the left-right dimension. Attitudes toward social conflict, for example, are—as we shall see in part III—related to the left-right continuum in both countries, but much more intimately so in Italy. Many of the democratic norms that will be examined in part IV are linked to this same dimension, but again the link is much tighter in Italy. There is, in a statistical sense, more "constraint" among the various elements of a political philosophy in Italy than in Britain.[2] By any measure, Italians are more ideological politicians, and this central fact needs explaining.

1. In an effort to discover the personal origins of political style and partisan hostility, I looked with care for consistent relations between these central variables and a variety of background characteristics—social class background, geographical origins, type and amount of education, occupation, career patterns, experience and status in local government, party organization, and trade unions. Several minor exceptions apart, this search revealed no consistent or significant patterns. Respondents with very little formal education tend to have a lower score on the ISI; no doubt some minimal educational exposure is necessary for one to become familiar with the abstract coinage of the realm of ideology. In Italy "professional," career politicians are notably less hostile and more ideological than their colleagues.

2. The use of "constraint" to measure ideology was introduced by Philip E. Converse in his "The Nature of Belief Systems in Mass Publics," in *Ideology and Discontent*, ed. David E. Apter (New York: Free Press, 1964). Note that on this, as on other measures, our British politicians, too, are considerably more ideological than the mass publics studied in previous research.

The single most important part of the explanation has to do with contrasting national values. Intellect is highly prized in Italian culture. Verbal and logical abilities are sought out and strengthened by the educational system.[3] Intellectuals are greatly esteemed. In the specifically political context my own data offer surprising confirmation of these cultural values.

"How would you describe the job of a party leader?" I asked my respondents. "What personal qualities does he need?" In both countries they offered a long and varied list of requirements. Many mentioned the capacity to conciliate differences. Others stressed the ability to inspire loyalty and confidence. Personal courage and integrity were demanded by some. Still others suggested skill and experience in practical or policy-related fields. One quality, however, was mentioned almost universally in Italy, but hardly at all in Britain.

A good party leader must have *una grande preparazione,* [*preparazione* means literally "preparation" but implies experience, education, and intellectual training] an excellent cultural background, so that he can see and understand fully the problems of modern society and can think how these problems can be resolved. It's a problem of thought and a problem of culture, of political culture and of culture in general, to know the problems as they are and to indicate the solution to them. (I90)

This is a conservative Italian Christian Democrat speaking. Far across the political spectrum, a left-wing Communist agreed with this prescription for party leadership.

I believe that today [a party leader] must have a great intellectual and theoretical capacity. You can't any longer be a socialist or communist leader just from the heart. Once the great European socialist leader was the one who could make women and children cry during his speeches. Today we face great historical, political, and economic complexities. . . . I insist on this: the communist movement has reached a point in which it needs a great period of theoretical elaboration. (I87)

Others phrased a similar requirement in terms of commitment to a set of beliefs.

Above all, he must be a man gifted with a very great faith in the ideal in which he believes and which he has embraced. (I76)
Above all, for us he has to have a knowledge of our doctrine. Thus, he must be able to make use of our doctrine to analyze situations and see what the possible initiatives of the Party are. This is the principal thing. (I42)

3. See Samuel H. Barnes, "Italy: Oppositons on Left, Right, and Center," in *Political Oppositions in Western Democracies,* ed. Robert A. Dahl (New Haven: Yale University Press, 1966), p. 317.

These politicians, the first a Christian Democrat and the second a Communist, like their two colleagues quoted earlier, share a belief that a reverence for ideals, an ability to relate these ideals to political action, and, in general, intellectual "weight" are essential qualities of political leadership. Slightly more than half of all Italian respondents make such a quality a central feature of their description of the ideal political leader, and only one in six fails to mention it.

By contrast, this characteristic is rarely emphasized by British respondents when they are reflecting on the traits of admirable party leaders. Fewer than one in twelve makes it a prominent part of his description. Indeed, for some British respondents, the crusading attitude that seems to them linked to intellectual traits is positively undesirable in their leaders. "The problems want to be dealt with as they arise . . . [and] in a rational and civilized manner. But I think the people who go on crusades usually find they've created as many problems as they've solved." (B38)

Thus, Italian political leaders are supposed to be intellectual, whereas British leaders are not. Nor is this a question of nominal values. The most important Italian politicians really are more "intellectual" than their less important colleagues, at least to judge by their scores on the Ideological Style Index. For the most important third of our sample in Italy (as rated by our panel of parliamentary journalists) the mean score on the ISI (with party controlled) is 6.2, as contrasted with a mean score of 5.2 for the lower two-thirds. In Britain, on the other hand, the more important politicians rank slightly lower on the ISI than their less important colleagues.[4]

The Italians' admiration for an ideological style of politics is often quite explicit. One Christian Democrat, a former minister and a former delegate to the Assembly of Europe, commented on the role of ideology and philosophy in politics this way:

> I know that in other countries they say that it isn't necessary, but every human act, every attitude, above all, every political attitude implies a way of thinking, implies a philosophy. And this is why we believe that an authentic democracy . . . must have a profound moral inspiration. . . . Politics must be founded on moral principles. (I88)

A similar view was presented by a Socialist with lengthy political experience.

> I wouldn't like to get to a situation where because of a sort of mania for specialization you get compartments which become watertight and particular. . . . I once visited America, and I noticed this. . . . Maybe it works in America, but I don't think it would be good for us—a kind of isolation around each

4. Among the major European nations, the Italian Parliament has the highest proportion of university graduates, the British Parliament very nearly the lowest. See Gerhard Loewenberg, *Parliament in the German Political System* (Ithaca, N. Y.: Cornell University Press, 1967), pp. 103–4.

problem, a desire for specialization around each particular aspect, to my mind at the expense of the possibilities for a synthesis of the whole situation. (I67)[5]

Some interesting linguistic evidence supports the point I am arguing. Clifford Geertz discusses the evaluative overtones of the word "ideology": "No one, at least outside the Communist Bloc, where a somewhat distinctive conception of the role of thought in society is institutionalized, would call himself an ideologue or consent unprotestingly to be called one by others."[6] Although this observation may be correct for some groups, it is not true of Italian politicians. The word "ideology" is quite common in Italian political circles; three-quarters of our respondents spontaneously used either the word itself or a cognate. Of those who used it, 41 percent did so in such a way that the coders agreed the respondent attached a positive evaluation to the word. Only 11 percent of those using the term did so pejoratively; 48 percent of the references were evaluatively neutral. (By contrast, only one Briton in five used the word, and nearly all the references were either pejorative or neutral.) To call a politician an ideologue is not, in Italy, to condemn him.[7]

In sum, then, the Italians' ideological style of political analysis is intimately related to basic values in the political culture. Rational consistency, "synthetic" comprehensiveness, adherence to explicit social and moral principles—the roots of these values lie deep in Italian history. To uncover these roots and to contrast them with the origins of comparable values in British elite political culture would require another and very different sort of inquiry. No doubt one strand of the historical explanation is the marked difference between the Roman law and common law traditions. (It is probably not accidental that lawyers in Britain score relatively low on the ISI; Italian lawyers, by contrast, are no less ideological in this sense than their colleagues who lack legal training or experience.) Probably another part of the explanation lies in the values and life styles of the aristocratic classes that ruled both countries until quite recently, historically speaking, for it seems likely that the national differences in political style predate the democratic revolutions of the last century. Part of the explanation can be found in the pervasive influence of French and German culture on Italy.

5. This respondent several minutes later argued just as strongly for compromise and consensus in political life, a nice illustration of the weakness of the hypothesis linking ideological style to fanaticism.

6. Clifford Geertz, "Ideology as a Cultural System," in *Ideology and Discontent,* ed. David E. Apter (New York: Free Press, 1964), p. 47.

7. Sometimes even the clichés of a nation reveal something of its values. And to judge by the responses to one of the closed-ended items on the questionnaire, this study uncovered at least one Italian cliché: "It is only when a person devotes himself to an ideal or cause that life becomes meaningful." Every single Italian agreed with this statement, 84 percent of them "strongly," surely the mark of a cliché. By contrast, only 31 percent of the British respondents agreed "strongly," and 15 percent disagreed.

Historians of modern philosophy have often noted the contrast between continental rationalism and British empiricism.[8]

In seeking to explain the differences in political style between Italy and Britain, I have so far emphasized values embedded in the two national cultures. But other explanations are also important.[9] Geertz has argued in a slightly different context that ideology arises as a response to the cultural and psychological strain that accompanies rapid and drastic social change. "It is in country unfamiliar emotionally or topographically that one needs poems and road maps."[10] Social, economic, and political change has been less dramatic in Britain's last hundred years than in Italy's. Theories left unstated and perhaps unformulated, values left unanalyzed, ideals left implicit—these are, perhaps, luxuries that only statesmen whose environment is changing relatively gradually can allow themselves.

Furthermore, there is probably a reciprocal relationship between social conflict and ideological style. Chapter 8 will show that the more conflict a politician sees in an issue, the more likely he is to treat that issue in an ideological style. And Italian history and contemporary Italian society are plainly cleaved by greater conflicts than is Britain. Intense social conflict calls for and seems to justify generalized explanations of social affairs. Political polarization drives men to the extremes of the political spectrum, where an ideological style of analysis is more common.[11]

Explaining Patterns of Partisanship

The cross-national contrasts in political style are more than matched in intensity by the differences in patterns of partisanship. Though Manichean views of the political world are not absent among British parliamentarians, the much greater frequency and depth of intolerance and partisan hostility in Italy is one of the central facts documented by this study. To take merely the crudest indicator,

8. A carefully qualified statement of this position can be found in Monroe C. Beardsley's "Introduction" to *The European Philosophers from Descartes to Nietzsche,* ed. Monroe C. Beardsley (New York: Modern Library, 1960), p. xxii.

9. The presence of large numbers of intellectuals in the Italian political elite is no doubt related to the value placed on ideology, as some have argued, but probably as result rather than cause. There is no evidence in our data that politicians from "intellectual" occupations are significantly more ideological than "nonintellectuals" in their political analyses.

10. Geertz, "Ideology as a Cultural System," p. 63.

11. One form of the proposition linking Italian ideological politics to conflict lays the blame at the feet of the Italian Communist Party. The single-minded "ideologism" of the PCI is supposed to have forced their competitors to "oppose Communist ideology with their own 'true' and, they hope, more attractive ideologies. Like increase of appetite, ideologism grows by what it feeds on" (Herbert Spiro, *Government by Constitution* [New York: Random House, 1959], p. 200). I do not find this explanation persuasive, for it treats ideologism as an aberrant malignancy, introduced into Italian politics by a foreign virus. I can find little evidence that non-Communist Italian politicians adopt an ideological style *a malavoglia* (despite their better intentions). On the contrary, the leaders of the PCI themselves faithfully reflect the intellectual values of the broader Italian elite political culture.

only one British respondent in five ranks above the global mean on the Index of Partisan Hostility; nearly four Italians in five rank that high. I want to examine both the historical factors that generated these contrasting patterns and the contemporary mechanisms that perpetuate them.

At the most basic level the historical explanation must be sought in the differing paths of British and Italian political development. Students of political change have described "crises of development," certain recurring problems that must be dealt with by a society as it moves from traditional to modern patterns of politics.[12] Broadly speaking, developing nations, now and in the past, have had to grapple with the crises of national integration and identity, of regime legitimacy, of the effective penetration of the state into society, of mass participation, and of the distribution of economic well-being.

In Western Europe Italy is probably "exhibit A" of a country that dealt with these successive problems inadequately. In the first place, all of these crises have been concentrated in the century since 1870, the year Italy was finally unified. A deep sense of national unity, a regime whose legitimacy is unquestioned, an effective national bureaucracy, a parliamentary democracy based on universal suffrage, and a broadly based welfare state—these marks of successful handling of the crises of development, earned by the British over perhaps ten centuries, are still in many ways absent in Italy. Moreover, the social and political conflicts that these crises inevitably entail were exacerbated in the Italian case by elites seemingly unwilling or unable to adopt the necessary reforms. As Mosca noted, with perhaps a touch of envy:

> [I]n the course of the nineteenth century England adopted peacefully and without violent shocks almost all the basic civil and political reforms that France paid so heavily to achieve through the Great Revolution. Undeniably, the great advantage of England lay in the greater energy, the greater practical wisdom, the better political training, that her ruling class possessed down to the very end of the past century.[13]

This perspective should remind us that the links between elite values and political development are reciprocal. But my concern here is with the cumulative effect of these unresolved crises, for the legacy of this past is the "fragmentation, isolation, and alienation" that characterize contemporary Italian political culture.[14] Chapter 9 will show that there is a direct relationship between partisan hostility and views about social conflict, and in chapter 11 we will examine the history of political and social strife in Italy and the impact that this strife has

12. See Lucian W. Pye and Sidney Verba, eds., *Political Culture and Political Development* (Princeton: Princeton University Press, 1965); and Joseph LaPalombara and Myron Weiner, eds., *Political Parties and Political Development* (Princeton: Princeton University Press, 1966).

13. Gaetano Mosca, *The Ruling Class,* ed. and rev. Arthur Livingston, trans. Hannah D. Kahn (New York: McGraw-Hill Book Company, 1939), p. 119.

14. Joseph LaPalombara, "Italy: Fragmentation, Isolation, and Alienation," in Pye and Verba, *Political Culture and Political Development,* pp. 282–329.

had on Italian beliefs about conflict and consensus. Those who believe—as many Italians do—that irreconcilable conflict is inherent in society do not treat their enemies with trust and tolerance. Furthermore, partisan hostility within the Italian political elite is also intimately related to the pervasive social distrust among Italians generally.[15]

Still another historical factor deserves emphasis here. The Italian experience with parliamentary democracy is short indeed, limited essentially to the postwar years. The impact of an authoritarian regime, like that achieved by the Fascists, on political tolerance and trust can hardly be exaggerated. One older Sicilian Christian Democrat, who had earlier expressed great distrust of the parties of the Left, reflected on the meaning of Italian history for contemporary politics.

> Look, democracy is a difficult thing to make work, especially when you come from different experiences. We come from a totalitarian experience, the Fascist regime, and practically speaking, I think that fascism has been stronger in the postwar period than during Fascism itself, because everyone is formed . . . there's nothing you can do. You'll get the result of what you have sown, there's nothing can be done. Political education bears indelibly the marks of the damage of the years in which those grave presuppositions were created. (I 28)

A strikingly similar analysis was offered by an older Communist, also from the South and quite hostile toward his opponents.

> We had a twenty-year period in which the more active antifascists were constrained to work in France and work clandestinely with the specter of the special tribunal always hanging over their heads. The others resisted passively, not concerning themselves with politics. Therefore, there was above all a lack of information and a loss of the habit of thinking about politics. This recent awakening of the university students illustrates well my thesis. That is, it's the young people, who were little kids—if they were even born then—during the Fascist period. Thus, they don't have a passive heredity to have to cope with, a monk's habit to have to change, and therefore, they are the bearers of new ideas. Instead vice versa the older classes, the older men still have much of the heredity—even involuntarily at times, even without knowing it—have much of the mentality of a regime which dominated absolutely for twenty years. (I93)

Such comments show remarkable insight into the origins of the closed mentality of many older Italians. If the analysis is correct, then there should be a considerable reduction in intolerance and dichotomous thinking among younger politicians reared under democracy, which is, of course, precisely what we have found.

15. Ibid.; and Gabriel A. Almond and Sidney Verba, *The Civic Culture* (Princeton: Princeton University Press, 1963), pp. 266–73.

Yet even among these younger parliamentarians the levels of hostility are higher than in Britain. Part of the residual explanation derives from the simple fact of political distance. As I have pointed out earlier, the further a politician is (and feels) from his opponents in terms of policy, the greater his distrust and hostility toward them. It is clear that the distances in Italian politics are simply greater than in Britain. This situation is, in part, a result of the presence of the PCI, which often claims for itself a distinctiveness that many of its opponents are all too happy to acknowledge, though with obviously altered evaluative overtones. Many on both sides of the Communist-anti-Communist cleavage have had tactical incentives to exaggerate the differences. But exaggerated or not, the apparent distance between the PCI and their opponents encourages and justifies high levels of distrust and intolerance.

In Britain, on the other hand, it is often argued that there are virtually no differences between the parties. Indeed, this view was so widespread at the time of our interviews that many of our respondents went out of their way to assert that the differences between the parties are greater than is commonly thought. These men are deeply involved in the partisan struggle, and they are sensitive to the many (though perhaps only marginal) policy differences that result when their party is in power. There is little doubt, however, that the British political spectrum is narrower than the Italian. Bagehot is still a guide without equal here.

> [I]t may seem odd to say so, just after inculcating that party organisation is the vital principle of representative government, but that organisation is permanently efficient, because it is not composed of warm partisans. The body is eager, but the atoms are cool. If it were otherwise, Parliamentary govern-ment would become the worst of governments—a sectarian government. . . . But the partisans of the English Parliament are not of such a temper. They are Whigs, or Radicals, or Tories, but they are much else too. They are common Englishmen, and as Father Newman complains, "hard to be worked up to the dogmatic level."[16]

Change may be coming in Italy, but processes of change are slowed by equally important processes of reinforcement. Attitudes toward opponents are inherent-ly reciprocal. Distrust breeds distrust and intolerance evokes intolerance. This factor was nicely illustrated by a number of respondents who expressed genuine regret about the coldness of cross-party relations, but blamed this coldness on the other side. One young Christian Democrat admitted that the attitudes of his party were not always as open as they could be, but argued that the origins lay in the tactics of the opposition.

We have had in Italy a strong Communist party which has always conditioned

16. Walter Bagehot, *The English Constitution* (1872, reprint ed., London: Collins, Fontana Library, 1963), p. 159.

all the attitudes of the Christian Democratic party in the sense that the DC has had to organize itself to combat this party and in forms which were perhaps not the best. Many of the characteristics of this, let's call it "Christian-Democratic regime," are imputable to this. (I77)

A leading Communist referred to the same problem from the other side, when she described the unsatisfying aspects of Italian political life.

The Italian Parliament today is profoundly politicized, "partisan-ized" [partiticizzato]. The parliamentarian is a representative of the people, but he is channeled by the large parties. The forces of the majority [parties] render the relationship between majority and opposition impermeable. They make everything a function of the government agreements and the relationship with the opposition is very closed, very blocked. (I87)

A left-wing Italian Socialist explained that he had several friends in other parties, "above all when there isn't that element which makes relations among deputies so unpleasant, that is, sectarianism, 'closedness.' When there aren't these things—and with a few deputies there aren't—then it's very easy." (I47)

Several of these comments hint that there is in part a structural basis for the persistence of high levels of interparty hostility. Much of the hostility is directed, not personally at the members of opposing parties, but at the parties as organized groups. In fact, when I asked whether they could trust members of other parties, nearly two out of five Italians indicated specifically that their personal relations were all right, but that this point was politically irrelevant because on all important matters party constraints supervened. Of course, viewing the system as a whole, this is not entirely an independent phenomenon, since part of the explanation for the rigidity of official party boundaries lies in the general climate of distrust and hostility. But it is relevant that in Italy the more important politicians tend to show relatively higher levels of partisan hostility.[17] (In Britain the more important politicians are slightly more tolerant than their followers.) The organizational strength and rigidity of the Italian parties increases the inertia of the political culture, thus reducing the speed with which tolerance and mutual respect might increase.

The origins of the pervasive atmosphere of distrust, recrimination, and intolerance in Italian politics are, in summary, numerous and varied. Ancient and recent political history, mass and elite political culture, political distance and political organization—all these seem to play a role. It may be wrong, however, to treat Italy as the deviant case. In world perspective the anomalous case is probably Great Britain and the fairly high levels of partisan trust found there. To some extent it is tolerance, not intolerance, that needs explanation.

17. The mean IPH score of the most important third of the Italian sample was 7.4, as compared to 6.3 for the rest of the sample.

Historically, the absence of unreconciled domestic cleavages is clearly relevant, for as Dahl points out, the record of grievances against the government is an important influence on patterns of opposition.[18] Long experience with pluralist politics is a factor. Perhaps too, early socialization in such institutions as the elite "public schools" has historically had an effect. If so, the effect is indirect, however, since there is no evidence in the present data that those from public schools are more tolerant than their less fortunate colleagues. Britain's higher levels of socioeconomic development have probably encouraged lower political temperatures. Above all, the origins of the British tradition of trust and mutual respect between political opponents can be traced to three centuries of relative political stability.

The "rules of the game" that developed in the predemocratic House of Commons continue to affect contemporary attitudes, particularly because these rules themselves strengthen the role of the House as a place of "postrecruitment socialization." When I asked what they found most appealing about being in politics and government, more than a third of our British respondents mentioned the conviviality of colleagues on both sides of the House or the club-like atmosphere in Parliament. (Only 1 Italian out of 83 mentioned anything of the sort.) One of the most vociferous members of the Tory right wing replied to my question: "Politics is a matter of personalities and people. I love the House of Commons because here are 630 men from all walks of life. I'm very friendly with large numbers of them in all parties." (B61)

Another member, who had left the House and returned at a later election, knew what he would miss when he left again.

Well, to be honest, I think probably the companionship. I really don't mean that in the sense of the Commons being a good club. It is of course a good club, but what is unique to it is that all the members of the club have the same interests. . . . When I left, I . . . well, it was pretty lonely there for a while. I of course got things sorted out in the end, but the first few months that you couldn't go over there, it was almost as if something had been cut off. (B47)

Most British politicians seem to share this sense of fellowship, even though political battles are often quite bitter. Indeed, it seems one of the sacred dogmas of the House that friendships and trust cross party lines—no doubt a relic from the days before parties entered parliamentary affairs, and perhaps based more on faith than fact, but nonetheless a significant part of the parliamentary culture. Partisan hostility would need deep personal roots to survive in this climate.

18. Dahl, "Some Explanations," in Dahl, *Political Oppositions in Western Democracies,* pp. 359–67. Northern Ireland is an important exception to this generalization about British political culture (as it is to most similar generalizations), but British politicians from all parties have usually succeeded in preventing the tensions arising in Ireland from disrupting politics at Westminster. For an extended treatment of this problem, see Richard Rose, *Governing Without Consensus: An Irish Perspective* (Boston: Beacon Press, 1971).

In this chapter I have been reviewing the causes of Italy's markedly higher level of ideological style and markedly lower level of partisan tolerance. Alert readers may have noted that there lies latent in this discussion a perplexing paradox. On the individual level of analysis, as we have repeatedly seen, there is essentially no connection between ideological style and partisan hostility. But if the unit of analysis is the nation, then the more ideological—Italy—is also the more hostile. Is this correlation mere chance or is there some intelligible connection between the political style of Italians and their tendency to distrust and revile one another?

The notion that two variables can be unrelated to one another at the individual level and yet related at the group level is not as illogical as it might at first glance seem.[19] In fact, social science methodologists have discovered here a trap for the unwary, the so-called ecological fallacy. Using American states as the units of analysis, it can be shown that there is a positive correlation between literacy and immigration: the states with the highest literacy rates are the states with the highest proportion of immigrants. Does this mean that immigrants are relatively well-educated? Quite the contrary—on the individual level of analysis, immigrants tend disproportionately to be illiterate. The reversed correlation at the state level is fallacious, a result of the historical accident that immigrants settled mostly in the urban Northeast, while literacy rates are lowest in the rural South and West.[20] This example may provide the proper pattern for interpreting our data. The fact that both more "ideologues" and more "intolerants" are found in Italy may well be pure happenstance, a trap set by History to snare students of politics into thinking that ideology and intolerance are linked at the individual level.

But the plot may be thicker still, for there are some examples in social science in which there is a genuine correlation at the group level but no such correlation exists at the individual level. In a study of the factors that cause people to drop out of book discussion groups, James A. Davies found no difference at all in the relative drop-out rates of men and women. But the drop-out rate *was* lower in groups in which men were more numerous. Something about groups that had relatively more men induced participants of *both* sexes to stay in the program. Intensive analysis led Davies to conclude that the mysterious something was "activity level." The presence of more men in a group seemed to stimulate more engaging discussions, which then led participants of both sexes to continue their affiliation.[21] Davies warns us that such " 'compositional' effects . . . present some interesting problems for interpretation. The influence process here

19. See the excellent discussion of the development of sociological understanding of this issue in James A. Davis, *Great Books and Small Groups* (New York: Free Press of Glencoe, 1961), pp. 1–25.

20. This example and the term "ecological fallacy" are taken from William S. Robinson, "Ecological Correlations and the Behavior of Individuals," *American Sociological Review* 15 (1950): 351–7.

21. Davis, *Great Books and Small Groups,* pp. 140–1.

may be thought of as acting in the absence of any individual trait difference. The effect may possibly be thought of as 'catalytic' in which the influence of the attribute works through affecting the group climate or milieu without influencing individuals directly."[22]

Davies' statistical analysis of "compositional" effects was possible because he had data from a large number of separate groups. With a "sample" of only two nations, it cannot be determined whether the apparent correlation between ideology and hostility at the national level is random or real. The possibility that the connection is real, however, is plausible enough to merit some brief consideration. But first of all, I want to stress one point.

The evidence examined thus far should refute the notion, implicit in much Anglo-American thought, that the link between ideological style and political intolerance lies through psychopathology. Some have argued that only psychologically marginal individuals adopt an ideological style and that the very marginality of such individuals predisposes them to paranoia, dogmatism, and intolerance. (Shils, for example, describes ideologues as "madmen.")[23] Our evidence shows, however, that although there may be some connection between political style and patterns of partisanship, it does not depend on individual psychopathology.

One indirect link between ideology and partisan hostility at the societal level has already been suggested. Both may be, in part, the heritage of a "high-conflict" society. In nations where social change has fractured most shared frames of reference and most bonds of mutual trust, both ideological politicians and intolerant politicians may find enthusiastic audiences.

A possible direct link between ideology and hostility at the societal level lies in the conflicting demands of idealism and pluralism. An ideological political style, such as the Italian, stresses words and principles, often at the expense of deeds and practical accomplishments. In such a culture intellectual consistency and coherence are also highly valued. These values need not preclude compromise, but a compromise must be shown to be consistent, or as the Italians say, *coerente,* with basic principles. Mere agreement on concrete policy, without the reconciliation of basic principles, is not self-justifying. The dictionary definition of a common Italian political epithet is revealing. "Possibilism," says the *Dizionario Garzanti,* is "the renouncing of the coherence of one's own ideological positions, in order to obtain certain results."

Not all Italians are ideologues; not all stress the importance of clear principles, explicit values, and rational consistency. But the ideologues have set the tone of Italian public debate. They have established the standards by which everyone's political behavior will be judged. Just as the male members of book discussion clubs "catalyze" lively conversations in which all take part, so the

22. Ibid., p. 20.
23. Edward Shils, "Ideology and Civility: On the Politics of the Intellectual," *Sewanee Review* 66 (1958): 464.

Italian ideologues have "catalyzed" a politics in which *coerenza* is demanded of all and by all.

Such a political style has important advantages, but in a pluralist society with competing groups and interests it will often prove impossible to satisfy its lofty demands. Policy, if there is to be policy at all, will sometimes have to violate the principles of some of the participants. Where principles are unstated and coherent justifications unnecessary, such violations will occasion little notice and still less distress. On the other hand, where the prevailing political style stresses the importance of clear principles and rational justifications, these violations will be highly visible and to many will seem to transgress basic cultural values. The result can easily be widespread cynicism about political motives and political standards—a cynicism shared by ideologues and non-ideologues alike. It is a short step from this cynicism to intolerance and hostility.

Our data provide some evidence that this sort of mechanism operates in Italian politics. Coders noted instances in which the respondent spontaneously referred to some disparity between the words of other politicians and their actions or true intentions.[24] This variable was called "cynicism." More than half of all Italian respondents made such a reference "clearly and explicitly" and seven out of eight did so at least in passing. In Britain, only one in eight made explicit such a reference and nearly three-fifths never made any reference of the sort. One could read these figures as showing that the British observe higher standards of political integrity. But an equally plausible explanation is that Italian behavior is no different, but that Italian norms are more demanding. Not only is cynicism in this sense common in Italy, it is also very closely related to partisan hostility and intolerance. The correlation between the "cynicism" measure and the Index of Partisan Hostility is gamma $= .70$. On the other hand, cynicism is completely unrelated to the Ideological Style Index, with gamma $= .02$. These are precisely the results one would expect if my speculations about the relationship between principle and practice in an ideological culture are correct.

This, then, is the most plausible link—if link there be—between partisan hostility and an ideological style of politics, a connection based not on individual neurosis, but on the inconsistent demands of a culture that values "coherence" and a society that is intractably "incoherent."[25] Whatever the worth of these speculations, however, it is important to stress the more certain and more important truth that the volcanic hostilities in Italian politics were generated years ago by the heat of friction along historical fault lines.

24. The reliability of this judgment was fairly high. Tau-beta for the two coders' judgments $=$ .52; 7 percent of the respondents were placed at opposite ends of the three-point scale.
25. Cf. Harvey Waterman: "The obligation to adhere to principle (or poetry) and to act consistently therewith, together with the sheer impossibility of doing so, have weighed heavily on the French, burdening them with a perpetual sense of their own corruption and a weakness for the correctives of reversion to principle and chastisement by the pure" (*Political Change in Contemporary France,* [Columbus, Ohio: Charles E. Merrill, 1969], p. 118).

PART II
POLITICIANS AND CONFLICT:
AN ESSAY ON COGNITIVE PREDISPOSITIONS

7 Conflict in Society: A Variety of Views

Is society fundamentally harmonious and based on cooperation and widely shared values and interests? Or are discord and conflict the essence of social relations? Do politics and government consist in the rational pursuit of collective goals or rather in the violent clash of conflicting demands for limited goods? These are questions that have divided political philosophers since the classic debate between Socrates and Thrasymachus and they form the basis of a continuing controversy in contemporary sociological theory. I shall argue in this chapter and those that follow that politicians, too, have opinions on these apparently recondite matters, and moreover, that these opinions—these cognitive predispositions—inform the politicians' approaches to their tasks, indeed inform their very definition of these tasks. A politician's orientation to social cleavage and social consensus is, in short, a fundamental characteristic of his view of the world.

The Philosophers' Views

Since many of the subtleties of the politicians' views on this issue will turn out to have clear antecedents in the philosophical controversies, it will be of some help to begin by considering the philosophers' analyses of social conflict and consensus.

Like many important issues in political philosophy, this question can be traced back to a divergence of view between Plato and his most illustrious student, Aristotle. A true society was, for Plato, no mere collection of self-interested individuals, but a communion of souls rationally united in the collective pursuit of moral ends. As Wolin argues, "[Plato's] vision of the Good, whether it was located with the philosopher-statesman or written into the fabric of the laws, decreed that the aim of the ruler's art was to nurture souls, an aim that could be attained only if the community were at one in feeling and sentiment."[1] While Aristotle shared with his mentor a fundamental belief in the moral basis of political life, he was more sensitive to the reality of conflicting interests and

1. Sheldon S. Wolin, *Politics and Vision* (Boston: Little, Brown, 1960), p. 63.

perspectives. "Accordingly, while justice remains the ordering principle of the political association, justice itself has been widened to embrace the notion of political conciliation. The political art has to do with the reconciliation of a wide range of valid claims."[2]

The polar position that irreconcilable conflict is inherent in social relations has been explored most extensively by Thomas Hobbes and Karl Marx. The two differ sharply about the origin of conflict. Hobbes links it to a psychological theory of motivations; Marx, to a sociological theory of property relations. But they are in full agreement that the essence of social relations is conflict. There is, according to Hobbes, a permanent enmity among men, "a perpetual contention for honour, riches, and authority."[3] For Marx, "the history of all hitherto existing societies is the history of class struggles." "Every class struggle is a political struggle," and under capitalism, "the executive of the modern state is but a committee for managing the common business of the whole bourgeoisie."[4] Each theorist also conceives a new and radically different type of society in which conflict would be muted or transmuted. Hobbes suggests that an omnipotent Sovereign impose order on social anarchy, while Marx offers a romantic vision of a distant classless and therefore harmonious society. But both agree that society as they (and we) know it is inherently discordant, and that conflict is the very essence of politics.

After Plato, the "consensual" pole of the argument was developed by such diverse theorists as Cicero and Burke. Throughout the Middle Ages and into the early modern period, the concept of "the commonwealth" was central to social and political theory. The origin of this notion, apparently, lay in Cicero's version of the Stoic doctrine of natural law. "The commonwealth, then, is the people's affair; and the people is not every group of men, associated in any manner, but is the coming together of a considerable number of men who are united by a common agreement about law and rights and by the desire to participate in mutual advantages."[5] A similar image of social relations is implied in Burke's later assertion that society is a partnership, "a partnership in all science, a partnership in all art, a partnership in every virtue, and in all perfection."[6]

More recently, several schools of thought have attempted to synthesize these differing perspectives on social conflict. The English liberal philosophers, for example, argued that because of the latent natural harmony of interests, free competition among self-interested individuals—"the simple principle of natural

2. Ibid., p. 64.
3. Thomas Hobbes, *Leviathan* (Oxford:Basil Blackwell, n.d.), p. 460.
4. Karl Marx and Frederick Engels, "Manifesto of the Communist Party," *Selected Works* (Moscow: Foreign Languages Publishing House, 1962), 1:34, 42–3, 36.
5. Cicero *Republic,* 1. 25, as quoted in George H. Sabine, *A History of Political Theory,* 3rd ed. (New York: Holt, Rinehart and Winston, 1961), p. 166.
6. Edmund Burke, *Reflections on the Revolution in France* (1790, reprint ed., New York: Liberal Arts Press, 1955), p. 110

liberty"—would automatically produce mutually beneficial outcomes, "the greatest good for the greatest number."[7] Experience of the nineteenth century raised some doubts about this natural harmony of interests, and Idealists like T. H. Green and Bernard Bosanquet strove to save the theory of social consensus by distinguishing between an individual's "apparent" will and his "real" will. Though there might be conflict among what different individuals or groups *think* they want, there is no conflict among their "real" interests. "If everyone pursued his *true* private interest," Bosanquet affirmed, "he would pursue the common interest."[8]

The kind of distinction between conflict and consensus models of society put forth in such classic statements can also be found in contemporary sociological theory. As summarized by Percy Cohen, the consensus or "integration" model

> attributes to social systems the characteristics of commitment, cohesion, solidarity, consensus, reciprocity, cooperation, integration, stability, and persistence, while the other [model] attributes to it the characteristics of coercion, division, hostility, dissensus, conflict, malintegration, and change. One could also say that the first model emphasises the significance of norms and legitimacy, while the second emphasizes those [*sic*] of interests and power.[9]

Up to this point I have spoken as if conflict and consensus were a simple dichotomy. In fact, as many proponents of each position have recognized, they are poles of a continuous dimension. One can imagine societies with varying mixes of conflict and consensus. Moreover, over time and across different policy domains the relative balance between shared interests and conflicting interests is clearly a variable, not a constant. Recently, some students of politics have drawn on the mathematical theory of games to illuminate this variable. With Robert Axelrod, let me informally define "conflict of interest" as "the state of incompatibility of the goals of two or more actors."[10] One can then imagine at

7. See, for example, Robert L. Heilbroner, *The Worldly Philosophers,* rev. ed. (New York: Simon and Schuster, 1961), pp. 39–40. Burke at times seemed to endorse this view, as when he admonished the French revolutionaries that in the discarded Estates General "you had that action and counteraction which, in the natural and in the political world, from the reciprocal struggle of discordant powers, draws out the harmony of the universe" (*Reflections on the Revolution in France,* p. 40).

8. Bernard Bosanquet, *Philosophical Theory of the State* (London: Macmillan, 1899), p. 114. Emphasis in the original. For an interesting Marxist synthesis of the contending views that distinguishes between "antagonistic" and "nonantagonistic" conflicts, see Mao Tse-tung, "On the Correct Handling of Contradictions Among the People," as exerpted in Stuart R. Schram, *The Political Thought of Mao Tse-tung,* rev. ed. (Harmondsworth, England: Penguin Books, 1969), pp. 304–306.

9. Percy Cohen, *Modern Social Theory* (New York: Basic Books, 1968), pp. 166–7. See also Ralf Dahrendorf, *Class and Class Conflict in Industrial Society* (Stanford: Stanford University Press, 1959), pp. 157–65; and N. J. Demerath III and Richard A. Peterson, eds., *System, Change, and Conflict* (New York: Free Press, 1967), pp. 261–311.

10. Robert Axelrod, *Conflict of Interest: A Theory of Divergent Goals with Applications to Politics* (Chicago: Markham, 1970), p. 5.

one extreme a game of pure conflict in which all the gains of one player come at the expense of his opponent, a "zero-sum conflict" in which the algebraic sum of wins and losses is zero. At the other extreme one can envisage a game in which two players are partners against "the house," sharing all winnings. This would be a game of pure cooperation, since either player could win only insofar as his partner won. In between these two extremes one can imagine a whole array of games with differing amounts of conflict, depending on the balance of shared or opposed interests.

Axelrod has used a diagram similar to figure 7.1 to elucidate this problem in the case of what are technically called "bargaining games."[11] Each axis represents the winnings of one of the two players and each of the dotted lines represents a set of possible outcomes for a given game. Line I represents a game of pure conflict (strictly speaking, a "constant sum" game), in which each player can only win the maximum amount if the other wins nothing, and each increment in one player's winnings comes at the expense of the other. Line II represents a game of pure cooperation, because with the outcome represented by point A both players can win their respective maxima. Line III represents an intermediate game of both shared and conflicting interests. Each player's maximum is compatible with his opponent's doing fairly well (as at point B_1 or B_2), but over the range of alternatives between B_1 and B_2 increased winnings for

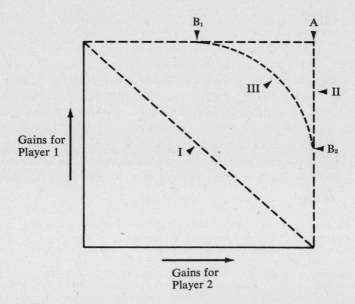

Figure 7.1: Conflict of Interest in Three Games

11. Ibid., chap. 2.

one are almost balanced by decreased winnings for the other. Axelrod offers a mathematical definition of conflict of interest based on this analysis and shows that the amount of conflict latent in an issue (or, presumably, in a society) could, in principle, be measured by the extent to which the curve of outcomes for that issue (or society) "bulges."

The analysis presented so far has been, from one point of view, overly static. One can imagine that during their interchanges the players might find a previously undiscovered solution (a new policy, perhaps) that would allow them both some gains. In graphic terms, this discovery would be equivalent to a restructuring of the game so that the "outcome line" would jut outward further to include the newly found solution. Insofar as the players in any game are engaged in attempts to find such new and mutually satisfactory outcomes, we could describe their activities as problem solving. Insofar as they assume a fixed set of outcomes and are merely contending over which one from this set will finally be selected, they are engaged in bargaining. This distinction between different kinds of behavior (or different kinds of games) has been noticed by a number of students of game theory; Schelling refers to "efficiency" and "distributional" bargaining, Walton and McKersie to "integrative" and "distributive" bargaining.[12]

Political philosophers and political scientists, therefore, have recurrently focused on the issue of conflict and consensus as central to their interpretations of society and politics. But what of the views of practical politicians?[13]

The Politicians' Views

"Some people say that there is always bound to be conflict among various groups in society and politics, while others say that most groups have a great deal in common and share basically the same interests. What do you think about this?" This query introduced a series of questions designed to elicit from our British and Italian politicians their interpretation of the relative importance of conflict and cooperation in society, politics, and government. Follow-up questions probed the respondent's view of the reconcilability of social and political

12. Thomas C. Schelling, *The Strategy of Conflict* (New York: Oxford University Press, 1963) Richard E. Walton and Robert B. McKersie, *A Behavioral Theory of Labor Negotiations* (New York: McGraw-Hill, 1965). For a more general treatment of this topic, see Edward P. Levine, "The Mediation of International Disputes" (Ph. D. diss. Yale University, 1971).

13. Recently several other political scientists have called attention to the need to study the conflict-consensus orientation of political leaders. See Gabriel Almond and G. Bingham Powell, *Comparative Politics: A Developmental Approach* (Boston: Little, Brown, 1966), pp. 55–6; Robert A. Dahl, *Polyarchy: Participation and Opposition,* (New Haven: Yale University Press, 1971), pp. 152–162; and Alexander L. George, "The 'Operational Code': A Neglected Approach to the Study of Political Leaders and Decision-Making," *International Studies Quarterly* 13 (1969): pp. 201–02. James C. Scott emphasizes a closely related notion, the "constant pie" orientation, in his study of the beliefs of Malaysian bureaucrats, *Political Ideology in Malaysia* (New Haven: Yale University Press, 1968), pp. 99–149.

conflict and his image of relations between social classes.[14] Most respondents found this an intelligible, if somewhat unusual, topic, and their views covered a wide range, encompassing nearly all of the classical philosophical arguments.

Not surprisingly, the clearest expression of the position that irreconcilable conflict of interest is at the heart of politics came from Marxists. "Listen," argued a working-class Italian deputy in the left wing of the Socialist Party,

> The capitalist class as a general rule never give anything to the workers spontaneously. If you want to get something, you only get it through hard struggles: strikes, arrests, prison, many times even blood. And there isn't ever a real victory, because even when you pass a law, there are always catches in it, so that in reality it turns out to be worthless. It's a continuous struggle. (I23)

A more variegated view of ubiquitous conflict was expressed by a Labour MP:

> There's always conflict—between employers and employees, manufacturers versus consumers, Labour people versus Tories. There's continual conflict. [*Do these various groups ever have anything in common?*] Yes, but even so, there is nothing that everyone shares in common. [*Is there bound to be conflict between the different social classes or can they get along together without any conflict?*] There's bound to be conflict. Those people who have mean to keep what they have and those who don't have a fair share are trying and demanding to get a fair share. (B22)

Expressions of this point of view were not limited to politicians in the Marxist tradition. The most graphic statement, in fact, came from a right-wing Italian:

> I look at it this way. In the jungle there's a sparrow pecking on the ground for something. A snake comes by and 'pop,' eats it up. There's a lamb, lying quietly; a lion passes and 'zap,' grabs a bite to eat. It's a continuous struggle. And then the other curious aspect of life is mimicry. Go to the jungle again. Why do certain animals take on the color of nature? In order to hide, because they recognize the dangers around them. There's always danger. (I95)

Life in this politician's world is remarkably Hobbesian—nasty, brutish, and (potentially) short.

At the other end of the continuum are those who believe in the essential unity and harmony of society. A number of Tories expressed this viewpoint quite clearly.

> Well, of course, the Marxian philosophy is that life is conflict between groups. I think this is nonsense. I think that in fact this idea of conflict between

14. This set of questions concentrates on conflict among groups and does not raise directly the issue of competition or cooperation among *individuals*. Thus, insofar as there is an empirically significant distinction between an "individualistic" theory of social conflict (for example, that of Hobbes) and a "collectivist" theory (for example, that of Marx), this set of questions will tend to evoke the latter more than the former. Note, however, that the groups in question need not be classes in the Marxist sense.

groups is based on lack of knowledge and perhaps lack of contact. I think the truth is that groups do have a great deal in common and when people from different groups meet, as in the old days at the Duke of York's camps and at present on some of the training ships where boys from all sorts of families get together, they're astonished to find how much they *have* in common and I think these do a very great deal of good. But of course it is an absolute part of the Marxist dogma that they have nothing in common and that there is a natural state of class warfare between them—I believe this to be rubbish. (B30)

But again, this attitude is not limited to any one position on the ideological spectrum. A Labour barrister was asked about differences, for example, between the political parties.

No, no, none at all. There are imaginary differences. Both parties have to pretend that there are differences and they have to exaggerate the differences, because to enable a democracy to work, it's no use to tell the people they want a different set of people. You have to tell the people that the new people have got a different policy which would enable them to avoid the mistakes of the old government. That's the essence. It doesn't mean having a different policy. It means pretending to have a different policy. But that's purely camouflage, in reality, because basically both parties want to do the same thing—produce the best Government for all the people. [*Conflicts and controversies are pretty important. . . I mean pretty common in politics. What's the most important . . .*] When you say they're important. . . [*Common, at any rate.*] People think they're important. The newspapers think they're important, but it doesn't mean that they're really important. *I* don't think they're important. (B27)

Between the extremes represented by such statements as these are a range of positions reflecting different mixes of conflict and common interests. One of the leaders of the postwar Italian Left reflected on my question:

From this point of view I am a Marxist, and I believe that there are class antagonisms, which must be resolved, naturally. The method isn't that of extermination, but it is one of struggle. And I don't believe that a democracy has an interest in camouflaging conflicts as mere adjustments. They're conflicts. [*Are they reconcilable?*] Yes, but it isn't a final reconciliation. You can find points of temporary contact, but between the position of the worker in industry, without any real power, and the industrialist, there isn't . . . well, they can reach an accord—after all, they do, on wages and so on, but you must recognize that there is a conflict. (I61)

A Labour backbencher presented a viewpoint somewhat further toward the consensus end of the spectrum:

> There are groups obviously that cooperate to the full, but there are groups that are in conflict. . . . I think a measure of conflict is a good thing—depends on how far you do it. The general policy in general outline—groups giving full support, of course, is a good thing, too, but when it comes down to detail I think there must be a good deal of disagreement. (B36)

Somewhat similar was the position of a Christian Democratic party activist, who remarked:

> I've got to say that both things are true, that collaboration arises from conflict, and conflict from collaboration. Depends on how you look at it. [*Are the conflicts of interest in your experience irreconcilable or not?*] Well, it's precisely the task of the politician to resolve them. The great politician is the one who reconciles, because if there's a permanent situation of conflict, the society remains stopped. Conflict and conciliation—that's the way you move ahead. Of course, there's the dictator who reconciles, too, but he simply represses the conflict—that's reconciliation at the price of liberty. (I77)

Finally, here is a British MP still further toward the consensus end of the continuum:

> I take the view that groups have most in common, but of course, it doesn't always appear that way, and I think what we've got to try and do is stress the fact that we are one nation and that our interests are indivisible. Obviously, there'll be differences within that general definition. (B75)

Even the most casual reading of these interviews reveals a spectrum of attitudes toward social and political conflict. To move beyond such gross generalities, however, one must subject one's impressions to the hard discipline of coding and counting. Each respondent's discussion of conflict and consensus was rated on a six-point scale according to the relative prominence of harmony or discord. The specific definitions of each point on the scale and the distribution of the British and Italian respondents along it are given in table 7.1.

The first conclusion to be drawn from this table is a negative one. Virtually no respondents fall in the most extreme categories; indeed, from a statistical point of view, these categories could be omitted. It is, however, useful in interpreting the meaning of responses in the less extreme categories to know what more extreme alternatives were rejected by the coders as inappropriate. In other words, virtually no British or Italian politicians take either the view that conflict of interest is all pervasive and totally irreconcilable or the view that there is *no* real conflict of interest in politics.

The respondents' familiarity with the prevalence of conflicting perspectives on policy problems, as well as their broader knowledge of social realities no doubt precludes complete agreement with Cicero's description of society and politics as "the coming together of a considerable number of men who are

Table 7.1: Images of Social Conflict in Britain and Italy
(in percentages)

QUESTION: "How prominent is conflict of interest in the respondent's view of society and politics?"

Categories	Britain (N = 39)	Italy (N = 60)
1. He sees virtually no real conflict of interest in politics.	0	0
2. He sees some conflict of interest, but conflict is generally deemphasized and clearly overshadowed by cooperation.	38	10
3. Pro-con. He sees both conflict of interest and areas of cooperation. These seem equally important.	13	15
4. Conflict of interest is more typical of politics as he sees it. This conflict is, however, limited and reconcilable so that cooperation is possible.	36	47
5. Conflict of interest is dominant of his view and difficult to reconcile, but it is possible to reach a modus vivendi.	13	25
6. Conflict of interest is dominant of his view and is irreconcilable. Cooperation is rarely, if ever, possible.	0	3

NOTE: The intercoder reliability was quite high, tau-beta = .60. In more conventional terms, 55 percent of all respondents were coded identically and an additional 36 percent were placed in adjacent categories by the two coders. Approximately half of each national sample were asked the series of questions on conflict described at the beginning of this section. The remainder were asked a slightly different series, culminating in: "Which is more typical of your experience in politics and government: conflicts and controversies, or situations in which everyone is cooperating on some common purpose?" Unfortunately, while the earlier "social analysis" question seemed to evoke general beliefs about society, this latter "political experience" question was interpreted much more narrowly and idiosyncratically. A variety of contextual and statistical evidence confirms that this alternative question does not tap underlying orientations to conflict; respondents asked only that version have, therefore, been excluded from most of the analysis that follows in the text.

united by a common agreement about the law and rights." On the other hand, their calling as parliamentary politicians probably precludes a belief in the total irreconcilability of social and political disputes. Society and politics is for these men a game of "mixed motives," as the game theorists say.

The most striking fact about differences among the respondents' views is that according to this measure—which I shall term the Social Conflict Index— Italians are considerably more sensitive to conflict in society and politics and British politicians are more impressed by areas of shared interest. Consensualists, deemphasizing social conflict, are nearly four times as common among the British, while twice as many Italians as Britons see conflict so pervasive as to be difficult to reconcile.[15]

The details of this picture must be sketched. In the first place, a number of respondents added an important qualification. Several in each country remarked that although there was in fact conflict in politics and society, this conflict was

15. This comparison, by the way, holds even if one removes from the Italian sample all Communists, who, naturally enough, are clustered toward the conflict end of the continuum.

really unnecessary. If men were intelligent and sincere, they would find themselves in agreement. One Italian argued:

> I believe that there are differences, because men are all different from one another, but if everyone had the possibility of a sincere evaluation of his interests, put in terms that he could understand, I believe that everyone would be in agreement. (I6)

A British Conservative reflected on conflict and coincidence of interest in society.

> I would have thought in fact that they probably have very similar interests . . . but I think you'll never persuade them of that. They think they're opposed. I mean, employers and employees think they're opposed. Obviously, they are not, in the sense that the prosperity of the firm is what matters to both; but I think it's a rather high-falluting view, that. You won't get many of them to see it. (B47)

An Italian Liberal also thought that shared interests were often overlooked, but he thought that more than ignorance lay at the root of this misperception.

> I think if we take, not pure politicians, but educated men, I believe that common ends are easily discoverable. If you take educated men and discuss things with these men, I think you could come to many more things that unite than things that divide. The trouble is precisely the political question, the rabid chasing after the voter. This chasing after votes makes us adopt attitudes which are really counterproductive. This is the dishonesty which leads us to more open divisions—because all of us are furiously seeking votes. (I27)

These respondents are arguing that apparent conflict of interest is in some sense an optical illusion. This is an interesting reprise of the philosophical argument made by the Idealists who distinguished between "apparent" interest and "real" interest. This distinction was also echoed in some of the game theory analyses referred to earlier. In game theory terms, these respondents are arguing that there is a mutually satisfactory point "out there" beyond the currently accepted "outcome line," a point that is presently obscured by ignorance or malevolence.

This point of view was stated explicitly more frequently in Italy than in Britain. Twenty-three percent of all Italians made such a qualification, while only 13 percent of the British did so. (In Italy, but not in Britain, such a qualification was much more characteristic of the Right than the Left, with less than 10 percent of the Italian deputies of the Left making such a statement, as contrasted with 30 percent to 40 percent of those of the Right.) The higher figure for Italy probably reflects the fact that Italian consensualists can hardly deny the existence of apparent conflict in Italian society; they can only deny that this conflict is genuine.

These respondents were a bit difficult to place on the basic continuum con-templated by the research, since they are essentially calling attention to two *different* continua, one in terms of the amount of conflict presently characteristic of society, the other in terms of the amount of intrinsically necessary conflict. They were generally placed toward the consensus end of the spectrum, since that seemed best to express their more fundamental attitude. Subsequent statistical analysis confirmed this decision, and the data presented in this and subsequent chapters include these respondents, although their exclusion would not signif-icantly alter our conclusions.

A second shading must be added to the picture. It is natural when talking of conflict in society to think of specifically class conflict, especially because for the orthodox Marxists in our samples, social conflict *is* class conflict. Many re-spondents were asked specifically about their views on class conflict, and the results are given in table 7.2. Once again, the difference between the countries is clear: nearly twice as many British as Italians stress class harmony, and two-fifths of the Italians claim that class interests are nearly always opposed.

Table 7.2: Images of Class Conflict in Britain and Italy
(in percentages)

QUESTION: "Do you think that there must be conflict among social classes or can they get along together without conflict?"

	Britain (N = 36)	Italy (N = 43)
Class harmony universally true; no real conflicts of interest	17	7
Class harmony typical, though there are some conflicts	31	19
Pro-con	8	7
Class conflict typical, though there are some common interests	33	28
Class conflict clear; no common interests	11	40

But this straightforward comparison does not tell the whole story. While Italians interpret the question in classical Marxist terms, many of the British, especially those of working class origin, interpret class conflict differently. For example, one Welsh ex-clerk answered the question this way:

Well, I think on the whole they will get along together. I mean, in many ways this is a snobbish country in some areas. I mean, I'm fortunate we live in Wales, because in Scotland and Wales it's not as great as it is in parts of England. (B99)

It is the "snobbishness" of the English upper classes that upsets him, not any exploitation of the workers à la Marx. A left-wing Socialist felt that

the greatest amount of class prejudice that is displayed is the prejudice that is displayed in suburbia against workers and trade unionists. . . . I don't

believe there is any class conflict between the really wealthy and the worker.
. . . The middle class is still climbing and therefore they feel they slip down
the ladder if they identify themselves with the workers and the Labour
Party. (B1)

Statistical evidence confirms the impression that class conflict means something
rather different to many Englishmen.[16]

Images of social conflict, then, are related to, but not identical with, images of
class conflict. It might be plausible, in addition, to assume that images of social
conflict are linked to a generalized distrust of a threatening social environment,
a sense that one's fellow man is basically hostile and dangerous. At least one
student of political belief systems has found empirical evidence of such a
syndrome.[17]

Among Italian and British political elites, however, misanthropy and conflict
images of society are *not* part of the same syndrome. Two items from a widely
used "misanthropy" attitude scale were included on the written questionnaire.
These items and the results from the two groups of politicians are given in table
7.3. The correlation between the Social Conflict Index and a Misanthropy Index
composed of these two items is gamma = .05 for Britain and gamma = −.13
for Italy. This negative pattern of findings is intelligible, if we consider the

Table 7.3: Misanthropy and the Social Conflict Index

STATEMENT 1:   "No one is going to care much what happens to you when you get right
down to it."

	Agree strongly	Agree	Disagree	Disagree strongly
Britain (N = 77)	1%	23%	61%	14%
Italy (N = 53)	4%	23%	53%	21%

	Britain	Italy
Correlation (gamma) with Social Conflict Index:	.14	−.22

STATEMENT 2:   "If you don't watch yourself, people will take advantage of you."

	Agree strongly	Agree	Disagree	Disagree strongly
Britain (N = 73)	8%	59%	30%	3%
Italy (N = 53)	19%	60%	15%	6%

	Britain	Italy
Correlation (gamma) with Social Conflict Index:	−.14	−.15

16. The correlation between the question on general social conflict and that on class conflict
is gamma = .76 in Italy and only gamma =.55 in Britain, even though the two questions were
contiguous in the interview.

17. See Scott, *Political Ideology in Malaysia,* p. 107.

correlation of each dimension with the left-right ideological continuum. In both countries, but especially in Italy, it is the Left that supports the conflict view of society. In both countries, but especially in Italy, the Left tends to be *more* optimistic about the trustworthiness of other individuals in society. In sum, the Social Conflict Index measures, not distrust and hostility towards other individuals in a personal sense, but the respondent's view of the relations among different social groups.[18]

We now have an overview of the basic dimension to be analyzed in this part of the study. Many British politicians, but fewer Italians, feel that in society and politics harmony and consensus are the norm. Further along the scale, many politicians in each country emphasize conflict, but emphasize also its essential reconcilability. And many Italians and a few Britons stress nearly unbridgeable conflicts of interest in social relations. Among the Italians this spectrum of opinion is closely tied to traditional notions of social class relations, while in Britain class conflict is interpreted in a less malignant way and views of social conflict or cohesion are not so intimately linked to specifically class images. Substantial numbers in both countries, though more in Italy, call attention to a distinction between apparent conflict, which may be quite intense, and real conflict, which they consider relatively insignificant. Finally, we have discovered, images of social conflict are not necessarily linked to generalized misanthropy.

18. The correlation between the left-right ideological spectrum and the Misanthropy Index is gamma = .22 in Britain and gamma = .27 in Italy. Three items on the written questionnaire were drawn from a scale proposed by Scott (ibid.) as a measure of the "constant pie" orientation. These items, especially the two that refer more to personal competition than to social conflict, seem on their face to tap a more "personalized" version of the conflict-consensus dimension. The items and the results from the two groups of politicians are as follows:

		Agree strongly	Agree	Disagree	Disagree strongly
1. "Any government that wants to help the poor will have to take something away from the rich in in order to do it."	Britain (N = 82)	12%	37%	39%	12%
	Italy (N = 55)	73%	24%	0%	4%
2. "When an individual or group gains, it usually means that another individual or group loses."	Britain (N = 80)	1%	28%	62%	9%
	Italy (N = 50)	8%	66%	24%	2%
3. "Those who get ahead usually get ahead at the expense of others."	Britain (N = 84)	4%	23%	63%	11%
	Italy (N = 51)	2%	24%	71%	4%

These data, of course, largely confirm the greater sensitivity of Italians to social conflict. But the pattern of intercorrelations among the Social Conflict Index, the index of "misanthropy," and this "constant pie scale" suggests that, especially in Italy, the "constant pie" measure taps the misanthropy dimension more directly than it does the social conflict dimension. Future research, especially if based on written questionnaires, will have to keep these two dimensions distinct.

Views of Conflict and Political Ideologies

Before turning to an investigation of the causes and consequences of this central dimension, it is helpful to examine its relationship to ideology in the traditional left-right sense. As explained in chapter 4, each respondent was rated on a five-point left-right scale according to his views on the proper role of government in regulating the economy and providing for social welfare.

In both Britain and Italy, but much more in the latter, a politician's perspective on social conflict and harmony is quite closely related to his ideological position in this left-right sense. Leftists stress conflict, rightists stress harmony, and centrists fall between. The correlation between the two dimensions is gamma = .60 in Italy and .29 in Britain.[19] (This markedly greater ideological "consistency" of Italian politicians has already been discussed in chapter 6.) The variation in images of society across the ideological spectrum is shown in table 7.4.

Table 7.4: The Social Conflict Index and the Left-Right Spectrum

	Far Left	Moderate Left	Center	Moderate Right	Far Right
Britain	4.2	3.2	3.0	2.6	3.8
	100%	50%	40%	11%	75%
	(N = 5)	(N = 16)	(N = 5)	(N = 9)	(N = 4)
Italy	4.9	3.8	3.5	3.3	4.5
	100%	70%	61%	57%	100%
	(N = 16)	(N = 17)	(N = 18)	(N = 7)	(N = 2)

NOTE: The first entry is the mean Social Conflict Index for respondents in each category; the second entry is the percentage of respondents in each category who are rated "4," "5," or "6" on the Social Conflict Index, that is, those in whose view of society conflict predominates.

The relationship shown in table 7.4 is not strictly linear; in both countries politicians on the far right are more sensitive to social conflict than are any others except the far left. Although the numbers involved are quite small, the consistency of this pattern and the size of the differences suggest that the phenomenon is really there. Part of the explanation may lie in the fact that moderate left governments were in power in each country at the time of the study. Those on the far right no doubt felt threatened by social trends in their countries. On the other hand, there may be some persisting "warp." Those on the ideological extremes may be more conflict-oriented than are more moderate men. Of course,

19. The correlation between the left-right dimension and the question on class conflict is higher still: gamma = .78 in Italy and .50 in Britain. Evidence from the questionnaire is consistent: Agreement with the statement that "any government which wants to help the poor will have to take something from the rich in order to do it" is correlated with the left-right continuum, gamma = .69 in Britain and .50 in Italy. This correlation between ideology in a left-right sense and images of sociopolitical conflict or harmony is probably a widespread phenomenon. See, for example, Arthur B. Gunlicks, "Representative Role Perceptions Among Local Councilors in Western Germany," *Journal of Politics* 31 (May 1969): 443–64.

even if there is such a warp, the data in table 7.4 show that the basic left-right correlation *also* exists, since in all cases respondents in the two left categories are more conflict-oriented than their "mirror image" counterparts on the right.

That conservatives stress harmony of interests and reformers stress conflict is not merely a function of each group's immediate goals—it is not simply that to reform involves conflict—for evidence will be offered later that the relationship exists even when conservatives and progressives are faced with identical social problems. In a broader sense, however, there is a link between ideological principles and orientations toward conflict. The Left, attacking an established social order, finds the origin of injustice in conflicting interests. The Right, defending the existing order, argues that no one is "really" disadvantaged by that order and that issues must be resolved, not by conflict, but "on their merits." It is obviously no accident that Burke, the great conservative, extolled social harmony, while Marx, the great revolutionary, stressed social cleavage.

Of course, extreme conservatives may not really be defending the existing order, but rather attacking it in the name of some supposed traditional order. Reactionaries may, paradoxically, be revolutionary. This may help to account for the anomaly that extreme conservatives seem to be relatively conflict-oriented.

Views on conflict and consensus are, thus, clearly an integral part of a broader network of views about state and society; it probably makes no sense to ask which is cause and which consequence. But in the discussion in the next three chapters of the origins and effects of the conflict-consensus syndrome, we will want to keep clearly in mind the close connection between this syndrome and the left-right spectrum.

8 Conflicts in Issues

For a politician conflict and consensus are not primarily philosophical matters. Shared interests and interests in conflict are latent in the concrete public problems he faces daily. Nor is his response to conflict an academic matter. Each disputed issue requires a decision: to reconcile, to resist, or to run. And every politician evolves a distinctive style of response to these recurrent demands for decision, evolves a characteristic orientation to his fellow players in the political game, evolves a personal interpretation of his fundamental political responsibilities. In this chapter and the next we shall examine how all these traits are linked to basic orientations to social conflict.

Latent Issue Conflict: An Introduction

Let us begin with an examination of the conflict latent in a politician's analysis of policy issues. As explained in chapter 3, early in each interview the respondent was asked to discuss two specific problems facing his country, one proposed by the respondent himself, the second supplied by the interviewer from a list of four: national economic planning, poverty, crime, and urban transport. Each respondent's discussion of "his" issue and the "suggested" issue was analyzed individually by the coders in terms of a set of substantive and stylistic categories. One of these items asked the analyst to rate "the prominence of conflicting interests in the respondent's discussion of this issue."[1] The specific coding instructions and the results for the two national samples are given in table 8.1. The meaning of this measure can be clarified by some illustrations.

Conflict of interest was very prominent in an older Italian Communist's discussion of the most important problems facing Italy.

> On the basis of my experience, I'd say that the fundamental problem is the problem of the Italian state itself—the public administration—which is neither modern nor interested in solving the problems of the Italian citizen, but which is slow, old, archaic. And it's made that way, not because it has to be that

1. The reliability of this code was rather high, given that it is not based on the manifest content of a specific response. The tau-beta correlation between the judgments of the two independent coders was .55; only 12 percent of the discussions were rated more than one point apart.

Table 8.1: Latent Conflict of Interest in Issue-Discussions
(in percentages)

QUESTION: "How prominent are conflicting interests in the respondent's discussion of this issue?"

Categories	Britain (N = 177)*	Italy (N = 161)*
1. *Absent.* There is no evidence he perceives groups with different interests or perspectives on this problem.	15	15
2. *Minimal.* No differing interests are mentioned. Differing opinions or perspectives are mentioned, but without the implication that these reflect conflicting interests; *or* discussion of "priorities" with no mention of conflicting interests.	35	30
3. *Present.* Conflict among interests is implicit and peripheral, but present (e.g. he mentions groups whose interests are opposed, but does not discuss conflict among these interests.)	34	20
4. *Important.* Conflict among interests is explicit, but not central; *or* central and implicit in the discussion.	11	21
5. *Very prominent.* Conflict among interests is explicit and central to the discussion.	5	14

*The unit of enumeration here is a single discussion of a given issue. Nearly every respondent was asked to discuss two separate issues; therefore, the Ns shown are approximately twice the total number of respondents in each national sample.

way, but because those who command in Italy want it that way. [*What are the origins of this problem?*] The origins are distant, but there is a fundamental cause: that those who have up till now dominated political, social, and economic life have an interest in maintaining a situation of this kind. (I75)

A Scottish miner discussing poverty in Britain displayed a similarly sharp sense of conflicting interests.

The causes of poverty in Britain are firstly that the nation has a wrong sense of values. If one looks at the entertainer who by singing some little song, sometimes sensible, sometimes silly, can earn from four hundred to five hundred pounds per week, . . . then this is a wrong criterion of values, because the miner upon whom the whole of the superstructure of society depends on the hewing of that coal . . . that particular person, speaking as far as Scotland's concerned, earns less than fifteen pounds a week. [*What could be done about this problem?*] I've always believed there should be a different income tax set of allowances for the miner and the steel worker and the heavy worker than there is for the entertainer or the others, the spokesmen, who enjoy fantastic salaries for very little effort. . . . This would mean, of course, that so far as some of these entertainers to whom I refer—I'm not castigating entertainers, I'm merely illustrating entertainers—I mean, of course, that their tax allowances will be decreased, very substantially, in order to make provision for the allowances for those who are indulging, not only in heavy work, but in work of real national importance. (B21)

Both of these men see clearly a conflict of interest at the heart of the problems they are discussing. To bring out most sharply the differences in the way issues can be conceptualized, let us turn to examples of discussions of the same two issues—administrative reform and poverty—that fall at the other end of the spectrum, discussions that give no hint of differing interests or perspectives, but treat these problems instead as straightforward technical matters.

First of all, a moderate Christian Democrat discusses the need for "reform of the state apparatus" in Italy.

The reform of the state has become more necessary than ever, because we find ourselves with an old state, which really goes on only by a miracle. But in the face of the progress in the world, this state organization can't keep up to the rhythm which this undeniably improved life demands of it. [We need] a reform of the bureaucracy, of the ministries, new structures which can really adapt themselves to the new times of our country. [*How did this come to be a problem?*] Look, if you examine what's happened in our country in the last twenty years, in terms of demography and in terms of development, I find it entirely natural that that which worked fine twenty years ago can't work any more today, with the same bureaucratic mechanism. We need a more dynamic bureaucracy. (I20)

Another working class Scot, this time a member of the Conservative Party, discusses the problem of poverty.

Well, my constituency is a relatively poor constituency. . . . I would say that what I have come across is not so much poverty, but an inability to manage money, and an inability to budget. . . . I honestly doubt if this is something the Government can solve. I think it's a question of giving people more responsibility. . . . I don't know why this is, but all the people I would say who are in this category are people who have no assets. None of them, I would say, are people who take a fantastic interest in their children's education. And I would say that often forcing responsibility on people or encouraging them to take it does have this effect of encouraging them to budget. The next thing is, of course, that none of them have bankbooks. And the only thing that perhaps the Government could do would be a compulsory "save as you earn" scheme. (B79)

Although this MP and his compatriot quoted earlier seem to be discussing the same problem, their analyses imply totally different images of the extent to which conflicting interests are involved.

The following discussions of the problem of urban transportation illustrate the full range of positions on the underlying continuum. First of all, here is a discussion rated a "5" (conflicting interest "very prominent"), an Italian Communist's explanation of the problem:

> For the causes you must always go back to the fact that transport policy is
> very strongly influenced by the almost total monopoly by FIAT of the automobile industry. FIAT needs to produce and sell cars, trucks, vehicles of all
> sorts. . . . The problem is one of conflicting interests. If you don't confront
> these groups, it's obvious that they will naturally seek their own interest.
> If I were in the position of Agnelli [the chairman of FIAT], probably I'd do
> the same. But if I were in the position of the State, I think I'd defend the
> interests of the rest of society. (I62)

The discussion of another Italian received a rating of "4," since although
conflict of interests is explicit, it is not central.

> The origins are the development of the automobile—everyone wants a car
> . . . and the cities, especially a city like Rome, are ancient. And too, a car,
> even a little one, only holds a few people and takes up too much room, in
> contrast to buses. The ideal would be to take the principal traffic arteries and
> restrict them to public transportation—taxis and buses. But it's a tricky
> problem, because the shopkeepers want people to be able to come with their
> cars to shop. It's a stupid thing, but you have to find a compromise with these
> shopkeepers' associations. (I48)

A British MP who happened to be particularly interested in urban transport
poured forth a torrent of suggestions for greater "coordination," more "planning," and so on, most of them technical and showing no hint of conflicting
interests. One of his more esoteric proposals, however, involved restricting
freight traffic to the night. "There might be some trouble with the transport
unions, I wouldn't know about this, but they would be paid night rates, so that
should obviate that, and they'd make up the difference in the more speedy
transport of goods." (B56) This vague reference to conflict was merely a hint,
but it was enough to qualify for a "3" rating.

Still lower on the scale came respondents who implied that the problem, as
they saw it, involved disparate priorities or values, but who gave no indication of
seeing conflicting interests among different groups or individuals. A young
British Conservative argued:

> You've either got to get to a situation where if people are going to take their
> cars into the city center, they've got to pay the cost of doing so, in one of these
> various costing schemes that have been put forward, or else it's a question of
> abandoning them and improving your public transport. [*What about this
> question of public versus private transport?*] This goes into one's basic political
> philosophy, that where one person's actions start affecting the actions of other
> people—which obviously happens when you get congestion in city centers—

this obviously is a sphere where state control must take over in order to protect the individual. This is where you must always remember that it is state control for the benefit of the individual and not for the sake of control. (B12)

Finally, an Italian deputy who was also leader of a left-wing trade union provided a discussion of the issue that gave no hint that conflicting interests might exist. After analyzing the origins of the problem in terms of the psychology of car ownership and patterns of urban growth, he considered possible solutions:

In the unions we've always said that it's a problem which the government and the auto industry have an interest in sitting down with the unions and legislators for a calm examination of the problem . . . I think the problem is solvable, both through urban planning and in terms of equipment . . . It's simply a matter of seeing whether it's more costly to have an efficient public transportation system or an efficiently planned arrangement of home and place of work (I74)

In summary, then, different respondents have different propensities to perceive conflicting interests in specific policy areas, and these ratings of their policy analyses indicate their underlying sensitivity to conflict. Obviously, there is some slippage inherent in this indicator. The slippage is partly the result of ambiguities about the amount of conflict latent in any given discussion. In addition, there is undoubtedly some variability in the relative "conflict sensitivity" of individual respondents across different issues. Respondent A may see more conflict than respondent B on one issue, but less on another. Moreover, it is conceivable that a respondent's brief remarks about an issue are uncharacteristic of his more basic orientation toward that issue. Nevertheless, there is across our sample as a whole a significant correlation (gamma = .23) between any given respondent's ratings on the two separate issue-discussions of the interview. Later evidence in this chapter will confirm the validity of this measure even more strongly.

The evidence presented in table 8.1 suggested that Italians display somewhat greater sensitivity to latent conflict of interest. The clarity of this cross-national difference was muffled, however, because discussions of very different issues were grouped together. Table 8.2 removes this source of ambiguity by presenting the data separately for each of the four "suggested" issues. On each of the four, Italians are significantly more likely than the British to refer to conflicting interests. Table 8.2 also shows for each country the amount of conflict seen in each of the specific "suggested" issues. Naturally, this varies markedly from issue to issue, and it is striking that the rank order is identical in each country.

Economic planning most clearly evokes images of conflicting interests, no doubt because it involves the highly salient cleavage between workers and management. This cleavage is not involved in the issue of urban transport, but this problem too is seen as involving conflicting interests. In both countries crime and poverty are seen as issues that do *not* involve competing interests among

Table 8.2: Latent Conflict of Interest in Issue-Discussions,
by Country and Nature of Issue

Issue	Britain		Italy	
Economic planning	2.7	15%	3.2	46%
	(N = 26)		(N = 26)	
Urban transport	2.6	17%	3.1	35%
	(N = 18)		(N = 17)	
Crime	1.9	5%	2.6	23%
	(N = 21)		(N = 22)	
Poverty	1.8	4%	2.6	31%
	(N = 24)		(N = 13)	

NOTE: First entry is the mean "latent issue conflict" score for respondents in each category. Second entry is the percentage of respondents rated "4" or "5" on this index, i.e. those seeing conflict "very prominent" or "important."

social groups. Instead they are seen as common problems facing the nation as a whole.

The relatively low ranking of poverty is startling. One would have thought that of all these issues poverty would surely be the one closest to being "zero sum" in character. Yet of the British politicians who discussed this issue fully 46 percent noted *no* differing interests or perspectives on the problem, and another 38 percent indicated that it was merely a question of different priorities or perspectives. In Italy 31 percent saw "no" conflict and another 31 percent only "minimal" conflict.

As a substantive problem, poverty is interpreted somewhat differently in the two countries. The British by and large see poverty as a problem of isolated individuals or "problem families" who have eluded the "safety net" of the welfare state. The most frequently cited causes of poverty were low wages, individual laziness or stupidity, "problem families," and old age. It seems natural, therefore, to conceive of this problem as a technical one involving patching holes in the net. The impact of this patching operation on the interests of other groups is, it seems, too distant to cause those groups (or the politicians) concern.

In Italy poverty is generally interpreted in a "sectoral" sense, that is, characteristic of backward regions of the country. Most Italians mentioned "lack of regional development" as one of the causes of poverty, with substantial minorities citing general economic underdevelopment and agricultural backwardness as well. Naturally, therefore, the Italians tended to seek the cure for poverty in national or regional economic development. As in the case of Britain, the impact of this sort of policy on the interests of other groups (though undeniable in a strict sense) seems too distant to arouse concern.

Thus, latent conflict (at least as measured here) arises most clearly when the interests of some particular group are more or less directly threatened by proposed policies. Once stated, this seems an obvious generalization. The corollary is, however, less obvious. A politician's sense of the amount of conflict inherent in an issue may not coincide with one's theoretical deductions. "Is anyone's ox being badly gored?" seems to be the question implicit in a politician's impression of conflict of interest. And that is probably not a bad operational indicator for the practicing politician.

A final conclusion to be drawn from tables 8.1 and 8.2 is that (at least as measured here) most politicians do not see very much conflict of interest in most issues. In neither of these countries on any of the issues did as many as half of the respondents discuss explicitly any conflict of interest. With some exceptions, most politicians discuss most issues in terms of differing priorities or differing solutions, rather than in terms of differing interests. In this limited but important sense most politicians, when they talk about policy, talk as if they were solving problems rather than resolving conflicts.

Latent Issue Conflict and Styles of Political Analysis

Politicians differ systematically in their propensity to detect conflicting interests in policy problems. My next concern is to ask how this propensity is linked to other aspects of what I have termed "political style." Do politicians who detect conflict in issues analyze those issues differently from politicians who see only common interests?

An economical way of answering this question is to consider the relationship between our Index of Latent Issue Conflict and the several dimensions of political style uncovered in chapter 3. Detailed analysis shows that in each country politicians who rank high on the former also rank high on the Ideological Style Index and on the Index of Partisan Style, based on the "partisanship" dimension which emerged from the factor analysis shown in Table 3.3.[2]

These characteristics fall together into an intelligible and interesting syndrome. The more conflict a politician sees involved in an issue, the more he generalizes and moralizes his analysis of that issue, and the more his proposals are argued in terms of distributive justice. Conversely, the less that conflicting interests seem involved, the more detailed and "objective" his discussion, and the more oriented his proposals to collective benefits.

It does not make sense at this stage in our evolving understanding of styles of policy analysis to ask about cause and effect. No doubt, as I suggested at the end of Chapter 5, an ideological style encourages a politician to discover conflicting interests that are obscured to more inductive analysts, and a preexisting partisan stance certainly increases the probability of finding something in each passing

2. Holding party and country constant, the average correlation (gamma) between the Index of Latent Issue Conflict and the Ideological Style Index was .21; that between the former and the Index of Partisan Style was .28. The Index of Partisan Style is the sum of the respondent's ratings on "moralizer,' "reference to group benefits," and "reference to practicality," standardized and weighted according to the factor loading of each on Factor 3, table 3.3. In terms of individual stylistic characteristics, across all issue discussions the average correlation (gamma) between latent issue conflict and generalizer-particularizer was .25; for moralizer, the average correlation was .50, while for reference to group benefits, the figure was .21.

issue to be partisan about. On the other hand, a basic sensitivity to social and political conflict probably in turn stimulates a wider-ranging, more *engagé* style of policy analysis. Sorting out the reciprocal interconnections between these two sets of variables is less important than recognizing the syndrome that together they comprise.[3]

Latent Issue Conflict and Political Responsibility

Why does a politician see more or less conflict latent in an issue? Up to this point, we have considered two aspects of the problem—characteristics of the issue itself and the politician's style of policy analysis. In chapter 9 I shall turn to the impact of his basic beliefs about social harmony and discord; to anticipate our conclusion, we will discover a marked tendency for those whose social philosophies are conflictual to detect latent conflict more readily than those whose basic beliefs stress consensus. But first there is one more important factor to be considered.

In any parliamentary system at any point in time some politicians will have more responsibility for policy making and policy outcomes than do their colleagues. In the first instance, members of the party or parties supporting the Government are more responsible for government policy than are members of the Opposition. And ministers are more directly responsible than are their backbench supporters. I shall argue that if basic beliefs about social conflict are held constant, then the more responsible an individual is for government policy making, the less likely he is to see conflicting interests in public problems.

The "social philosophy held constant" provision is crucial whenever a left-wing party is in power, as, for example, in Britain at the time of this research. Labour politicians are, it will be recalled, more likely to have conflict models of society than are Conservatives, and therefore tend to see more conflict latent in specific issues. But if one controls for this effect, by comparing Labour and Conservative MPs having the same basic images of social conflict, the Conservatives (in Opposition at the time of this study) tend to see *more* latent conflict of interest than the Labourites. In Italy the factors of social philosophy and responsibility for policy making both tend to sharpen the contrast between the Government coalition and their primary Opposition, the Communist Party. On the other hand, in the case of the right-wing Opposition in Italy, as in Britain, the two factors of social philosophy and lack of governmental responsibility tend to offset one another. Again, when Government and Opposition deputies who

3. This correlation between an ideological style and sensitivity to conflict does not extend to the fundamental orientation measured by the Social Conflict Index. Ideologues of the Right tend, by and large, to have more consensual images of society, while ideologues of the Left have more conflictful models, as contrasted in each case with their less ideological party colleagues. This finding reflects, no doubt, a tendency for ideologues to exhibit more clearly the basic correlation noted in chapter 7 between ideology in the left-right sense and the conflict-consensus dimension. Ideologues are more consistent in their ideology.

have identical images of social conflict are compared, members of Opposition parties—at *both* ends of the ideological spectrum—see more latent conflict than do Government supporters. Finally, although the numbers involved are quite small, the evidence suggests that in both countries ministers are apt to see less latent conflict in issues than their own backbenchers.

Although responsibility clearly has an impact on perceptions of latent issue conflict, there is no evidence at all of a similar impact on social philosophy. Ministers do not have less conflictful images of society than their backbenchers—indeed, in Britain, those ministers interviewed happen to have *more* conflictful images. Nor, as shown by comparisons between Labour and Conservative Members or between supporters of the *centro-sinistra* (the Italian Center-Left Government) and their opposition on the Right, are members of Government parties *ipso facto* apt to have more consensual views of society than their opponents. All this is, of course, consistent with my contention that social philosophy is more basic and less mutable than perceptions of conflict in particular issues.[4]

It is entirely natural that those with responsibility for formulating and applying policy tend to see little conflict of interest latent in the problems with which they are dealing. Faced with the need to solve policy dilemmas, they come to see them as technical rather than political, as problems facing the country as a whole and not as issues involving the conflicting interests of different groups. It is surely more congenial to deny (implicitly) any conflict, for then the policy chosen can be seen as in the public interest, rather than in the interest of one group or another.[5]

Extending the argument beyond data of this study, it is possible to imagine that those whose whole careers involve "responsibility" would show most clearly this tendency to deny real conflict of interest. Civil servants should, for example, fall at the extreme nonconflict end of the spectrum, claiming that their work is "technical," not "political." It also would seem to follow that as individuals or parties came to share responsibility for policy making, they would come to see problems less in terms of conflicting interests and more in terms of national

---

4. Of course, responsibility might have an impact on social philosophy in the long run. An interesting test case would be a left-wing party, like the Swedish Labor Party, that has been in power for many years. If responsibility breeds consensualism in the long run, such a party should come to have less conflictful models of society than their Opposition on the right.

5. Of course, this "responsibility" effect may reflect not lower perception of conflict on the part of the more responsible, but their inhibitions in discussing conflict with an interviewer. But several factors argue against this interpretation: (1) The latent-conflict measure is based on coders' judgments, not overt questions. Thus, any bias would have to have been anticipatory. (2) Few Government backbenchers were shy about their disagreements with Government policy. (For example, three-quarters of the Labour MPs disagreed with their own party at some point in the interview.) Thus, the interparty comparison is quite unlikely to be artifactual. (3) Finally, in one sense the difference between my explanation and the artifactual one is a matter of degree. The artifactual argument supposes that someone with responsibility finds it uncomfortable to discuss conflicting interests with an interviewer. I add only that he also finds it "uncomfortable" to contemplate such conflicting interests in his private reflections.

interests, though their basic social philosophy would change much more slowly. This is, of course, the logic behind the common observation that "there is more in common between two deputies, one of whom is a revolutionary, than between two revolutionaries, one of whom is a deputy."

9 Views of Conflict as Cognitive Predispositions

In chapter 7 we discovered that politicians profess quite divergent philosophies of social conflict and harmony; in chapter 8 we learned that they differ systematically in the extent to which they discern conflicting interests in public problems. In this chapter I shall examine the links between this pair of findings, consider the sense in which the social philosophies we have discussed are "cognitive predispositions," and more broadly, investigate whether it makes any difference if a politician stresses conflict or consensus in his interpretation of society and politics.

Social Philosophy and Political Analysis

As I adumbrated at the end of chapter 8, there is a strong correlation in the expected direction between a politician's philosophical view of society and the amount of conflict latent in his discussion of specific issues. The more prominent conflict is in his social philosophy, the more likely he is to spot conflicting interests in everyday issues. Conversely, the more harmonious his view of society, the more likely he is to discover mutual interests in policy problems. The statistical evidence is provided in table 9.1.

Table 9.1: Social Conflict Index and Latent Conflict of Interest in Issue-Discussions

	Britain (N = 39)	Italy (N = 60)
Conflict latent in discussion of "his" issue	.58	.54
Conflict latent in discussion of "suggested" issue	.28	.48
Summary measure of latent issue conflict in both issue-discussions	.55	.60

NOTE: Entry is gamma for correlation between respondent's general view of social conflict or consensus and the amount of conflict of interest latent in his discussion of issues.

Left-right ideology is, as we have seen, very closely bound up with a respondent's assumptions about social discord and harmony, and a respondent's position on the left-right spectrum is also closely related to his sensitivity to latent issue conflict.[1] Therefore, one might suspect that the correlations shown in table 9.1 are in some sense spurious and the result of the impact of ideology or party affiliation. The basic correlation between image of society and latent issue conflict remains strongly positive, however, even when partisan affiliation is held constant.[2] The evidence strongly suggests that the way a politician inter- prets policy problems is significantly influenced by his normally unarticulated assumptions about social harmony and discord.[3]

The importance of this relationship between social philosophy and political analysis can best be illustrated by considering our respondents' discussions of one specific issue—crime. In both Britain and Italy crime is a recognized public problem, one which these politicians were willing to discuss as "another im- portant problem facing this country today." In neither country, however, was this issue very "hot" at the time of the interviewing. No politician mentioned it as among "the two or three most important problems facing this country today." Coverage of the issue in the national news media in both countries at the time was also relatively low key, directed at the rising statistical indices of crime. In other words, in both countries crime was for politicians an issue like many others. It was recognizable as a public problem, one to which they had given some casual thought, but it was not at the center of their attention.

The respondents for whom crime was the "suggested" issue (roughly a quarter of each national sample) were asked about the origins of the problem and about their suggestions for solutions. Naturally, there was a great variety of responses, precisely because the terms of discussion on this issue had not already been set by an extended public debate. It is especially revealing, therefore, that the causes and cures of crime offered by individual politicians depended in part on their general image of social harmony or social discord.

As shown in table 9.2, "consensual" or "low-conflict" politicians tended to attribute the rise in crime rates to a breakdown in the family and in moral authority, whereas the "high-conflict" group put the blame on social change and social injustice. The low-conflict group argued for individual moral rebirth or education and child development programs as promising solutions, while the high-conflict group suggested broad social reform as the most effective answer.

1. In Britain the correlation (gamma) between the left-right scale and the summary measure of latent conflict is .34; in Italy the correlation is .64.

2. The correlation is weakest (.15) for the members of the PCI, but this is partly a result of the low variance in the independent variable. More than any other party, the Communists are concentrated in a few positions on the Social Conflict Index.

3. There is virtually no chance that these correlations result from the inter-item assimilation discussed in chapter 2. The bases for the two codes were well separated in the interview and in the coding process; the issue discussions (the more susceptible to unconscious bias) came at the beginning, the discussion of conflict and consensus, toward the end. The "cross-coder cor- relation technique" only slightly reduces the correlation coefficients. The correlation between one coder's judgment of latent issue conflict and the other coder's judgment on the Social Conflict Index is gamma = .36 in Britain and .45 in Italy.

Table 9.2: The Social Conflict Index and Analyses of Crime,
Both Countries Grouped

	Social Conflict Index*		
Selected causes of crime	High conflict (N = 10)	Medium conflict (N = 17)	Low conflict (N = 12)
Social change (urbanization, industrialization, etc.)	40%	24%	8%
Social injustice (poverty, unemployment, etc.)	50%	35%	17%
Breakdown of the family	10%	24%	33%
Breakdown of morals and authority	40%	59%	58%
Selected cures for crime	(N = 10)	(N = 17)	(N = 10)
Individual moral improvement	10%	24%	60%
Education and child development	10%	35%	40%
General social reform (redistribution of income and/or power)	40%	24%	0%

NOTE: Entry is percentage of each subsample who volunteer the cause or cure of crime indicated at the left. The first three causes and the first two cures suggested by a respondent were recorded. Causes and cures other than those listed here were cited, but these other suggestions were unrelated to the conflict-consensus dimension.
*"High" conflict means a rating of "5" or "6" on the Social Conflict Index; "medium," a rating of "4"; and "low," a rating of "2" or "3."

In short, the evidence is striking that a politician's views about social conflict and social consensus have a direct and substantial impact on his explanation of social problems, as well as on the specific policy proposals he supports.[4]

If one believes in the essential harmony of society, then crime can only be attributed to individual immorality, ignorance, or psychopathology, and the cure must be sought in changes in the individual, through education or through moral improvement. If, on the other hand, one is convinced of the reality of social conflict, it is natural to seek the sources of crime not in the individual, but in social tension and social change, and to seek solutions in altered social conditions.

An adherent to a consensual, harmonious model of society, like the Labourite whose statement follows, can only attribute violation of the norms of society to moral or psychological fault in the violator.

In my opinion, the moral standard of the people has not kept pace with the material standard of living . . . I don't know what the Government can do. It's more of an individual problem. . . the individual realizing his responsibilities and facing up to his responsibilities in the community. . . . I think that this runs in the realm of the Church and the social workers and schools . . . . I wonder sometimes if some subjects could be dropped and these sort

4. In order to enlarge the samples and thus increase the stability of the estimates, I have grouped data from both countries in table 9.2, but in fact the sharp differences between "consensualists" and "conflictualists" persist within each country considered separately.

of social subjects, of responsibility to the community, to the home, and to the nation should be taught. (B46)

On the other hand, a politician operating with a conflictful image of society, stressing malintegration and coercion and change, seeks the fault neither in selves nor in stars, but in social relations. An Italian whose image of society was primarily conflict-oriented explained rising crime rates in these terms:

Italy is making the leap from a predominantly agricultural civilization to an industrial civilization later than other countries. This leap has created new tensions, new sufferings, and transmigrations of masses from zone to zone of the country, and it has put in crisis certain old values and old conceptions of morality on which was founded a fundamentally retarded society, without yet establishing new values of civilization and morality. . . . In general, I think that this is a problem which will be resolved only if the great problems of social reform are confronted. Specifically, I would say that our magistrature is retarded with respect to the exigencies of a modern country. It is drawn from privileged strata of the country, lacking in ties to the lower classes [gli interessi popolari]. It comes more from the agricultural world and not from the industrial world, and therefore it doesn't understand an industrial society. (I21)

Naturally, not every political issue is so resonant to social philosophy as is the issue of crime. The substance of proposals for dealing with more technical issues like urban transport is less likely to be affected by these basic social perspectives, although, as we have already seen, the form of the analysis of such issues is so affected, and there are no doubt instances where form determines substance. But on issues like crime (and possibly economic planning) even the substance of the analysis is directly informed by basic cognitive predispositions.

Conflict and Compromise

A natural question when considering the correlates of a politician's perspectives on conflict concerns his attitudes toward compromise and conflict resolution. Theoretically, if one imagines the full continuum from a belief that there is no real conflict in society to the belief that there are no genuine shared interests, the most plausible hypothesis is that there should be a curvilinear relationship between this dimension and attitudes toward compromise.

A person who believes that there are no real conflicts and that, therefore, there is an objectively correct policy for any given problem would tend to reject compromise, because there should be no compromising of "truth" or "the public interest." "Truth is a thing, not of divisibility into conflicting parts, but of unity. Hence, both sides cannot be right."[5] On the other hand, a person who believes

5. John Taylor, *A Definition of Parties* (Philadelphia, 1794), as quoted in Samuel H. Beer, *British Politics in the Collectivist Age* (New York: Alfred A. Knopf, 1965), p. 42.

that there are no common interests and that the interests of other groups are diametrically opposed to his own would also tend to reject compromise as inevitably harmful to his own cause. Those with more balanced views, sensitive to both shared and antagonistic interests, might be relatively more open to the possibility of constructive compromise.

The set of indicators of orientations to compromise that are available in our data was discussed in chapter 4. Figure 9.1 shows how average scores on that chapter's summary measure of the respondent's attitude to conflict resolution vary according to scores on the Social Conflict Index.[6] The graph shows that in both countries the relationship approaches the curvilinear pattern of our hypothesis. None of our respondents fell at the extreme consensus end of the spectrum, so it is not possible to confirm that adherents to a view that excludes

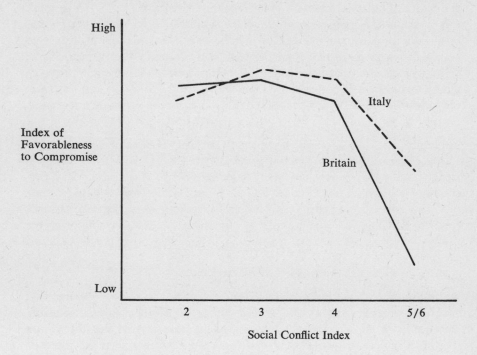

Figure 9.1: The Social Conflict Index and Attitude toward Compromise
Weights have been used to hold constant party affiliation.
For unweighted Ns, see table 7.1.

6. Because both the Social Conflict Index and our measures of orientation to compromise are systematically related to the left-right ideological continuum. I have used a system of weights in constructing figures 9.1 and 9.2; the weights have the effect of holding constant the partisan composition of the subsamples at each point on the Social Conflict Index. Thus, one can see the direct impact of attitudes toward conflict on attitudes toward compromise, with partisan ideology controlled.

all genuine social conflict would be distinctly less favorably disposed to compromise. (Empirically, the evidence in chapter 7 suggests that few, if any, politicians in pluralistic societies would hold that polar view.) For the rest of the range of the Social Conflict Index, the pattern is as predicted, although the differences among the central categories are slight.

Even more striking confirmation of the hypothesized curvilinear relationship comes from evidence concerning attitudes toward political opponents. The relationship between the Social Conflict Index and the Index of Partisan Hostility described in chapter 4 (with the standard controls for party affiliation) is shown in figure 9.2. In each country, respondents with views evenly balanced

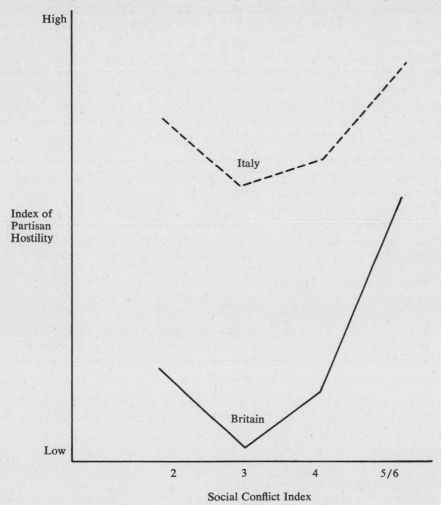

Figure 9.2: The Social Conflict Index and the Index of Partisan Hostility
Weights have been used to hold constant party affiliation.
For unweighted Ns, see table 7.1.

between conflict and consensus show the lowest average hostility to opponents, followed by respondents rated "4" on the Social Conflict Index, that is, those for whom limited and reconcilable conflict is the essence of politics. In each country, those respondents ranged toward the two extremes of the conflict-consensus spectrum show significantly more hostility toward their partisan antagonists. A politician's basic views about conflict in society are, then, closely related to his general orientation toward political opponents and his willingness to seek compromise solutions to disputes with them.

Whether a politician will be willing to accept a compromise in particular circumstances will, of course, depend in part on the specific features of the case. A person generally open to compromise might be unwilling to accept a particularly disadvantageous proposal, and someone generally reluctant to compromise might in certain circumstances be willing to reach an accommodation with his opponents. But relatively speaking, the propensity of some politicians to cooperate and compromise with their adversaries is greater; their "cooperation threshold" is lower. And as we have just seen, politicians' "cooperation thresholds" and their images of society are linked in an intimate, if slightly complex, relationship. Some implications of this relationship for theories of democratic stability will be considered in chapter 12.

Conflict and Political Roles

One way of summarizing much of the preceding discussion of the consequences of the conflict-consensus orientation is to consider the relationship between the Social Conflict Index and each respondent's general perspective on political action, his implicit definition of his own political role. William Gamson has characterized two such perspectives in the following terms.

> One view takes the vantage point of potential partisans and emphasizes the process by which such groups attempt to influence the choices of authorities or the structure within which decisions occur. The second view takes the vantage point of the authorities and emphasizes the process by which they attempt to achieve collective goals and to maintain legitimacy and compliance with their decisions in a situation in which significant numbers of potential partisans are not being fully satisfied.[7]

Gamson attributes to those adopting the perspective of "potential partisans" the belief that conflict of interest is a real and necessary part of politics and that power is a zero-sum (strictly speaking, a constant-sum) concept. To those adopting the perspective of "the authorities," on the other hand, he attributes the belief that conflict is unimportant and undesirable in politics and that power is by nature a positive-sum concept.

Evidence from the present study strikingly confirms Gamson's speculations.

7. William A. Gamson, *Power and Discontent* (Homewood, Ill.: Dorsey Press, 1968), p. 2.

Every respondent was rated by the coders according to his emphasis on what was termed a "tribune" role, "focusing on protesting injustices or other wrongs and fighting for the interests of a social group, class, or cause," and on what was termed a "trustee" role, "focusing on defense of national or collective interests."[8] Although Gamson's analysis was not available at the time this part of the research was carried out, these two roles are virtually identical to his categories of "potential partisans" and "the authorities."

The correlation between the respondent's view of social conflict and his apparent adoption of a "tribune" role is very strong, gamma = .61 in Britain and gamma = .62 in Italy. Respondents who see conflict as the essence of society focus their attention on righting social and political wrongs. Those who see society as essentially harmonious rarely adopt this role.

The correlations between images of social consensus and apparent adoption of the "trustee" role are are also strong, gamma = .35 in Britain and gamma = .59 in Italy. Those convinced of the reality of social harmony focus on the defense of the general interests of society and the nation, while conflict-oriented respondents rarely adopt this perspective.[9]

Cognitive Predispositions and Politics

The central discovery of this chapter seems at first glance a remarkably simple one. Politicians differ in the basic assumptions they make about the extent of conflict inherent in society. Nearly all of them, in the language of game theory, believe that they are playing games of "mixed motives," games in which there are areas of both common interest and conflict. But for some of them the areas of common interest seem more important, while for others, conflicts predominate. And these orientations, stressing harmony and cooperation or discord and controversy, seem to guide their thought and behavior across a remarkably wide range of activities.

I have from time to time referred to these basic orientations as "cognitive predispositions," and it is now possible to say more precisely what I mean by this phrase. Some of the beliefs that guide men's political behavior are consciously held and easily articulated. A socialist's belief in the inequity and ineffi-

8. Since these role names are current in the literature on legislative behavior, I must stress that their operational definition here is strictly that quoted from the coding instructions. These ratings are not based on any explicit question or set of questions, but rather on the coders' summary judgments of the transcript as a whole. The correlation between the coders' judgments of the tribune role was tau-beta = .48, with 9 percent of the respondents rated at opposite ends of the three-point scale; for the trustee role, tau-beta = .40, with 6 percent at opposite ends.

9. These pairs of correlations persist when controls are introduced for partisan affiliation. To some unspecifiable extent these correlations may be a function of the method of coding, since the judgments of role were based on the interview as a whole, including that section dealing with social conflict and consensus. Although the correlations substantiate one's general impression that these aspects of a politician's view of society, politics, and his own role "hang together," it would be desirable in a more rigorous study to use more independent measures.

ciency of capitalism is of this kind, and so is an Italian deputy's belief that real power lies with the party organizations, not the Parliament. But some important political attitudes rarely if ever reach the stage of explicit formulation. Such unstated assumptions, or "cognitive predispositions," silently structure more explicit and more ephemeral political thinking and political action.[10]

These predispositions serve as implicit premises for the conscious reasoning that leads men to act as they do. They bear a family resemblance to the perceptual predispositions that psychologists have studied under the rubric of "set." A standard textbook explains this notion in the following terms:

> The perceiver's state as he encounters a given stimulus-pattern is never completely 'neutral.' He brings to the situation various readinesses and expectations that help to govern the manner in which the stimuli are perceived and organized. In a word, he is *set* to perceive something more or less specific.[11]

Solomon Asch, a social psychologist sensitive to the rationality in man's social behavior, stresses nonetheless the extent to which these perceptual sets operate below the level of consciousness.

> We expect our neighbor, when he opens his mouth, to speak in English; we would be much surprised if he spoke to us in Latin. . . . We do not ordinarily think of all the strange possibilities that might happen; we are often not even aware of the expectations we do have. But this is all the more impressive an indication of the operation of sets; they function most reliably when they are not present to consciousness.[12]

Students of the psychology of perception have demonstrated in myriad ways that sets play a crucial role in structuring our awareness of our environment. Told to expect names of animals and presented momentarily with the nonsense word "sael," subjects will perceive "seal." Told to expect terms from navigation, they will perceive the same stimulus as "sail." And all this, apparently, without the subject even realizing his "creative misperception."[13]

The gulf between the primitive perceptual task I have just described and the incredibly sophisticated judgments that politicians make daily about their political and social environment is very great. My purpose in glancing briefly

10. Cf. an anthropologist's view that "a cognitive orientation provides the members of the society it characterizes with basic premises and sets of assumptions normally neither recognized nor questioned which structure and guide behavior in much the same way grammatical rules unrecognized by most people structure and guide their linguistic forms" (George M. Foster, "Peasant Society and the Image of Limited Good," *American Anthropologist* 67 [1965]: 293). Foster deals in this article with a "cognitive orientation" very much akin to the orientation to social conflict I am here discussing.

11. David Krech and Richard S. Crutchfield, *Elements of Psychology* (New York: Alfred A. Knopf, 1959), p. 96. Emphasis in the original.

12. Solomon E. Asch, *Social Psychology* (Englewood Cliffs, N.J.: Prentice-Hall, 1952), p. 584.

13. This example is drawn from a classic experiment on perceptual set conducted by E. M. Siipola in 1935, and summarized in Krech and Crutchfield, *Elements of Psychology,* p. 102.

across this gulf is simply to clarify the sense in which I describe attitudes toward social conflict as "cognitive predispositions." From time to time these attitudes can be made explicit. Indeed, this has been the contribution of political philosophers throughout the ages—to make explicit and consistent the judgments that most of us "make" unwittingly. Part of the methodology of this study has involved an attempt to get politicians to articulate, at least vaguely, their own implicit assumptions about social relations. But most men most of the time act and think without this kind of artificial self-consciousness. And in this, politicians are not exceptional.

To forestall some confusion, I should add that some politicians have in their repertoire of conscious beliefs an image of a kind of society different from the contemporary one in which they act. Such utopian visions, like those of Marx and Hobbes, often include the characteristics of perfect peace and social concord. Many politicians of the Left in both Britain and Italy see themselves as working toward some such "new society." But these utopian visions generally have very little empirical connection with the cognitive predispositions that I am discussing here. In working toward their new and better world, as well as in thinking about hundreds of everyday political and social issues, these men typically operate with models of contemporary society that stress conflict. Nor should their complex set of beliefs be confused with the perspectives of the politicians discussed in chapter 7 who seem to believe that in contemporary society there is little inherent conflict of interest and who describe observable political conflict as unnecessary and even bogus. In all cases the crucial question is what assumption the actor makes about the structure of interests in the environment in which he acts.

One other suggestive analogy with the perceptual set of the psychologists can be risked. Researchers have found that in general the impact of set on perception increases with the ambiguity and unfamiliarity of the stimulus. Thus, "sael," but not "seal," is misperceived as "sail." In the political arena many issues are relatively ambiguous in their implications for the well-being of society and its component groups. Some issues, especially those not immediately at center stage, are relatively unfamiliar, even to the politically knowledgeable. And in many cases much of the controversy is over what the issue *is,* rather than over what should be done about "it." My argument has been that the cognitive predispositions of political leaders function like perceptual sets, influencing, though seldom wholly determining, the way in which issues are conceived and analyzed. One may reasonably suppose that this assumption will be more true of issues that are relatively ambiguous and unfamiliar. Thus, the issue of crime seems particularly subject to variable interpretations, depending on one's cognitive predispositions. But no doubt a similar process is constantly at work, informing our political judgments on all sorts of matters.

There is, no doubt, a wide range of different types of cognitive predispositions that interact to influence the way we see the world. Some authors have stressed

temporal and spatial premises, others metaphysical and epistemological pre-
sumptions.[14] I have concentrated on the single theme of social conflict and
harmony, because this theme seems to play a central role in structuring the
political thought and, ultimately, the political action of politicians in Britain and
Italy. Our intensive investigation of this one dimension may serve as an example
of a particularly promising kind of inquiry for students of comparative political
behavior.

14. The approach here sketched owes a great deal to the work of Robert E. Lane on the
"cultural premises" of political thought. A lucid statement of his theoretical perspective as well
as a more comprehensive list of different types of "cultural premises" is found in his *Political
Ideology* (New York: Free Press, 1962). See also Florence R. Kluckhohn and Fred L. Strodt-
beck, *Variations in Value Orientations* (Evanston, Ill.: Row, Peterson, 1961).

10 The Personal Sources of Perspectives on Conflict

In this chapter and the one that follows the focus shifts from consequences to origins. In the broadest terms, our search for the roots of a politician's perspective on social harmony and discord will follow the guidelin suggested by Lucian Pye when he argued that "political culture is shaped on the one hand by the general historical experiences of the society or system and on the other hand by the intensely private and personal experiences of individuals as they become members of first the society and then the polity."[1] Although my data do not reveal the psychogenetic sources of the attitudes under consideration, I will follow Pye in examining both personal history and social history for influences on a politician's orientation toward conflict. Chapter 11 examines the impact of contrasting national histories. In this chapter I shall discuss the personal origins of these attitudes in political ideology, in prepolitical socialization, and in political experience.

Political Ideology

No other factor is more important in explaining a politician's views on social conflict and consensus than his position on a left-right ideological continuum. As we have already seen in chapters 7 and 9, politicians of the Right are typically consensualists, whereas politicians of the Left have a much greater propensity to discern conflicting interests. The personal origins of a politician's ideology are, in turn, almost infinitely various, though such factors as parental loyalties, social class background, religion, and region obviously are important. Inextricably entangled with this process of acquiring a set of substantive policy positions or a full-fledged ideology is the process of developing perspectives on social conflict and social consensus.

Social Background

One social background characteristic—social class—is quite strikingly related to the respondents' images of social harmony or discord. The lower a politician's social origins, the more likely he is to have a conflictful image of society.

1. Lucian W. Pye, *Politics, Personality, and Nation Building* (New Haven: Yale University Press, 1962), p. 121.

The background data available for the two countries are rather disparate and not quite comparable. In particular, more extensive information is available on the social class of the British MPs at different stages of their careers. The British correlations between the Social Conflict Index and these various measures of social class are given in table 10.1. These data show not only that there is a consistently high relationship between class and social philosophy but also that the relationship is closer with the class of origin than with the Member's class at the time of his election to Parliament. Although these data are too scant to be probative, they suggest that perspectives on social conflict and consensus are set fairly early in life, and that subsequent social mobility (especially upward mobility) has relatively less impact.

Table 10.1: Social Class Background and the Social
Conflict Index in Britain

Parental social class*	.43
	(N=33)
MP's initial social class†	.47
	(N=39)
MP's present social class‡	.34
	(N=39)

NOTE: Entry is gamma, positive when low social class is linked to high Social Conflict Index.
*Based on father's occupation.
†Based on MP's first full-time occupation.
‡Based on MP's present nongovernmental occupation or, if none, then on last occupation prior to election.

These correlations remain high even when controls for partisan affiliation are imposed. Figure 10.1a (on p. 132) illustrates this point, using a measure of class based on the respondent's first full-time occupation. Working class Labour Members and "non-U" Tories both have more conflictual images of society than do their upper class colleagues. Indeed, this figure suggests that when one controls for the class origins of the Members, there is virtually no consistent difference between the parties in their perspectives on social conflict.

Roughly comparable Italian data on social class and images of conflict are given in table 10.2. The results are consistent with the British findings, although the pattern is less clear-cut.

Table 10.2: Social Class Background and the Social Conflict Index in Italy

Parental social class*	.08
	(N=43)
Highest educational level attained	.50
	(N=56)
MP's present social class†	.34
	(N=60)

NOTE: Entry is gamma, positive when low social class is linked to high Social Conflict Index.
*Based on father's occupation.
†Based on deputy's present nongovernmental occupation or, if none, then on last occupation prior to election.

No parental social class is known for nearly a third of the Italians, which may help to explain the low correlation there. In any event, in Italy, too, the impact of social class (as measured by present occupation) persists when controls are added for party affiliation. Working class Socialists or Christian Democrats are more sensitive to social conflict than are their colleagues from higher social strata. (Attitudes on this dimension are much more uniform in the PCI, so that the correlation between class and the Social Conflict Index virtually vanishes if we consider Communists alone. Upper class recruits to the PCI have assimilated the conflict ideology of the Party as much as their working class comrades.)

Studies of the images of the social structure held by various social classes have found at the mass level, too, this tendency for working class respondents to have more conflictful perspectives on society than do middle and upper class people.[2] No doubt the explanation for the relationship is fairly simple. The world of a child growing up in a working class family is, in a very real sense, more "zero-sum" and therefore more conflictful than the world of his middle class compatriots. The size of the "pie" in a working class home is really more "constant," and philosophies of social harmony must ring truer spoken in upper class accents to upper class children.

The interesting and surprising fact revealed by the present study is that this relationship between social class and social philosophy persists among members of the political elite despite their specialized training and experience. In fact, in Britain the impact of class on mental models of society seems even more direct than the comparable impact of class on ideology in the conventional left-right sense. The sample here is distressingly small, but the contrasts are striking. Figure 10.1 shows the relationship between class and the left-right scale and that between class and the Social Conflict Index, in each case holding party constant.

The evidence is unambiguous. Figure 10.1a shows that in each party the relative predominance of conflict models rises sharply as we move down the social hierarchy. Indeed, the curves are nearly identical for the two parties. In other words, Tories and Labourites from similar social backgrounds have, on average, similar models of society. Figure 10.1b presents comparable data for the Members' positions on the left-right continuum. There is no tendency within either party for those from upper class backgrounds to be more conservative than those from middle class or working class backgrounds. Whereas social philosophy is shared across party lines by Members from the same social class, political ideology is shared along party lines and across class lines.

It would be very interesting to be able to sort out the pattern of causal relations among these four variables: class, party, ideology, and model of society. My

2. See Ralf Dahrendorf, *Class and Class Conflict in Industrial Society* (Stanford: Stanford University Press, 1959), p. 284, and the works cited there. See also Donald Stokes and David Butler, *Political Change in Britain* (New York: St. Martin's Press, 1969), pp. 92–4.

a. Class and the Social Conflict Index

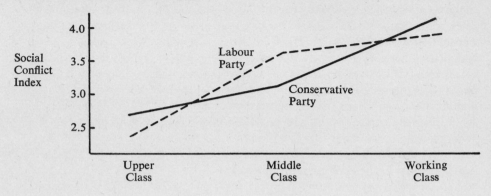

b. Class and the Left-Right Ideological Scale

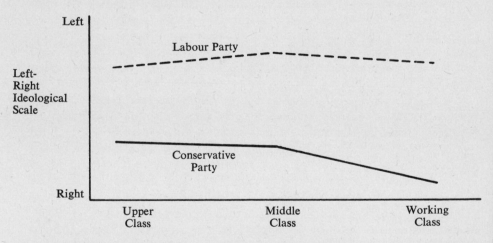

Figure 10.1: The Impact of Social Class on Images of Society and on Political Ideology, by Party (British respondents only)
   Class is based on the respondent's first full-time occupation. "Upper" refers to higher managerial and professional positions; "middle" to all other nonmanual occupations; "working" to all manual occupations. For fig. 10.1a, the Ns for Labour (upper, middle, and working class, respectively) are 5, 9, 10; for the Conservatives, 7, 6, 1. For fig. 10.1b, the Ns for Labour are 13, 22, 19; for the Conservatives, 23, 13, 1.

evidence here must be considered quite tentative, but figure 10.2 offers the model that best fits these data.[3] Perhaps most significant is the absence of any direct connection between social class and ideology; this finding, of course, reflects the evidence presented in Figure 10.1b. Apparently class directly affects one's image of society and one's party loyalty; one's ideological stance on policy problems is affected by class only indirectly, via one or both of these prior links.[4] In sum, the present evidence strongly suggests that among British politicians the impact of class on images of social conflict and consensus is more immediate and more durable than the impact of class on left-right ideology. (Unfortunately, the Italian data are not adequate to support a comparable analysis, partly because of problems with data on class, partly because of the dilemma of too many parties and too few respondents.)

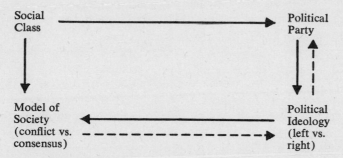

Figure 10.2: Causal Relations in Britain among Class, Party, Ideology, and Images of Society
Solid arrows indicate paths of influence confirmed by the data. Dotted arrows indicate paths of influence consistent with the data, but not required by the pattern of intercorrelations and therefore not conclusively confirmed.

Like any interesting result in social inquiry, this finding raises more questions than it resolves. How exactly does social class have its impact on images of social harmony or discord? I have implied so far that the basic orientation is set by

3. The basic technique used here is that outlined by Hubert M. Blalock, Jr., in his *Causal Inferences in Nonexperimental Research* (Chapel Hill: University of North Carolina Press, 1964). Those familiar with this technique, which is based on an examination of partial correlation coefficients, will recognize that several of the statistical assumptions of the approach are probably not met by the present data. Therefore, the diagram presented in figure 10.2 is offered with more than usual diffidence in the hope that it serve as a heuristic device for others interested in this problem.
4. A similarly indirect linkage between social background and partisan attitudes, mediated by party identification, has been discovered by Arthur S. Goldberg, using United States mass survey data. See his "Discerning a Causal Pattern Among Data on Voting Behavior," *American Political Science Review* 60 (1966): 918–20.

events during childhood and adolescence.[5] On the other hand, the proximate cause of the basic attitude could be subsequent adult experience, such as social discrimination, which is in turn derived from the stigmata or the deprivations associated with lower class origins. The issue cannot be resolved without longitudinal studies of the development of orientations to conflict and consensus.

One can also ask why attitudes toward social conflict seem so durable. One possibility is that these attitudes are somehow bound up with basic personality traits. Most theories of psychodynamics imply that attitudes integrated into the self are especially resistant to change. An alternative theory would stress not motivation for persistence, but the absence of an occasion for change. Unlike policy attitudes ("Are you in favor of Medicare?") or programmatic and ideological orientations ("Are you in favor of free enterprise?"), cognitive predispositions are rarely the subject of public discussion and debate. Indeed, as we discussed in chapter 9, these orientations to social conflict or social harmony are rarely even articulated. One would therefore expect them to be less subject to "resocialization" in normal political life.

One exception to this attitudinal longevity would be found in the case of a party whose ideology was explicit on the topic of social conflict and whose processes of indoctrination were particularly intense. The fact that members of the Italian Communist Party show the weakest link between social origins and present attitudes is quite consistent with the modest theory sketched here.

Social class seems, then, to affect cognitive predispositions more directly than it affects political ideology. The Parliamentary Labour Party provides an interesting example of the impact that this phenomenon can have on the structure of opinion within a party. Previous work has shown that one of the main lines of cleavage within the PLP is between Members sponsored by the Constituency Labour Parties and those sponsored by trade unions.[6] However, evidence in the present study suggests that in the 1966 House there was no consistent difference on the simple left-right scale between union-sponsored and CLP-sponsored Members.[7] This similarity exists despite the fact that CLP candidates are from higher status backgrounds and have higher status occupations. But the two groups seem to have rather different outlooks on social conflict and consensus. Compared with union-sponsored Members, CLP Members seem markedly less likely to endorse conflict models of society and markedly less likely to detect

5. There is some evidence that attitudes of this sort do develop during late adolescence. See Joseph Adelson and Robert P. O'Neil, "The Growth of Political Ideas in Adolescence: The Sense of Community," *Journal of Personality and Social Psychology* 4 (July–December 1966): 295–306.

6. S. E. Finer et al., *Backbench Opinion in the House of Commons 1955–1959* (New York: Pergamon Press, 1961).

7. Finer and his colleagues found—broadly speaking—CLP Members to be on the left on humanitarian and foreign issues and on the right on social welfare issues, and trade union Members the reverse. Our left-right dimension excludes the former type of issue as a basis for placement, but includes in addition to welfare attitudes, attitudes toward state control of the economy. The mean score on this scale was 1.9 for each group.

conflicting interests latent in policy problems.[8] The samples are too small to allow more detailed analysis, but these differences are too sharp to be the likely result of chance. One of the unrecognized sources of tension between these two wings of the PLP is probably a disparity in the basic models of society with which they operate, for the CLP-sponsored Members tend to interpret as non-conflictful and "technical" many issues which the union-sponsored Members see as conflictful and "political."

In British and Italian politics of the first half of the twentieth century social class has played a starring role. Asked to name "the two or three most important problems facing this country," the overwhelming majority of our respondents in each country cited issues involving economic management and social welfare. Substantial minorities also referred in Britain to national morale and in Italy to governmental institutions. But virtually no one mentioned such historic matters of dispute as religion and the role of the Church.[9] Money may not be the root of all politics, but in Britain and Italy today socioeconomic disputes nearly monopolize the attention of political leaders. Hence, in this examination of attitudes toward social conflict we have concentrated primarily on socioeconomic factors.

In principle, it is easy to imagine that background factors other than social class might influence a politician's orientation toward conflict. Religion is an obvious possibility, but one our data were not adequate to test. Distinctive regional tradition is another candidate. Some tantalizing hints of the impact of regional origins appear in our data. In each British party respondents from rural backgrounds and rural constituencies tend to be more consensual than their urban counterparts. Or to take another example, Welshman and Italians from the traditionally leftist "Red Belt" provinces seem especially sensitive to social conflicts. Sample size prevents testing whether these factors operate independently from other influences, such as class origin and party affiliation, but they

8. On the Index of Latent Issue Conflict 44 percent of the 32 CLP-sponsored Members are relatively insensitive to conflict, as contrasted with only 9 percent of the 21 Union-sponsored Members. On the Social Conflict Index 54 percent of 11 CLP-sponsored Members stress consensus, as contrasted with 17 percent of the 12 Union-sponsored Members asked this question. Despite the low Ns, both these differences reach statistical significance, using a Chi-square test corrected for continuity for the first and Fisher's exact test for the second. See Sidney Siegel, *Nonparametric Statistics for the Behavioral Sciences* (New York: McGraw-Hill, 1956), pp. 96–110.

9. Only 2 of the 83 Italians mentioned divorce or other Church-related topics. Similarly, only 5 of 33 Italians named Church-related problems, like education or family law, when asked about "the most important political conflict you remember in your experience." Of course, after 1970 the religious cleavage was evoked by the debate over divorce, but very few Italian politicians seem interested in reviving the moribund religious dispute. For evidence that the cleavage does persist at the mass level, see Samuel H. Barnes and Roy Pierce, "Public Opinion and Political Preferences in France and Italy," *Midwest Journal of Political Science* 15 (1971): 643–60. In the British case, Northern Ireland is an exceptional issue, but one that Westminster politicians themselves have tried to keep off the agenda. Even in a second series of interviews in the spring of 1971 relatively few MPs named it among "the most important problems facing this country."

serve to remind us of the possibility that a wide variety of forces may affect a person's view of society.

Political Experience

The social class background of a politician has an important effect on his view of social harmony or discord. By contrast, there seem to be no consistent connections between the Social Conflict Index and features of the politician's political experience. The length of time served in Parliament, past experience as a minister or leader in Parliament,[10] activity in local government, experience and status in party organizations—none of these factors has any measurable impact on the respondents' perspectives on social conflict.

The general conclusion seems to be that these perspectives are laid down fairly early in life and are relatively immune from the impact of later, more overtly political experience. Of course, it would be quite surprising if this immunity were as complete as our evidence seems to indicate. To be sure, the effects of later experience are normally muted by the cognitive predisposition itself. Chapter 9 showed that a politician's interpretation of contemporary public affairs is influenced by his basic perspective on social conflict. Thus, there is probably a tendency for the events of one's adult political life to be "experienced" in such a way as to confirm the original orientation. But dramatic personal or political events might trigger a reassessment of one's social philosophy. Perhaps, too, more sensitive measures of certain aspects of a politician's career would reveal some gradual impact.

10. Though former ministers are not basically lower on the Social Conflict Index, they seem to detect less conflict latent in issues. This probably reflects the continuing impact of "responsibility," as discussed in chapter 8.

11   Conflict in Britain and Italy:
Contrasts and Origins

By nearly every test, Italians see more conflict in society than do the British. This sharp and consistent difference is one of the central facts to emerge from this analysis, yet it is also annoyingly ambiguous. For one must somehow try to distinguish the effects of cognitive predisposition from the effects of social reality. Examining two photographs taken through different lenses of different scenes, we want to know which differences between the pictures are the result of objective differences between the scenes and which are the result of the distortions peculiar to each lens.

Lewis Coser has put this problem in broader perspective.

> The objective bases of social conflict must be sharply separated from subjective elements. Failure to do so results in excessively psychologistic explanations, which cannot do justice to the structure of conflict or to the situations that give rise to it. . . . [But] . . . hostile attitudes do not necessarily result in conflict; nor need we expect that objective discrepancies in power, status, income, and the like will necessarily lead to the outbreak of conflict, although they can be conceived as potential sources of conflict. Here, as elsewhere, the way men define a situation, rather than the objective features of the situation, must be the focus of analysis.[1]

The "Real" World

Why are Italians so much more sensitive to conflicts of interest in society and politics?[2] Part of the answer obviously can be sought in the contrast between Italian and British society. At least until very recently the Italian economy has both produced much less than the British economy and distributed what was produced less evenly. Moreover, the social structure of Italy has been and still

1. Lewis A. Coser, "Conflict: Social Aspects," in the *International Encyclopedia of the Social Sciences* (New York: Crowell Collier and Macmillan, 1968), 3:233.
2. One obvious possibility can quickly be excluded. The cross-national differences are not the result of differential social class composition of the parliaments. In fact, there are fewer working class members of our Italian sample than of our British sample.

is more rigid and inegalitarian than the British. These generalizations can be substantiated in part by some admittedly crude statistical indicators. The per capita GNP of Italy in 1957 was $516, less than half the $1189 of Great Britain. The average official unemployment rate in Italy in the late 1950s was 3.4 percent; the official figure for Britain was less than half that, 1.4 percent.[3](These official figures surely understate the real difference, when one considers underemployment, emigration, and the probable accuracy of the respective national statistics.) Cross-national data on income distributions are quite inadequate, but such evidence as we have indicates that even before taxes British income distribution is markedly more egalitarian than Italian.[4] Access to higher education is both more limited and less equitably distributed by social class origins in Italy than in Britain.[5] Available data on social mobility suggest that equality of opportunity is greater in Britain than in Italy.[6]

Clearly, then, part of the explanation of the greater sensitivity of Italians to conflict is that the socioeconomic "pie" in Italy is both smaller and less equally distributed than in Britain. There is in some sense simply more potential conflict in Italian society. But this fact cannot be the whole explanation for the cross-national difference. First of all, the postwar economic growth rates of the two countries have been sharply different, and different in a direction that ought to make Italian social and economic games markedly less zero-sum in quality than the British games. During the 1950s and 1960s real GNP rose at an average annual rate of 5.7 percent in Italy, as contrasted with 2.7 percent in Britain. In the ten years prior to our interviews Italian living standards rose from under half to more than two-thirds those of Britain. At these relative growth rates, Italian per capita GNP will have surpassed British per capita GNP by 1980.[7]

3. Bruce Russett et al., *World Handbook of Political and Social Indicators* (New Haven: Yale University Press, 1964), pp. 155, 189.

4. The Gini index of inequality is .403 for Italy,. 366 for Britain. Ibid., p. 245. See also Giuseppe Di Palma, *Apathy and Participation: Mass Politics in Western Societies* (New York: Free Press, 1970), pp. 164–6 and the works cited there.

5. See C. A. Anderson, "Access to Higher Education and Economic Development," in *Education, Economy, and Society,* ed. A. H. Halsey et al. (New York: Free Press, 1961), pp. 252–65, as cited in Di Palma, *Apathy and Participation,* pp. 168–70.

6. J. R. Hall and W. Ziegel, "A Comparison of Social Mobility Data for England and Wales, Italy, France, and the U.S.A.," in *Social Mobility in Britain,*ed. D. V. Glass (London: Routledge and K. Paul, 1954); Peter Blau and Otis Dudley Duncan, *The American Occupational Structure* (New York: John Wiley & Sons, 1967), pp.432–435; S. M. Miller, "Comparative Social Mobility," *Current Sociology* 9 (1960): 1–89; and Joseph Lopreato, "Social Mobility in Italy," *American Journal of Sociology* 71 (1965): 311–14. Calculations of S. M. Miller's "index of inequality" based on the most recently available data confirm that there is somewhat more equality of opportunity in Britain. The British data are those reported in David Butler and Donald Stokes, *Political Change in Britain* (New York: St. Martin's Press, 1969), pp. 96–7. The Italian data, as yet unpublished, are from the national survey reported briefly in Samuel H. Barnes, "Left, Right, and the Italian Voter," *Comparative Political Studies* 4(1971): 157–75. I am grateful to Professor Barnes for allowing access to his data; I alone am responsible for the use I have made of them.

7. See *The Economist* (London), September 5, 1970, p. 69–70, quoting an OECD report. See also *The Times* (London), February 26, 1971, supplement on the Italian economy.

Clearly, except for the viscosity of people's views of the world, the struggle over shares of the growing Italian economic pie ought to have been less intense than the comparable struggle in Britain.

Of course, at certain stages of economic development the process of growth itself gives rise to conflict. In Italy, for example, there is some reason to believe that growth has been paid for by the lower social classes—through low wages, migration, and so on. On the other hand, the increased wealth available for distribution should have reduced the potential for conflict. Indeed, evidence is presented later in this chapter that precisely this development seems to have occurred, affecting in turn the outlooks of some politicians.

A second reason to look beyond social reality for an explanation of contrasting national perspectives on conflict is that these differences are marked even where the objective problems facing the two countries seem fairly similar. It is far from obvious, for example, that the Italian urban traffic problem inherently involves greater conflict of interest than does the British problem. (That the former involves more conflictful *behavior* is obvious to anyone who has driven in both London and Rome, but only circular reasoning would allow this observation as evidence of greater genuine conflict of interest.) Yet, as discussed in chapter 8, Italians see considerably more conflict in this issue than do the British.

To take another example, economic planning in a rapidly growing economy such as Italy's ought to be inherently less conflictful than in a stagnant economy such as Britain's. To be sure, planning for growth brings problems and conflict. Capital must be accumulated by limiting consumption. Investments must be located in certain areas at the expense of others. But all this is as true of British planning as of Italian planning. The crucial economic difference is that British planners have had to operate at a closer margin, with a considerably smaller "growth dividend" to lubricate squeaking wheels. One must conclude that the realities of contemporary society explain only a part of the difference between the British and Italian perspectives.

The Legacy of History

The political history of the two countries is surely another part of the explanation for the cross-national differences in beliefs about conflict. One important historical factor involves the relationship already discovered between images of conflict and participation in governmental responsibility. Both major British parties have borne direct responsibility for public policy for extended periods over the last half century. In contrast, none of the three largest political groups in postwar Italy had ever participated in the government of the country before 1945. The Catholics had been excluded from power in pre-Fascist Italy, first by the Pope's *non expedit,* forbidding involvement with the Liberal government of the Risorgimento, then by the political chaos at the end of World War I. The Socialists and then the Communists became powerful politically just as Fascism was shutting off all opportunity for democratic politics.[8] Since the reestablishment of a parliamentary regime, the Catholics and subsequently the Socialists have gained government power and with it responsibility, but old perspectives are slow to change. The Communists, of course, have had little national responsibility to incline them to a less conflictful view of the world.[9]

Clearly, another part of the historical explanation has to do with the patterns of social conflict each country has endured over the last century. There have been deep and bitter social conflicts in recent British history, but for duration and intensity these conflicts cannot match those in Italy.

I argued in chapter 10 that a politician's cognitive predisposition toward conflict and consensus is set fairly early in his adult life, and that thereafter this perspective is slow to change. If this is so, then the views of politicians from different generations may reflect in some detail the recent history of the two countries. In order to increase the size of our samples and thereby the stability of our estimates, each respondent, whether asked about social conflict in general or about his own political experience, was rated on a single six-point scale according to the relative prominence his discussion gave to conflict or consensus. The average score on this measure was then calculated for each of four decennial age cohorts, with appropriate weighting to hold constant the partisan composition of each cohort. Figure 11.1 plots the relative prominence of conflict for each of these cohorts.

Two questions must be put to these data. First of all, how reliable are the estimates for the individual cohorts? Because the numbers involved are fairly small, caution is necessary. But roughly similar shapes obtain for each of the political parties considered separately and for each of the two different interview questions that underlie the composite index. It is fairly likely that the broad outlines shown in figure 11.1 would be confirmed if larger samples were available. Although the differences between successive cohorts in Britain are less striking and less straightforward than the cross-national differences, for example, tests of statistical significance suggest that the differences between successive points on the British curve are unlikely to be the result of random sampling error.[10]

If one accepts the general accuracy of the data shown in figure 11.1, a second

8. The Socialists were, of course, politically quite influential during the Giolittian era, and Giolitti himself aimed at bringing them into full political citizenship. However, during that period the Socialist Party never reached positions of responsibility, as that term is defined in the present study. A similar analysis applies to the role of the Communist Party in contemporary Italian politics.

9. I could find no evidence in these data to support the hypothesis that responsibility at the local level has tended to lead some Communists to a more consensual view of society and politics. This hypothesis, however, remains highly plausible.

10. Despite the low Ns involved, both the difference between the oldest pair of British cohorts and the difference between the two middle cohorts are significant at the .10 level or better; the difference between the youngest two cohorts is significant at the .15 level, using throughout a one-tailed difference-of-means t-test. In other words, there is less than one chance in ten that the successive differences among the three oldest cohorts are due to random sampling error, and less than one chance in six that the difference involving the very youngest group is accidental.

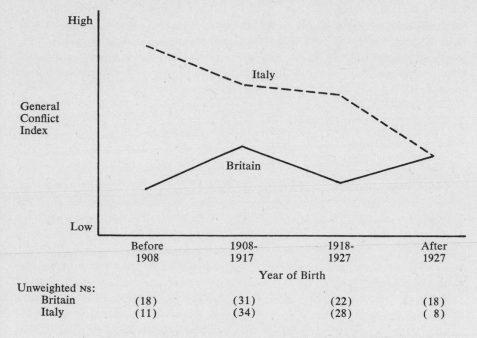

Unweighted NS:	Before 1908	1908-1917	1918-1927	After 1927
Britain	(18)	(31)	(22)	(18)
Italy	(11)	(34)	(28)	(8)

Figure 11.1: Images of Society and Political Generations
Weights have been used to hold constant party affiliation.

query must be faced. What is the most plausible explanation for the forms these curves take?

As I have already discussed in chapter 5, interpreting age-cohort differences is always problematic, for in principle "life cycle," "natural selection," and "generational" explanations are all possible. If the life cycle explanation were applied to these data, the Italian curve would mean that as politicians get older in Italy, their perspectives on society and politics change systematically. When they first enter politics, this interpretation would argue, they are fairly sanguine about the possibilities for cooperation, but with age comes greater sensitivity to social and political conflict. Although this explanation is not wholly implausible, the comparable explanation for Britain is less credible, for the saw-tooth shape of the British curve would, according to this explanation, indicate that age and experience first lower a young politician's emphasis on conflict, then raise it, and finally, in his old age, lower it again.

Nor would a pair of natural selection explanations be more persuasive. One could conceive that Italian consensualists might have less "staying power" in Parliament, but the correlation between age and perspectives on conflict persists virtually undiminished when controls for seniority are imposed. And a natural selection explanation in Britain would founder again on the highly irregular shape of the British graph.

Let us turn, therefore, to the alternative explanation for data such as these. Karl Mannheim in his essay "The Problem of Generations" has discussed the persisting effect that historical events can have on individuals in their formative years.

The fact of belonging to the same class, and that of belonging to the same generation or age group, have this in common, that both endow the individuals sharing in them with a common location in the social and historical process, and thereby limit them to a specific range of potential experience, predisposing them for a certain characteristic mode of thought and experience, and a characteristic type of historically relevant action.[11]

The result of such a phenomenon, viewed later through a cross-section of the population, would be a distinctive pattern of beliefs for the generation exposed to the crucial events.

The evidence presented in chapter 10 suggested that cognitive predispositions toward conflict are to some extent set early in adult life, perhaps at about the time a future politician comes of age, legally and politically. This presumption is consistent with the accumulating evidence that orientations of this sort seem to emerge during a "critical period" between the ages of roughly 17 and 25.[12] The youngest group of our politicians reached their legal majority (and, we are assuming, acquired their first relatively stable notions about social conflict and consensus) in the 1950s. Those 41 to 50 at the time of the interviews constitute from this point of view the generation of the late 1930s and early 1940s; those 51 to 60, the generation of the late 1920s and early 1930s; and those now over 60, the generation of the first two-and-a-half decades of the century. If then we map the contours of British and Italian social history during the critical periods of the respective cohorts, suddenly the odd shape of the British curve, as well as the smoother shape of the Italian, becomes more intelligible.

Our earliest generation of Englishmen had grown up in Edwardian England, as average real wages were rising, though not at the pace of the Victorian years.[13] More importantly, structural unemployment was relatively slight, certainly by

11. Karl Mannheim, *Essays in the Sociology of Knowledge*, ed. Paul Kecskmeti (London: Routledge and K. Paul, 1952), p. 291.

12. For two reviews of this literature, see T. Allen Lambert, "Generational Factors in Political-Cultural Consciousness" (paper delivered to the Annual Meeting of the American Political Science Association, Chicago, September 1971); and Neal E. Cutler, "Aging and Generations in Politics: The Conflict of Explanations and Inference," in *Public Opinion and Political Attitudes,* ed. Allen R. Wilcox (New York: John Wiley, forthcoming, 1973). The most directly relevant study is Joseph Adelson and Robert P. O'Neil, "The Growth of Political Ideas in Adolescence: The Sense of Community," *Journal of Personality and Social Psychology* 4 (July-December 1966): 295–306.

13. Much of this account of twentieth-century English social history is taken from a standard text by David Thomson, *England in the Twentieth Century* (Baltimore: Penguin Books, 1965). For economic data and interpretations, I have consulted principally Sidney Pollard, *The Development of the British Economy: 1914–1967,* 2nd ed. (London: Edward Arnold, 1969). Some relevant statistical evidence is provided in Brian R. Mitchell and Phyllis Deane, *Abstract of British Historical Statistics* (Cambridge: Cambridge University Press, 1962).

later standards. Lord Beveridge estimated that during the last three decades before World War I, unemployment had averaged 6 percent, as contrasted with more than double that throughout the years from 1921 to 1938.[14] To be sure, the last years of the Long Peace saw increased violence from suffragettes, a short-lived strike wave, and growing tensions over the Irish Question, but these were problems facing a people still confident the pie was growing.

This earliest generation came of age during and just after the Great War and the period of the Coalition Government. These years saw full employment, inflation, and a somewhat frenetic prosperity. Average real weekly wages of the fully employed rose by probably 20 to 25 percent from the prewar boom year of 1913 to the postwar boom year of 1920–21.[15] The average member of this cohort was 18 years old as World War I ended and the triumphant conservative coalition swept the successive General Election; he reached his legal majority as the postwar boom reached its peak.

But the locust years had arrived and the General Strike of 1926 symbolized the approach of an era of social and industrial strife. Unemployment rose (temporarily, it was thought) to the crisis level of 11 percent in 1923; it was not to fall below that figure for the next sixteen years. And for those lucky enough to retain jobs, average real weekly wage rates, which had risen about 3 percent per annum in the eight years before 1921, were to rise only 0.2 percent per annum in the next seventeen years.[16] It was during these years of hope decaying into despair that our second group of politicians came of age. The average politician in this group, about 55 at the time of our talk, was just 20 in 1932 when unemployment nationally reached a peak of 23 percent and 6 or 7 million of his fellows were living "on the dole."[17]

The continuing impact of these wretched years on the attitudes of politicians of that generation was illustrated by the response of one of them to a question about "what you find most appealing about being involved in politics and government."

> Well, I don't find anything terribly appealing in my politics. It's not something I want to do in order to find pleasure in it. This is terribly serious. Always has been a terribly serious thing for me. Prewar Scotland was 33 percent unemployed, was a place you grew up where politics was bread and butter. You weren't on a question of considering what you were going to make your career; you were in this [because] it meant your next day's breakfast, your next week's work. I don't look at politics this way. I think it's a very serious business. I still think it's a very serious business. (B72)

14. William H. Beveridge, *Full Employment in a Free Society* (New York: W. W. Norton, 1945), p. 335.
15. No single statistical series covers exactly this period; I have interpolated from two related series in Mitchell and Deane, *Abstract of British Historical Statistics,* pp. 344–5.
16. Ibid.
17. The interwar Depression hit the working classes with disproportionate force; this fact is consistent with our evidence, for the rise in the General Conflict Index among the generation of these years is sharper among Labour Members than among Conservatives.

The advent of war at the end of the decade, though its human and material costs were enormous, brought a striking change in the social climate of Britain. Historian David Thomson describes the impact of the war in this way:

Socially, the war was a mighty crucible, melting many pre-war contrasts and softening (though not always removing) old rigidities. Experience of evacuation, of mutual aid in air-raids, of great collective sacrifice and service, of stringent rationing and controls in the cause of "equal shares," all helped to strengthen a tide of egalitarian sentiment that had been generated before war began. Common humanity began to seem more important than distinctions of wealth or birth. Participation in so great a common effort made the pre-war years of insecurity and social hardship seem in retrospect grossly unjust. A new resolve was born to build, from the sacrifices of the war, a better society wherein none should be deprived of the necessities of life, and where the opportunity to work and live in decent surroundings should be opened to all citizens.[18]

Nor was impact of the war on public attitudes merely "atmospheric," for the economic basis of renewed social confidence was real enough. Unemployment fell from 13 percent in 1938 to less than 1 percent in 1944, while real average weekly wages were rising by roughly 30 percent.[19] The pie was growing once more. The average politician in our third cohort, 45 at the time of our conversation, was just 18 during the Battle of Britain in 1940 and came of legal age as the coalition Government produced the series of white papers promising profound social reform.

But, inevitably, the unity created by the shared hardships of the war gradually gave way, as the "better society" of which Thomson wrote turned out to involve continuing sacrifices, especially in a Britain whose economy bore the seemingly ineradicable marks of a half-century of wartime damage and peacetime neglect.

This gradual slipping away of a sense of social solidarity was reflected in the musings of one middle-aged Conservative about the kind of Britain he would like to see for his grandchildren. "I think you'd have all the good characteristics, the better characteristics which developed in the War. Good neighborliness, and a ready willingness to help people that you hardly knew, and a feeling of oneness. That's disappeared now." (B48)

This man had been just 22 during the Battle of Britain, but the average member of the youngest cohort in our sample was only a child then. A respondent 35 at the time of our interview was just 19 as the Conservatives were coming back into power in 1951 to "set the people free" from the socialist bondage imposed in the previous six years.

This picture of British social history in this century, though sketched admittedly in bold strokes, seems to make sense of the otherwise unintelligible varia-

18. Thomson, *England in the Twentieth Century*, p. 206.
19. Pollard, *Development of the British Economy*, p. 343; Beveridge, *Full Employment in a Free Society*, p. 110.

tions in the Social Conflict Index among contemporary British politicians of different ages. Similarly, an examination of Italian society in the twentieth century makes equal sense of the Italian data.[20] The first two decades saw the gradually rising power of parties at the extremes of the political spectrum, representing the bitterly opposed forces of labor and capital. World War I intensified these cleavages, and the postwar aftermath was not, as in England, the peaceful electoral inauguration of a coalition Government, but rather the violent accession to power of an authoritarian dictatorship. Real wages had fallen 35 percent from 1913 to 1918, and by the time the relationship of prices and wages had regained the prewar parity, in 1920, unemployment, labor disorder, and political violence had made wages virtually irrelevant as an index of well-being.[21] The average Italian politician in our oldest cohort was just 19 in 1921 when Mussolini's *squadristi* fought left-wing trade unionists in the piazzas.

The cleavages of the first two decades were by no means healed by the Fascist regime, but their open manifestations were suppressed. It is difficult from our present vantage point to gauge popular attitudes at the time, but Denis Mack Smith reflects the consensus of most historians on the impact of fascism on the Italians:

> Economically and politically, [fascism] may have been in the long run their ruin, but at the time it gave them reassurance and self-importance. . . . One way or another, so long as fascism offered an ordered regimen, an end of class war, and the fruits of victory without war itself, ordinary citizens seem to have been content.[22]

Social harmony in the corporate state was superficial and misleading, but Italy was "orderly" and overt political and social conflict sharply less than in the earlier years of the century. The average politician in our second cohort was 18 in 1929 when the Lateran Pacts were signed, formally reconciling Church and State; he was 19 in October 1930, when Mussolini announced the advent of the corporations, which were institutionally to embody Fascist social harmony.

The decade of the 1940s and the collapse of the Fascist regime brought a radically different social climate to Italy, more conflictful in many ways, but more genuinely harmonious in others. Political forces that had been surviving clandestinely emerged and immediately dominated Italian social and political life, initially in uneasy unison. A grand coalition (excluding only the Fascists) expelled the Germans and wrote a new national Constitution. This unity, of course, soon crumbled as the ideological cleavages of the Cold War split Italy, culminating in the election of 1948. The average Italian in the third cohort, 45

20. For the standard treatment of this period of Italian history, see Denis Mack Smith, *Italy* (Ann Arbor:University of Michigan Press, 1959). For economic history, see Shepard B. Clough, *The Economic History of Modern Italy* (New York: Columbia University Press, 1964).

21. Clough, *Economic History of Modern Italy,* p. 197.

22. Smith, *Italy,* p. 431.

at the time of the interview, was 21 in 1943 when the Resistance united the newly emerging political forces in uncertain, but hopeful alliance.

Postwar Italy has been, from the point of view of the present inquiry, a remarkably ambiguous period. There has been, of course, great and bitter national controversy, as my interviews revealed. But answers to my questions about the changing balance of conflict and cooperation also revealed a nearly universal sense that conflict had diminished from the peaks of the late 1940s. Perhaps more relevant is the data on economic growth presented earlier, for this ebullient prosperity, accompanied though it was by great social dislocations, gave many Italian leaders across the ideological spectrum a sense that society and politics is potentially a positive-sum game.

One young left-wing Christian Democrat illustrated this fact in expressing his optimism about the future.

> From this point of view, I share fully the opinion expressed by a leader who is politically my adversary, the leader of the Liberal Party, who often argues that Italian society for the first time since the Renaissance is facing all its problems and has the means to resolve them. In this I am fully in agreement with Hon. Malagodi. (I12)

It is relevant in this connection that only 6 of the 77 Italians who were asked were pessimistic about chances for substantial progress for their country in the future, a proportion less than half the British.

This sketch of the recent social and economic history of the two countries suggests an obvious explanation for the patterns shown in figure 11.1. A political leader's sense of the relative salience of social harmony and social discord is drawn from his interpretation of the world as it appears to him as he reaches maturity. If his society seems cleft by bitter conflict, he is likely to keep throughout his political career a basic assumption that the essence of politics is conflict. If on the other hand the political world as he first experiences it seems essentially harmonious, the chances are good that a consensual perspective will inform his views on politics in later life.

The discussion to this point has been phrased so as to suggest a once-for-all setting of social perspective at an early age, much as naturalists tell us "imprinting" takes place in young animals. It would be misleading to imply, however, that subsequent experience has no impact whatsoever. Although I have found no evidence that requires me to postulate such later "relearning," the data presented in figure 11.1 are not inconsistent with the hypothesis that adult experiences have some effect. The earliest generation of Italians, coming of age during the social disorders after World War I, may indeed have been mellowed somewhat by the affluence of the second postwar era, but most plausible learning models would still predict that the views of this generation would continue to be more conflict-laden than the views of the generations who had never experienced the earlier upheavals. In other words, one need only assume a continuing, not a literally indelible, effect of the social conditions at the time of passage into adulthood. As I discussed in chapter 10, precisely how liable the basic orientation is to the molding influences of a lifetime of political involvement is a question to which my data offer only a muffled answer.

How History Matters

The evidence and inference of this study suggest strongly that social change is ultimately reflected in the outlooks of political leaders. But built into this process is a time lag of considerable significance. The data in figure 11.1 on the most recent generation of Italian and British politicians show very little difference in their basic perspectives on social conflict. But at any point in time the political elite of a country may be composed of recruits from generations spanning nearly half a century, and the marked differences between Britain and Italy in the first decades of the twentieth century are still reflected in the attitudes of today's leaders. Even if in some objective sense Italian society is no longer inherently more conflictful than British society, that convergence will not be reflected in their respective political elites for several decades. Nor, it should be added, is there any determinism in history that requires present trends to continue. If contemporary Italian society should become more conflict-ridden—as a result of a slowing of economic expansion, for example—my theory implies that the future politicians now just reaching adulthood will bear the marks of that conflict when they assume positions of leadership at the turn of the next century.

Cognitive predispositions do, in other words, respond to changes in the social environment. But in the aggregate, this response takes the form of a lagged, moving average, because the politicians of any given period are drawn from a number of earlier political generations. Just as today's wheat price is a function of a lagged, moving average of weather conditions in the previous three years, so the attitudes of the contemporary political elite are a function of a lagged, moving average of objective social and political conflict several decades ago.[23] To demonstrate the truth of the latter generalization in the way that economists have demonstrated the validity of the former would require both accurate time-series data on these attitudes and a fairly precise barometer to measure the objective social and political climate. But if one adopts for a moment a bene-volent suspension of disbelief, it is possible to investigate some interesting im-plications of this theoretical model.

The fact that the independent variable is lagged and averaged over a number of decades means that short-term changes in the objective social environment tend to be damped in their political impact by the lingering outlooks of older

23. A moving average of a series of numbers is the average of (say) the first, second, and third; then the second, third, and fourth; and so on. "Lagged" in this context means that one variable at one point in time (e.g. price in 1960) is a function of the value of a second variable at some earlier time (e.g. weather in 1957–1959). For a presentation of the wheat price example and an extended discussion of the mathematics involved in this type of analysis, see Gerhard Tintner, *Econometrics* (New York: John Wiley & Sons, 1952), esp. pp. 288–300.

leaders. If a country whose social and political climate had long been relatively conflictful began to experience greater social harmony, because of increased economic prosperity, for example, the effects of this change would be relatively slow in coming at the level of political leadership. Political leaders would continue for some time to interpret public problems in terms of a cognitive set appropriate to an earlier era. This hypothetical example fits contemporary Italian politics in many respects and may well describe the political prospects of other countries as they arrive at a relatively affluent stage of economic development.

On the other hand, it is also possible to imagine the converse case. If a country whose social and political relationships had been relatively consensual moved into a period of heightened social tensions, the political effects of the changed environment would for some time be minimized by the continuities of cognitive predispositions at the elite level. Political leaders would still tend to expect and to seek communalities of interest. Elite political culture would change only slowly, exerting a "stabilizing" influence. Parts of this hypothetical illustration may parallel some aspects of contemporary British politics, although admittedly the case does not match the model in all respects.

One of the two key parameters in this model is the turnover of elite personnel. If generations of political leaders moved rapidly onto and off the political stage, the collective culture of the elite would respond quickly to social change. If, on the other hand, a given generation of leaders monopolized positions of power for a long period, the lag between social and attitudinal change would be greater.[24]

The second parameter is the volatility of the predispositions, their susceptibility to "relearning." If individuals' cognitive sets changed easily in response to changes in the environment, then the discontinuity between social reality and elite political culture would be slight. There is, however, reason to believe that the cognitive predispositions that are under discussion here are relatively resistant to change. Other, more peripheral and more conscious beliefs, such as those about economic policy or about the role of legislatures in the modern world, are probably much more rapidly responsive to environmental changes, although they may well fit the general model of cultural change elaborated here.

Organizational variables might also sustain attitudinal inertia. A party with an effective program of indoctrination and a corporate commitment to a philosophy of social conflict (or one of social harmony) might slow down change in beliefs that would otherwise occur among its cadres. As it happens, there is no evidence that the Italian Communist Party has played this role in slowing down change in its members' perspectives. The age gradient of the Social Conflict

24. Cf. Walter Bagehot's discussion of the effects of the longevity of "the pre- '32 statesmen" on nineteenth-century politics. He concludes, "what we call the 'spirit' of politics is most surely changed by a change of generation in the men than by any other change whatever." (*The English Constitution* [1867, reprint ed., London: Collins, Fontana Library, 1963], p. 269).

Index is, in fact, sharper within the PCI than in any other Italian party. The theoretical principle, however, might well apply in other national or organizational contexts.

The theory sketched in these pages is proposed tentatively. Too little is known about the processes of political socialization as they apply to attitudes of the sort under discussion to assert with complete confidence that the assumptions of the theory are accurate. Nevertheless, this provisional theory does help explain how events and conditions long since vanished can live on in the attitudes and behavior of contemporary political leaders. The violence in Italian public life at the end of the First World War persists in the attitudes of contemporary leaders, even in the relative affluence of "il boom." The social cohesion generated in the blitz of London and Coventry survives in an era of industrial tensions produced by current economic and financial insecurity.

Though these persisting perspectives may appear in some ways anachronistic, they are nonetheless significant for understanding contemporary politics. Young Italian leaders and their older colleagues are looking at the same world, but they are not seeing the same world, for their lenses—their cognitive predispositions—are quite different indeed. Both young and old recognize the importance of economic growth and economic planning, but where the young see the exploitation of mutual interests, the old see only mutual exploitation. British and Italian politicians facing comparable situations react differently, in part because they operate on different assumptions about the underlying structure of interests.

In some discussions of national political traditions or national political cultures, whether at the mass level or among elites, culture has been used as a residual category, one whose contents were unique to the given nation and virtually inexplicable except by vague references to the importance of history.[25] The most important lesson of this chapter is that political culture need not be treated as a question-stopper, as an uncaused first cause. Careful investigation of particular cultural patterns in more than one national setting may provide the leverage necessary to enable us to move beyond the despairing generalization that "history matters" to more precise indications of *how* it matters. There can be few tasks more important or more fascinating than unraveling the complex connections between the past we have almost forgotten and the future we barely discern.

25. For a trenchant criticism along these lines, see Erwin Scheuch, "Society as Context in Cross-National Comparisons," *Social Science Information,* 6 (October 1967): 5ff.

12 Views of Conflict and
Patterns of Politics

In chapter 11, I asked how national history molds the outlook of the political elite. In this chapter, I want to ask the obverse question: what differences do elite perspectives on conflict make for patterns of national politics?

Views of Conflict and the Policy-Making Process

While discussing game-theory analyses of conflict and consensus in chapter 7, I introduced a distinction between two different kinds of behavior in a game or in a political situation. On the one hand, there is "problem solving," that is, the search for Mary Parker Follett's "integrative solutions," policies that meet the interests and desires of all the parties involved.[1] On the other hand, "bargaining" implies a struggle over the allocation of values in a situation in which not all can win, or at least not all can win completely. "In problem-solving, it is assumed that objectives are shared and that the decision problem is to identify a solution that satisfies the shared criteria. . . . Where bargaining is used, disagreement over goals is taken as fixed, and agreement without persuasion is sought."[2]

One important determinant of whether participants in a game will engage in cooperative problem solving or conflictful bargaining is their image of the extent of shared or conflicting interests in the game. If the players believe that mutually beneficial solutions are possible, they will search cooperatively for them, even if the solutions are initially unknown. On the other hand, if the players believe that the discovery of new points beyond the present "outcome line" is unlikely, there is little incentive to engage in problem solving, and instead their attention will be directed at achieving maximum individual gains in the bargaining process.

These speculations are indirectly supported by a growing literature on experi-

1. Mary Parker Follett, *Dynamic Administration: The Collected Papers of Mary Parker Follett*, ed. Henry M. Metcalf and L. Urwick (New York: Harper, 1942), pp. 239ff., as quoted in Charles E. Lindblom, *The Intelligence of Democracy*, (New York: Free Press, 1965) p. 210.

2. James G. March and Herbert A. Simon, *Organizations* (New York: John Wiley & Sons, 1958), pp. 129–30.

mental studies of behavior in game situations.[3] Our findings encourage the hope that similar propositions apply at the level of national politics. The application of the theory to the present case is charmingly simple. The more that politicians expect to find common interests in society, the more they will engage in problem solving. Conversely, the more that they expect to find conflicting interests, the more they will resort to bargaining. The fit with the British and Italian cases is pleasingly snug.

Comparative studies of the policy-making processes of European countries are, alas, virtually nonexistent, and one must rely therefore on the anonymous authority of "most informed observers" if one is to contrast patterns of decision making in Britain and Italy. But most informed observers would doubtlessly agree that problem solving—the cooperative search for mutually beneficial solutions to national problems—is characteristic of British policy making. To be sure, no one could suppose that British policy is formulated simply in cordial and mutually deferential discussions over sherry. No one could doubt that representatives of interest groups abound in Westminster and haunt the corridors of Whitehall. No one could deny the importance of strategems and gambits and ploys, all characteristic of an intensely political bargaining process. Yet, the fact remains that the consulations that lie at the heart of the British policy process—consultations between bureaucrats and politicians, between ministers and backbenchers, between Government and interest groups—have an aura of cooperative problem solving about them that is, in comparative perspective, quite remarkable.[4] And the effectiveness of British government in dealing with public problems is due in large part to the unusual frequency with which the partlulpants engage in problem-solving behavior.

The party battles of Westminster would seem to introduce an uncomfortably large element of conflictful behavior. But what must be stressed is that normally the partisan contest takes precisely the form of a competition in problem-solving skill. Relatively rare are the issues of British politics that cleave the parties on substantive grounds; nationalization has this exceptional quality. Much more frequently partisan battles concern the abilities of the respective sides to grapple with a common problem. The issues of economic stability and of race both fit this category.[5] In sum, party competition is not an important exception to our generalization that problem solving is peculiarly characteristic of British decision making.

3. See the studies cited by Robert A. Dahl, *Polyarchy: Participation and Opposition* (New Haven: Yale University Press, 1971) pp. 156–7.
4. Some sense of the behavioral patterns that underlie my generalizations can be gleaned from the comprehensive reader edited by Richard Rose, *Policy-Making in Britain* (New York: Free Press, 1969).
5. Cf. the distinction that Donald Stokes and David Butler draw between "position" issues and "valence" issues in their *Political Change in Britain* (New York: St. Martin's Press, 1969), esp. p. 189.

The British example is placed in perspective by examining the Italian case. Our proverbial informed observers would probably not dissent from a description of decision making in Italy that stressed bargaining instead of problem solving. The confrontations that rocked Italian society in 1969 and 1970 offer a convenient and only slightly exaggerated example of the way Italian policy making works. Massive strikes are certainly not rare in other Western countries, and even political strikes are not unknown. But what is characteristic of the Italian decision-making process is that important policy departures rarely occur *without* upheavals of this sort.

The decade of the 1960s, which closed with massive confrontations over accumulated social ills unresolved by the Center-Left governments, had opened with massive confrontations over the possible installation of a right-wing Goverment led by Fernando Tambroni. Both of these episodes marked important turning points in recent Italian public life, and as in all such *svolte,* the dominant motif was not problem solving, but hard and often unproductive bargaining. Italian postwar history seems, to a jaundiced eye, a continuous oscillation between periods of stagnation in which no effective policies are offered or implemented and periods of innovation that occur only through dramatic and often quite costly games of political "chicken." While party competition in Britain usually takes the form of a contest in problem solving, Italian parties are preoccupied with bargaining and rarely devote energy to the analysis of problems in terms of common social interests and values.

The contrast drawn here is perhaps too stark to be wholly true. Problem solving is not unknown in Italy, any more than bargaining is absent in Britain. In some areas in postwar Italy problem-solving behavior has been dominant and bargaining less important. The development of the Italian South seems to illustrate this countertendency, although the evident failures in implementation raise doubts about the effectiveness of the decision-making process. But on a wide range of issues, from economic policy to the legalization of divorce and from university reform to social security legislation, the process of reaching decisions has been characterized by the unrelieved clash of sectional interests untempered by any sense of common purpose.

These examples should not be misread as referring simply to the prominence of mass public violence. Riots and mobs are, to be sure, more obvious features of Italian than of British politics. But this is not the point I want to make. Rather, I am arguing that even in more private arenas Italian policy-makers have engaged in cooperative problem solving only rarely, and indulged in adversary bargaining all too often. Bargains may be struck, but the problems remain unsolved.

The explanation for the relative lack of problem-solving behavior in Italian public life is no doubt complex, but the predominance of conflictful perspectives on social relations is clearly an important contributing factor. Between attitude and behavior there is naturally a reciprocal effect. Italians, more than the British, are looking for a fight, not because they *want* one, but because they *expect* one. And in part because they expect one, they find it. To politicians operating with conflict models of society, areas of shared interest seem more limited and cleavages seem deeper, on everyday issues as well as on grand matters of high politics.

Thus, a paradox. The Italians are *not* in principle less willing to compromise their differences than the British. If involved in a sharp political controversy, only 32 percent of the Italians said they would always or usually "stick to their guns" rather than "seek a solution acceptable to both sides." Thirty-three percent of the British made the same choice. (Comparable results were obtained for nearly all our indicators of a "compromise orientation.") But despite their endorsement of the principle of compromise, the Italians are less able to compose their differences, because these differences seem so much greater and because every problem seems to involve more conflict than mutual interest.

To some students of Italian history and politics, the willingness of Italian politicians to entertain compromise solutions will be no surprise at all. These observers, scholars and commentators alike, remind us of the long, if disreputable Italian tradition of *trasformismo* and *connubio,* of unprincipled political transformations and opportunistic marriages of political convenience.[6] There is a dilemma here in the usual critiques of Italian politicians, for they are said to be both too ready to compromise and too individualistic to do so, too willing to strike bargains and not willing enough, too unprincipled and too principled by half.[7]

Our evidence suggests that neither position in the argument is valid, that Italians are neither more nor less open to compromise than the British. But this statement is not a sufficient reply to the historians and commentators, for there seems clear evidence that many Italian leaders have been willing, indeed eager, to strike mutually (and personally) profitable bargains, often at the price of ignoring urgent national issues. Conversely, there is abundant evidence that many pressing social problems have festered because of the Italians' inability to arrive at constructive, mutually acceptable solutions. This Italian malaise is sometimes traced, especially by Italians themselves, to low standards of political morality, to a political class that does not measure up to its responsibilities. There may be some truth to this indictment, but the present study suggests another way of unraveling this skein of dilemmas.

6. For a summary of this argument, see any standard history of Italy, for example, Denis Mack Smith, *Italy* (Ann Arbor: University of Michigan Press, 1959), esp. pp. 110–12.

7. For the position that Italians are insensitive to the virtues of compromise, see, for example, Robert A. Dahl, "Some Explanations," in *Political Oppositions in Western Democracies,* ed. Robert Dahl (New Haven: Yale University Press, 1966), p. 354. Sometimes both halves of this contradictory condemnation appear in the same argument. Denis Mack Smith, for example, has criticized the *Democristiani* for minimizing internal conflicts in the interests of remaining in power and in the very next sentence berated the Socialists for failing to recognize that "politics is the art of the possible, not just the desirable." See his fascinating analysis of contemporary Italian politics in *Ls'Epresso* 15 (July 13, 1969): 4.

What is lacking among Italian political leaders is not, it seems, a willingness to cooperate for mutual benefit, but rather the belief that such cooperation is possible on the major social issues. The sense that these issues involve irreconcilably opposed interests, the fear that society may virtually fly apart if they are raised and faced openly, might lead a prudent politician to put them aside as quietly as possible—to "bury them in the sand," as the Italians say—perhaps hiding the deed behind a cloud of vaporous words. Disposed to believe that these problems involve irreconcilable conflicts of interest, politicians content themselves with sharing out smaller pies. Cooperation in dividing up what Americans call "the spoils" is relatively easy, because the possibilities of mutual advantage are clearer. (Here, too, however, there is probably an implicit assumption that the game is zero sum, with the losses of the *fesso,* or sucker, simply discounted.)

With larger issues, on the other hand, the stakes are higher, the players more numerous, and the interests less mutual. The possibility of an "integrative solution" is ruled out in advance. Given these assumptions, one response that makes psychological sense, if not always logical sense, is the avoidance of agreement, a refusal even to play the immensely important and potentially productive games that lie at the heart of politics and government. The result is continuing unreconciled conflict, which has among its side effects a tendency to confirm everyone's original assumptions.

Views of Conflict and Stable Democracy

So far in our discussion of the consequences of cognitive predispositions, I have argued that perspectives that stress conflicting interests are likely to inhibit problem solving and encourage hostile bargaining instead. Effective and stable government would thus seem to depend on belief systems that stress communalities of interest. It seems fairly clear, for example, that the stability and effectiveness of Italian democracy has been impaired by the Italians' predisposition to see conflicting interests in public problems.

Another face of the argument, however, is illuminated in Ralf Dahrendorf's superb study of *Society and Democracy in Germany*.[8] While I have to this point argued the disadvantages of a perspective that ignores common interests in society, Dahrendorf points out that comparable dangers to democratic stability inhere in a perspective that denies the reality of social conflict.

Wherever there is human life in society, there is conflict. . . . Wherever conflicts are suppressed as awkward obstacles to arbitrary rule or declared abolished once and for all, these fallacies produce unexpected and uncontrollable responses of the suppressed forces. Different attitudes toward conflict have ramifications for views and policies of liberty. . . . Since no man

8. Ralf Dahrendorf, *Society and Democracy in Germany* (Garden City, N. Y.: Doubleday, 1969).

knows all the answers, it is all-important to avoid the dictatorship of false answers. The best way to accomplish this is to see to it that at all times and everywhere more than one answer may be given. Conflict is liberty, because by conflict alone the multitude and incompatibility of human interests and desires find adequate expression in a world of notorious uncertainty.[9]

Dahrendorf's argument is particularly interesting for our present discussion because he claims that the historic German inability to support liberal democracy can be traced in large part to a view of society that is insufficiently sensitive to conflicting interests. In other words, he proposes an explanation of German political history that is precisely the mirror image of the explanation that I have offered for the Italian case.

Dahrendorf offers examples in brilliant profusion of the tendency of Germans to overstress social harmony and oneness. The notion of the unity of truth recurs insistently in the epistemology of German academic philosophers. Industrial relations and, in particular, the policy of "codetermination" similarly illustrate this overemphasis on concord. ("There are traces everywhere of the deep aversion of all participants in industry to conflict, and the untiring search for ultimate solutions.")[10] Since Lasalle the broader German labor movement has been hypnotized by the myth of the State and the image of national unity. A view of political action as the search for "truth," as the defense of indivisible national interests, has pervaded German legal and political philosophy.

Whether or not Dahrendorf's description of German political culture is accurate today, his theoretical argument is quite pertinent: orientations toward social conflict are among the factors that affect a people's aptitude for democracy.[11] Democracy requires participation,

> but chances of participation for citizens are of little use if they are not expressed in lively conflicts of interest. Even the effective equality of citizens loses its consequence if institutions of controlled conflict are missing. . . . Aversion to conflict is a basic trait of authoritarian political thought, which means in effect that government loses control of change, and the citizens lose their freedom.[12]

It is temptingly symmetrical to argue that the relationship between democratic stability and the Social Conflict Index is curvilinear, as suggested in figure 12.1. A country whose political leaders are insensitive to conflicting interests is likely to be subject to a regime that is authoritarian, though perhaps stable in some limited sense. A country whose political leaders are insensitive to commu-

9. Ibid., pp. 138, 140.
10. Ibid., p. 161.
11. Some current research of mine suggests that Dahrendorf's description is *not* accurate as applied to German elites in the 1970s, but given the apparent stability of the Bonn regime, this finding does not invalidate his theoretical proposition.
12. Dahrendorf, *Society and Democracy in Germany,* pp. 170, 184.

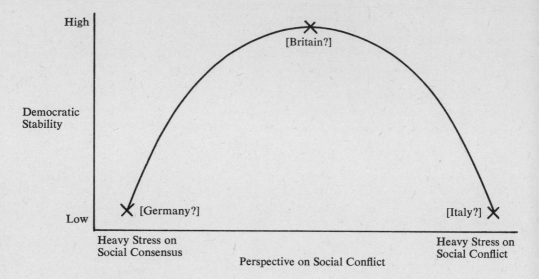

Figure 12.1: Democratic Stability and Perspectives on Social Conflict

nalities of interest is prone to the politics of instability, and, ultimately, runs the risk of an authoritarian reaction. The prospects for stable democracy are best where leaders are equally sensitive to social conflict and social concord.[13] That these three positions may be exemplified by Germany, Italy, and Britain respectively will not, I hope, seem too convenient to be true.

The propensity for cooperation with political opponents is linked in a curvilinear fashion to the Social Conflict Index. (See figures 9.1 and 9.2.) The logic that underlay our discussion of that phenomenon is exactly parallel to the logic that leads me now to argue more generally that the country will be most hospitable to democracy whose leaders have a balanced perspective on conflict and consensus in politics and social relations. The critical judgment on Italian politicians that gains support from this study is not that they see conflict in Italian society and politics. Only fools or knaves would not. It is instead that their general disposition to *chercher le conflit* may hinder the recognition of shared interests and the resolution of national problems.

13. A similar proposition has recently been suggested by Robert A. Dahl in his *Polyarchy: Participation and Opposition*, pp. 152–62. As his example of a political class oversensitive to conflicting interests, he uses Italy; to exemplify insufficient sensitivity to conflict, he uses India. A recent study of Mao's impact on Chinese political culture argues essentially that Mao set out to overturn the traditional Chinese aversion to social conflict. See Richard H. Solomon, *Mao's Revolution and the Chinese Political Culture* (Berkeley: University of California Press, 1971). See also Gabriel Almond and Sidney Verba, *The Civic Culture* (Princeton: Princeton University Press, 1963), pp. 389–93; and Harry Eckstein, *Division and Cohesion in Democracy: A Study of Norway* (Princeton: Princeton University Press, 1966), pp. 192–6.

PART III
POLITICIANS AND DEMOCRACY:
AN ESSAY ON OPERATIVE IDEALS

13 Democratic Practice and
     Democratic Theories

Democracy, more than any other political arrangement, requires its practitioners to follow an intricate, stylized, and often unnatural code of behavior. To be sure, other political systems are based on mutual expectations and inhibitions; members of the Politburo only rarely murder their competitors, for example. But the norms of democratic political behavior are both less obvious and more constraining. Democratic politicians follow rules of behavior every bit as "odd" as those that guide the performance of a highly stylized Japanese Nō play. That men should be allowed to say whatever they wish about the rulers of a country, that they should be allowed to mobilize opposition to those rulers, that rulers should be chosen by balloting in which the entire population takes part, that those who win this contest should accede to power without hindrance by their opponents—these principles so contradict patterns of behavior that have been "normal" historically that it is remarkable that they are ever followed at all.

Theorists of democracy who pondered this puzzle before the advent of behavioral science came to the conclusion that the success of democracy depends on widespread understanding of and support for these fairly subtle "rules of the game." Consensus on democratic procedures, that is, was said to be a precondition for stable democratic politics.[1] Empirical studies of mass publics have, however, cast doubt on the extent to which national electorates really support these supposedly critical norms. American voters, for example, support "free speech" in the abstract, but apparently fail to see the connection between this principle and the right of a communist to speak publicly in their town.[2] Despite popular endorsement of the general principles, there is little popular understanding of the practical implications of these principles.

1. See, for example, Ernest S. Griffith, John Plamenatz, and J. Roland Pennock, "Cultural Prerequisites to a Successfully Functioning Democracy: A Symposium," *American Political Science Review* 50 (1956): 101–37.
2. James W. Prothro and Charles M. Grigg, "Fundamental Principles of Democracy: Bases of Agreement and Disagreement," *Journal of Politics* 22 (1960): 276–94. See also Samuel Stouffer, *Communism, Conformity, and Civil Liberties* (New York: Doubleday, 1955).

Recent students of democracy have focused, consequently, on the possibility that effective support for the norms of democratic politics is concentrated among the political elite.[3] Some empirical research has tended to confirm this proposition.[4] On reflection, one should perhaps not be surprised that politicians are better able to draw practical conclusions from abstract political principles, for their familiarity with complex political reasoning is necessarily greater than that of their constituents. I support the principle that clean carburetors make for better gasoline mileage, but my garage mechanic is much better than I am at drawing practical conclusions from that principle.

There are two general lessons to be learned from this recent research. First, the values and attitudes of political leaders are particularly important in understanding stable democracy. Second, the findings about attitudes of the mass electorate call attention to the important distinction between the "name" of a norm and the "meaning" of a norm, between "free speech" and "allowing Communists to speak here." Part III will investigate politicians' support for democratic norms, but more precisely, their understanding or interpretation of these norms.

In most modern countries today the accepted standard of judgment for political arrangements is "democracy." As a UNESCO committee studying "democracy in a world of tensions" in 1949 said (with only slight overstatement):

> For the first time in the history of the world, no doctrines are advanced as anti-democratic. The accusation of antidemocratic action or attitude is frequently directed against others, but practical politicians and political theorists agree in stressing the democratic element in the institutions they defend and the theories they advocate.[5]

Everyone supports "democracy," but, as the work of the UNESCO committee itself reveals, there is little agreement on what democracy means. If the "basic agreement" cited by the committee is important, so too is the diversity of interpretations their work underscored. Working at the height of the Cold War, they were concerned primarily with the contrast between what they called "Western" and "Eastern" conceptions of democracy. But within Western countries, too, there are markedly different notions of what democracy means.

Giovanni Sartori has argued trenchantly that "in the final analysis, our political behavior depends on our idea of what democracy is, can be, and should

3. See Robert A. Dahl, *Who Governs?* (New Haven: Yale University Press, 1961), pp. 311–25; and V. O. Key, Jr., *Public Opinion and American Democracy* (New York: Alfred A. Knopf, 1964), pp. 535–58.

4. Herbert McClosky, "Consensus and Ideology in American Politics," *American Political Science Review* 58 (1964): 361–82. See also Ian Budge, *Agreement and the Stability of Democracy* (Chicago: Markham, 1970), for evidence supporting the theory in the British case.

5. "Statement of the Members of the Committee concerning the Importance of the Problem," in *Democracy in a World of Tensions: A symposium prepared by UNESCO,* ed. Richard McKeon (Chicago: University of Chicago Press, 1951), p. 522.

be.''[6] If this is so, then it is important to examine politicians' ideas of democracy. As a way of orienting this inquiry, let us look briefly at several important strands of traditional democratic philosophy.

How Theorists Conceive Democracy

The literature on theories or conceptions or models of democracy is almost literally endless. Even if we restrict our attention to those notions of democracy that have some currency in the world of political practice as well as the world of political theory, any simple summary of the contending views is bound to do violence to certain features of each. Indeed, it is difficult to arrive at any straightforward list of what the contenders *are*. Nevertheless, if we are to understand how politicians view democracy, we must first ask how theorists have viewed it.

The earliest, the simplest, and in some ways, still the most attractive notion of democracy is that it is "government by the people" in a fairly literal sense. Mass participation in the activities of politics and government—for all "to rule and be ruled in turn," as Aristotle said[7] —is the essential of what has come to be called the "classical" conception of democracy. This conception is perhaps best exemplified by the democracy of the Greek city-states, the essential features of which were public deliberation and decision by all citizens and the filling of most executive offices by lot. Some Enlightenment theorists of democracy, most notably Jean Jacques Rousseau, argued that this kind of direct popular participation in public decision making and decision execution was the *sine qua non* of democracy. Representative democracy was, on their terms, a logical absurdity. Political practitioners inclined toward this view of democracy have argued for methods and procedures that would increase popular involvement in government. In the United States, for example, such innovations as the initiative and referendum, recall, and direct primaries stem from the Populist movement and reflect a classical conception of democracy.[8]

In recent years another, quite different conception of democracy has gained much support, especially among social theorists familiar with empirical findings about the low levels of political interest and involvement characteristic of mass publics in modern nation-states. Joseph A. Schumpeter usually receives credit for the most concise formulation of this alternative model. "The democratic method is that institutional arrangement for arriving at political decisions in which individuals acquire the power to decide by means of a competitive struggle for the people's vote."[9] This model of democracy, for which we will borrow

6. Giovanni Sartori, *Democratic Theory* (New York: Frederick A. Praeger, 1965), p. 5.

7. Aristotle *Politics* 1317b, trans. Benjamin Jowett (New York: Modern Library, 1943), p. 260.

8. This conception is closely related to the model Dahl analyzes under the name "Populistic democracy." Robert A. Dahl, *A Preface to Democratic Theory* (Chicago: The University of Chicago Press, 1956).

9. Joseph A. Schumpeter, *Capitalism, Socialism, and Democracy* (New York: Harper & Row,

Robert A. Dahl's term, "polyarchal democracy,"[10] insists that all that can reasonably be expected of "the people" is that they vote periodically for teams of leaders who will then run the nation's affairs. Thus, in many ways this theory retains a predemocratic, hierarchic conception of authority, with a sharp distinction between the roles of leader and led. The element of novelty is the voter's choice between competing teams, for this competition—oligopolistic though it is—encourages the teams' leaders to formulate and carry out policies designed to have the widest popular appeal. Anthony Downs has provided a logical calculus that explains the behavior of both leaders and followers in such a system.[11]

Between the restatement of the classical theory by Rousseau and the formulation of the polyarchal theory by Schumpeter another interpretation of democracy arose and came to dominate both theory and practice. This third model, which I shall call the "liberal" model, after the political movement that fostered it throughout Western Europe, stressed above all the importance of representative institutions. Public decision making was the responsibility of elected parliaments. Governments served at the will of parliamentary majorities. Liberals, even as late as John Stuart Mill, were not wholly convinced of the propriety of universal and equal suffrage, but from the theoretical point of view, the liberal model of democracy easily accommodates the notion of "one man, one vote."

The liberal model also underscored the importance of liberty, claiming that political or civil liberties—freedom of speech, of assembly, of the press, and so on—were essential to democracy. Democracy also included, in this interpretation, protection of certain basic legal rights, as embodied in the notion of the rule of law. Finally, certain advocates of the liberal model of democracy argued that limited government—the absence of state interference in socioeconomic affairs—was part of the notion of democracy.[12] The most important theorists of the liberal model, like its most influential practitioners, were found in Britain. Parts of the model can be traced to Locke, but Bentham and the two Mills honed it to its sharpest. In America the liberal model—with a few modifications—has dominated public rhetoric as well as political institutions. The most important modifications were those introduced by James Madison and embodied institu-

---

1950), p. 269. See also Walter Lippmann, *The Phantom Public* (New York: Harcourt, Brace, 1925), esp. pp. 54–62.

10. Dahl, *A Preface to Democratic Theory,* pp. 63–89. There are always dangers in appropriating terms from other authors. In this case there are some significant differences between the model of Schumpeter and that of Dahl. Nonetheless, it probably does little violence to current usage among American students of politics to term this family of models "polyarchal."

11. Anthony Downs, *An Economic Theory of Democracy* (New York: Harper & Row, 1957).

12. It may reasonably be objected that no important philosopher of liberal democracy has ever included laissez faire among the defining characteristics of democracy. However, among less philosophic adherents to this model such a connection is often made. One Tory, for example, argued that it would be "undemocratic" for the Government to interfere with private education in the English "public schools." (B75)

tionally in the separation of powers and in the system of checks and balances.[13]

These three models of democracy have concentrated on political institutions, as indeed have most theorists of democracy. Toward the end of the nineteenth century, however, another conception began to take shape, one that stressed not political or governmental arrangements, but rather social and economic justice. Democracy, this theory argued, is about equality, including social and economic equality. A real democracy would be one in which social distinctions—at least distinctions of rank—would be abolished, and economic exploitation and inequality replaced by social ownership and widely shared wealth.[14] I shall term this conception the "socioeconomic" model of democracy.

Other, fairly distinct conceptions of democracy have appeared in Western political theory over the last several centuries. In Britain, for example, the Idealists and their successors argued for a definition of democracy in terms of "reasoned discussion," and the Guild Socialists offered a distinctive variant of socioeconomic democracy.[15] But these four models—classical democracy, liberal democracy, polyarchal democracy, and socioeconomic democracy— have provided the main themes of both public discussion and philosophical analysis of the nature of democracy.

Interpretations of democracy differ in a number of ways. They fall on different sides of two closely related dichotomies: prescription versus description and ends versus means. Some conceptions of democracy, including in particular the liberal and the polyarchal, purport to be more or less accurate descriptions of the functioning of actual political systems. These conceptions focus on the methods of democracy, on how democracies work, rather than on the ideals— perhaps utopian—that inspire democrats. Other models, including the classical and the socioeconomic, are prescriptive in intent, stating values that democracy embodies rather than institutions that embody democracy. These models state goals or norms toward which democrats should aspire and strive, rather than methods for achieving democracy.

13. See Dahl's treatment of this variant of the liberal model, under the heading "Madisonian democracy" in *A Preface to Democratic Theory*. An interesting statement of the American version of liberal democracy can be found in the guidelines that the American military government formulated for the reconstruction of German democracy after World War II. These guidelines are reproduced in Herman Finer, *Theory and Practice of Modern Government*, rev. ed. (New York: Henry Holt and Co., 1949), p. 90.

14. Perhaps the best discussion and defense of this model of democracy appeared in Harold Laski's article on "Democracy" in the *Encyclopedia of the Social Sciences* (New York: The Macmillan Co., 1935), 5: 76–84. The rise of this conception was closely associated with the rise of Marxist socialism, and there has been some tendency to refer to it as the "Marxist" conception. I believe, however, that what Marx and his successors mean by "democracy" is closer to the model I have termed classical democracy. See Sartori, *Democratic Theory*, pp. 416–44, where the Marxist conception is attacked and Paul M. Sweezy, in *Democracy in a World of Tensions*, ed. Richard McKeon (Chicago: University of Chicago Press, 1951) pp. 391–424, where it is defended.

15. For a careful and concise statement of the positions of the Idealists and the Guild Socialists, including comparisons with the other models here described, see A. H. Birch, *Representative and Responsible Government* (Toronto: University of Toronto Press, 1964).

Sartori has argued that Anglo-American definitions of democracy differ from continental definitions along precisely these lines. The former—what Sartori calls the "empirical democracies"—are content with "pragmatic and instrumental" definitions. "The Anglo-Americans do not need to worry about essence; it is sufficient that they concentrate on procedures." By contrast, the "rational democracies" demand an abstract, idealized interpretation.[16] In chapter 14 I will present some evidence bearing on this argument.

There are also other variations from country to country in the interpretations given the concept of democracy. In his classic essay on "The Two Democratic Traditions," George H. Sabine characterized the Anglo-American tradition of democracy as based ultimately on the value of liberty. Tracing the origins of this tradition to the revolutionary upheavals of seventeenth-century England and to the philosopher of that era, John Locke, Sabine argued that "what the English Revolution contributed to the democratic tradition was the principle of freedom for minorities, together with a constitutional system both to protect and to regulate that freedom."[17] By contrast, according to Sabine, the continental conception of democracy derives from the French Revolution and its philosopher, Rousseau. This tradition emphasizes the value of equality. The French Revolution, argues Sabine, ". . . put at the center of modern politics the concept of equal national citizenship and as its counterpart the concept of the sovereign national state, supreme over every other form of social organization."[18] While the English stressed freedom of association as the very root of democracy, the French followed Rousseau in viewing "partial" associations of members of the body politic as insidious threats to real democracy. Sabine is careful not to overstate the contrast he draws, for the Anglo-Americans have not been blind to the imperative of political equality, nor the French deaf to the demand for political liberty. Nevertheless, as he concludes, "ideals that have been embedded for centuries in a culture are not discarded with impunity."[19]

Sabine illustrated how conceptions of democracy differ across national boundaries. Others have investigated changes within one country over time. Samuel H. Beer has cast British constitutional history in terms of five broad conceptions of the proper organization of state and society: Old Tory, Old Whig, Liberal, Radical, and Collectivist. The three most recent of these theories bear a close, if not perfect, correspondence to the models I have termed liberal democracy, classical democracy, and polyarchal democracy. Beer's work, as he says, "lights up continuities in British political culture that are fundamental

16. Sartori, *Democratic Theory,* pp. 228–46. The quoted sentence appears at p. 242.

17. George H. Sabine, "The Two Democratic Traditions," *Philosophical Review* 61 (1952): 457.

18. Ibid., p. 462.

19. Ibid., p. 474.

to an understanding of contemporary British political behavior,"[20] but it also illustrates that the ideals of a nation are not immutable. A similar analysis is offered by A. H. Birch, who provides additional detail on the development of democratic theory and practice in nineteenth-century Britain.[21] His typology, too, closely parallels the one I am using here, and he, too, stresses the impact of political theories on political practice.

A. D. Lindsay said that it was the business of philosophers to study "operative ideals."[22] But if Sartori is right that conceptions of democracy affect political behavior, then perhaps empirical students of comparative politics, too, may learn from an analysis of the operative ideals of political leaders in modern democracies. That is the task to which I now turn.

20. Samuel Beer, *British Politics in the Collectivist Age* (New York: Alfred A. Knopf, 1965), p. x.

21. Birch, *Representative and Responsible Government*.

22. A.D. Lindsay, *The Modern Democratic State* (London: Oxford University Press, 1943), p. 3.

14   How Politicians Conceive Democracy

Democracy as a Symbol

"The word 'democracy' is one of the most loosely-used words in politics. What to you personally are the essentials of a 'democracy'?" This question, asked of each respondent in both countries and followed by a series of more specific probes, provides the basis for our analysis of conceptions of democracy held by British and Italian political elites. Before looking in detail at the responses to this question, however, we should confirm that democracy is, at least in Britain and Italy, the universally acclaimed symbol that the UNESCO committee believed it to be.

British support for democracy is nearly unanimous. Except to a very few right-wing Tories "democracy" is a term with wholly favorable connotations. Even the odd exception helps in a curious way to confirm the extent of the consensus. One Tory responded hesitantly to a question on the disadvantages of a democratic system of government.

> Well . . . I don't . . . well, I mean, this is very revolutionary—what I'm going to say . . . I think that . . . that the one man, one vote system is all right, but I cannot help thinking that . . . there's something wrong in the system when a man like Lord Nuffield [late British automotive tycoon], we'll say, has as much say in the country and the working of the country as a man on relief . . . I think the weakness in a democracy really is that you get a mass of people who really take a short-term view of what their immediate benefits are, as opposed to the person who thinks and takes a long-term view for the sake of the country, and I think that's always a weakness in a democracy. (B10)

The obvious hesitation and the recognition that this is a "very revolutionary" sentiment are powerful evidence of the depth of support for democracy in Britain. (In fact, this respondent nearly confiscated the tape at the end of the interview for fear that this view would be attributed to him by name.)

On the other hand, his statement does reveal some personal dissent from the norm of democracy, and a careful reading of all the interviews uncovers a few other MPs who have similar, if limited, reservations about democracy. A total

166

of 6 percent of the British sample were so classified by the coders. This is some measure of the extent to which democracy is positively valued by British politicians.

An analysis of the Italian interviews suggests a comparable conclusion. Among the older and more conservative members of the Italian parliament there are some erstwhile supporters of the avowedly antidemocratic Fascist regime. It is, therefore, no surprise to find a slightly higher level of hostility to the concept of democracy than in Britain. Five of the Italian politicians discussed democracy in a way that suggested partial or complete antipathy to this notion, and another four evinced approval for the word "democracy," but defined it in such an idiosyncratic fashion as to indicate lack of real sympathy or at least a total lack of comprehension of the term. One older member of the neo-Fascist party, for example, denied that liberty or equality were any part of "true democracy"; those values pertain only to "the democracy of the plebes." True democracy, he argued, requires limits on liberty and the recognition of the inevitability of human inequality. (I6)

I shall consider these seemingly antidemocratic or authoritarian interpretations of democracy a bit later in this study, but this appropriation of the term by those who, on almost any of the conventional definitions, are actually antidemocratic illustrates the extent to which in Italy, too, democracy is a positive symbol. Even if these latter respondents are included, still only 11 percent of the total Italian sample can be said to oppose democracy even in part. And even the neo-Fascist just quoted revealed some ambivalence toward democracy at a later point in the interview:

> Democracy, whether it pleases you or displeases you, must be the form to which you have to orient yourself. You can discuss how it should operate. This is another problem. But the alternative between democracy and totalitarianism really isn't a live option. . . . Democracy, good or not so good, feasible or not so feasible, is always "plannable." (I6)

There are exceptions, then, but for the overwhelming majority of both British and Italian politicians, democracy is a central, positively valued political ideal. To be sure, this study also confirms earlier evidence that democracy is not nearly so salient a political concept in Britain as in Italy.[1] Italians are much more likely than the British to talk about democracy, and their conceptions are better articulated. Reflecting on the essentials of democracy, one of the most thoughtful leaders of the Italian Socialist Party suggested this explanation: "Because of our very geographical situation, because of our history, because of the difficulties which we have undergone in this country, we have been led to meditate on this problem often." (I21)

1. For other evidence on this point see Jack Dennis et al., "Political Socialization to Democratic Orientations," *Comparative Political Studies* 1 (1968): 77–9, and Ithiel de Sola Pool, *Symbols of Democracy* (Stanford, Calif.: Stanford University Press, 1952), esp. pp. 9–12.

Some of our data illustrate the relative salience of democracy and democratic ideals in the two countries. *Democrazia* and *democratico* are among the most common words in the vocabulary of an Italian politician. Four-fifths of our Italian respondents spontaneously used the term "democracy" or a congate somewhere in the interview prior to the point at which the interviewer introduced the subject. Such terms are much less common in British political discourse; only one in five of the British respondents referred to "democracy" spontaneously. A second, rather different indication of the relative salience of this concept lies in the fact that more than half of all Italian respondents—Communists and non-Communists alike—said that one of the most important differences between the major parties was differing commitment to democracy. Not surprisingly, not a single British respondent mentioned this as a distinction between the British parties. This evidence illustrates the familiar fact that democracy is a much more frequent topic of political controversy in Italy.

In summary, then, in both countries democracy is a highly valued political symbol, and especially in Italy it is a common yardstick for judging political activities. The British seldom debate about democracy (at least about political democracy). But the British discussions of the essentials of democracy leave little doubt that there, too, this is the central standard of judgment for political behavior.[2]

Democracy Defined

A rough initial impression of the variety of interpretations and connotations of this concept in the two countries can be gained from table 14.1, which summarizes responses to the central question about "essentials of democracy." The very diversity of definitions suggests caution in summarizing, but I shall highlight several of the more interesting cross-national comparisons.

"Government by the people" is, of course, the root meaning of "democracy," and responses under this general heading were very common in both countries. But this gross similarity conceals an exceedingly important difference, for Italians interpret this notion more literally. Direct popular participation is a much more frequent defining characteristic there. British explications of "government by the people" imply much less direct public involvement and control; instead such things as responsible government or public attention to political affairs are mentioned. Indeed, a number of British respondents went out of their way to *reject* direct popular participation as a defining characteristic of democracy.

2. It must be remembered that fully 20 percent of the British MPs *did* spontaneously use this term in the earlier parts of the interview. Such alternative standards of judgment as "constitutional" or "traditional" are much rarer. My impression is that for the present generation of British politicians, "democracy" is a more commonly used political standard than previously it was.

Table 14.1: Definitions of Democracy in Britain and Italy

	Percentage of respondents citing given characteristic as an "essential of democracy"	
	Britain (N=93)	*Italy* (N=83)
1. Direct popular participation in government	14	42
2. Popular sovereignty*	57	35
a) Responsibility to the electorate	(24)	(10)
b) Dialogue between government and the people	(17)	(8)
c) Other aspects of "government by the people" in a limited sense: public attention to politics; decentralized government; no secrecy in government; etc.	(28)	(21)
3. Voting*	55	36
a) Elections	(45)	(30)
b) Political equality; one man, one vote	(10)	(2)
c) Majority rule	(6)	(8)
4. Parliamentary government*	46	36
a) Representative government in general	(29)	(22)
b) Parliamentary control of the executive	(22)	(14)
5. Political liberties*	30	36
a) Freedom of speech and/or the press	(24)	(19)
b) Other political liberties	(10)	(19)
6. Limits on government power and discretion*	33	12
a) Rule of law; due process; constitutionalism	(20)	(5)
b) Other aspects of limited government: laissez faire; minority rights; religious freedom; checks and balances within government	(16)	(8)
7. Liberty (generic comment only)	6	30
8. Political competition and choice*	46	23
a) Possibility of changing the Government	(32)	(12)
b) Party competition; multiparty system	(11)	(10)
c) Other aspects of political competition	(8)	(4)
9. Socioeconomic democracy*	18	34
a) Equality of opportunity	(5)	(12)
b) Social and economic security	(1)	(12)
c) Public ownership/control of economy	(4)	(11)
d) Other aspects of socioeconomic justice: classless society; workers' control; etc.	(10)	(14)
10. Pluralism and government by discussion*	10	28
a) Social pluralism; "associationism"	(3)	(19)
b) Consultation and discussion	(8)	(8)
c) Other aspects of pluralism	(4)	(10)
11. Mature, educated, thoughtful citizenry	8	25
12. Duties, responsibilities, controls	5	20

NOTE: Up to six separate responses were coded, sometimes more than one in a single category; therefore, percentages cannot be directly summed.
*Subheadings show the responses included under this general heading.

References to specific political institutions such as elections and parliamentary government were very common in both countries, though more so in Britain. In both countries political liberties, such as free speech and freedom of association, were very popular nominees. But there is a noticeable national difference with regard to other kinds of liberties and limitations on government power and discretion. References to the rule of law, dispersed governmental powers, laissez-faire social and economic policy, and the like were common in Britain and relatively rare in Italy.

"La democrazia è la libertà," said a number of Italians; "the essence of democracy is liberty." Whenever such references were further defined, they were classified in the more specific form, but some Italians offered only the generic comment. We will see evidence later in this chapter that these references probably conceal a rather sinister conception of democracy.

One of the most interesting cross-national differences involves references to political competition and choice. Nearly half of the British respondents refer to party competition or the existence of an alternative Government—the ability to "chuck one side out and have the other lot in"—as the essential of a democracy, whereas less than a quarter of the Italians mention such characteristics. Italians are not necessarily opposed to political competition and choice, but relatively few of them see this as essential to democracy.

Aspects of social welfare and social justice are commonly mentioned in Italy among the defining characteristics of a democracy, but such references are much rarer in Britain. Similarly, Italians were more likely to define democracy in terms of social pluralism and "associationism." Much has been made in recent years, especially in Britain, of the rise of a new kind of "neocorporativist" democracy, but few of our respondents in either country defined democracy in terms of such characteristics as "consultation" or "government by negotiation."

Many Italians said that one essential of a real democracy is a mature, educated, or intelligent citizenry, while others stressed individual duties and responsibilities or the need for government limits on political behavior. As in the case of the generic references to "liberty," later evidence will suggest that these comments about duties are not always what they seem.

Much of this evidence confirms earlier speculation about differing national interpretations of democracy. Two broad contrasts are evident. In the first place, Sabine's distinction between two democratic traditions, the British and the continental, one centered on liberty and the other on equality, is clearly revealed. Both social equality (in references to social welfare and social justice) and political equality (in references to popular political participation) bulk much larger in the Italian comments than in the British. On the other hand, references to the rights of citizens and limitations on government are much more typical of Britain. Further evidence supporting Sabine's judgment will be offered later.

A second and perhaps even more striking finding confirms Sartori's observation that Anglo-American interpretations of democracy are instrumental and procedural, while the so-called "rational democracies" focus on goals and general principles. Table 14.2 summarizes this aspect of the cross-national differences, showing how each respondent's discussion was rated on a five-point scale, from an emphasis on methods and institutions to an emphasis on ideals

Table 14.2: The Focus of Conceptions of Democracy
(in percentages)

	Britain (N = 93)	Italy (N = 83)
Wholly instrumental	50	5
Mainly instrumental	31	29
Mixed	14	24
Mainly normative	5	32
Wholly normative	0	10

NOTE: Entry is percentage of each national sample rated at indicated point on scale, ranging from exclusive emphasis on methods and institutions to exclusive emphasis on ideals and values.

and values.[3] Asked about democracy, British politicians talk about Parliament and elections and party competition. Asked about democracy, Italian politicians talk about equality and justice and liberty and responsibility.

Conceptions of Democracy

In chapter 13 we considered the contrasting theories of democracy that philosophers have offered. Each of the four prominent interpretations of democracy outlined there also appears in the politicians' discussions.

The most consistent proponents of the classical theory are found among the Italian Communists.

The concept of democracy necessarily involves the concept of popular "coparticipation." This is the first thing—participation—let's say physical participation and ideal participation. As far as I'm concerned, there isn't democracy if there isn't this participation. . . . Secondly, a democracy isn't made only of forms and structures for this participation—and at all levels— but also of contents. And therefore a democratic government not only has a parliament, and elections, and local governments, but also in practice makes it possible for the population to intervene in the decisions, to accomplish certain things, and as a people to "realize themselves." (I68)

This view of democracy was not restricted to the Far Left in Italy. One moderate Christian Democrat felt that democracy

should be a system in which citizens are taken from their condition as subjects and are all helped a little to become protagonists. . . . The way in which they represent their interests should allow the direct exercise of "self-representation" in the widest measure possible. (I15)

Not all proponents of this model shared Rousseau's antipathy to pluralism and civic organizations or his rejection of representative institutions. One Communist argued that

3. The intercoder reliability of this rating was tau-beta = .53; only one out of eight respondents was placed more than one point apart by the two coders.

A democracy isn't only a society in which you vote every five years to choose a communal, or provincial, or regional council or a national deputy; rather it is that which—by means of a high level of education of the people, by means of the widest and freest forms of association and participation in the life of society—allows the citizen day by day to participate at every level of the institutions and agencies which preside over the life of the society. (I91)

A few British MPs also endorsed the classical model of democracy. One university lecturer newly arrived on the Labour backbenches made his view quite clear.

My own conception of democracy is a Rousseauesque conception, which I realize is not practicable within a mass society. We can't have, you know, direct democracy in this sense, it must be a representative system. Now given the framework of a representative system, I would nevertheless like to see our institutions so framed that individuals are in a position to have a much more effective say in the actual decision-making process than they are in a position to do now. . . . I think we might consider, for example, the direct initiative, plebiscites, which one finds in Switzerland. . . . You've also got to make people aware of the vital importance of politics. You've got, as it were, to try and create a political milieu. This is being done in the Soviet Union . . . . They are conscious of a political dimension which the average person in this country is not aware of. . . . You could say it's biased—of course it is, but nevertheless they are conscious of politics as an important dimension within their lives. (B42)

Each of these men stresses the importance of widespread public involvement in political and governmental affairs. Some betray pessimism about the practicality of direct democracy in a full sense, but they all argue that the more one can achieve effective popular participation in decision making, the closer one moves toward "real" democracy.

These classical democrats differ markedly from their colleagues who adopt the polyarchal model. Many British MPs are quite outspoken in their support of a conception of democracy as simply electoral competition between alternative teams of leaders. One miner with many years' experience in the Labour movement argued that

The essential thing I think in democracy is a General Election in which a Government is elected with power to do any damned thing it likes and if the people don't like it, they have the right to chuck them out. I don't like government by committee. I do believe—this is basic to all my thinking—that democracy means that you have an election and decide by the election to give somebody the power to do it, and for God's sake, give them the power. But at a suitable opportunity, you have the right to say, "you either have abused the power, or you haven't done what you ought to do," and chuck them out and put somebody else in. (B108)

Another, much younger Labourite phrased a similar notion of democracy in more instrumental or institutional terms.

The essentials of a democracy? Well, the right of an opposition to organize against the government, and to have free expression of its views . . . ; election at fixed terms, or, you know, within a certain period of time; and the basic choice being presented to the people at those elections in order to turn the government out. (B71)

One older, rather aristocratic Member answered my question tangentially.

Well, I can't think of any other practicable method. I mean, I personally consider myself capable of coming to decisions without having to fight an election once every four or five years, but on the other hand, the people must be allowed to feel that they can exercise some control, even if it's only the control of chucking somebody out that they don't like. [*So what makes a government democratic or undemocratic?*] Oh, the fact that every now and again they've got to go to the country and ask for a renewal or vote of confidence. (B50)

This view of democracy was common on both sides of the House. One well-read Conservative referred explicitly to Schumpeter's definition, calling it "one of the most perceptive of all time."

Although this interpretation of democracy is less frequent in Italy, there too some respondents offered definitions that fit the polyarchal model. One Italian centrist, for example, said

Democracy is for me the possibility that there exists a majority which governs and a minority which is in opposition, and the possibility therefore that this minority can tomorrow become the majority. And this is guaranteed by free elections, the secrecy of the ballot, by freedom of the press. These are some very important elements, but all of them elements, let's say, as a means toward this possibility I spoke of. (I83)

In summary, then, a number of respondents in each country hold classical or polyarchal conceptions of democracy. In terms of the defining characteristics enumerated in table 14.1, classical democrats emphasize "popular participation and involvement in government" and polyarchal democrats stress "political competition and choice." Of course, there is no reason why a given individual should hold only a single model of democracy, and there was no constraint in the interview to prevent a respondent from offering a wide variety of "essential characteristics." However, some statistical evidence suggests that, in empirical terms, these first two models tend to be self-sufficient and mutually exclusive.

The definitional components of these models were negatively correlated not only to each other, but also to other commonly offered defining characteristics. People who said that an essential of democracy was "popular participation" tended not to say that "limited government" or "political competition" or "liberty in general" were also essentials. Similarly, people who said that "political competition" was an essential tended not to add "popular participation" or "parliamentary government" or "social democracy" or "civic duties." (By way of contrast, "elections," for example, as a defining characteristic tended to be virtually uncorrelated with any other characteristic. Elections are not the basis of any distinctive conception of democracy.)

Moreover, both "popular participation" and "political competition" tended to appear in shorter, simpler definitions. Respondents who gave these as essentials of democracy tended to give *only* them. By contrast, such essentials as "elections" or "representative government" tended to appear in relatively longer lists; that is, respondents who offered them as defining characteristics tended to offer other characteristics as well. Thus, the classical and polyarchal conceptions of democracy seem to be self-sufficient. Some of our respondents are, in other words, clear and distinct polyarchal democrats and others are clear and distinct classical democrats.

It is also possible to find socioeconomic democrats in our samples, although few define democracy solely in these terms. Some of the clearest statements of this model came from members of the Labour Party, even though it is not a very common model in Britain. One leading Labour backbencher argued that

I would say that what you want, what most people who believe in democracy are really aiming at, is a society in which exploitation of one group by another or one class by another, and in which secrecy—which is just one variation of exploitation in one sense—privilege, which is another—this kind of thing, in which they are eliminated. If you've got a society in which all the individuals and all the groups into which they form themselves feel equal, if they don't feel maltreated, . . . if you get this kind of thing removed, then I think you've got what most people are aiming at, democracy. A thing which provides opportunity. (B55)

A colleague of his offered a similar answer, which also illustrated the point that the socioeconomic model often coexists with more specifically political models.

Well, the essentials to me is that . . . in a democracy, one's own ability, no matter how young or how far it goes, is the thing that matters, where the ability to do the job, or the ability to do a certain profession, or the ability to learn or things of this nature, are the things that matter and are the things that matter most. Traditions I have no time for, as you can say; I would do away with all these more or less in one clean sweep. But as far as democracy in this country is concerned, if we can get to a system like this, . . . I think everything else—a democracy as we know, freedom of speech, this, that, and the other—will just go on. (B15)

For both these men, democracy involves more than merely political or governmental arrangements. But their emphasis on equality of opportunity differs from the more explicitly socialist conceptions often offered in Italy. One older Communist, for example, attacked "formalistic" conceptions of democracy, and argued that

True democracy should require the disappearance of the differences of social and economic classes. True democracy is that which—how shall I put it—can represent the effective, if not the total majority. A society without classes, this is the socialist ideal. . . . As long as there are groups or classes in society which aim to realize profit—earnings on earnings—at the expense of another part of the society, you will never have a true democracy. (I42)

One of his colleagues expanded on this notion that democracy involves socioeconomic rights.

I mean a real democracy, on the economic plane, which means recognition of the rights of the workers, of the citizens—to work, to social assistance, to education, to have a decent house, to live in a city which isn't prey to speculators, to buy products which aren't adulterated, a whole series of things. (I32)

Several Italians all along the political spectrum distinguished between "substantive" and merely "formal" rights. One Christian Democrat, for example, proposed that

The essential element is the liberty of the citizen, and the possibility that the citizen can develop his own qualities. I'm speaking above all of moral and intellectual qualities, with complete liberty, without constrictions which violate his will. Naturally, from a moral point of view this must have its counterpart in a social structure which allows the citizen not to face the problem of the little piece of bread for himself and his children, because I can't give liberty to the citizen if I don't first of all enable him to live. This is undeniably a basic element. (I16)

A few Italians of the Left defined democracy explicitly in terms of public ownership of economic enterprises.

[Democracy is] the accentuation of a direct and permanent relationship between the citizen and the authorities. [It is also] the accentuation of the effective capacity of public agencies to be determinant, not merely at the level of political affairs . . . but also at the level of political economy. Hence, the accentuation of the effective capacity on the part of the leading public organs to exert power over all the spheres of economic and social life. (I103)

This last discussion also illustrates that in Italy, as in Britain, social conceptions of democracy were very often linked to more specifically political conceptions. Unlike references to "popular participation" or "political competition," references to "socioeconomic democracy" tended not to stand alone. Adherents to the socioeconomic model tended not to see the political aspects of democracy in polyarchal terms. Rather, there was some tendency in both countries—stronger in Britain—for socioeconomic democrats to adopt classical perspectives, too. In addition, there were scattered references by socioeconomic democrats to such political characteristics as civil liberties, elections, or parliamentary government.

Examples of the last of the four theoretical models, liberal democracy, can also be found among our respondents. One young British Conservative phrased a liberal conception primarily in institutional terms.

Well, my conception of democracy [is] parliamentary democracy. There is participation of the electorate in government through free elections, and through voting freely their representatives to Parliament; with a legal system which is independent and which is respected and which can operate independently of the government; where you have freedom of expression, and to a certain extent the freedom of choice. (B109)

An older Labour MP, a barrister, stressed a different aspect of the liberal model, but seemed to have most of the same central elements in mind.

As little interference with individual liberty as possible—I would have thought that was the essential, when you get down to bedrock. Now it's true we talk about democracy—representing all the interests, rights of a minority, freedom of speech, and all the rest of it, but when you get down to bedrock, wouldn't you think that that's your most important point? As little interference with the rights of the individual, the freedom of the individual, as is compatible with good government. (B84)

A young Tory from Scotland also stressed laissez faire, but added to this another important element of the total model.

My belief is, and this is particularly in the economic sphere, I believe that a great many of the decisions must be left to the private person, whether it's in terms of the private individual or whether it's the board of directors in a firm. . . . In the political sphere, as I see it, the danger at the present time is the growth of the power of the civil service and of the minister, and the declining control of Parliament. . . . I think it's absolutely essential . . . to try and find better ways of controlling the power of the minister and of the executive generally. I think this [power of the parliament to control the executive] is the absolute number one essential of democracy. (B12)

A number of Italians, too, expressed fairly clearly most of the central features of the liberal model.

The central features of a true democracy for me are, above all, liberty—liberty of the press, liberty of action, liberty of discussion. These are the fundamental presuppositions of democracy, as far as I am concerned. Democracy also implies that the people, through their representatives, can have the possibility of expressing their problems with great clarity and with decisiveness. (I14)

The conservative Christian Democrat just quoted was joined by a right-wing Socialist, who added a note of laissez faire to the tune.

The essential elements of a democracy? First of all, the concrete possibility of a direct and secret popular expression—hence, free, secret elections. This, then, implies freedom of expression. But beyond these fundamental constitutional pilasters, I believe that for a true expression of democracy, this liberty must be transferred on the economic plane, too; hence free enterprise also on the economic plane. (I67)

The incidence of the liberal model, however, was rather different from that of the other three models. The central themes in the liberal model, as described in the traditional literature, are parliamentary government, limited or constitutional government, and civil or political liberties. As table 14.1 has already revealed, each of these individual themes appeared frequently among the definitions of democracy given by the respondents. Indeed, considered separately, these were among the most common defining characteristics.

However, the term "liberal model" assumes that these elements together form a single syndrome. Unfortunately, in neither country does this seem to be the case. Indeed, references to parliamentary government were *negatively* correlated with references to the two "libertarian" elements, political liberties and limited government, and these latter two elements were essentially uncorrelated with each other.[4]

The explanation for this state of affairs seems to lie in the fact that the liberal model of democracy as articulated in the nineteenth century has become so widely diffused in the political cultures of both Britain and Italy that many people have come to share parts of the model, even though they do not support it in its entirety. For example, most of the individual elements that (theoretically) compose the liberal model tend to appear in longer lists of defining characteristics. That is, these elements tend to appear only in the company of other defining characteristics, rather than standing alone. (This generalization is not, however, true for references to "limited government," which seems in that sense to be the one element from the original model that has *not* become widely diffused.)

4. In this generalization I have grouped together a number of different kinds of references, as perusal of table 14.1 will reveal. However, the generalization offered in the text remains valid no matter how one narrows or redefines the three categories of "parliamentary government," "political liberties," and "limited government."

Unlike the basic elements of classical and polyarchal conceptions of democracy, then, the basic elements of the liberal model do not in general form a clear and distinct unit. In each country a significant number of respondents linked several of the individual elements in such a way that it is natural to describe these politicians as adherents to the liberal model of democracy. Nevertheless, in the discussion that follows, one must keep in mind that the liberal model is the least cohesive and discrete of all the models studied.

After noting the defining characteristics offered by each respondent, the coders rated on a three-point scale the extent to which each of the four models appeared in the respondent's discussion. A given model could be rated "prominent in the discussion of democracy," "present in the discussion but not prominent," or "not present in the discussion."[5] The models were not conceived as necessarily mutually exclusive or collectively exhaustive interpretations of democracy. Hence, a respondent could receive positive ratings on more than one model; conversely, he could receive negative ratings on all.

Empirically, however, the models do tend to be mutually exclusive. Relatively few respondents offered more than one model "prominently"—10 percent of the British and 16 percent of the Italians. On the other hand, these four models far from exhaust the conceptions of democracy found in our sample; 39 percent of the British and 34 percent of the Italians displayed none of the four "prominently."[6] Let us consider for a moment these respondents who were "unclassifiable."

The natural question to ask about these respondents is "If they don't interpret 'democracy' in either classical or liberal or polyarchal or socioeconomic terms, how do they conceive of it?" Early in the analysis of these residual respondents, one important subgroup attracted attention. This subgroup was composed of those respondents, especially Italians, who defined democracy in terms of "duties" and "controls." One conservative Italian, for example, answered my question about the essentials of democracy in this way:

Well, it seems to me you need the capacity for self-criticism and self-control. . . . Every people has its own psychological and cultural level. Now democracy withers or malfunctions if the government—if the staff of governors—doesn't have an exact perception of the cultural and psychological level of the people. [*Is there some way in which Italy could be more democratic*

5. The intercoder reliability coefficient (tau-beta) for these judgments is as follows, with the percentage ranked at opposite ends of each three-point scale given in parentheses: classical democracy, .60 (3 percent); liberal democracy, .48 (5 percent); polyarchal democracy, .65 (3 percent); socioeconomic democracy, .70 (2 percent). The lower reliability of the judgments regarding the liberal model reflects the empirical diffuseness of this model, as discussed in the text. Overall, these reliabilities are quite high; more than 70 percent of all judgments were made identically by the two coders.

6. On the other hand, nearly all our respondents share to *some* extent one or more of these four models; all but one of the Britons and two of the Italians mentioned some elements of at least one of the models.

than it is today?] Yes, I would say democracy, not in the sense of liberty—because we already have too much of that, liberty which isn't real liberty, but license—but in the sense of training for democracy. For training in democracy I maintain that you need a little bit of force [*forza*]. [*In what sense?*] A little bit of force in order to make certain laws obeyed, to impose certain . . . Look, democracy must not, out of fear of being undemocratic, neglect to exert authority, the authority which the people need in order to become a litle more mature. (I34)

Another right-wing member of the Christian Democratic party offered a similar analysis of democracy.

Democracy, for me, means the conscience of the citizens, self-control. That is, I, a citizen, must be aware of my duties and of my rights, of that which is coming to me and of that which is coming to the other citizens, and I must limit my liberty so that it doesn't damage the liberty of others. And then, too, democracy is patience, above all, patience. It all rests on maturation in a civic sense, self-control, conscience. (I99)

A conservative Christian Democratic minister illustrates clearly the paternalism inherent in such views.

The essential elements of a true democracy, to my mind, are determined by the equilibrium between rights and duties which must be established in the conscience of the citizens and of the government which administers the citizens. Because the excessively generous use of the word "democracy" doesn't alert some people that from "democracy" one passes quite easily to "demagogy." And demagogy means an entirely different thing. It means indulging the people, the electorate, the members of the parties, indulging the workers in your ministry, giving in to their uncontrolled wishes, without imposing the criterion of responsibility and hence of duty. (I44)

The contrast that a number of these Italians drew between liberty and license also appeared in the discussions of a few right-wing British MPs.

I think [democracy] can be well-summarized by something which Monty once said—that liberty, true liberty, is not the freedom to do just as you like, but freedom to do the right thing. And it's that which has got lost sight of. (B49)

This conception of democracy, on further analysis, turns out to have all the characteristics of a distinctive model. "Duties," when offered as a defining characteristic of democracy, tends to stand alone. Moreover, this element—like the basic elements of the classical and polyarchal models—tends to be negatively correlated with the other main defining characteristics. Those who defined democracy in terms of duties and controls tended not to refer to such things as parliamentary government, popular participation, political competition, or socioeconomic justice and welfare. (The one exception to this pattern involves those mysterious generic references to "liberty" we noted earlier. Those who defined democracy in terms of duties and controls tended also to refer to "liberty," without specifying further what "liberty" meant to them. Evidence from other parts of the interviews confirms that those Italian respondents who gave only this generic reference to *libertà* are in fact relatively hostile to orthodox democratic norms and ideals.)

Since those who defined democracy in terms of duties and controls seem to be operating with a fairly consistent and distinct conception, we can simply add this to our list of models. Something of the intellectual heritage of this conception of democracy, at least in Italy, is captured by Benito Mussolini's definition of Fascism as "organized, centralized, authoritarian democracy."[7] I will, therefore, borrow the term "authoritarian democracy" to refer to this model.

Operationally, this model differs from the other four, since its existence was inferred only after the coding had been completed. Respondents who had offered "duties and controls" as a defining characteristic of democracy *and* who had been rated "prominent" on none of the four earlier models were rated "prominent" on authoritarian democracy. Those who referred to "duties or controls," but whose discussions displayed one of the other four models "prominently" were rated as "present" on authoritarian democracy. Subsequent analysis suggested that this procedure erred, if at all, on the conservative side, by assigning to the "present" category of the authoritarian democracy model respondents for whom that model was probably quite central.

Of course, a number of orthodox philosophers of democracy have stressed the importance of citizen self-discipline, and the mere mention of this factor would not impugn the democratic faith of our authoritarian democrats. But a variety of evidence presented below will show that they have a quite distinct view of the proper balance between liberty and order. For many, there can be little doubt that their reference to "duties" concealed a conception of democracy that Mussolini would have found congenial.

The classification of these additional respondents as authoritarian democrats reduces the number of respondents who evince no clear model of democracy. However, even then, 37 percent of the British and 18 percent of the Italians display none of the five basic models "prominently." Attempts to uncover additional novel models of democracy were fruitless. Further analysis, however, afforded a somewhat more precise profile of these residual respondents. In both Britain and Italy their definitions tended to be shorter and more "instrumental" or "descriptive" than those of the respondents who gave one of the five basic models. In Britain—where these "misfits" (in a statistical sense) were more common—they were concentrated among the older, less-educated Members. All this suggests that in Britain these remaining respondents are simply less

---

7. *The Doctrine of Fascism* (1932), as reproduced in *The Social and Political Doctrines of Contemporary Europe* ed. Michael Oakeshott (New York: Cambridge University Press, 1949), p. 173.

sophisticated and less able to formulate the kinds of abstractions that would have enabled the coders to classify their conceptions of democracy.

Among the less-educated Italians the rate of "unclassified" conceptions is much lower—about one in eight among those without university education, as contrasted with about five in eight among the less-educated British respondents. For these Italians—mainly Communists and Socialists—Marxist ideology and party indoctrination probably serve the same purpose as university education in providing relatively sophisticated conceptions of democracy. In Britain there seems, from this point of view, no substitute for a university education. The lower salience of democracy in British politics is probably also part of the explanation for the greater difficulty that some British politicians seem to have in formulating an abstract conception of democracy.

A few of these "unclassified" respondents may have had genuinely idiosyncratic or at least unusual interpretations of democracy. For example, in both countries, respondents who defined democracy in terms of social pluralism tended to fall into this "unclassified" category. However, so few respondents in all proposed that conception that for the purposes of further analysis they must be ignored.

Another example of an attitude toward democracy that failed entirely to fit our schema was offered by one Tory.

Well, I'm not particularly interested in democracy in the abstract sense, because after all, we are a mixed constitution—we still have an hereditary element in the House of Lords; and we still have the monarchy, although the political activities of the monarchy are very limited. But we are not supposed to be democratic; we are supposed to admit of a share in legislation of a house which is still to a great extent hereditary. So if you're a constitutionalist in this country, you're not a democrat in the strict sense of the word. . . . I'm interested in our system of constitutional monarchy, much more than in some demo . . . I mean, if you'd like to say we are a monarchical democracy, I'm quite happy with it. (B90)

Such attitudes as this persist among a few quite sophisticated British politicians, but they are vanishingly rare. In sum, then, we do no great injustice to this group of "unclassified" respondents if we think of them collectively as the unsophisticated and the idiosyncratic. Chapter 15 will provide a more detailed analysis of the five modal conceptions of democracy.

15 Britain and Italy:
Contrasting Operative Ideals

Interpreting Democracy

Authoritarian democracy, polyarchal democracy, liberal democracy, classical democracy, and socioeconomic democracy—these are the models of democracy used by most British and Italian politicians. The order in which I have listed them is not casual, for the models do not have a purely random relationship to each other. If classical democracy can be characterized as "government by the people," then liberal democracy is "government by parliament," and polyarchal democracy is "government by party leaders." Authoritarian democracy may be seen as yet another step toward the accentuation of the role of political leaders and diminution of the role of followers. There is here, in other words, a continuum from political egalitarianism to political elitism. (Socioeconomic democracy is the only one of these models that does not fit clearly on this putative dimension, because it is based on a relatively nonpolitical conception of democracy.) There is more to this dimension than rhetorical convenience.

I have earlier pointed to the relatively low overlap among these five basic models.[1] In general, overlap is most marked between models which are adjacent to one another on the egalitarianism-elitism dimension. Overlap between polyarchal and classical conceptions of democracy is fairly rare, whereas overlap between polyarchal and liberal or between classical and liberal conceptions is less rare. There is, in other words, a scalar quality to these models. (Overlap between the socioeconomic and classical conceptions is relatively high, but this is a special case, because the socioeconomic model does not fit clearly on the underlying dimension.)

The first question to ask about these conceptions of democracy concerns

1. "Overlap" here means merely that a respondent was given a positive score ("prominent" or "present") on more than one model. Whether this is because he actually holds two distinct images of democracy or rather because his own particular conception "falls between" the two standard models is irrelevant at the moment. Only one British respondent in ten and fewer than one Italian in six seem to operate with more than one "prominent" model. On the other hand, two-thirds of the Italians and three-fifths of the British have at least two models "present" in their discussion.

their incidence in the two countries. Figure 15.1 presents the relevant data in graphic form. The solid part of each bar represents the relative frequency with which each model appeared "prominently"; the clear part refers to instances in which elements of the model were "present, but not prominent." A number of striking conclusions can be drawn from this chart.

In Britain polyarchal and liberal models are by far the most frequent. Authoritarian democrats are quite rare and classical and socioeconomic democrats are not much more common. These conclusions hold whether one considers only instances in which a given model was "prominent" or all instances in which elements of the model were "present." Of all British politicians, 97 percent show some signs of either the polyarchal or the liberal model (or both), and 53 percent display one (or both) of these two models prominently. On the other hand, 87 percent of all the British respondents display none of the other three models "prominently" and 66 percent make no reference to any of the other three models. Thus, there is in Britain a fairly clear national consensus in favor of the polyarchal and liberal interpretations of democracy and an even stronger consensus against any of the other three conceptions considered here.

In Italy, by contrast, the most common model is classical democracy. As in Britain, elements of the liberal model are given quite frequently, but the model as a whole is less common. The next most frequently mentioned model is socioeconomic democracy, but there are also significant numbers of authoritarian democrats and (to a lesser extent) polyarchal democrats.

In general there is greater dispersion across the variety of models in Italy than in Britain. More significantly, while the British respondents fall mostly into two categories adjacent on our underlying continuum from authoritarian through classical democracy, large numbers of Italians endorse models at the poles of this continuum. Fifty-two percent of all Italians are either authoritarian democrats or classical democrats; the figure for Britain is 10 percent. This analysis reveals the strikingly greater dissensus on the meaning of democracy in Italy than in Britain. This is the other face of the controverted and salient status of "democracy" in Italy that we noted earlier. Italians use the word more and agree less what it means.

More light can be thrown on this issue by examining the extent of cross-party dissensus on the meaning of democracy. Table 15.1 presents the frequency of each of the five basic models among members of the major party groupings in the two countries. The British data reveal some cross-party disagreement about classical and socioeconomic democracy. These models are virtually unknown among Conservatives, while they are upheld by a small but significant minority of Labour MPs. Similarly, there is some mild cross-party dissent over the liberal model, since it is more common among Conservatives. Both polyarchal democrats and authoritarian democrats are found in virtually identical proportions in the two parties. Thus, there is some interparty disagreement in Britain about the meaning of democracy, but intraparty disagreement is almost as high.

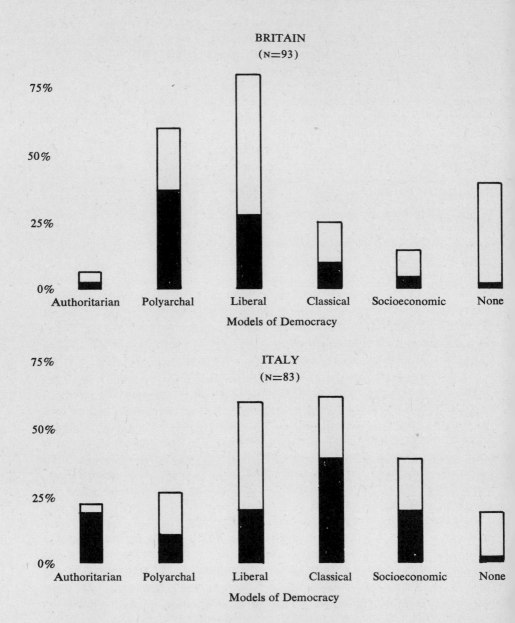

Figure 15.1: Models of Democracy in Britain and Italy
    Solid bar = percentage of sample rated "prominent" on model. For bar marked "None," "prominent" means that none of the other models was rated even "present."
    Clear bar = percentage of sample rated "present" on model. For bar marked "None," "present" means that none of the other models was rated "prominent."

Table 15.1: Interpretations of Democracy, by Party Affiliation
(in percentages)

| | Model of Democracy | | | | | | | | | |
| | Authoritarian | | Polyarchal | | Liberal | | Classical | | Socioeconomic | |
Party	Prom.	Ab.	Prom.	Ab.	Prom.	Ab.	Prom.	Ab.	Prom.	Ab.
Labour (N=54)	2	93	33	43	18	29	11	65	6	78
Conservative (N=37)	3	97	38	43	38	16	0	97	0	97
Communist (N=20)	0	100	0	85	20	65	75	5	40	30
PSIUP (N=4)	0	100	0	100	0	75	75	0	25	75
Socialist (N=14)	14	71	7	93	21	29	36	43	14	64
Christian Democratic (N=33)	27	70	9	70	18	33	15	58	12	73
Liberal (N=5)	0	100	60	20	20	20	20	40	0	100
Other Rightist (N=5)	40	40	20	60	20	40	0	60	0	60

NOTES: Prom. = prominent; Ab. = absent. Entry is percentage of each party that received the indicated score on the indicated model of democracy.

Interparty differences in Italy, by contrast, are striking.[2] Most Communists and most members of the left-wing Socialist Party of Proletarian Unity (PSIUP) are clear classical democrats, and virtually no one in these parties is without some trace of this model. Members of the centrist parties and especially members of those of the Right are much less likely to offer elements of classical democracy. (To keep the cross-national differences in perspective, however, it must be noted that along the whole spectrum of Italian parties, classical democracy is much more commonly endorsed than in either British party.) On the other hand, the bulk of Italian centrists and rightists endorse at least elements of the liberal model, while most members of the Far Left show no tendency to endorse this model at all. The polyarchal model is still more narrowly confined in partyterms, at least in our sample. Members of the Italian Liberal Party seem very open to this model, while members of the other parties are quite unlikely to suggest it. Authoritarian democrats are concentrated in the Christian Democratic Party, in parties of the Extreme Right, and to some extent in the Socialist Party; in the other parties there are none.[3] Finally socioeconomic democrats are most common among the Communists. They are relatively rare among the Socialists

2. Naturally, with a total sample of 83 the numbers of respondents from the individual Italian parties are quite small, and hence the probability of sampling error is relatively high. On the other hand, the differences shown in table 15.1 are so marked—and so intelligible—that they can hardly be written off as the products of chance.

3. Although it is not shown in table 15.1, the Demochristian authoritarian democrats are to be found primarily within that party's right wing.

and Christian Democrats and virtually unknown in the parties further to the right.[4]

The analysis shown in table 15.1 sharpens still further the contrast between Britain and Italy. Not only are the Italians less agreed among themselves on the proper interpretation of democracy, but their disagreements are more likely to fall along party lines. A British politician is likely to find nearly as much support for his conception of democracy among his opponents as among his party colleagues. The Italian politician, by contrast, is apt to find that most of his party comrades share his interpretation of democracy, but that few of his opponents are sympathetic toward it. Although the consequences of this phenomenon will be discussed in chapter 18, it is already clear why democracy is much more controversial in Italy than in Britain. It is not that some parties favor democracy and some oppose it. Rather, all are "prodemocratic" by their own interpretation, yet they cannot agree what that means, making the debate all the more confused and embittered.

More Democracy?

Locke, Mills, and Schumpeter versus Rousseau, Marx, and Mussolini—this is the contrast between Britain and Italy.[5] Different intellectual and political traditions have led to strikingly different interpretations of the democratic ideal. The focus of this study is, however, operative ideals. If these interviews are tapping more than mere verbiage, these democratic ideals must have a dynamic, impelling quality. How do these politicians apply their ideals to contemporary realities?

After each discussion of the essentials of democracy, the respondent was asked, "Are there any ways in which this country could or should be more democratic than it is today? How is that?" Table 15.2 shows how respondents in each national sample replied. Clearly, the Italians are much less satisfied with the state of democracy in their country. Only one Italian in nine saw no

---

4. It is striking that disagreements over the proper interpretation of democracy tended to divide the Socialists in my sample along precisely the lines of the 1947 schism, which had been patched up at the time of these interviews, but which was to reemerge two years later. None of the former members of the right-wing Italian Social Democratic Party (PSDI) showed any support for the classical model of democracy, while eight of the ten former members of the more progressive Italian Socialist Party (PSI) favored this model. On the other hand, half of the right-wing Socialists were clearly liberal democrats, while only one in ten of the left-wingers gave that interpretation of democracy. On measures to be introduced in chapter 16 the members of the PSDI are markedly less egalitarian. (They also show higher scores on the Partisan Hostility Index and lower scores on the Ideological Style Index.) On all these variables the PSDI members are closer to the Liberals or Christian Democrats than to their erstwhile party comrades. Despite the tiny samples, all these differences reach or approach statistical significance, and one cannot avoid speculating that our findings strike close to the heart of the explanation for the schism.

5. The greatest distortion in this formula is the slighting of the liberal element in Italian conceptions of democracy.

Table 15.2: Desire for More Democracy in Britain and Italy
(in percentages)

QUESTION: "Is there some way this country could or should be more democratic than it is now?"

The respondent wants:	Britain (N=91)	Italy (N=82)
Major change*	2	28
Important change	19	44
Modest change	43	17
No change	32	5
Less democracy than at present	4	6

*He answers the question before it is asked.

significant way in which Italy should be more democratic, and three-quarters thought there were important improvements to be made. Indeed, more than one-quarter of the Italians felt so strongly about democratization that they answered the question before it was asked. By contrast, three times as many British respondents were wholly satisfied and only one-third as many demanded important changes.

It is not surprising that the Italian politicians are less satisfied with the state of democracy in their country than are the British. Democracy in Italy obviously does not yet function as smoothly as it does in Britain. More significantly, responses to this question are related to the respondent's conception of democracy. Figure 15.2 shows that in each country changes were most insistently demanded by classical democrats, closely followed in each case by those endorsing the socioeconomic model. Liberal democrats and polyarchal democrats in each country are considerably more satisfied with the status quo, and the authoritarian democrats are still less eager for more democracy. In fact—although it does not appear in figure 15.2—more than a third of the Italian authoritarian democrats indicated that there is perhaps too much democracy in Italy already! (Figure 15.2 and this discussion of it are based only on respondents rated "prominent" on a given model, but a similar pattern emerges if we include respondents rated "present" on each model.)

Thus, as we would expect theoretically, descriptive models of democracy, such as the liberal and the polyarchal, are linked to considerable satisfaction about contemporary democracy, whereas prescriptive models, such as the socioeconomic and the classical, are associated with discontent about current political and social institutions. Here, too, is the first of a series of confirmations that (at least in Italy) the authoritarian democrats' verbal attachment to democracy masks considerable disaffection from the realities of democracy.

To understand better the perspectives of those who want more democracy, one must turn to table 15.3, which summarizes responses to the follow-up query about suggested reforms. Since we have already seen that most British politicians are relatively satisfied with the state of democracy in their country, the fact in

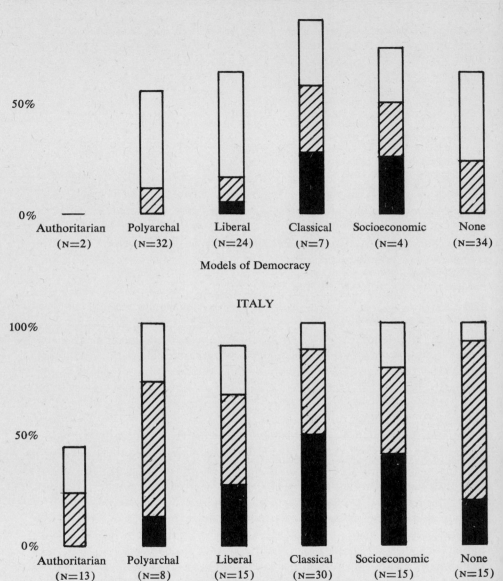

Figure 15.2: Models of Democracy and Demands for More Democracy
Solid bar = percentage demanding major change.
Hatched bar = percentage demanding important change.
Clear bar = percentage demanding modest change.
All data based on those using given model "prominently."

Table 15.3: Proposed Democratic Reforms in Britain and Italy

	Percentage of respondents proposing given reform as means to greater democracy	
	Britain (N = 91)	Italy (N = 82)
1. More public participation and/or control*	46	50
a) More direct participation in government	(9)	(26)
b) More participation in local government only	(13)	(1)
c) More public interest in politics	(14)	(9)
d) More responsive government	(15)	(7)
e) Other: initiative; referendum; participation in party activities; etc.	(4)	(13)
2. Socioeconomic reforms*	22	35
a) Educational reforms	(5)	(11)
b) End poverty; increase economic security	–	(15)
c) Other: workers' control; more public ownership/ control of economy; greater equality of respect; etc.	(18)	(20)
3. Less arbitrary government interference	7	4
4. Decentralization or devolution of government	14	20
5. More powerful Parliament or MP	25	13
6. Reform of electoral system	10	2
7. Miscellaneous government reforms: reform local government; reform upper chamber; more efficient bureaucracy; etc.	10	7
8. Changes in party politics*	–	23
a) Change party system; more party turnover in power	–	(11)
b) Reduce power of some particular party	–	(12)
9. More pluralism; more "associationism"	1	12
10. More mature, responsible, capable citizenry	4	27
11. Other miscellaneous reforms: more dispersed press ownership; less corruption; etc.	10	15

NOTE: Up to three separate responses were coded, sometimes more than one in a single category; therefore, percentages cannot be directly summed.
*Subheadings show the responses included under this general heading.

table 15.3 that Italians are more represented in nearly every category of reform is not unexpected. The only important exception is that the British are more concerned about the power of the parliament, a fact that is consonant with the relatively greater salience of the liberal model of democracy in Britain. About half of each national sample suggest that democracy would be served by greater public participation in or control over the affairs of government. This gross similarity, however, hides the fact that the reforms proposed by the Italians call for a more active public, consistent with the greater popularity in Italy of the classical model of democracy.

In three specific areas the Italians show more concern than the British. First, half again as many Italians as Britons propose socioeconomic reforms. Secondly, various changes in party politics are proposed by a quarter of the Italians, but by none of the Britons. Some Italians propose changes in the party system to provide, for example, more opportunity for parties to alternate in power; others argue that greater democracy will be reached only through a reduction in the power of some particular party, generally either the Communist Party (PCI) or the Christian Democratic party (DC). "More democracy?" said an older Communist. "That's easy—cut off the claws of the DC." (I75)

The third suggestion made more frequently by the Italians than by the British is a demand for a more mature, responsible citizenry. Detailed analysis confirms that this proposal comes predominantly from the authoritarian democrats. Logically, of course, this comment might have been made by classical democrats in the context of a demand for more widespread involvement of the citizens in government, but in fact these two proposals were rarely linked. These demands for "maturity," one suspects, betray an attitude toward the mass public that is more than slightly paternalistic.

These reforms are associated in the manner one would expect with the various conceptions of democracy. Suggestions for greater public participation came from classical democrats, those for more parliamentary power from liberal democrats, those for social and economic reforms from socioeconomic democrats, and those for reforms in the Italian party system from the relatively few Italian polyarchal democrats. When authoritarian democrats made any suggestions at all for increased democracy, these were primarily demands for greater civic maturity and responsibility.[6]

Procedural Consensus in Britain and Italy

So far in this chapter I have been talking about some rather basic philosophical differences in political values. I want now to move closer to the everyday world of our politicians and consider their evaluations of the existing political institutions in their respective countries.

Students of British political culture have often alleged that political consensus is so high that a rigid procedural conservatism results. James B. Christoph argues that "whereas they may display flexibility and a willingness to bargain over the content of public policy, the British often show an unbending dogmatism in regard to the process by which policy is established."[7] Harry Eckstein says simply that the British "behave like ideologists in regard to rules and like

6. This coincidence between models of democracy and specific proposals for reform suggests the extent to which these discussions of democracy were coherent, but it is not, strictly speaking, independent confirmation of the models themselves, since the coders knew what reforms had been proposed by a respondent when they were assessing his general model of democracy. Independent evidence of the differential conative impact of these models comes from responses to a later question about desires for the future. Twice as many classical democrats as authoritarian democrats express a wish for a more democratic political system; liberal and polyarchal democrats fall in between. The same pattern occurs in each country.

7. James B. Christoph, "Consensus and Cleavage in British Political Ideology," *American Political Science Review* 59 (1965): 636.

pragmatists in regard to policies."[8] Although these generalizations may have been true in the past and may continue to be true for some sections of the political elite, in the spring of 1967 a majority of British MPs were surprisingly ready to entertain ideas of reform in the system of government.[9]

Two questions in the interview touched on this issue. One was the query about "ways in which Britain could or should be more democratic." In another section of the interview I asked some respondents for a fairly detailed description of the pattern of power in British politics as they saw it, involving the Government, the civil service, Parliament, outside groups and organizations, and so on. After this discussion I asked, "Do you think this is all as it should be, or do you think there are any major changes needed in this pattern of influence and power?" The general shape of answers to these two questions was quite similar.

Eagerness for governmental reform in Britain is not universal, of course. The Tory quoted here epitomizes the procedural conservatism often attributed to all British politicians:

> Well, I'm not going to say the present system's perfect, and I know an awful lot of suggestions that have been made, but I don't think many of them are worth very much. I think really they'd create more difficulties than they would solve. Oh, there are little things that you could change, but on the whole I think it's pretty good. (B30)

Even this statement could hardly be described as procedural "dogmatism." But many other Members could easily think of ways in which they would like British politics to be more democratic and of changes they would like to see in the existing pattern of power. Indeed, two-thirds of the British sample—majorities in each party—wanted changes that went beyond mere improvements in institutional efficiency to affect influence relations.[10]

By far the most common suggestion was for increased parliamentary power in policy making. It was mentioned by more than half the respondents. In 1966 two new specialist committees with the power to question civil servants had been established as an experiment in parliamentary reform, and this innovation found warm welcome among the Members with whom I spoke. Other common suggestions for reform included decentralization and the creation of a more responsive bureaucracy.

8. Harry Eckstein, *Division and Cohesion in Democracy* (Princeton, N.J.: Princeton University Press, 1966), p. 265.

9. I found a similar openness to institutional reform among a sample of British civil servants interviewed at this same time. For further evidence of reformism among Members of the Parliament elected in 1966, see Anthony Barker and Michael Rush, *The Member of Parliament and His Information* (London: George Allen & Unwin, 1970), pp. 378–86.

10. Reformers did not seem confined to the backbenches. In fact, there was a slight positive correlation between receptivity to reform and our measures of political importance, both reputational and positional.

Since many of these proposals would involve strengthening the position of the individual MP, they are not wholly selfless in intent. Indeed, many of the suggestions are formally reactionary, for they recall a simpler age of decentralized, genuinely parliamentary government of a type no longer practical. But in many details the Members' proposals resemble the sorts of reforms that have been urged by many British academics and commentators—specialist committees, devolution of certain powers to regional authorities, admission of more lateral, politically appointed entrants to the civil service, and so on. Of course, most Members would welcome more staff and better office space, too, but most of their proposals go further, challenging many of the shibboleths that have grown up around the British Constitution. The changes suggested would be incremental, not revolutionary, but they would seem to imply a substantial shift in the distribution of influence in British government. Widespread support for such innovations must be taken as evidence against procedural "dogmatism" and "ideologism."

It is interesting to ask why this thesis of British procedural conservatism has been so widely accepted. In part, of course, it can be traced to the slowness with which established procedures have in fact changed. But this evidence is hardly conclusive, for procedural change comes slowly even in "experimentalist" America; established procedures naturally accumulate powerful supporting pressures. A generational change may be involved, for the "reformers" on both sides of the House tend to be drawn from the younger, less-experienced Members. Another, perhaps even more important part of the explanation must be sought in terms of party affiliation. My impression is that many of the standard descriptions of British political culture apply much better to Conservative than to Labour politicians; for instance, Conservatives are, on the whole, more suspicious of procedural change. No doubt it is relevant to an understanding of the received interpretation of British attitudes toward governmental reform that until 1964 the Conservatives had ruled Britain for 28 of the previous 34 years. British elite political culture does not look so typically "British" when examined in a Parliament with a Labour majority of 100 and more than 200 new Members.

Only time (and subsequent research) will tell whether the reformism of 1967 reflected merely the enthusiasm for change characteristic of any new recruits before they get settled in. It would be a mistake to read more into this evidence than is there, for it only qualifies the basic truth that the British are agreed on basic political values to an extent that is remarkable in comparative perspective. Nevertheless, the qualification is important: this fundamental consensus need not—does not—preclude demands for institutional reform.

If the British consensus on political institutions is somewhat less complete than is commonly thought, the opposite is true of Italy: there is a good deal more agreement within the Italian political class on the institutions of government than many recognize. Norman Kogan states the accepted view, in concluding his review of the prospects for Italian democracy. "The major long-run political weakness is the absence of a sense of legitimacy of the Republic and its institutions."[11] Whatever force this generalization has when applied to mass attitudes, it is not an accurate statement of the attitudes of the political elite.

Very few Italian political leaders interviewed in this study expressed any desire to abolish the institutions of the Republic or even to modify them in any fundamental way. In fact, there seems to be developing among Italian politicians something of the "Constitution-worship" that characterizes American politics. Of course, Italians do not agree on exactly what the Constitution requires any more than Americans historically have. And American history serves as a distressingly apt example that universal commitment to "the Constitution" is compatible with fratricidal controversy over what the Constitution "really" means. Nonetheless, even nominal agreement on the fundamental law of a political system is a significant political fact, especially if the actors in that system are willing to let disputes over the interpretation of that law take place within the constitutional framework.

This nominal agreement on the Italian Constitution can be most strikingly illustrated by quoting at some length from an interview with a deputy widely reputed to be one of the leading "unreconstructed" Stalinists in the PCI. I began by asking him about "the most important problems facing Italy."

Well, really the most important, most general, most basic problem . . . is that of carrying out the Constitution. We find ourselves facing a crisis of the Parliament, and basically, also of the Italian State, because we have a Parliament which is different from the earlier ones, even the pre-Fascist ones, different because its composition is, first of all, more lower class [*popolare*]; there is no longer a monopoly of certain economic or professional castes. . . . And then there is the problem that the individual as such has a very limited weight in the present Parliament, whereas previously he had a good deal more. Then there is the problem of the parties, which, like it or not, constitute a guarantee of greater democracy, and of more impersonal independence. Therefore, the Parliament today is a thing absolutely different. However, the Parliament should be developed in correspondence to the vision of the Constitution. Sure, the Constitution claims to conserve the fundamental bases of the present society from the economic point of view. But the Constitution also anticipates a development of this society in the direction of greater social justice, of greater defense of labor, and of greater involvement of the people in the affairs of state and therefore of the Parliament. But this isn't happening. Parliament has stopped in midstream. . . . Why? There is strong pressure from the past, from past laws, past conceptions, and there is strong pressure from the groups with economic power who influence various parties, and in particular, the Christian Democrats, who accept verbally the idea of the

11. Norman Kogan, *The Government of Italy* (New York: Thomas Y. Crowell, 1962), p. 186.

implementation of the Constitution, but in fact always put on the brakes, delay, keep us from going ahead. We have a crisis of the Parliament, yes, and of the State, but it is a crisis of immobility. [Later, speaking of his attitude toward the Christian Democratic party:] It isn't really that we have things in common with the Christian Democratic party. But we did make this Republic in common and we did create the Constitution together. (I42)

As this man fully recognizes, verbal agreement on the Constitution barely hides deep disagreement over how it should be implemented. But the fact that his disagreement is framed in terms of the constitutional mandate (as he sees it) for social change illustrates my point that there is at least nominal agreement on the legitimacy of the Constitution. That the more moderate parties are also defenders of the Constitution does not need documentation. To be sure, this verbal consensus is not shared by some right-wing extremists, nor by some splinter groups of the Far Left, but these groups are virtually irrelevant in today's national politics.

Agreement on the written Constitution, of course, does not preclude demands for political reform. In response to my several questions on this topic, nearly all Italians suggested modifications in the present pattern of power. As in Britain, the most common demand was for increased power for the individual deputy, either through internal reforms, or by loosening party control over individual legislators. As in Britain, the next most frequently mentioned reforms were decentralization and increased control over the bureaucracy. The Italians were more vehement in demanding reforms, but the *kinds* of reforms they proposed are strikingly similar to the British suggestions.

Only 10 percent of the Italians proposed changes in the existing institutions that the coders thought were "revolutionary in effect, if not in method," and these few respondents were heavily concentrated in the oldest age groups. The corders could find among our 83 deputies only one whose attitude to the existing regime was one of "total, passionate rejection," and only another 16 percent who fell into the category "rejects the system, but proposes ameliorative reforms." The vast majority of Italians were judged to "accept the system, but propose ameliorative reforms."

I believe that these judgments accurately reflect the attitudes of the Italian political class. It cannot be proved that respondents were not concealing more revolutionary sentiments.[12] But the present evidence is in fact consistent with the postwar history of Italy. No major political party in republican Italy has

12. Whether or not the PCI is a genuinely revolutionary *party* is still a matter of some scholarly dispute, though there is an emerging consensus that it is not. The PCI *deputies* I spoke with were very radical in their proposals for social and economic change; one might justifiably say they are asking for revolutionary social reforms. But no more than one or possibly two of the twenty Communists I spoke to seemed even a potential revolutionary in political terms. A few deputies of the Far Right, by contrast, might be willing to overthrow the institutions of the Republic, but it would be purest daydream to believe that they have the ability to do so without massive assistance from outside the Italian political class. And these rightist deputies know that.

publicly called into question the basic institutions of government, except for some right-wing authoritarians who are almost universally dismissed by the rest of the political class as irrelevant. (This point represents a difference between Italian politics and the politics of Fourth Republic France that is not always fully recognized.)

Of course, many Italians want to improve the functioning of their institutions, but this desire is no more revolutionary than contemporary demands for reform of the American government and the American party system. If I may borrow David Easton's distinction between the institutions of the "regime" and the incumbent "authorities," there is in Italy today much dispute over the latter, but surprisingly little dispute over the former, at least among the major parties.[13]

One absolutely central fact about postwar Italian politics is that this distinction between the positions of legitimate power and the incumbents of those positions has been difficult to make, since a single party has dominated all postwar Governments. Attacks on the Christian Democrats may seem (perhaps even to some of the attackers) equivalent to attacks on the regime. The potential consensus on institutions of which I speak will not be finally confirmed until an alternation of parties in power allows the distinction between "the regime" and "the authorities" to be seen clearly by all. (To their credit, a number of Christian Democrats put precisely this point in private conversation.) Nevertheless, even in today's Italy there is a surprising level of agreement on the institutions of the Republic among politicians of all major parties.

13. David Easton, *A Systems Analysis of Political Life* (New York: John Wiley & Sons, 1965), pp. 190–219.

16 Equality and Liberty
in Britain and Italy

This investigation of the operative ideals of British and Italian politicians has moved from an examination of their contrasting interpretations of democracy to a more detailed survey of their assessments of the political institutions in which they act. In this chapter I shall discuss their commitment to two values central to democracy—equality and liberty.

Equality: Three Variations on a Theme

Equality has been one of the keystones of democratic theory since antiquity. Today's proponents of "participatory democracy" draw on a long tradition of speculation about how to make man effectively the political equal of all his fellows. The origins of the modern concern with political equality lie in the ferment of the English Civil War and the radical doctrines espoused by the Levellers. However, as we were earlier reminded by Sabine, the value of equality came to take second place to liberty in the Anglo-American democratic tradition. Meanwhile, on the Continent Rousseau was restating the moral imperative of equality and analyzing the conditions necessary for its realization. Throughout Western Europe, the theoretical and practical controversy about equality soon spilled beyond the bounds of political institutions to involve broader social and economic issues.

It is clear that equality, especially political equality, is a critical topic in any inquiry about democratic norms. How do these politicians feel about political equality? To answer that question I shall in this section draw on three distinct, but complementary, sorts of evidence.

One way of getting at the politicians' basic orientation is to ask what role in politics and government they attribute to the average citizen. Presumably, those most strongly committed to the value of political equality will be most inclined to welcome and encourage widespread, active involvement in public affairs. "Ideally speaking," I asked, "what would you say is the proper role for the public generally in politics and government?"

Well, I don't know. I should have thought that on the whole we've got it quite well arranged here in England. I mean we're not a very political country, you know. . . . People are not interested in that way. I think it's a good thing, in a way, that they're not. They do have the feeling, I think, that when a General Election comes along, they pay attention, they elect their man, and they say to him, 'Now we've put our trust in you. Go get on with it.' (B31)

This older Tory reflects one common view. Except for the handful of respondents in each country who had some doubts about the whole idea of universal suffrage, his position—that public involvement in government should end at the voting booth—represented the lower end of a continuum. As my earlier discussion of classical democrats indicated, a number of Englishmen and Italians spoke out for the opposite end of the continuum—constant and active public participation in the affairs of government at every level. Not all had a clear idea how this goal could be achieved institutionally, but there were suggestions for town meetings, widespread use of the referendum, and part-time citizen involvement in public administration.

Between these two extremes stretched a range of suggested levels of participation. One common response called for an informed public that from time to time communicates its feelings to its representatives, but little more.

First of all, they send a representative. By all means keep him informed. You can threaten him if you like. . . [but] keep a sense of perspective, which they seldom do. . . . They must select a person—and I think they could well afford to express themselves at the choosing stage a lot more than they do. Take more interest in this, but having done so, having got a person whom you reckon is a reasonably intelligent person, you must take his judgment as a whole. (B48)

A rather more active role was suggested by others, represented here by a leading moderate in the PCI.

[The present political situation] leads many citizens to stay away from political things. . . . But in a changed situation it would be necessary that the citizens get it in their heads that they too must be present, must contribute, must be vigilant, must make their voice heard and not just leave everything to the politicians. . . . If they give a blank check, it's so much the worse for them, but if instead they are present, active in the parties, in the unions, in the various democratic organizations, then they have the possibility to make their voice heard, to exercise a control. If they don't do this, there is always the danger of the political class becoming detached from the people. (I4)

Not every one of our respondents was asked this question explicitly, often because the answer had been given in earlier conversation. But on the basis of the entire discussion about democracy and political participation, it was possible to estimate in general terms the attitude of each respondent toward the role of the public in politics and government. Table 16.1 presents for each national

Table 16.1: The Public's Role in Politics
(in percentages)

QUESTION: "Ideally speaking, what do you think is the proper role of the public generally in politics and government?"

	Question asked explicitly		Overall rating of interview	
	Britain (N=65)	Italy (N=37)	Britain (N=92)	Italy (M=81)
Voting or less	23	19	25	8
Interest in politics and/or communication to representatives	63	39	70	41
More direct activity (in parties, associations, local government, etc.)	14	43	5	51

sample the pattern of attitudes toward political participation, giving first the data based only on the explicit question and then those based on the overall rating.[1] The panorama of answers is here reduced simply to a trichotomy, distinguishing among those who advocated the role of voting (or less), those who argued for a sustained interest in politics, coupled perhaps with occasional communication to political leaders, and finally, those who suggested still more active involvement.

Most Italians project a much more active political role for the public than do the British. Three to ten times as many Italians as Britons argue for a role that goes beyond the proverbial American advice to "write your Congressman." This finding is quite consistent with the greater tendency for the Italians to endorse the classical model of democracy. The findings for Britain show a reflection in the political elite of the oft-discussed deference of the British electorate. By and large, both leaders and followers expect that the latter will play only a modest role in public affairs. The British responses are more "realistic"; they describe more accurately the role that mass publics typically do play in contemporary democracies. The implications of the more "idealistic" pattern of answers in Italy will be considered later.

Discussions about the proper level of popular participation in politics are one way of measuring attitudes about political equality. Another, quite different

1. The intercoder reliability for the global judgment was almost as high as for responses to the explicit question. The tau-beta coefficient for the global judgment was .65, with 1 percent of the respondents rated at opposite ends of the three-point continuum; the coefficient for responses to the explicit question was .69; no one was placed at opposite ends of the continuum by the two coders. Note that expressing a global judgment about a respondent's attitudes is often as easy as deciding how to classify an explicit answer. The differences in the distributions between the overall rating and the responses to the explicit question are attributable to two factors. First, some of those not asked the explicit question had in fact already answered it, usually by assigning a relatively active role to the public; this was especially true in Italy. Hence the explicit question tended not to be asked of those who most strongly favored increased participation. Secondly, from time to time a respondent's full discussion revealed that his response to the explicit question had been unintentionally misleading. The coders were able to take this into account in the overall rating.

Table 16.2: Questionnaire Items Composing the Index of
Political Egalitarianism

		Agree strongly (%)	Agree (%)	Disagree (%)	Disagree strongly (%)
1. Every citizen should have an equal chance to influence government policy.	Great Britain (N=81)	26	55	18	1
	Italy (N=56)	50	41	7	2
2. It will always be necessary to have a few strong, able people actually running everything.	Great Britain (N=82)	2	37	48	13
	Italy (N=52)	6	27	31	36
3. Certain people are better qualified to run this country because of their traditions and family background.	Great Britain (N=83)	4	16	53	28
	Italy (N=53)	11	42	32	15
4. People ought to be allowed to vote even if they cannot do so intelligently.	Great Britain (N=81)	27	64	9	0
	Italy (N=55)	36	53	7	4
5. In this complicated world the only way we can know what is going on is to rely on leaders or experts who can be trusted.	Great Britain (N=83)	4	25	52	19
	Italy (N=55)	4	20	49	27
6. Few people really know what is in their best interests in the long run.	Great Britain (N=83)	4	36	57	4
	Italy (N=49)	29	47	22	2
7. A few strong leaders would do more for this country than all the laws and talk.	Great Britain (N=84)	7	17	48	29
	Italy (N=55)	4	6	38	53

method for tapping these attitudes comes from answers to several items on the written questionnaire, designed to gauge orientations toward political equality and authority relations in general. Table 16.2 presents the seven items and the responses to them by each national sample. Each item measures a slightly different aspect of the putative syndrome of political egalitarianism. The set, however, does cohere; empirically, these items measure a single dimension.[2]

2. One statistical yardstick for this coherence is that the Spearman-Brown internal reliability coefficient for the set of seven items is .66 for Britain and .68 for Italy. (See n. 8, chap. 4.) When all items from both countries are grouped for a factor analysis, the mean communality of variance is .36, and the dominant factor that emerges accounts for 62 percent of the total common variance. Items 1 and 4 were reversed in the scoring. Virtually identical results are obtained when one considers each national sample separately. The Italian data seem to some extent subject to "acquiescence" response set, reducing slightly correlations between items phrased in opposite directions and inflating slightly correlations between items phrased in the same direction. However, since the findings reported are confirmed by using each of the items separately,

Each respondent's position on this continuum can be measured by an Index of Political Egalitarianism (IPE), based on his responses to these seven statements.[3] Figure 16.1 shows how the two national samples are distributed along this dimension.

Two obvious conclusions can be drawn from this figure, which summarizes more succinctly the evidence in table 16.2. In the first place, scores on the Index of Political Egalitarianism are strongly skewed toward the egalitarian end of the continuum. At least in their responses to these questionnaire items most British and Italian politicians are quite favorable to political equality. Secondly, the two national distributions are remarkably similar, but as with the responses to the interview question on participation, the Italians tend to be somewhat more egalitarian.

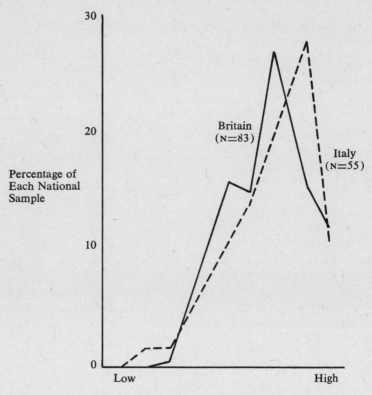

Figure 16.1: The Index of Political Egalitarianism in Britain and Italy

no bias is introduced by grouping them into a single scale. It is possible, however, that since five of the seven are phrased so that to agree is to be "inegalitarian" the scale tends to underestimate the relative egalitarianism of the Italians.

3. Staticstially, the IPE is simply the respondent's factor score on the dominant factor emerging from the matrix of intercorrelations.

Authority relations within political parties offer a third focus for our investigation of attitudes about political equality. After a series of questions about the nature of party leadership respondents were asked about the relative balance of obligation between the leader of a party and his followers. Images of these reciprocal rights and duties varied considerably. One Tory, for example, was asked, "How would you describe the obligations and responsibilities of a party leader to his supporters?"

Well, . . . he's just got to be a good leader. He's got to be highly intelligent and capable. He's got to be a good speaker. . . . I think that's all there is to it. [*Well, how about the obligations and responsibilities of his supporters to the leader?*] The obligation of a supporter to a party leader is complete and utter loyalty and to work and work loyally behind him. (B10)

A leading Italian politician had a similar interpretation of this relationship between leader and followers.

It is the [leader's] obligation to bring his forces to success, just as generals must lead their armies. [*What are the obligations and responsibilities of the supporters to the leader?*] Not to weaken the action of the party by internal divisions, or personalisms, or power struggles. To have clearly in mind the political function of a party. (I57)

Others had a different notion about the relative obligations of leaders and followers. A Labour MP offered this analysis.

I think that the leader has the obligation of carrying [the followers'] collective thought forward and making out of this some kind of coherent policy . . . . His policy has got to be a reasonable cross-section of the things that the people in his party want. [*How about the other way around? What are the obligations and responsibilities of the supporters to the leader?*] I don't think that they have any obligations to a leader at all. Responsibilities? They have the responsibility, I think, to be loyal to him, provided that he is expressing their collective views. If he is not, then they have no responsibilities to him whatever. I think they must always be free to criticize their leader. (B66)

Similar views were expressed by several Italians. One Socialist, for example, argued that the leader of a party

must always take account of the feelings of the people, because whoever wants to govern cannot ignore—even in a party—the state of mind, the popular will. [*And the obligations and responsibilities of the supporters to the party leader?*] Look, I'll say this right away: never give a blank check. Trust, but never mythology, okay? (I65)

Responses to this question were rated on a five-point scale, ranging from heavy emphasis on the obligations of followers to the leader, to great stress on the obligation of the leader to his followers.[4] The distribution of the two national samples on this dimension is given in table 16.3. As with the other measures of egalitarianism that we have examined, the British seem more willing than the Italians to endorse an asymmetrical distribution of power and influence. We saw earlier that British politicians are reluctant to attribute an active political role to the average citizen, and it is now apparent that they are similarly reluctant themselves to interfere with the prerogatives of their party leader. This pattern of norms—deference by followers and autonomy for leaders—recurs throughout British political culture.

Table 16.3: Balance of Duties in Leader-Follower Relations
(in percentages)

QUESTION: "What are the obligations and responsibilities of a party leader to his followers, and what are the obligations and responsibilities of the followers to the leader?"

	Britain (N=78)	Italy (N=37)
Followers' duties heavily stressed	3	5
Followers' duties emphasized	50	22
Mixed	27	38
Leader's duties emphasized	20	32
Leader's duties heavily stressed	0	3

Most Italians, on the other hand, are unwilling to give their party leaders such a wide margin of independence. A few Italian respondents explained this attitude by referring to their experience with autonomous political leadership under Fascism. Whether or not this explanation applies to their colleagues, the individualism manifested in these attitudes to party leadership may be one source of the recurrent factionalism that plagues Italian parties.

The cross-national comparison for each of our three indicators of political egalitarianism is the same. The Italians are always on average more egalitarian, although the spread of Italian scores is always wider, reflecting the existence in each case of a cluster of dogged opponents of political equality. The statistical evidence for this statement is that on each measure of egalitarianism, both the mean and the standard deviation of the Italian scores are greater.

One might wonder, however, whether these indicators do indeed measure the same basic orientation to political authority and equality. Table 16.4 gives for each country the intercorrelations among these three measures. The concordance shown in this table strengthens considerably one's confidence that there is a single basic dimension of political egalitarianism.

Politicians, it seems, are consistent about the kind of power distribution that they approve. Some prefer asymmetrical influence relations in party affairs and argue for a relatively restricted role for the general public in politics and government. Others, by contrast, demand an egalitarian distribution of power

4. The intercoder reliability coefficient for this rating was tau-beta = .49; 4 percent of all respondents were rated more than one point apart on the five-point scale.

Table 16.4: Intercorrelations among Three Measures of Support for Political Equality

	Britain	Italy
Index of Political Egalitarianism vs. public's role in politics	.55 (N=85)	.46 (N=55)
Index of Political Egalitarianism vs. leader-follower relations	.25 (N=72)	.52 (N=23)
Public's role in politics vs. leader-follower relations	.13 (N=78)	.56 (N=37)

NOTE: Entry is gamma.

within the party and welcome widespread popular participation in public affairs. Only a few politicians in Britain and Italy are overtly hostile to political equality, but the rest vary considerably in the warmth with which they embrace this value.

Democracy and Equality

In chapter 15 I speculated that the basic models of democracy could themselves be ranged along a continuum according to the pattern of power posited by each. Classical democracy implies the most egalitarian distribution of influence, whereas authoritarian democracy seems to imply a narrowly restricted pattern, in which citizens are subject to manifold duties and controls. Polyarchal democrats attribute a moderately passive role to ordinary citizens, while liberal democrats appear to support a distribution of influence less egalitarian than that endorsed by the classical democrats, but more egalitarian than that supported by the polyarchal democrats. Let us try to confirm these speculations by examining where the adherents to each of these models stand on the dimension of political egalitarianism.

To begin with the relationship between models of democracy and attitudes toward popular participation, figure 16.2 shows a neat and unbroken progression as one moves along the continuum from authoritarian democrats through polyarchal and liberal democrats to classical democrats. Respondents at each step along this continuum advocate a higher and higher level of involvement and influence for members of the mass public.[5]

The evidence from the Index of Political Egalitarianism and from the question on intraparty authority relations confirms this systematic relationship between conceptions of democracy and attitudes to political equality. In each country on each measure classical democrats (and the closely related socioeconomic democrats) are the most insistent on egalitarian distributions of authority, authoritarian democrats the most insistent on hierarchy, with liberal and polyarchal democrats in between. Table 16.5 presents this evidence, grouping

5. The one partial exception to the unbroken progression is the British authoritarian democrats, but there are only two of them and therefore the probability of sampling error is very high.

BRITAIN

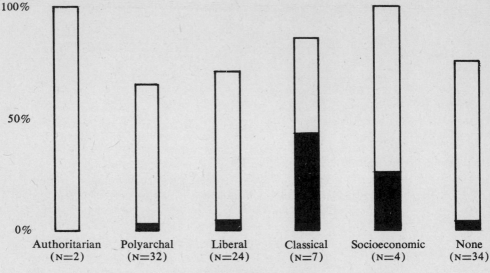

100%

50%

0%

| Authoritarian | Polyarchal | Liberal | Classical | Socioeconomic | None |
| (N=2) | (N=32) | (N=24) | (N=7) | (N=4) | (N=34) |

Models of Democracy

ITALY

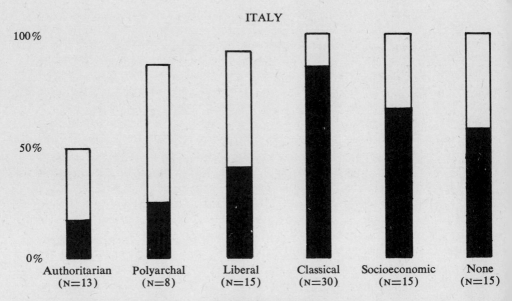

100%

50%

0%

| Authoritarian | Polyarchal | Liberal | Classical | Socioeconomic | None |
| (N=13) | (N=8) | (N=15) | (N=30) | (N=15) | (N=15) |

Models of Democracy

Figure 16.2: Models of Democracy and the Public's Role in Politics
    Clear bar = percentage advocating public interest in politics and occasional communication to leaders.
    Solid bar = percentage advocating more direct participation.
    All data based on those using given model "prominently."

Table 16.5: Models of Democracy, the Index of Political Egalitarianism,
and Leader-Follower Relations

	Models of Democracy					
	Authoritarian	Polyarchal	Liberal	Classical	Socioeconomic	None
IPE	5.4	6.6	7.2	7.6	7.4	6.5
	(N=12)	(N=35)	(N=35)	(N=23)	(N=13)	(N=42)
Leader-	87%	55%	40%	31%	17%	34%
follower	(N=9)	(N=29)	(N=24)	(N=23)	(N=10)	(N=32)

NOTE: First entry is mean score on the IPE; second entry is percentage of respondents who emphasize duties of followers to party leader. All entries based on respondents holding given model "prominently." British and Italian respondents grouped, weighting each national entry equally to hold national effects constant.

data from both countries, with appropriate weights to control for national effects; as indicated, the form of the relationship is identical in the two countries.

Political equality is a value that can be variously interpreted and applied. A politician's orientation to this value is basic to his response to a wide range of authority relationships, those in which he himself is subordinate as well as those in which he is superior. It would be futile and perhaps meaningless to ask which is cause and which effect, but attitudes to equality and interpretations of democracy are intimately connected.

Liberty

Political liberty is a complex and ambiguous concept, but the central element is the freedom to oppose, to dissent, to criticize established policies, practices, and people. Liberty in this sense is not a sufficient condition for democracy. There have been liberal but undemocratic regimes; nineteenth-century England is a good example. Moreover, Sabine's discussion of the continental democratic tradition, as well as some of the evidence from the present study, should alert us to the fact that not all conceptions of democracy place so extreme a stress on civic freedoms as does the Anglo-American version. But if we are to understand the operative ideals of democratic politicians, we must investigate their attitude toward political liberty.

The broad principle of political liberty enjoys virtually unanimous support among the political leaders of Britain and Italy. This fact is illustrated by responses to one of the questionnaire items, "Unless there is freedom for many points of view to be presented, there is little chance that the truth can ever be known." This paraphrase of John Stuart Mill's essay "On Liberty" was agreed to by every single British respondent, 55 percent of them doing so "strongly." The Italian consensus was only slightly less complete; 94 percent agreed, 68 percent strongly. No other statement in the 29–item questionnaire evoked such agreement in Britain, and in Italy only an item calling for a life built around "ideals" was more popular. (A glance back at table 16.2 will show that not even an item endorsing universal suffrage was so uniformly accepted.)

In the broadest comparative perspective this universal endorsement of the freedom to dissent is significant, for it is the foundation upon which more specific protections for political liberties may be built. It is necessary, however, to discover how deep this support for civic freedoms is, how ready these men and women are to limit the right to oppose, to criticize, to dissent. This task is complicated by the unanimous nominal support for these rights. A respondent whose tolerance for dissenting minorities is low might be reluctant to reveal this intolerance, especially if there were some question about the position of the interviewer. The strategy I used, therefore, was to make it as easy as possible for the respondent to express his reservations about complete political liberty.

I began by asking, "Some people say that there are certain political groups which engage in tactics which are unfair, or illegitimate, or even dangerous to the country's welfare. How do you feel about this—do you think there ought to be more careful controls over any activities of this sort?" If the respondent accepted my suggestion, and supported the imposition of certain controls, I probed to find out just which groups he opposed, and what sort of controls he favored.[6] On the other hand, if—as was fairly common—he hesitated or denied knowledge of any dangerous groups, I went on to suggest a particularly vocal group at the opposite end of the ideological spectrum from the respondent. Thus, for example, I asked British Conservatives about the activities of the left-wing Campaign for Nuclear Disarmament (CND), and asked Labour Members about the right-wing, crypto-racialist pro-Rhodesian lobby. In Italy I referred generically to the activities of "the extreme Left" or "the extreme Right." Once again, responses to this further query were probed to learn just what groups the respondent had in mind, and what kinds of controls, if any, he favored.[7]

This method of inquiry has the advantage of lowering considerably the threshold for the expression of intolerance, but this advantage has a counterpart danger. From the respondent's point of view, I was virtually asking if he thought subversives should go uncontrolled. A defense of political liberty in this situation will be particularly good evidence of strong support for that value, but the converse is not necessarily true, since there might have been some "false intolerance" expressed to accommodate the interviewer.[8] I was in fact trying to push

6. The Italian verb *controllare* is ambiguous. It can have the English meaning of "control," but it can also be used in the more limited sense of "keep track of" or "be vigilant about." However, the further probes allowed the coder to judge to what extent the respondent favored overt controls of some sort.

7. These additional probes are important, for it is necessary to understand exactly how the respondent interpreted the question if one is to judge his overall tolerance for political freedoms. For example, certain extremist groups in Italy have carried out violent attacks and bombings against their opponents. Clearly, a respondent who argued that bombings should be stopped should not be placed in the same category as one who wanted to stop the distribution of an opposition newspaper.

8. Obvious cases of this sort would have been caught by the detailed probes and the coders' judgment; there were, in fact, few cases in which the coders discerned such "false positives."

support for civic freedoms to the breaking point. That I could find such a breaking point is not proof that the individual in question is antilibertarian, for the
strains of ordinary political life may seldom reach his limit. On the other hand,
in times of real stress the pressures for restricting political liberties are surely
greater than those I could generate in a calm, reflective interview situation.

Disguise it as I might, a good many respondents saw quite clearly that controls
of the sort suggested violated a fundamental norm. This response was most
striking when the respondent himself obviously disagreed completely with the
group in question. One Conservative in our sample had won some limited re-
nown for his patriotic defense of the Queen and the Union Jack. He caught the
drift of my opening probe immediately.

> Well, I suppose if you oppose it very violently, you would say that the CND
> is in fact endangering the country and the state. I think in all these things, if
> one can, one wants to try and allow a good deal of conscience. . . . You see,
> otherwise you stifle . . . look, you know, I disagree entirely both from the
> CND and Vietnam [war protesters], intensely! I mean, I am entirely the
> opposite to them, but I think that you injure things by stifling the personal
> expression which they have a personal right to express. (B18)

Another example, from the opposite end of the ideological spectrum, arose when
a Labour Member happened to get on the subject of racialist electoral appeals
during a different part of the interview. When I tried to follow up his lead, both
the virulence of his anger and the depth of his support for civil liberties were
revealed.

> I think what happened in Smethwick was an abuse of the democratic process
> by people who were quite selfishly intent on their own political advancement,
> and didn't give a damn about the political damage they did, or about the shift
> they stirred up in the community's feelings. [*Do you think there should be more
> careful controls over that kind of activity?*] You know you can't do that, be-
> cause once you start interfering with any man's right to get up and say what
> he wants to say, then you are changing the form of democracy. . . . You just
> have to live with this and hope that other chaps will come along or better
> ideas will come along and remove the damage, and the danger. No, you can't
> interfere with it. (B26)

The commitment of other respondents to civil liberties was much weaker. The
initial tolerance of one older Italian rightist, for example, dissolved before he
could complete his first sentence.

> As far as I am concerned, in the case of propaganda and demonstrations, if
> there isn't fraud, if there isn't a crime, if there isn't really a denial of the
> truth . . . no one has the right to make use of instruments like the press, or
> television to tell lies. He must tell the truth. Therefore, the state has the right
> at a certain point to prevent someone from systematically lying. (I6)

Sometimes the conflict between a respondent's own inclinations to repression and his knowledge of the principle of political liberty was plainly visible, as in the case of the following Christian Democrat.

> Those people who come here in front of Montecitorio [the Chamber of Deputies] are all bought. We all know it. . . . From the point of view of trustworthiness, it seems to me they should be—I don't say eliminated, but should be, I would say, disciplined. These demonstrations should really represent something true, not just counterfeit ballyhoo, a farce. [*How could you exert a more careful control?*] I don't know. Look, there is a law that these demonstrations require a special permit . . . , but in a democratic regime certain things . . . [*you can't . . . ?*] I don't know. They would be considered suffocations by the opposition. In this sense, you must have tact, balance, because sometimes, it would be considered . . . I don't know. (I28).

The norm of freedom of expression is recognized here, but more as a fact of political life than as an internalized value.

Communist deputies responding to this question were in a rather special position, for the Party has always called for the implementation of the clause of the Italian Constitution that prohibits the formation of a neo-Fascist party. Many simply wrapped themselves in the Constitution and demanded that the Italian Social Movement—widely acknowledged to be neo-Fascist—be dissolved. Some Communists, however, were reluctant to take such drastic action.

> You could say that the Constitution should be faithfully applied. . . . [*and therefore the MSI should be forbidden, you think?*] Oh, I wouldn't forbid the idea of any organization, of any party, because I am for the maximum of democracy and liberty. However, look here. What is forbidden is the old Fascist Party . . . but if you call yourself MSI, and want to be a party of the Right, carry out your activities, you're free to do so. We will confront our ideas, make clear our conflicts of class interest, fine. But the introduction of the method of violence, however, is excluded; that isn't admissable.

These quotations give some flavor of the range of responses to this set of questions. Aligning the variety of "breaking points" on a single dimension was not simple, but the coders were able to reach high levels of consistency using a four-point scale.[9] Table 16.6 shows how each of the national samples was distributed along this dimension.

The national differences are truly remarkable. From nine-tenths of the British politicians, it is impossible to elicit any support for restrictions on extremist political activity; and more than half justify their refusal by referring explicitly to the value of political freedom. The vast majority of Italians, on the other hand, are willing to contemplate suppression of certain political activities, and

9. Intercoder reliability for this judgment is tau-beta = .70; only 9 percent of the respondents were rated more than one point apart.

Table 16.6: Support for Political Liberties in Britain and Italy
(in percentages)

QUESTION: "Some people say that certain organizations engage in activities which are unfair, or illegitimate, or even dangerous to the country. . . . Do you think there should be more careful controls over such activity?"

	Britain (N=62)	Italy (N=60)
1. Respondent is willing to impose certain limits.	0	30
2. Respondent is willing to impose limits, though reluctantly.	10	42
3. Respondent unwilling to impose limits, but makes no explicit reference to value of political liberty.	36	10
4. Respondent unwilling to impose any limits, and refers explicitly to value of political liberty.	54	18

fully a third show little or no reluctance to do so. Part of the explanation for this difference can probably be found in the objective differences in the political climates of each country, although Italian demands for the control of physical violence were *not* counted as infringing political liberties. The Italians are simply much less wholehearted supporters of political liberties. However, what most needs explaining is not so much the Italian readiness to consider controls, but rather the astonishing strength of the British norms of free speech and fair play. [10]

Before turning to that conundrum, however, I want briefly to indicate how support for the norm of political liberty is related to the other values discussed in this chapter. The British data are, from this point of view, quite frustrating, for correlational analysis is virtually useless. In Britain support for political liberties is not a variable at all, but a constant.

Such is not the case for Italy, however. Contrary to the notion that libertarianism and egalitarianism are competing strands of democratic theory, among contemporary Italian politicans these two traits are positively correlated. Those who favor a more participant citizenry are also less inclined to repress dissident groups.[11] Classical democrats are the high scorers on the "political libertarianism" variable; only 14 percent of them rank in the most repressive category. Authoritarian democrats, by contrast, are the least libertarian; 54 percent of them rank among the most repressive. Looked at another way, only about a fifth of the total Italian sample are authoritarian democrats, but they provide half of the most antilibertarian respondents.

Indeed, those Italians most ready to limit political liberty are rather distinctive on a variety of measures. They rank relatively high on the index designed to

10. The case of Northern Ireland deserves special treatment here, for although the policy of internment would seem to contradict my generalization, urban guerilla warfare raises peculiar moral and practical issues. For an instructive interpretation of British problems in Northern Ireland, see Richard Rose, *Governing Without Consensus: An Irish Perspective* (Boston: Beacon Press, 1971).

11. Support for political liberties correlates (gamma) .17 with the IPE, .19 with "leader-follower relations," and .22 with "role of the citizen in politics."

measure an "end justifies the means" orientation, and they score relatively low on indices tapping "social trust" and "political trust."[12] On the basis of their discussion of democracy (*not* on the basis of their response to the queries about political liberties), they were judged among the least sympathetic to the whole idea of democracy.[13] This total syndrome—intolerance, suspicion, ruthlessness, antipathy to democracy—is familiar to students of Italian history. More surprising and disturbing is the size of this group in contemporary Italy; table 16.6 shows that approximately a third of the Italian parliamentarians fall into the lowest category on our measure of political libertarianism.

These national differences in the depth of support for political liberties are long standing. In 1859 John Stuart Mill published the classic philosophical defense of these rights.

If all mankind minus one were of one opinion, and only one person were of the contrary opinion, mankind would be no more justified in silencing that one person, than he, if he had the power, would be justified in silencing mankind. . . . We can never be sure that the opinion we are endeavouring to stifle is a false opinion; and if we were sure, stifling it would be an evil still.[14]

Three decades later in Rome Leo XIII, one of the more openminded Popes, explained to the Italians that

right is a moral power which—as we have before said and must again and again repeat—it is absurd to suppose that nature has accorded indifferently to truth and falsehood, to justice and injustice. Men have a right freely and prudently to propagate throughout the State what things so ever are true and honourable, so that as many as possible may possess them; but lying opinions, than which no mental plague is greater, and vices which corrupt the heart and moral life, should be diligently repressed by public authority, lest they insidiously work the ruin of the State.[15]

As has happened previously in this study, after establishing the existence of national differences in elite attitudes and tracing these differences to contrasting national traditions, we begin to lose the trail in the mists of history. The differential impact of religious beliefs is probably part of the story, for chapter 17 will show that the value of political liberty continues to be foreign to many Italian politicians who claim inspiration from Catholic doctrine. The national differences in levels of partisan hostility discovered in chapter 4 are also relevant, since it is difficult to be tolerant of those one distrusts as much as many Italian politicians distrust their opponents. Moreover, the higher levels of tension and

12. See chapter 4 for a detailed presentation of these scales. The correlations referred to here are all between gamma = .22 and gamma = .44.

13. Gamma for this relationship = .58.

14. Mill, *On Liberty* (New York: E. P. Dutton, Everyman's Library, 1910), p. 79.

15. From the encyclical *Libertas,* reprinted in Michael Oakeshott, ed., *The Social and Political Doctrines of Contemporary Europe* (New York: Macmillan, 1942), p. 63.

intrigue in Italian politics may seem to many basically reasonable men to justify vigilance.

But the more fascinating mystery concerns the obstinacy with which the British defend civic freedoms. In one sense the explanation is clear, for the consensus on this point is so solid that it would be almost literally impossible for a member of the British political elite to dream of infringing these freedoms. A potential deviant would find virtually no social support for his views. Through a multitude of socialization and selection procedures a consensus of this sort is self-perpetuating. To discover how the consensus itself came to develop, however, one must look to a different kind of evidence than that avilable in the present study.[16]

But if the causes of the national differences in norms are not wholly clear, the effects are. British toleration for political dissent is legendary, and if comparative evidence be needed, it is supplied by Herbert Hyman's study of American and British policy on internal security during the decade of the 1950s.[17] Overt political repression in Italy in the postwar period has been minimal, at least if we limit our attention to the formal agencies of government. But the dim outlines of the SIFAR case, involving dossiers on political leaders, plans for concentration camps, and possible blackmail, is perhaps sufficient testimony to the fragility of Italian political tolerance.[18] Italy has been and continues to be a

16. The English constitutional historians have much to say that is relevant to this topic. See, for example, the standard work by Sir David L. Keir, *Constitutional History of Modern Britain Since 1485,* 7th ed. (London: A. & C. Black, 1964). The older generation of constitutional historians spoke in a different idiom, but spoke to this issue nonetheless. See, for example, F. W. Maitland, *The Constitutional History of England* (Cambridge: Cambridge University Press, 1920). A recent study of profound importance to this topic is J. H. Plumb, *The Origins of Political Stability: England 1675–1725* (Boston: Houghton Mifflin, 1967).

17. Herbert Hyman, "England and America: Climates of Tolerance and Intolerance," in *The Radical Right,* ed. Daniel Bell (New York: Doubleday, 1963). Hyman, by the way, explains the national differences in terms of what I am here calling "elite political culture," although he is forced to rely more on inference than on evidence. For the argument that even in England political liberty is sometimes infringed, especially, but not only, during wartime, see H. R. G. Greaves, *The British Constitution,* 3rd ed. (London: George Allen & Unwin, 1955), pp. 235–40. The two most important peacetime limitations are the very strict law on defamation, which inhibits personal attacks on public figures, and the Official Secrets Act, which is often used to prevent *insiders* from presenting a dissenting case.

18. This case has been the cause of much heat in Italian politics since it surfaced in 1967, but firm information on it is still lacking. Apparently certain officials in a security agency of the Italian armed forces had been systematically compiling files of personal information on leading public figures, including the President of the Republic. The purpose of these dossiers was never wholly clear, but it does not seem to have been an academic interest in documenting current history. At the same time, in a tangentially related series of events, other officials seem to have been discussing the possibility of a *coup d'etat,* complete with midnight internments of opposition politicians. The issues of the Italian journal of opinion *L'Espresso* for 1967 and 1968 are replete with lurid accounts of the rumors and counterrumors that circulated. The report of a parliamentary inquiry into the affair has been indefinitely delayed, and so the full facts are still unknown. But the smoke–fire principle probably does apply here, and in any event, the more significant fact in regard to the comparison with Great Britain is that Italian politicians all accept that the allegations *could* be true. For a useful discussion of the recent Italian record in the area of civil liberties, see John Clarke Adams and Paolo Barile, *The Government of Republican Italy* (Boston: Houghton Mifflin, 1966), pp. 217–25.

relatively open and democratic polity, and the nominal consensus on the *principle* of political freedom has no doubt inhibited the repressive urges of some leaders. The tensile strength of this consensus is, however, incomparably weaker than in Britain.

17 Some Sources of Democratic Norms

In the last three chapters I have examined a wide variety of democratic norms and values, including interpretations of the concept of democracy itself, attitudes toward equality in public affairs, and support for political liberties. In a search for some of the antecedents of these attitudes, I will now restrict my attention for the most part to the two dominent themes of liberty and equality.[1] Why do men come to believe what they believe about the rights of opposition and participation?

Ideology

The best predictor of attitudes toward political equality is party affiliation or left-right ideology. Table 17.1 displays the relationship between the left-right spectrum and support for popular political participation, while table 17.2 shows that for each of our three indicators of political egalitarianism, the further to the right a politician is (defined, as always, in terms of his position on the issues of social provision and economic management), the more likely he is to favor hierarchical authority patterns and to view political equality with some suspicion, if not hostility. For each measure of egalitarianism the correlation is stronger in Italy, again a familiar finding. This basic correlation between partisan or ideological position and attitudes toward equality naturally includes the various conceptions of democracy. In both countries classical democrats are heavily concentrated on the left of the political spectrum, and the other models are concentrated in varying degrees on the right.

That the Left favors greater political equality is no surprise. Historically, equality has been the *summum bonum* of radicals. "Socialism," said the Labour revisionists, "is about equality." And it could equally well be said that con-

1. The relatively small number of adherents to each model precludes a detailed investigation of the roots of specific conceptions of democracy. But since the models themselves can be ranged along the egalitarianism dimension, in seeking the sources of a respondent's position on this dimension, one will *ipso facto* come to understand the sources of the respondent's conception of democracy. Socioeconomic democracy differs from the other models in stressing nonpolitical values. In both countries socioeconomic democrats are predominantly older, left-wing working class radicals. The newer generation of radicals is no less concerned with social justice, but their conceptions of democracy are more specifically political.

Table 17.1: The Left-Right Spectrum and Support for Popular Political Participation
(in percentages)

	Extreme Left	Moderate Left	Center	Moderate Right	Extreme Right
Role of public: Britain					
Voting or less	8	21	25	39	27
Interest	67	74	75	61	73
Direct involvement	25	5	0	0	0
	(N=12)	(N=38)	(N=8)	(N=23)	(N=11)
Role of public: Italy					
Voting or less	0	0	14	36	0
Interest	4	57	57	46	100
Direct involvement	96	43	29	18	0
	(N=24)	(N=23)	(N=21)	(N=11)	(N=2)

Table 17.2: Support for Political Equality and the Left-Right Spectrum

	Britain	Italy
Public's role in politics	.41	.77
	(N=92)	(N=81)
Index of Political Egalitarianism	.39	.65
	(N=86)	(N=56)
Leader-follower relations	.36	.39
	(N=78)	(N=37)

NOTE: Entry is gamma for correlation between the measures of support for political equality and the measure of left-right ideology, positive when those on the left are more egalitarian.

servatism, in Italy as in Britain, is about inequality. Even in the age of the "democratic consensus" in Western Europe, this basic value—political equality —continues to divide the Right from the Left. Reconciled, most of them, to universal suffrage, conservatives continue to fear the ignorance of the masses and to believe that politics and government is properly the business of an able, educated, wise, and responsible elite. Across the chamber radicals continue to decry the persistent element of oligarchy in modern democracies and to demand expanded popular participation and power in all levels of government.

This network of values is closely tied up with the distinction that we discussed in chapter 9 between politicians whose point of view is that of the "authorities" and those who adopt the perspective of "potential partisans." Respondents rated high on our measure of the "tribune" orientation, the "potential partisans," also ranked high on all measures of support for political equality. Those rated high on the "trustee" orientation, the "authorities," were, conversely, low scorers on the various egalitarianism measures.[2] The antithesis of conservation and reform, of "power and discontent," of hierarchy and equality pervades the world of European politics now as it did a century ago and more.

2. The mean correlation between the three measures of egalitarianism and the measure of "tribune" perspective is gamma = .33. The mean correlation between the egalitarianism measures and the measure of "trustee" perspective is gamma = −.48.

Politicians in Britain and Italy are, above all, party politicians. It may be useful, therefore, to see how this correlation between ideology and attitudes to democracy works out to provide each party with a distinctive orientation toward democratic values. Figure 17.1 summarizes the evidence, indicating the relative standing of each party's members on the three measures of egalitarianism and the measure of support for political liberties.[3]

Ignoring the virtually identical support of the two British parties for political liberties, we see that Labour MPs are marginally, but consistently more favorable to political equality than the Tories. Samuel Beer's classic analysis of British politics describes the historical evolution of the contrasting conceptions of democracy in the two British parties.

> Old Tory authoritarianism . . . adapted to successive waves of voluntarism and liberalism until finally there emerged that curious hybrid—contradictory in name, but operational in practice—Tory Democracy. Giving a large initiative to leaders and the largely passive function of control to followers, while joining to the modern idea of mass participation the older doctrines of independent authority, class rule, non-programmatic decisions, and strong government, this conception characterized with reasonable fidelity the mode of governance of a typical Conservative Government as well as the Conservative Party. On the other hand, insisting that not merely control, but also the initiative itself must in some real sense be exercised by the rank and file, the Socialist ideal of democracy sharply departed from the Tory.[4]

Beer shows that "in practice as in theory, in the actual distribution of power as in their reigning conceptions of authority, the two parties were deeply opposed."[5] These differences are clearly reflected in the operative ideals of our politicians from the two parties, but the differences are limited. The accession to power of Labour during this century and its tenure at the time of these interviews have blurred the original philosophic divergence. "Governments must govern and be seen to govern" is a favorite aphorism on both sides of the House, and one that no doubt seems more compelling when the Government is of one's own party. In comparative perspective, the similarities in outlook of British politicians from the two parties are as striking as their traditional differences.

---

3. In order to get sufficiently large groups to allow fairly stable estimates of the distribution of attitudes, I have done with a flick of the computer that which all the efforts of Italian politicians have not accomplished: I have grouped together deputies from all three Socialist parties, and I have combined all the smaller parties of the Right. The only injustice this works is to the Italian Liberal Party. The Liberals in my sample were noticeably more egalitarian and libertarian than their colleagues in the parties to their right. But they were less egalitarian and libertarian than the parties on their left, so the broad outlines of the party system are not greatly distorted by my simplification.

4. Samuel Beer, *British Politics in the Collectivist Age* (New York: Alfred A. Knopf, 1965) pp. 387–8.

5. Ibid., p. 388.

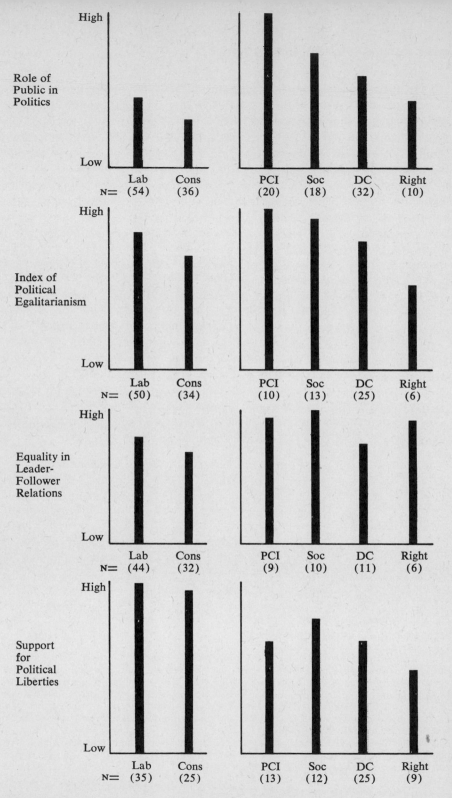

Figure 17.1: Democratic Attitudes, by Party Affiliation
Lab = Labour Party   PCI = Italian Communist Party
Cons = Conservative Party   Soc = all Italian Socialists
                                  DC = Christian Democratic Party
                                  Right = all Italian rightist parties (PLI, MSI, PDIUM)

The differences among the Italian parties are both sharper and more complex. On two of the three measures of egalitarianism there is the expected steady decline from left to right across the party spectrum. If support for mass participation in politics and hostility to elitism in government be the criterion, the Communists are the most democratic force in Italy, followed closely by the Socialists. Christian Democrats are quite heterogeneous on this as on most political dimensions, and some of them are no less egalitarian than the most fervid Communist. But in our sample (as in the councils of the party itself) these Christian Democratic radicals are outnumbered by conservatives suspicious of political equality and mass participation. (Seventy percent of the authoritarian democrats are found in the *Democrazia Cristiana*.) Further across the party spectrum, the operative ideals of the right-wing parties are consistent with their formally elitist ideologies.

The third measure of egalitarian attitudes, which deals with intraparty authority relations, yields more ambiguous results, in part because the number of respondents asked this question in each party was quite small. The evidence suggests that the Socialists are the most individualistic and egalitarian; this finding is consistent, of course, with the repeated fragmentation of Italian socialism. Unlike the other two measures of egalitarianism, this one does not rank the Communists at the top, a fact that seems consistent with the common portrayal of Communists as authoritarian in party affairs. This observation must be kept in perspective, however, for the Communists in our sample demand more control over their party leaders than do either the Christian Democrats or the rightists.

The final party comparison that can be drawn from figure 17.1 concerns support for political liberties. Socialists seem, on balance, the most libertarian of Italian politicians, and rightists the least libertarian. Christian Democrats and Communists get identically mixed marks here. I have already remarked upon the presence in the DC of significant numbers of authoritarian democrats, whose commitment to political liberty, as to political equality, is nominal at best. On the other hand, these politicians are balanced by many who fully understand and support this value. The case of the Communists is similar. It would occasion no special comment, except that this evidence belies the common impression that the Communists are peculiarly hostile to the freedoms of Western democracy. Italian Communists are, to be sure, not so libertarian as British politicians, and their support for the free expression of divergent views stems as much from a simple recognition of the realities of Italian politics as from a philosophical commitment to political liberty. But in this, they are not so much typically Communist, as typically Italian.[6]

6. The attitudes and values of Italian Communists are treated in more detail in my paper on "The Italian Communist Politician," prepared for the Conference on French and Italian Communism, American Council of Learned Societies, Cambridge, Mass., October 13, 1972, and to be published in a forthcoming volume edited by Donald L. M. Blackmer and Sidney Tarrow. For

Social Class

If the role of partisan ideology as the first and most important antecedent of political egalitarianism is straightforward and expected, the second factor is less anticipated. "Working class authoritarianism" has been discussed so frequently that many accept as proven that "the lower classes are much less committed to democracy as a political system than are the urban middle and upper classes."[7] But in this study British and Italian politicians from the lower classes are more committed to political equality than those from the upper classes and no less supportive of political liberties.

The evidence is summarized in table 17.3 which gives the correlations between our various measures of egalitarianism and libertarianism and a measure of social class background. (For Britain I use a measure based on the respondent's father's occupation. Weaknesses in the Italian data on father's occupation compel the use of a measure based on the respondent's own occupational background.) With only one exception, those from lower class backgrounds are consistently more opposed to authoritarian political arrangements than their upper class colleagues.[8] The explanation is probably quite simple. These men are relatively

Table 17.3: Equality, Liberty, and Social Class

	Britain	Italy
Public's role in politics	−.54	−.54
	(N=75)	(N=81)
Index of Political Egalitarianism	−.34	−.44
	(N=71)	(N=56)
Leader-follower relations	−.38	.06
	(N=62)	(N=37)
Support for political liberties	−.29	−.06
	(N=49)	(N=60)

NOTE: Entry is gamma for correlation between the measures of support for political equality, the measure of support for political liberties, and a measure of social class background, based on parental occupation in Britain and on respondent's occupation in Italy. Entry is positive when higher class background is associated with greater support for the relevant democratic norm.

comparable views of other scholars, see Tarrow's "Political Dualism and Italian Communism," *American Political Science Review* 61 (1967): 39–53; Gordon J. Di Renzo, *Personality, Power, and Politics* (Notre Dame, Ind.: Notre Dame University Press, 1967); Timothy M. Hennessey, "Democratic Attitudinal Configurations Among Italian Youth," *Midwest Journal of Political Science* 13 (1969): 167–93. Blackmer himself has focused on a rather different set of questions, but my findings are consonant with his in *Unity in Diversity: Italian Communism and the Communist World* (Cambridge, Mass.: M.I.T. Press, 1968). For a useful comparative perspective, see Thomas H. Greene, "The Communist Parties of Italy and France: A Study in Comparative Communism," *World Politics* 21 (1968): 1–38.

7. S. M. Lipset, *Political Man* (London: Mercury Books, 1963), p. 102. In fairness, it should be noted that most of Lipset's argument is directed at the mass level; working class leaders are discussed only tangentially.

8. The entry for intraparty authority relations in Italy does not fit the hypothesis; this anomaly may be due to the relatively small number of Italians who were asked this question.

sophisticated about the facts of political life, and they are no doubt well aware that the more restricted power and participation is to a small circle, the greater will be the representation and power of the upper class.[9]

Conversely, members of the upper classes of European society are often bound to older, aristocratic views of politics and tend to be pessimistic about the intelligence and wisdom of the average citizen. The upper class Italian who said that the Italian people needed *"un po' di forza"* ("a little bit of force") shared this basically paternalistic perspective with an English aristocrat who felt that

> the trouble with democracy as it's working out at the moment is it tends to assume, in a horseracing analogy, that every horse has got to be fit to run in the Derby, when in fact a draft horse may pull the brewer's dray better than a thoroughbred would. Similarly, a cart horse cannot win the Derby. But cart horses and thoroughbreds are both immensely valuable. (B49)

Rarely do these upper class respondents display open contempt for the masses, at least in Britain. More often there is simply a low estimate of the political competence and interest of the average citizen, often expressed with an almost audible parental sigh.

The relationship between class and support for civil liberties is less clear-cut, but there is certainly no evidence to support the theory that working class politicians are more intolerant and insensitive to the value of these liberties. As one Labour MP with long experience in working class organizations put it, "Well, if one argued there should be controls over that, then some of us would have been stopped a long while ago. I mean, after all, that's been our one area of freedom for many, many years." (B11) Precisely the same argument was made by a left-wing Italian Socialist: "Look, we are for the maximum liberty, the maximum democracy, because we're the ones who have suffered, who have learned what the absence of liberty and democracy means." (I23) Working class authoritarians were not absent from our samples, but neither were middle class authoritarians nor upper class authoritarians.

The connection between class and democratic attitudes obviously is linked to that between party ideology and democratic attitudes. Sorting out the relationships among these variables is not simple with our fairly small samples. Figure 17.2 maps out the most probable interrelations, showing that class has both a direct impact on egalitarianism and an indirect effect via party affiliation and ideology. Like its counterpart in chapter 10, this diagram should be taken as an aid to understanding the possible and probable relations among these variables, rather than as a definitive statement. As one examines the relationships using

9. Studies of the social backgrounds of political elites, for example, find with monotonous regularity that the higher up the political ladder one looks, the greater the disproportionate representation of upper status social groups. See W. L. Guttsman, *The British Political Elite* (New York: Basic Books, 1963); and Giovanni Sartori, *Il Parlamento Italiano* (Naples: Edizioni Scientifiche Italiane, 1963).

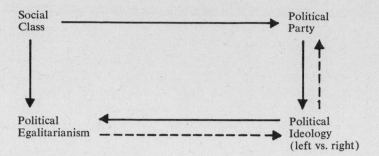

Figure 17.2: Causal Relations in Britain among Class, Party, Ideology, and Political Egalitarianism
    Solid arrows indicate paths of influence confirmed by the data. Dotted arrows indicate paths of influence consistent with the data, but not required by the pattern of intercorrelations and therefore not conclusively confirmed.

different indicators of political egalitarianism, sometimes the impact of class seems mostly direct; that is, not mediated by party and ideology; sometimes mostly indirect; and sometimes there seem to be both direct and indirect effects. But in every case the joint relationship between these variables and egalitarianism is very substantial.

A range of other features of social background and political experience were tested: region, education, occupation, political importance, experience in local government, past or present tenure in positions of legislative or executive or party leadership, and so on. None of these characteristics appeared to have a clear and consistent impact on attitudes toward democracy.[10] In both countries and for all measures of egalitarianism the class-party-ideology complex was by far the strongest influence.[11]

Age and Experience

Only one other variable was significantly related to egalitarianism: age. Younger politicians seem to be more egalitarian than older ones. (The zero-order correlations are shown in table 17.4.) The negative correlation between age and egalitarianism is not sizable, but it persists across all the various measures of egalitarianism and under various kinds of statistical controls.

To explore this intriguing pattern further, one must first sort out the "life

10. The one oasis in this desert of negative findings is not unexpected. More important politicians in both Britain and Italy are relatively less egalitarian in their attitudes to intraparty affairs. They are *not* less egalitarian on the other measures, but this question strikes especially close, and they are at pains not to restrict unduly the autonomy and initiative of the party leader.
11. These findings are wholly consistent with Timothy M. Hennessey's conclusions, based on a study of socialization in Italian adolescents. See his "Democratic Attitudinal Configurations Among Italian Youth."

Table 17.4: Age and Support for Political Equality

	Britain	Italy
Public's role in politics	−.28	−.21
	(N=92)	(N=81)
Index of Political Egalitarianism	−.12	−.16
	(N=86)	(N=56)
Leader-follower relations	−.10	−.05
	(N=78)	(N=37)

NOTE: Entry is gamma for correlation between age and the measures of support for political equality, positive when older respondents are more egalitarian.

cycle," "natural selection," and "generational" hypotheses. Does a lifetime of political experience tend to efface initial egalitarianism and to mold one's attitudes toward authority relationships into a more hierarchical pattern? Or are more egalitarian politicians weeded out earlier, leaving the older, more experienced cohorts staffed predominantly by elitists? Or is the generation of the 1940s and 1950s enduringly more open to political equality, the earlier generations enduringly more suspicious of it?

Choosing among these alternatives is, as we have already learned, not a simple matter, but in the British case there is one useful clue. The correlations between years in Parliament and the egalitarianism measures are systematically stronger than those with age. There are technical reasons why this set of relations must be treated with care, but the evidence suggests that older British politicians are less egalitarian, *not* because of their age (or generation), but because of their experience.[12]

It is still impossible to choose between the natural selection and life cycle alternatives, and in all probability both are at work. As we have seen repeatedly in previous chapters, the culture of British parliamentary politics is rather elitist. Most MPs expect that their constituents will not question their judgment, and in turn they do not expect to control the activities of their party leader. This is, of course, more true on the Conservative benches, but it is not untrue on the Labour side. Newcomers arriving with more egalitarian views find these views inappropriate to their new station. Those who persist in their demands for widely shared power may find Westminster less hospitable than do their more malleable colleagues. While the interviewing for this study was in progress, Prime Minister Wilson tried to forestall backbench revolts by telling the Parliamentary Labour Party that "Dogs who bite can only expect to have their licenses renewed once." But one of my respondents replied (privately) that Wilson was barking

12. The correlation between seniority and the role assigned to the public in politics is gamma = −.31; the correlation between seniority and the Index of Political Egalitarianism is gamma = −.21; the correlation between seniority and attitudes to leader-follower relations is gamma = −.19. The correlation between age and seniority is r = .73, raising the spectre of "multicollinearity." When two variables are closely related it becomes difficult to distinguish the effects of one from the effects of the other, especially with small samples.

up the wrong tree. He was probably right. Informal socialization is almost surely more effective than overt sanctions in generating the attitudes toward equality and authority characteristic of experienced British politicians.

In Italy, by contrast, age is more strongly correlated with attitudes toward democracy than is seniority. The generational hypothesis is intrinsically more plausible in the Italian case. Philip E. Converse has speculated on the relationship between time and political stability.

> While we know of no systematic chartings of such developments, it is impressionistically clear why the consolidation of a newly established democracy is slow and unsure with respect to elite attacks. In most such situations, there is initially a residuum of elite personnel, which either poorly understands the constraints of democratic values, or which is downright hostile to them. As these older cohorts die out and are replaced by younger generations of potential elites, socialized from the outset in the fundamental "rules of the game" characteristic of democratic values, the balance of ideologies shifts progressively and the new forms find increasingly firm footing.[13]

A strikingly similar analysis of the Italian experience was offered by one of the Italian politicians I interviewed. My question: Was there any way Italy could be more democratic than it is now?

> Sure, sure. It's a question of education, a question of experience. . . . The real democracy will be made by those who were born in the democratic regime, not those who came to democracy thirty or forty years old. I am convinced that when we have in power those born after 1945, they will really be rid of the past, and therefore will apply the rules of democracy better than we do. . . . We come from a different experience, and therefore we have a concept of authority which is not typically democratic. We call ourselves democrats, but in practice we aren't democrats. [We're] little dictators who come from this experience, who in practice bear the marks of this mentality. (I28)

One way of testing these intuitions is to compare the conceptions of democracy held by respondents from different generations. Following Converse, I shall consider both those whose outlook is essentially antidemocratic and those who seem simply not to have a clear conception of democracy. Figure 17.3 charts the generational ebb and flow of these two types, the authoritarian democrats and those who hold none of the five basic models of democracy.

As an aid to interpretation, I have also shown on the same coordinates the percentage of each cohort having one of the four basic "sympathetic" conceptions of democracy and the proportion of each age group's adolescence and adulthood that has been spent under a democratic regime.[14] This proportion is

13. Philip E. Converse, "Of Time and Partisan Stability," *Comparative Political Studies* 2(1969): 141.
14. I assume here that conceptions of democracy are not fully formed until at least early

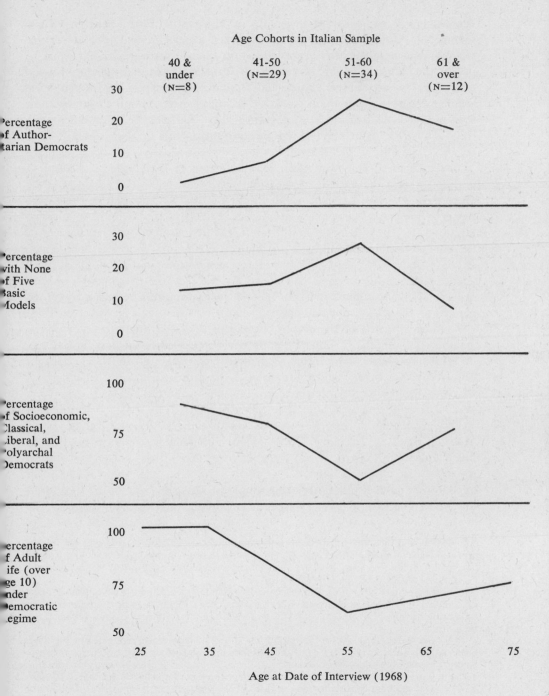

Figure 17.3: Models of Democracy and Political Generations in Italy

100 percent for all those who were 10 or younger in 1943 when the Fascist regime fell. For the next older groups the relative exposure to democracy drops, reaching the minimum for those who were just 10 when Mussolini came to power in 1922. In 1968 this generation of Italians—I shall term it the "Fascist generation"—had still spent barely half their sentient years under a democratic regime. The oldest generation, however, has been relatively more exposed to at least the forms of democracy, since their earliest years were spent in pre-Fascist Italy. Thus, for them, the line representing proportion of years under a democratic regime begins to rise again.

The correlation among the four lines in figure 17.3 is uncanny. All Italian parliamentarians have lived at least twenty-five years under democracy. But the more exposed a politician was to life under the Fascist dictatorship, the less he seems to understand democracy and the more likely he is to define it in authoritarian terms. The differences here are not merely marginal. Only 12 percent of the youngest cohort fail to have a genuinely democratic model of democracy, as contrasted with 52 percent of the Fascist generation. And the political significance of these differences is heightened by the fact that more than a quarter century after Mussolini's fall this Fascist generation still comprised over 40 percent of the Italian political class.

The characteristic of the graphs that speaks most strongly in favor of the generational hypothesis is the rise in prodemocratic sentiments among the very oldest group, those who presumably had formed certain attitudes and conceptions about democracy before the onset of Fascism. All the evidence suggests that the negative correlation between age and egalitarianism in Italy reflects percent a genuinely generational phenomenon.[15]

Thus, two quite different processes seem to underlie the basic age gradients in Britain and Italy.[16] Younger politicians in both countries are more egalitarian, but in Britain this characteristic seems to result from their shorter exposure to the relatively elitist parliamentary culture, while in Italy the younger men appear to be more egalitarian because they were less exposed to the authoritarian culture of Fascism. If these diagnoses are correct, then the prognoses for the

---

adolescence, and therefore, I base the proportion on a man's lifetime after the age of 10. For some evidence on this point, see Jack Dennis, Leon Lindberg, Ronald McCrone, and Rodney Stiefbold, "Political Socialization to Democratic Orientations in Four Western Systems," *Comparative Political Studies* 1 (1968): 71–101.

15. The other measures of egalitarianism show essentially the same trends as those in figure 17.3, though the individual patterns are less clear-cut. The curvilinearity of this relationship is one reason why the coefficients in table 17.4 are only moderate, for these measures assume linear relations.

16. These correlations involve the egalitarian strand of democratic thought, not the libertarian strand. There is no evidence in either country that support for political liberties is lower among the older generations. On the contrary, there is in both countries, all else held constant, a slight positive correlation between libertarianism and parliamentary experience. The differences are small but consistent, and they hint at the possibility that exposure to the rules of the parliamentary game increases tolerance for the right of opponents to speak their minds.

two countries are rather different. For Britain one would predict no net change in commitment to political equality. Assuming that the basic processes persist, the incoming generations will undergo the same slow slump in egalitarianism shown by their older, more experienced colleagues.[17] In Italy, on the other hand, there should be a general rise of egalitarian sentiments within the political elite over the next twenty years, as the Fascist-influenced generations leave the scene. If this set of assumptions is met, the national differences will widen, as the Italian "lead" on the egalitarianism dimension grows.

Of course, events might well upset our assumptions. The most probable perturbation would be a rise in demands for more effective political equality in Britain. Revolts against elite consensus and technocracy have been common in Europe in the last several years; the Netherlands and France provide the most prominent examples. At least one rising British politician, often touted as a future Labour Prime Minister, has spoken of the need to develop a more participatory democracy. Such a shift in a nation's political ideals is inordinately difficult, but it is not impossible. On the other hand, should British elites become more egalitarian, probably the net effect would be merely to keep pace with the Italians. National differences in democratic ideals are not likely to disappear soon.

17. There is in the data a hint of a generational change among British politicians *away from* egalitarian interpretations of democracy. Polyarchal models of democracy are more common among the younger British generations, and this correlation, unlike the correlations involving egalitarianism, is not a function of their inexperience.

18 Democratic Ideals in
Britain and Italy

Equality, liberty, democracy—these are the three primary themes of the fugue in political values developed in the last five chapters. As in any proper fugue, now one, now another of the themes has led, the others providing contrapuntal background. In this final chapter I shall recapitulate the interplay among these three themes and discuss the links between operative ideals and the nature of politics in Britain and Italy.

At the outset of chapter 13 we noted the historical singularity that political elites do abide by the norms of democratic politics. Most British and Italian politicians today accept the principles of political liberty and political equality. They accept them with varying degrees of enthusiasm, and they apply them in varying ways, but to an extent that is without parallel historically in these countries, they do accept them.

In examining the operative ideals of contemporary British and Italian politicians, we are looking at the alluvial sediment deposited by several centuries of political and cultural change. Of the two themes at whose juncture democracy lies—liberty and equality—the former is the older, at least in its implementation. The expediency, and more slowly, the intrinsic value, of toleration for dissenting views was accepted throughout most of Western Europe several centuries before reasonable men came to believe that all the subjects of a realm ought, of right, to play some role in the formulation of public policy. Liberty's longer pedigree is undoubtedly part of the explanation for the relatively more enthusiastic reception it encounters among today's politicians. Virtually none of the respondents could be induced to deny the basic principle involved, even though many Italians were less than eager to implement that principle. This cross-national contrast, too, can be traced in part to the fact that the value of liberty has been embedded in the British political culture much longer than it has in the Italian.

The principle of political equality is also widely accepted in these two nations, but here the dissenters are not so invisible, and even the supporters show considerable pessimism about the practicality of pushing this value too far. Equality in the polling booth has few critics, but many doubt that political equality ought to be interpreted in any wider sense than that.

The evidence of this study suggests that attitudes toward equality are consistent over a range of political relations. Those politicians who feel more comfortable with relatively hierarchical authority patterns express this attitude in their expectations about consultation with their leaders as well as with their followers. Those who demand more participation for themselves in the decisions of their leaders also accord a more active political role to average citizens.

This evidence represents a special case of the theory, advocated most notably by Harry Eckstein, that there is a strain toward consistency in the various authority patterns in which a person plays a role.[1] Of course, there is more to an authority pattern than the operative ideals we have here described. Actual behavior in authority relations might diverge, perhaps quite considerably, from the ideals and values that the participants articulate. The extent of this divergence is itself a variable of some political significance. Before discussing this point, however, let us compare briefly the "value profiles" for the two political elites in this study.

Liberty in London, "Equality" in Rome

The British value liberty and accept equality; the Italians value equality and accept liberty. This contrast is well documented by these data. British politicians are much more concerned than Italians about political freedoms. As much as any political norm is ever inviolable, this one is in Britain. Of course, a good deal of dissent is characteristic of Italian politics, more indeed than exists in British politics. But in Italy dissent is tolerated less because tolerance is thought morally right than because it is thought politically necessary.

Historians will rightly point out that this pattern is a familiar one in the "natural history" of a norm. Religious freedom in the Anglo-American nations was a necessity before it was a right. A similar process may be underway in regard to political freedom in Italy. Communists who initially protested their commitment to free speech for tactical reasons may come to have a "functionally autonomous" commitment to this value. Conservatives who tolerated Communist political activity in order to avoid revolutionary discontent may come to accept the moral imperative of tolerance. But political leaders in Italy today do not yet share the libertarianism of the British.

Nor do the British share the Italians' normative commitment to political equality. Political practice in the two countries is not so divergent, but political philosophy is. As Sabine suggests, the explanation for these philosophic differences seems to involve the contrasting intellectual traditions of the two countries. It is no accident, I believe, that half of the small band of classical democrats in Britain are academics by profession, several of them sociologists. These are men

1. Harry Eckstein, *Division and Cohesion in Democracy* (Princeton, N.J.: Princeton University Press, 1966), esp. pp. 255–6.

and women whose prepolitical experience exposed them to rather "un-English" doctrines of democracy. Rousseau is a familiar figure in social and political theory, but the egalitarian tenets of his doctrine are in a fundamental sense foreign to British political thinking.

In Italy, by contrast, Rousseau's theory of democracy seems to have been quite influential. The influence of his stress on mass participation in politics is obvious; the Italians in this study emphasize relatively high levels of popular involvement in public affairs. But other parts of his theory, for example his antipathy to "self-interested" participation, have had a similar impact, as one of the questionnaire items used in this study revealed. "Groups of citizens have a perfect right to lobby for legislation which would benefit them personally" was a perfectly unexceptionable sentiment in Britain; only 2 respondents in 85 disagreed with it. Forty-three percent of the Italians, however, found this proposition unacceptable. These nay-sayers were not necessarily unsympathetic to democracy. A number explained their objections by underlining the words "which would benefit them personally." As one of the staunchest Italian defenders of democracy said, "Well, I agree that people should be actively involved in politics, but their involvement should not be self-interested. They should be seeking the common good, not their personal good." (I61)

This viewpoint mirrors Rousseau's central distinction between "the general will" and "the will of all" and his belief that "nothing can be more dangerous than the impact of private interests on public affairs."[2] Caught between their commitment to popular participation in politics and their fear of self-interested participation, many Italian democrats registered opposition to this questionnaire item. In so doing, they revealed the continuing power of the continental conception of democracy.

The British cherish liberty, the Italians equality. The most important qualification that must be made to this generalization is that the consensus among British politicians on these values is considerably greater than that in Italy. By consensus here I do not mean simply agreement on the existing political institutions. Indeed, as chapter 15 showed, that sort of agreement is, in fact, surprisingly great in Italy. Rather the Italian dissensus involves more basic values, the values that can undergird or undermine support for particular institutions or regimes. This dissensus derives primarily from the existence within an egalitarian political culture of a substantial number of politicians who find political equality not simply implausible, but downright obnoxious. These men and women—the authoritarian democrats—find the discussion of democracy difficult, for they are too aware of the emotive value of this term to attack it explicitly. They are forced, therefore, to redefine the term so as to stress the continuing importance of hierarchy, authority, and control. They are not opposed to the word "democracy," but in a fundamental sense they are opposed

2. Rousseau, *The Social Contract*, trans. Willmoore Kendall (Chicago: Henry Regnery, 1954), p. 73.

to democracy itself. We have examined some evidence that suggests that this set of beliefs may be associated with a political generation reared under Fascism and destined to pass off the political stage in the coming decades. If this suggestion is borne out, the level of dissensus in Italy on basic political values will concomitantly decline.

Italy is not, however, likely to reach in the foreseeable future the level of agreement on these fundamental political values that presently characterizes Britain. Tories in England have shown a remarkable ability to steal the clothes of their political opponents, but perhaps even more remarkable has been the willingness of English radicals to don the more traditional garb of the Conservatives. Eric Nordlinger's remark that "even in a democratic age, the pre-democratic Tory tradition has easily made a larger contribution to the English [mass] political culture than has the Socialist tradition" applies at the elite level, too.[3] The rationales offered for elitist interpretations of democracy vary from Member to Member. Some are drawing directly on an older tradition of aristocratic rule and *noblesse oblige*. Others are simply disillusioned about the possibility of greater mass involvement in public affairs, especially in an age when the complexity of government decisions is great and growing. The few populists in the House of Commons are a tiny (and largely inexperienced) minority.

The Functions of Operative Ideals:
Weapons, Rules, and Goals

I have been talking about some basic philosophical differences in political values. However, our interest is in neither comparative linguistics nor academic philosophy, but in operative political ideals, the standards and values that men bring to bear on political institutions and political behavior. Are philosophical principles relevant to practical politics at all? To answer this question requires that we consider, finally, the functions of operative ideals.

One common use of the concept of democracy, especially in Italy, is as a weapon in partisan combat. Ithiel de Sola Pool has pointed out that democracy "is to modern political controversies what God and the Church were to medieval thought, i.e., an end by which all programs are justified," and he might well have added, a standard for judging heresies.[4] I have already noted that more than half of our Italian politicians use commitment to democracy as one of the most important ways of classifying the various parties. Naturally, there is just as much disagreement about which parties are the undemocratic ones as there is on the meaning of democracy. In the Italian interviews the word "democracy" often had very little cognitive content. It was used simply to legitimate the respondent's own political objectives or to attack those of his opponents.

3. Eric Nordlinger, *The Working Class Tories* (Berkeley: University of California Press, 1967), p. 17.
4. Ithiel de Sola Pool, *Symbols of Democracy* (Stanford, Calif.: Stanford University Press, 1952), p. 1.

A member of the Italian Republican Party: "I engage in politics as a moral duty, like a soldier, morally obliged to conduct the *democratic* battle." (I57) Or a Christian Democrat: "Planning is necessary because we must coordinate the participation of the healthy, *democratic* forces of the country." (I9) Or a Communist: "These problems of social injustice are felt by all the *democratic* parties, excluding naturally the Italian Social Movement and the Monarchist party." (I17) The word "democracy" is part of the arsenal of every Italian politician, regardless of his interpretation of the concept. In fact, it appeared more often in the conversations of authoritarian democrats than in any other interviews. "The Devil quoting Scripture" is the way Pool's medieval men referred to the comparable phenomenon in their world.

This use of the notion of democracy is interesting from the point of view of intellectual history. But if the only role that this word played in practical politics were that of a convenient synonym for "policies (or parties or people) of which I approve," this linguistic fact would be of little interest to students of politics. However, some politicians use the concept of democracy in more significant ways.

Notions of democracy can serve as guides to the rules of an ongoing political game. Sartori seems to have this function in mind when he points out that "a clear understanding of what democracy is about is a major condition (although not the only one) for behaving democratically. For wrong ideas about democracy make a democracy go wrong."[5] Many respondents use their conception of democracy as a guideline to appropriate political behavior. "In a *democracy* it is impossible to impose a strait-jacket incomes policy, you just can't do it," or again, in the same interview, "We should have clear-cut lines between the parties, as clear-cut as possible, because . . . where the lines between the parties merge, *democracy* falters because the electorate does not get a clear choice." (B3) Or another MP, talking about extremists: "If they want to put their point of view, well, it isn't any good arguing that you're living in a *democratic* society if you don't allow them to." (B88) These respondents are using the concept of democracy as a basis for evaluating political tactics, their own and others'. Their syllogism is explicit: democratic norms prescribe (or proscribe) conduct of a certain sort; I support democratic norms; therefore, I support (or oppose) that sort of conduct.

The concept of democracy serves this function much more frequently for British than for Italian politicians, a natural consequence of the different focus that democratic theory has in the two countries. As discussed in chapter 14, the British conception of democracy heavily emphasizes institutions and procedures; the Italian conception does not. Both the polyarchal and the liberal models of democracy are well suited to this purpose, as they stress procedures and institutions. A politician who interprets democracy as the free com-

5. Giovanni Sartori, *Democratic Theory* (New York: Frederick A. Praeger, 1965), p. 5.

petition of opposing teams or as parliamentary control over the executive knows that certain kinds of political activities are legitimate and that others are not. A politician who interprets democracy as "maximum individual self-realization" cannot easily use this notion as a standard for judging his own political actions or those of his opponents.

As guides to appropriate political behavior, polyarchal democracy and (to a lesser extent) liberal democracy have another important advantage. They fit well with traditional, more elitist patterns of authority. If people's attitudes toward authority change only slowly, then the transition from predemocratic to democratic patterns of politics must be a difficult one for leaders and followers alike. British political development is a classic example of how this transition can be eased if the newer conceptions of authority are similar in some respects to the older conceptions they are replacing. Liberal and polyarchal versions of democracy can be assimilated to older orientations relatively easily, because each stresses autonomous leadership. Furthermore, as Harry Eckstein has pointed out, hierarchical conceptions of democracy (like those characteristic of Britain) are more consonant with authority patterns found elsewhere in society—in the family, in the factory, and so on.[6]

The modal Italian conceptions of democracy are at a considerable disadvantage on these counts. The philosophical egalitarianism of Italian politicians and the ideal of direct democracy embodied in the classical model are wholly alien to the authority patterns of traditional society, in Italy as elsewhere. There are no orienting similarities between these egalitarian attitudes and nonpolitical social relations in today's Italy.

Furthermore, neither of the two most characteristic Italian interpretations, classical democracy and authoritarian democracy, offers a resolution of the knotty problem of leadership in a democracy. As Gabriel Almond and Sidney Verba have phrased this issue:

> The maintenance of a proper balance between governmental power and governmental responsiveness represents one of the most important and difficult tasks of a democracy. Unless there is some control of governmental elites by nonelites, it is hard to consider a political system democratic. On the other hand, nonelites cannot themselves rule. If a political system is to be effective— if it is to be able to initiate and carry out policies, adjust to new situations, meet internal and external challenges—there must be mechanisms whereby governmental officials are endowed with the power to make authoritative decisions.[7]

It is precisely this dilemma that Italian governments have often failed to resolve,

6. Harry Eckstein, "A Theory of Stable Democracy," as reprinted in his *Division and Cohesion in Democracy*.

7. Gabriel Almond and Sidney Verba, *The Civic Culture* (Princeton, N.J.: Princeton University Press, 1963) pp. 476–7.

and it is precisely this dilemma for which neither classical democrats nor authoritarian democrats have a satisfactory answer. The former cut this Gordian knot by denying the need for leadership, the latter by denying the value of democracy.

The argument here must be carefully phrased, for (as I will argue in a moment) the classical conception of democracy may play a very important role as an operative ideal. But classical democracy (and the authoritarian and socioeconomic models, for that matter) cannot easily serve as a guide to the practice of contemporary politics, in Italy or elsewhere. There is, inevitably, a wide gap between practical politics and this conception of democracy, a disparity recognized quite explicitly by some Italians.

> Look, in terms of conception, in terms of principle, I believe that despite the youth of our democracy, in terms of the conception of democracy, we are in the vanguard. In terms of capacity to achieve it, perhaps we are not in the vanguard. Perhaps we affirm it more than we achieve it. (I18)

The danger in this disparity between ideals and reality is the possibility that a virulent cynicism may develop about the ideals. For many Italian leaders, and still more, for many ordinary citizens, the gap between the democratic ideals to which the leaders pledge allegiance and the reality of the politics they practice is too great to be bridged by a tolerant realism. The ideals seem hypocritical, the reality illegitimate. By contrast, British conceptions of democracy and the realities of British politics are virtually identical. The political ideals serve to legitimate and sustain the political system.

Mosca called attention to the importance of what he called "the political formula," the moral and legal principles used to justify any political regime. The political formula may be based on supernatural beliefs or on secular doctrines, but in either case, the basis is essentially nonrational. "And yet," Mosca was at pains to point out,

> that does not mean that political formulas are mere quackeries aptly invented to trick the masses into obedience. Anyone who viewed them in that light would fall into a grave error. The truth is that they answer a real need in man's social nature; and this need, so universally felt, of governing and knowing that one is governed not on the basis of mere material or intellectual force, but on the basis of a moral principle, has beyond any doubt a practical and a real importance.[8]

When the correspondence between the political formula and the political system is close, as it is in Britain, the need of which Mosca speaks is satisfied. On the other hand, if the correspondence is not close—perhaps because the formula is stated in such a way that no political system in the real world could

8. Mosca, *The Ruling Class*, ed. and rev. Arthur Livingston, trans. Hannah D. Kahn (New York: McGraw-Hill, 1939), p. 71.

fit it—both the rulers and the ruled will doubt the authenticity of the regime. Many will believe that the formula is indeed a fabricated quackery. Mosca himself pointed out that this peril was inherent in the Italian tendency to interpret democracy in Rousseau's terms.[9] In the three-quarters of a century since he wrote, the danger has not diminished.

There may be, as I have suggested, substantial agreement on Italian institutional arrangements. But this agreement is fragile, lacking the adamantine qualities imparted by a widely shared conviction that the institutions "fit" one's most fundamental political values. When you ask a British politician about democracy, he tells you about British politics, about "how we do things here." When you ask an Italian politician about democracy, he tells you about another world, about what a better Italy would be like. This contrast explains why Italians do not typically use their conceptions of democracy as guides to appropriate behavior and why those conceptions do not serve effectively to legitimate the existing regime.

The Italian conception of democracy may, however, be better suited for one final function, for one's concept of democracy may also serve to guide and sustain a critique of existing social and political institutions. Historically, this function has been the most important that models of democracy have performed. Even the relatively realistic conceptions now current in Britain once served in this way. A. H. Birch points out, for example, that "in the past 130 years the Liberal theory of the constitution has passed through three phases. It has been successively the basis of a programme of reform, a slightly idealized version of an existing situation, and a set of traditional principles to which practice no longer corresponds."[10]

A few British respondents seemed to be reaching for a conception of democracy that would give them some critical leverage. One, for example, said that the most important problem facing Britain was the task of involving people in social activities, raising their sights from the trivialities of everyday life. He used the phrase "participatory democracy" several times, and struggled to express more precisely the kinds of changes he had in mind. Finally, he stumbled to a halt: "I'm not particularly articulate so far as this is concerned." (B28) I believe he was overly harsh on himself. His culture simply does not provide him with conceptual tools for thinking about that different, more democratic kind of society that he wanted. Knowing "how we do things here" is not enough if you want to do them differently.

By contrast, many Italians who felt a similar discontent with contemporary society used their more idealized conceptions of democracy to help them formulate their desires fairly explicitly.

Basically, I believe that the biggest problem is how to create a new democratic

9. Ibid., p. 258.
10. A. H. Birch, *Representative and Responsible Government* (Toronto: University of Toronto Press, 1964), p. 66.

life in our country. . . . [There are] deficiencies in many fields, deficiencies in the economic field, in the social field, but above all, deficiencies in the field of new institutions for democratic participation, which would permit greater participation and not the kind of tutelary democracy which in certain respects still exists in our country. Woe to us if we become absorbed only by the economic and social objectives of our economic planning. . . . These must be means, and not ends, means toward the realization of [greater] participation, [greater] sensitivity, so that the citizen participates increasingly actively in the democratic life. (I74)

This respondent went on to describe ways of increasing popular participation through decentralization, local autonomy, more active and politically independent trade unions, workers' councils in industry, and so on. His image of this future, more democratic society was not complete in all details, but it was incomparably more articulated than the vision of his British counterpart.

Of course, in some ways Italian conceptions of democracy are irrelevant to several of the most important problems facing Italy, for they fail to provide the ideas and ideals needed to overcome political instability and decay. The British historian Denis Mack Smith has recently argued that Italian government will remain unstable and ineffective so long as there is no alternation of different parties in power. And yet, as I have shown, this notion of competition and alternation in power is a relatively insignificant part of the Italian concept of democracy. In this respect, Italian democrats do not have the same critical leverage that Mack Smith's notion of democracy affords him.[11]

The causal chain here is tangled, for the absence of partisan alternation in Italian politics is both effect and cause of the failure of Italian politicians to interpret democracy in polyarchal terms. And both factors are, in turn, bound to the widespread Italian criticism of *partitocrazia,* or rule by parties. Britain, too, is ruled by parties in which decision making is highly centralized, but the British do not consider this a fault, partly because it is consonant with their conceptions of democracy and partly because the reality of competition for governmental power makes for genuine, if limited, public influence on policy.

The classical conception of democracy so common in Italy is essentially irrelevant to this problem; it provides no basis for critical understanding and creative response. Some may argue that this conception is similarly irrelevant to any problem in the real world. Whether one accepts this argument depends on one's projection of the future of Western society and politics. Any casual observer of the contemporary scene is aware of widespread demands for "participation" and "involvement" and "control over one's own life." As the decade of the 1970s opens, such phrases are on the lips of prominent politicians on both sides of the Atlantic. All this may be simply a passing cultural fad, more pom-

11. Denis Mack Smith's discussion appeared in *L'Espresso* 15 (July 13, 1969): 4.

pous than Beatle records and miniskirts, but no less ephemeral. But there are some reasons for suspecting otherwise.

Most people do not participate actively in politics, because they lack the competence, the interest, and the time. But social and political change in the West during the last several generations may well have modified these conditions substantially. Studies of mass political behavior have found that interest, competence, and participation rise with rising levels of education.[12] And everywhere in the West levels of education are rising, often very rapidly.

Lack of leisure has always been a formidable obstacle to mass political participation. The opportunity cost of engaging in political activities when basic physical needs are not satisfied is very great; the poor will seldom choose to participate in politics. But in a world of affluence and leisure, political participation (or more broadly, social participation) would be less costly and more sensible. To be sure, most people have not yet achieved the levels of well-being that could allow them to devote large amounts of their time and energy to political activity, but this may not be an immutable condition of human existence.

Finally, the growth of government intervention in social and economic affairs increases the incentives for political participation. As people feel their lives more directly affected by the activities of government, they naturally demand greater influence over those activities.[13] Bigger government is also more complex government, of course, and the growth of science and technology does threaten to widen the gap between the experts and the rest of us. But the task of politicians in our age is to design bridges for this gap, to reconcile complexity and responsiveness.

More education, more affluence, more leisure, more government—these well-established trends in modern society make it plausible that demands for effective popular involvement in public affairs are likely to be a persisting feature of politics in the future. If this is so, politicians whose operative ideals help them comprehend and respond to these demands are likely to be more effective leaders than those whose images of the good polity are elitist and hierarchical.[14] In the coming decades those attitudes toward democracy and equality that characterize Italian elite political culture may become increasingly relevant to politics throughout the West. To be sure, Italy is not itself one of the nations of Western Europe that will reach the requisite levels of affluence, education, and leisure most rapidly. And in the shorter run, Italian operative political ideals have

12. See, for example, Almond and Verba, *The Civic Culture,* esp. pp. 379–87. In the Italian case, see also Samuel H. Barnes, "Participation, Education, and Political Competence: Evidence From a Sample of Italian Socialists," *American Political Science Review* 60 (1966): 348–53.

13. For an extended treatment of this proposition, see S. M. Lipset, *Political Man* (London: Mercury Books, 1963), pp. 186–90.

14. Asked whether there should be more popular participation in politics and government 36 percent of the British respondents said flatly "no." Only 4 percent of the Italians responded similarly. There are a variety of interpretations for these data, but the figure for Britain surely does not suggest wholehearted welcome for mass involvement in public affairs.

grave deficiencies. But although Keynes' oft-quoted dictum that "in the long run we are all dead" may be an appropriate guide for economists concerned with the business cycle, students of comparative politics and history may find a longer perspective useful. Some of the younger politicians I have spoken with in this study will lead their countries into the twenty-first century, guided in large measure by their beliefs about the proper relationship between men and their government.

Epilogue   Elite Political Culture and Its Sources

Politicians and their beliefs have been the subject of this volume. Our purpose has required that we decompose the several elements in elite political culture, that we pull apart the individual strands in a man's carefully woven fabric of political ideas and ideals. No doubt one of the respondents, glancing over the reader's shoulder, would find much that is unfamiliar, perhaps even alien, about my descriptions. For it is precisely in the mix a man makes of his beliefs that his individuality is found. I have hoped only to illuminate certain central and recurrent themes in the mixes most men have made.

And I have tried to treat these men seriously—not always sympathetically, but always seriously. Students of politics have not always adopted this stance toward political leaders.[1] Some have seen madness at the root of political activism. Indeed, much of the behavior of politicians is nonrational, and some of it may be irrational. But—though I can offer no data to demonstrate this—my impression is that politicians are, on balance, less at the mercy of maniacal impulses than most of us. It seems to me, as it did to Harold Lasswell, that "it is probable that a basically healthy personality is essential to survive the perpetual uncertainties of political life."[2]

If the actions of political leaders are more self-controlled than psychically compelled, then it makes sense to study the attitudes, values, and habits that they use to orient themselves in their world. I have suggested that these orientations can best be understood in terms of three broad categories. The goals a man seeks in his political activity and the rules he follows are informed by his *operative ideals*. We have examined together the way the operative ideals of democracy, liberty, and equality are interpreted and evaluated and used by British and Italian politicians. The empirical judgments a man hazards about a complex and ambiguous world are structured by his *cognitive predispositions*.

1. An otherwise fascinating study of Italian elite political culture seems to me badly flawed by a failure to take seriously the beliefs expressed by politicians and by a consequent tendency to explain quite rational political behavior in terms of dubious mechanisms of ego-defense. See Gordon J. Di Renzo, *Personality, Power, and Politics* (Notre Dame, Ind.: Notre Dame University Press, 1967).

2. Harold Lasswell, "The Selective Effect of Personality on Political Participation," in *Studies in the Scope and Method of "The Authoritarian Personality"* ed. Richard Christie and Marie Jahoda (Glencoe, Ill.: Free Press, 1954), p. 223.

We have investigated one important example—attitudes to social conflict and consensus—and I have tried to illustrate how this pre-perceptual presumption about the structure of interests in society affects the outlook and the behavior of our respondents. The way a man combines his normative commitments and his empirical judgments is regulated by his *political style*. We have considered one salient dimension of style, involving the role of ideology in politics.

For each of these particular examples of style, cognitive predispositions, and ideals I have illustrated the way the beliefs of a man and the culture of a nation influence the patterns of their politics. In thus seeking the consequences of these cultural themes, we have paid particular attention to implications for the responsiveness, stability, and effectiveness of British and Italian democracy. In our quest for the origins of elite political culture, we have also discovered several recurring patterns. Four particular variables emerged with surprising regularity as we searched for the correlates of cultural traits: age, social class, partisan ideology, and country.

The consistent discovery of significant divergences among the outlooks of different generations cries out for interpretation in historical terms despite the methodological ambiguities inherent in such evidence. Cohort analysis is a poor substitute for genuinely longitudinal research. But patterns we have found for each of our themes—attitudes to democracy, to conflict, to opponents, and to style—compel attention to the nature of cultural change. One of our central conclusions must be that the study of elite political culture offers unique opportunities for students of history and politics to investigate the impact of the past on the future.

If correlations with age recall the importance of history, the recurrent correlations with class underline the significance of social structure. At the urging of sociologists and under the aegis of Marxist and neo-Marxist social theories, countless scholars have counted the social background characteristics of political leaders. But there have been persistent complaints that these studies assume the unproved: that social background conditions behavior.[3] Recently, these murmurs of discontent have been amplified by evidence that many aspects of the belief systems of political leaders are virtually unrelated to their social origins.[4] The present study adds another refinement to the argument. If one wants to predict a politician's position on economic planning or European integration, his social background may well be irrelevant. But if, on the other hand, one wants to predict his orientation toward social conflict or his commitment to political equality, his social background may be considerably more important. The day of blanket assumptions that social background characteristics are

3. An early statement of this reservation can be found in Donald Matthews, *The Social Background of Political Decision-Makers* (Garden City, N.Y.: Doubleday, 1954).

4. See Lewis J. Edinger and Donald D. Searing, "Social Background in Elite Analysis," *American Political Science Review* 61 (1967): 428–45; and Donald D. Searing, "The Comparative Study of Elite Socialization," *Comparative Political Studies* 1 (1969): 471–500.

politically relevant has passed. The time has come for more carefully defined inquiries into the effects of specific background characteristics on basic orientations.[5]

The third important correlate of the attitudes we have investigated has been partisan ideology. Here, too, recent studies have raised doubts about long-assumed relevance. Soundings of mass attitudes in many nations have revealed how little understood and little used are the great systems of ideas through which scholars have traditionally interpreted political behavior. As I stressed at the outset of this volume, most people are not interested in politics, and it is not surprising, therefore, that their conceptions of politics are impoverished and unconstraining. But on this dimension, too, elites are different, for at least in Britain and Italy their orientations toward many diverse features of the political world are linked through the ideology they have embraced. Like history and social structure, political ideologies—"forensic ideologies," in Lane's felicitous phrase[6]—are an important element in the complex causal background of cultural orientations.

Political scientists who take seriously the "comparative" in comparative politics can be terrible simplifiers, for their desire to discover uniformities in political behavior can blind them to the equal significance of national peculiarities. I claim no exemption from this indictment, for I have been intent on describing the similarities in the behavior of British and Italian politicians. But the data demand that I close by stressing the cross-national differences. For throughout our investigation the most persistent predictor of these politicians' basic attitudes has been country. The political style, the cognitive orientations, and the operative ideals of Italians and Britons continue to show the tug of national tradition. But this fact should not engender simple awed reverence for the ineffable uniqueness of cultures. The task of social science is rather to discover why cultures differ as they do.

5. Cf. Searing's statement that "we have found that expressed specific attitudes (and most likely specific attitudes as well) cannot be forecast with currently employed background variables. But these sorts of attitudes may have little relationship to elite behavior patterns over time in any event. Underlying orientations on the other hand—which probably hold more relevance for elite behavior patterns—may perhaps be more easily forecast among elite populations. If they are to be adequately forecast, however, it will be necessary to refine background categories by way of generating data closer to relevant socialization experiences." ("The Comparative Study of Elite Socialization," p. 495).

6. Robert E. Lane, *Political Ideology* (New York: Free Press, 1962), p. 16.

Appendix A
Coding Conversational Interviews

Because the coding procedures used in this study are not common in political science, some comments on methodology may be useful. In the present context coding means simply some technique for placing all respondents along a given dimension or within a given classification scheme, on the basis of their responses in an interview situation. Let us consider a range of four different types of coding.

"Closed" questions require the respondent to choose among a fixed set of alternatives. The coding of responses to such questions is essentially automatic. If the respondent "agrees" with the statement that "most people can be trusted," he is implicitly, but automatically, classified as "low on misanthropy." Apart from clerical errors, the coding reliability of this procedure is perfect; repeated coding of a given response will always give the same result.[1] But the validity of responses of this sort is much more questionable; for reasons discussed in chapter 2, it is far from clear that responses to "closed" items accurately measure the presumed underlying attitude.

The second type of coding involves classifying answers to explicit, but open-ended questions. One can ask a respondent what he thinks should be the role of the public in politics and government, for example, and categorize his answer. Coding reliability for this sort of operation is high, but it is far from perfect, for a number of respondents may give answers that fit poorly into the categories that have been devised. Reliability can be improved by careful construction of the classification system, but inevitably some respondents will have given incurably idiosyncratic or ambiguous responses, which independent coders may not interpret in exactly the same way.[2]

1. Effective response reliability may be much lower, of course, since if the respondent is dissatisfied with the alternatives offered, his choice may be essentially random, displaying very low consistency from one time to another in his reaction to the identical stimulus. For the distinction between "reliability" and "validity," see, for example, Claire Selltiz, Marie Jahoda, Morton Deutsch, and Stuart Cook, *Research Methods in Social Relations,* rev. ed., (New York: Holt, Rinehart and Winston, 1959), pp. 146–186.
2. This problem can always be solved, of course, by allowing a large "unclassifiable" category, but this defeats the purpose of the coding operation, which is to align respondents in terms of a single, consistent set of categories.

Two distinct tactics can be allowed in coding answers of this sort. The coders can be instructed to record either what the respondent *says* in response to a single question or what he seems to *mean,* taking into account his entire discussion of the topic. The former tactic is, clearly, more conservative, but it is not always more reliable in a statistical sense. For example, coders in this study were asked both to rate the explicit response to the question on political participation and to rate the respondent's overall attitude toward participation, basing their judgment on his entire discussion of a series of questions on this topic, including *obiter dicta.* The intercoder reliability of these two separate coding operations was virtually identical.[3] The coders did not always believe that what was said in response to the single question was precisely what was meant, and when they judged what was meant, they were as often in agreement as when they judged what was said.

In summary, then, coding answers to open-ended questions of this sort can often be very reliable, though not perfectly so, and this reliability may not be reduced by allowing coders to base their judgment on more than merely the explicit answer to a single question. The validity of these codes is, of course, harder to measure, but there is every reason for believing that it can be quite high, perhaps even higher if the coders are allowed to express their broader judgment.

A third type of coding can be termed "latent feature" coding. Suppose one wants to know not what a respondent thinks about poverty, but how he thinks about it. One might want to know, for example, the extent to which he "moralizes" his discussion by attributing blame for the problem to someone. The reliability of coding such latent characteristics is, not surprisingly, lower than the reliability of coding manifest responses to explicit questions. However, the evidence presented in part II illustrates that carefully instructed coders using a carefully defined set of categories can achieve impressive levels of agreement, well above the level of chance.

The validity of latent feature coding must be demonstrated in any given case. But there are some theoretical concerns that logically require this type of coding; political style is a good example. Asking a politician whether he is an "ideologue" may produce a reliably codable response, but that response tells you virtually nothing about his political style. If latent-feature coding is based on a fairly precise section of the interview (for example, the discussion of a single policy issue) and if the coding criteria can be made similarly precise and explicit, the results are often relatively easy to interpret.

This ease of interpretation is not, by contrast, always characteristic of the fourth type of coding operation, which requires the coders to make a global judgment about certain traits of the respondent, based on the interview as a whole. To discover some features of a political belief system, this type of coding is useful. If one wants to know "the extent to which the respondent applies to all discussions of political topics a single, simplified conceptual or explanatory scheme"—or more simply, the extent to which he has a comprehensive *Weltanschauung*—"global coding" is essential.

This type of coding is both difficult and dangerous. It is difficult, because the criteria for the judgment are not easily made explicit nor is the basis of the judgment easily specifiable, since relevant evidence may be found in any part of the interview. In fact,

3. See n. 1, chap. 16. The generalization in the text holds true even for interviews in which the explicit question was not asked in the appropriate form; hence, it is not a spurious result of ratings on the first judgment directly influencing ratings on the second judgment.

coders in the present study were able to achieve a rather high degree of concordance in their judgments about the *Weltanschauung* trait just mentioned. But this sort of coding is also dangerous, precisely because the criteria are largely implicit. It may be difficult even for the coders themselves to know just what it is that they are agreeing on. In other words, the validity of these judgments is often questionable. Some of these problems can be dealt with by careful statistical analysis, but global codes of this sort, though sometimes essential, must always be treated with caution.

These last two types of coding bear a close family resemblance to the technique called content analysis. Some forms of content analysis, particularly the more recently developed automated versions, stress word counts, but under the rubric of content analysis some researchers have carried out operations logically identical to what I have here called "latent feature" and "global" coding.[4]

The guide for analyzing the interviews in the present research is given as appendix B. Perusal of that codebook will give the reader some of the flavor of the judgments that the coders were asked to make; examples may be found of each of the four types of coding I have mentioned. As described in chapter 2, every interview was coded separately by two coders. Their independent judgments were then confronted, and the coders discussed the differences and arrived at an agreed final judgment. The analyses reported in this volume are based on these consensual assessments.

There are a number of advantages to be drawn from the double coding of each interview. The most obvious benefit is that it provides statistical evidence on the reliability of the judgments being made. Throughout this volume I have systematically reported the intercoder reliability coefficients for all problematic judgments.[5] A second advantage of comprehensive double coding is that it allows the technique of "cross-coder correlation" to be used; as described in chapter 2, this technique permits one to detect and control for inter-item assimilation.

Several equally important advantages of double coding are less obvious. If coders are forced continually to confront their divergences in judging individual interviews, they come to understand better the implicit criteria they are using, and therefore to understand better the way they are interpreting the underlying, theoretical variables. This procedure can be especially helpful if the primary researcher becomes involved, for he is then able to clarify for himself some of the unexplored aspects of his "primitive" conceptual formulations.

Finally, comprehensive double coding encourages the development of a community of coders with common standards. It is essential to this sort of coding that the codebook itself be as clear and explicit as possible. Nevertheless, in any large-scale coding

4. Much of the methodological literature on content analysis is highly relevant here. A concise, but comprehensive introduction to this literature is the article by Matilda White Riley and Clarice S. Stoll in the *International Encyclopedia of the Social Sciences* (New York: Crowell Collier and Macmillan, 1968) 3: 371–7. An excellent discussion of the problems of coding can be found in D. P. Cartwright, "Analysis of Qualitative Material," in *Research Methods in the Behavioral Sciences,* ed. Leon Festinger and Daniel Katz (New York: Dryden Press, 1953), chap. 10.

5. Since the final judgments used in the analyses for this study were based on a discussion between the two independent coders, which tended to "weed out" obvious mistakes by one or the other of the two coders, the final judgments are somewhat "purer" and therefore presumptively more reliable. Hence, the reliability coefficients given in the text above may safely be taken as the *lower limits* of actual reliability.

operation a body of "common law" is built up that deals with how to treat particular sorts of ambiguous responses and how to delimit the thresholds between adjacent categories on certain dimensional codes. (For example, how intense must distrust toward partisan opponents be to be rated "total"?) Double coding and frequent collective discussion of recurrent problems ensure that this body of common law is understood and applied consistently by all coders.

Appendix B
The Codebook

The following is the codebook used to guide analysis of each interview transcript. Coders entered on codesheets numbers corresponding to their judgments on each separate coding item. When a given item was inappropriate for a given transcript or when no answer was possible (NA), a code of "0" was assigned. When an answer was given that did not fit into any of the specific alternatives in the codebook, the respondent was put in an "other" category, and a notecard was filled out, giving details. (Thus, the abbreviation "MAC" stands for "make a card.") All topics covered in the interview are also covered in the codebook, and the interview question is reproduced for each coding item. Hence, the reader can easily reconstruct the interview schedule by leafing through this codebook. A mass of information was gathered that is not reported in this volume. Sometimes the categories that appear in the codebook for a given variable are not identical to those presented in the text because certain variables (e.g. deck 3, column 76, "Political Liberties") were collapsed in order to simplify analysis and presentation.

Column Number	Code
01–02	*Study Number* (33)
03–04	*Deck Number* (01)
05	*Country*

    1.   Britain
    2.   Italy

06–08	*Respondent Number*
09	*Questionaire Version*

    1.   AC (Parties and crime discussed)
    2.   AT (Parties and transport discussed)
    3.   BE (Pattern of power and planning discussed)
    4.   BP (Pattern of power and poverty discussed)
    5.   Mixed (Some other combination of topics)
    0.   NA; Inap.

10–11,   *Likes about Politics*

12–13,   Q. 2.   "What do you find most appealing about politics?"
14–15   Code up to three mentions.

General or undefined

    11.   Life commitment; like everything about politics.
MAC————18.   Other.

Sociability

    21.   Conviviality with colleagues in Parliament.
    25.   Life or atmosphere in Parliament.
    27.   Contact with "great men."
MAC————28.   Other.

Power/influence/"center of things"

    31.   Political fun; "center of things."
    33.   Fun of attacking opponents or debating.
    35.   Power or influence on decisions or political affairs.
    36.   Freedom of action.
    37.   Chance to express opinions or share in public discussion.
MAC————38.   Other.

Prestige/respect

    41.   Contact with people, the masses, constituents.

Column
Number   *Code*

10–15   43.   Honor, prestige, acclaim.
Cont.   47.   Entree; access to important people.
MAC———48.   Other.

Moral/philosophical

        51.   "Citizen-duty"; contribution to solving national problems (no issue content).
MAC———58.   Other.

Ideological

        61.   Fighting for ideals, a program, a cause.
        63.   Fighting for the interests of a particular group, class, or party.
        65.   Opposing a group, class, or party.
MAC———68.   Other.

Problem-solving

        71.   Solving concrete social, technical, or legislative problems.
        75.   Service to constituents, "casework," "ombudsman."
MAC———78.   Other.

Miscellaneous

        81.   Intellectual satisfactions; educational experiences.
        83.   Diversity of experience.
MAC———88.   Other.
        91.   Nothing; no attractions. (This code is not inconsistent with other codes in these columns; it is a priority code, however; i.e. if it appears, it must appear in cols. 10–11.)
        00.   NA; Inap. No further mentions.

16–17,   *Dislikes about Politics*
18–19,   Q. 3.   "What do you find least appealing about politics?" Code up to
20–21   3 mentions.

Working Conditions and Opportunity Costs

        11.   Time constraints in general; hecticness.
        12.   No time for family; privacy gone; no time for culture, reading, relaxation.
        14.   General working conditions: lack of facilities; lack of assistance; irregular schedule.
        15.   Financial problems.
        16.   Wasted time.
        17.   Boredom; routine; drudgery.
MAC———18.   Other.

Impotence with Respect to Other Political Actors

        21.   Lack of influence of parliamentarians on policy-making.
        22.   Lack of influence of parliamentarians on bureaucracy or administration.
        23.   Party domination of parliament; *Partitocrazia.*

16–21   24.   Lack of influence of Opposition on policy-making.
Cont.   26.   Unfulfilled desire for more powerful position (in Government).
           27.   Lack of opportunity for speaking in Chamber on subjects of
                 interest.
MAC————28.   Other.

Political Institutions and Leadership

           31.   Organization, methods, and slowness of Parliament.
           32.   Slowness and other inadequacies of political institutions in
                 general.
           37.   Lack of educated, technically prepared political leaders.
MAC————38.   Other.

Public Pressures and Attitudes

           41.   Servicing constituents' demands; "casework."
           42.   Elections and electioneering.
           43.   Publicity, public attention, general public demands.
           44.   Undue pressure from particularistic groups, from demanding
                 constituents (on policy, not "ombudsman"-demands).
           45.   Necessity of making lots of contacts; "the social side of it."
           46.   Lack of popular esteem for politicians.
           47.   Gap between leaders and the country; popular apathy.
MAC————48.   Other.

Limitations on Solving Problems or Reaching Goals

           51.   "Talk, not action." Priority of abstract discussion over concrete
                 problem-solving.
           52.   "Partisanship." Priority or necessity of partisan maneuvering or
                 partisan bickering over concrete problem-solving.
           53.   Uselessness of activity; problems never solved; decisions never
                 made; nothing concrete ever accomplished; no sense of accom-
                 plishment.
           54.   No time or opportunity for studying concrete problems.
           55.   Frustration of getting others' agreement to policy proposals;
                 political realities taking precedence over ideals.
           56.   Lack of progress toward political ideals.
MAC———— 58.   Other.

Ambition, Antagonism, and Distrust

           61.   General, diffuse fear and distrust of others.
           62.   Personal antagonisms; difficulties in personal relations.
           63.   Personal and factional ambition or lust for power or intrigue.
           67.   Social life made difficult for person with integrity.
MAC———— 68.   Other.

Political Morality

           71.   General political corruption; low level of morality.
           72.   Demagogy; *trasformismo*; pandering to the base desires of
                 the electorate; *clientelismo*.

Column
Number   *Code*

16–21   73.   Lack of political ethics; unfair tactics; personal attacks.
Cont.   74.   Special interests taking priority over the general interest.
               75.   Cynicism; hypocrisy; bad faith.
MAC————78.   Other.

               Miscellaneous

               81.   Other politicians boring or uninteresting.
MAC————88.   Other.
               99.   No dissatisfactions.
               00.   NA; Inap. No further mentions.

22   *Overall Attractiveness*

               Qs. 2–3.   What is his overall assessment of the attractiveness of being
               involved in politics?
               1.   He likes it very much. No important dissatisfactions.
               2.   On balance he likes it. Some dissatisfactions, but satisfactions
                     more important.
               3.   Pro-con. Satisfactions and very important dissatisfactions.
               4.   On balance, he dislikes it. Some attractions, but dissatisfactions
                     are more important.
               5.   He dislikes it very much. No important satisfactions.
               0.   NA; Inap.

23   *Use of "Democracy" in Discussing Career*

               Qs. 2–3.   How often does the word "democracy" or cognates appear in
               his discussion of his likes and dislikes? Code actual number from 0–7.
MAC———— 8.   8 times or more. (MAC for 9 times or more.)
               9.   NA; Inap.

24–25,   *Most Important Problem*

26–27,   Q. 4.   "What are the three or four most important (domestic) problems
28–29   facing this country today?" Code up to three mentions, listed according to
               importance, if there is some indication of relative importance given; in
               order of mention, if no specific indication of importance given. Code
               based on the entire description given of the problem, not simply on the
               label the respondent gives the problem.
               Production
               11.   General type of economic development of the country (e.g.
                      socialist or capitalist economy).
               12.   Economic growth and productivity and stability.
               13.   Balance of payments; pound sterling, etc.
               14.   Prices and incomes policy; inflation.
               15.   Agricultural development.
               16.   Regional economic development.
MAC————18.   Other.
               Distribution
               21.   General direction of social development; type of society to
                      create; the general social situation.

Column
Number   *Code*

24–29   22. Social-economic planning; *programmazione*.
Cont.   23. Social justice; redistribution of national income.
             24. Setting priorities in governmental expenditure.
             25. Limiting governmental expenditure; lower taxes; greater incentives.
             26. Poverty; raising workers' (or other low) standards of living.
             27. Unemployment or underemployment.
MAC————28. Other.

            Services

             31. Allocation of resources to social welfare or social security; general references to welfare programs.
             32. Particular social welfare services (e.g. family allowances; aid to the blind).
             33. Pensions; aid to the aged.
             34. Education; the schools. (But *not* schools-and-religion, which is coded 82, below.)
             35. Housing.
             36. Medical care; hospitals.
             37. Problems connected with urbanization and the cities.
MAC————38. Other.

            Industrial Relations and Regulation of Business

             41. Regulation of business activities.
             42. Regulation of trade unions; trade union reform.
             43. Industrial relations.
MAC————48. Other.

            Form of Government and the Constitution

             51. Consolidation or development of democracy.
             52. General reform of the State or the Constitution. N.B. As used here "Constitution" refers specifically to the organization of government. If the respondent refers to "implementing the Constitution," but it is clear that he means more than simply governmental reform (for example, broader social reform) code under category 21 above.
             53. Decentralization or regional government or local government.
             54. Bureaucratic reform.
             55. Parliamentary reform.
             56. Excessive power of executive; need to protect individual freedom.
             57. Power or authority or autonomy of the State (vs. other groups— e.g. cabals); *partitocrazia*.
MAC————58. Other.

            Political Problems

             61. Equilibrium among the political forces (parties); relations of alliance, etc.
MAC————62. Elimination or reduction of influence of certain party or parties.

Column
Number   *Code*

24–29   63.   Corruption or malpractice in political life.
Cont.   64.   Gap between political leadership and the country—bringing
                    workers into full citizenship.
MAC————68.   Other.

Moral or Psychological Problems
             71.   Sense of purpose; sense of identity.
             72.   Mass participation in social and political activities.
             73.   Subordination of selfish interest to national welfare.
             74.   Moral decline; crime.
             75.   Overcoming traditionalism and conservatism.
             77.   Racialism; racial problem.
MAC————78.   Other.

Miscellaneous
             81.   Emigration.
             82.   Religion; Church-State relations; Church schools.
             83.   Divorce.
             84.   *Alto Adige* [Italo-Austrian border problem].
             85.   Problems of youth.
MAC————88.   Other.
             00.   NA; Inap. No further mentions.

30–31   *First Problem Discussed*

             Qs. 4 and 5: "How did this come to be a problem?" What is the problem
             which was *actually* selected for discussion? Use code outline given for
             columns 24–29.

32   *Breadth of Problem Discussed*

             Qs. 4–5. As the respondent describes (not just names) the problem se-
             lected for discussion, does it involve a *general social goal* or philosophical
             principle (e.g. greater social participation, "what kind of society do we
             want?"), a *broad policy area* (e.g. economic growth, reform of the State),
             or a *narrow policy area* (e.g. trade union reform, hospital reform, parlia-
             mentary reform)?
             1.   General social goal or philosophical principle.
             3.   Broad policy area.
             5.   Specific policy area.
             0.   NA.

33   *Foreign Policy—Defense*

             Q. 4. Does he mention foreign policy, international affairs, or defense
             in his list of important problems?
             1.   Yes, as the first problem mentioned.
             2.   Yes, but as a secondary problem.
             3.   Yes, but only as an adjunct to a domestic issue.
             5.   No.
             0.   NA.

Column
Number   *Code*

34   *Generalizer-Particularizer—His Issue*

Qs. 5 and 6–9. "How did this come to be a problem? What can be done about it? What do you think of the positions of the other parties on this issue?" Does the respondent generalize or particularize his discussion of this issue? Does his discussion focus on the general principles involved or on the specific details of the problem? Use this code as a continuum, not a set of discrete categories.

1. Extreme generalizer. (Focuses on the general philosophical principles involved, with little or no attention to specific details of the problem.)
2. Moderate generalizer. (Focuses on the general principles, but there is some discussion of relevant specifics.)
3. Pro-con. (Generalizes and particularizes, with no clear predominance of either.)
4. Moderate particularizer. (Focuses on specifics, though some general principles are mentioned.)
5. Extreme particularizer. (Focuses on details of problem, with little or no discussion of general principles.)
0. NA.

35   *Historical Context—His Issue*

Qs. 5–9. Does he place his discussion in a historical context by referring to historical trends?

1. Yes, explicitly. This is a central element of his discussion.
3. Yes, but only vaguely or in passing. (A simple recounting of the recent history of the problem and attempted solutions justifies a code of 3.)
5. No.
0. NA.

36   *Moralizer—His Issue*

Qs. 5–9. Does he moralize his discussion by assigning *blame* for the problem? Is it someone's fault?

1. Yes, explicitly. This is a central element of his discussion.
3. Yes, but only vaguely or in passing.
5. No.
0. NA.

37   *Utopias—His Issue*

Qs. 5–9. Does he refer to some ideal future or past society as a goal or standard in discussing this issue? Does he act politically with respect to this issue by moving towards a predefined goal or ideal *or* rather by reacting to existing problems?

1. Yes, refers to ideal explicitly and in some detail. Future.
2. Yes, explicitly and in some detail. Past.

Column
Number   *Code*

37   3.   Yes, but only vaguely or implicitly. Future.
Cont.   4.   Yes, but only vaguely or implicitly. Past.
              5.   No.
              0.   NA.

38   *Nature of Solution—His Issue*

              Qs. 5–9.   What is the nature of his solution to this problem?
              1.   Major changes in social, economic, or political institutions.
              2.   Programmatic. Specific proposals linked by some programmatic statement or general principles.
              3.   Statement of general principles which should guide policy, without particular policy proposals.
              4.   Particularistic. One or more specific, but unrelated proposals, lacking an integrative framework.
              9.   No solution proposed.
              0.   NA.

39   *Reference to Ideology—His Issue*

              Qs. 5–9.   In discussing this issue, does he refer to a specific, *named* ideology or doctrine as a criterion for proposing or opposing policies?
              1.   Yes, this is a central element of the discussion.
              3.   Yes, but this is not central or not explicit.
              5.   No.
              0.   NA.

40, 41   *Which Ideology—His Issue*

              Qs. 5–9.   What is the ideology referred to? Code up to 2 mentions.
              1.   Communism; Marxism.
              2.   Socialism; Social-Democracy.
              3.   Capitalism; Free Enterprise.
              4.   Conservatism.
              5.   Liberalism; laissez faire.
              6.   Fascism; totalitarianism; Nazism.
              7.   Catholicism; Christianity.
MAC———————— 8.   Other.
              0.   NA. Coded 5 or 0 in col. 39.

42   *Deductive-Inductive Thinking—His Issue*

              Qs. 5–9.   Does he use some general, abstract political or social or economic theory to explicate his problem? Is a chain of reasoning, including certain theoretical premises, given for reply to the question "Why do what you propose?" (i.e. not simply "because that's the problem.")? How distant is the solution from the problem? A solution which gets at the "roots" of the problem implies some theory about what those roots are; a solution which treats symptoms implies no such theory. Use code as a continuum.
              1.   Yes, definitely. Use of a general, abstract theory is explicit and central to his argument.

Column
Number   *Code*

42   2.   [Intermediate high].
Cont.   3.   Yes, but the theory is not general or abstract, and is not central
                    to the argument.
              4.   [Intermediate low].
              5.   No. He analyzes the problem without using any abstract theory.
              0.   NA.

43   *Reference to Group Benefits—His Issue*
              Qs. 5–9.   In discussing this issue, does he refer to benefits or losses to
              certain specific social groups as a relevant criterion for proposing or op-
              posing policies? Is the reference *direct* (help group for group's sake) or
              indirect (help group as means to solve some separate problem)?
              1.   Yes. Reference is central to argument and direct.
              2.   Yes. Reference is central to argument and indirect.
              3.   Yes, but reference is peripheral to argument. Direct.
              4.   Yes, but reference is peripheral to argument. Indirect.
              5.   No.
              0.   NA.

44–45,   *What Groups Mentioned—His Issue*
46–47,   Qs. 5–9.   What is the social group referred to above? Code up to 4 men-
48–49,   tions. N.B. Code first the group reference(s) which justified the code in the
50–51   previous column. Code in order of prominence.

              Social Class
              11.   Social classes in general.
              12.   Proletariat; working class.
              13.   The masses; *masse popolari.*
              14.   Bourgeoisie.
              15.   Middle class.
              16.   Aristocracy.
              17.   The privileged.
MAC————18.   Other.

              Occupation Groups
              21.   Miners or other unskilled or semiskilled heavy workers.
              22.   Workers.
              23.   Management; industrialists.
              24.   Peasants; farm workers.
              25.   Farmers.
              26.   Trade unionists.
              27.   The unemployed.
MAC————28.   Other.

              Income Groups
              31.   The poor [low priority on poverty question].
              33.   Lower-paid workers.
              35.   The rich; wealthy.
MAC————38.   Other.

Column
Number   *Code*

44–51   Psychological/Moral/Personal Characteristic-based Groups
Cont.   41.   The capable; the intelligent; the talented.
                42.   The ambitious; "self-starters".
                43.   "Inadequate," "unfortunate," "people in difficulty," "life's failures."
                45.   Criminals (to be rehabilitated).
                46.   The sick; the disabled; the blind; the infirm.
                47.   The family.
MAC————48.   Other.

                Geographical Groups
                51.   Geographical groups in general.
                52.   *Il Mezzogiorno* [the Italian South].
                53.   Scotland.
                54.   Wales.
                55.   The North of England.
                56.   Sicily and/or Sardinia.
                57.   Northern mountain regions of Italy.
MAC————58.   Other.

                Age Groups
                61.   The old.
                63.   Pensioners.
                65.   Youth; young people.
                67.   Children.
MAC————68.   Others.

                Sectors of Economy
                71.   Sectors of economy in general.
                72.   Agriculture.
                73.   Industry.
                74.   Export industry.
                75.   Other particular industries.
                77.   Consumers.
MAC————78.   Other.

                Miscellaneous
                81.   Emigrants.
                82.   Taxpayers.
MAC————88.   Other.
                00.   NA; no further mentions; coded 5 or 0 in col. 43.

52   *Acceptability—His Issue*
                Qs. 5–9. In discussing this issue, does he explicitly refer to political feasibility or acceptability as a relevant criterion for proposing or opposing policies?
                1.   Yes. This is a central element of his analysis.
                3.   Yes, but this is not central.

Column Number	Code
52	5. No.
Cont.	0. NA.

53   *Practicality—His Issue*

Qs. 5–9. In discussing this issue, does he refer explicitly to technical practicality or administrative efficiency as a relevant criterion for proposing or opposing policies?

Scale as in column 52.

54   *Cost—His Issue*

Qs. 5–9. In discussing this issue, does he refer explicitly to financial practicality or cost as a relevant criterion for proposing or opposing policies?

Scale as in column 52.

55   *Tradition—His Issue*

Qs. 5–9. In discussing this issue, does he refer to tradition or custom as a relevant criterion for proposing or opposing policies?

Scale as in column 52.

56   *Conflict of Interest—His Issue*

Qs. 5–9. How prominent are conflicting interests in his discussion of this issue? Conflict of interest implies at a minimum that one policy would be good for one group, another policy for another group. Assume for the sake of this coding item that the respondent's own position reflects one set of interests, so that if he mentions some other set of interests in conflict with "the right" solution, count this as a (low-level) perception of conflicting interests. N.B. Use this code as a continuum, not a set of discrete categories. Take into account two factors: (1) how central is the conflict of interest to his analysis? (2) how explicit is the reference to conflict of interest?

1. Very prominent. Conflict among interests is explicit and central to his discussion.
2. Important. Conflict among interests is explicit, but not central; *or* central and implicit in his discussion.
3. Present. Conflict among interests is implicit and peripheral, but present (e.g. he mentions groups whose interests are opposed, but does not discuss conflict among these interests.)
4. Minimal. No differing interests are mentioned. Differing opinions or perspectives on the problem are mentioned, but without the implication that these reflect conflicting interests. Discussion of "priorities" (with no mention of conflict of interest) would justify a code of "4."
5. Absent. There is no evidence that he perceives groups with different interests or perspectives on this problem.
0. NA.

Column
Number   *Code*

57   *Zero-Sum Conflict—His Issue*

Qs. 5–9.   Is the conflict of interest mentioned explicitly seen as zero sum? (Zero-sum conflict is a conflict of interest such that what one side gains the others involved necessarily must lose.)
1. Yes.
5. No.
0. NA. Coded 3, 4, 5, or 0 in column 56.

58   *Conflict Resolution—His Issue*

Qs. 5–9.   If he is aware of differing interests in this problem, what is his reaction?
1. He seeks a resolution of the conflicting interests. (Nobody loses; there is something for everyone.)
3. No resolution is explicitly sought, but none of the interests involved is rejected explicitly.
5. He explicitly rejects one or more of the interests or desires involved. (Somebody loses; nothing for somebody.)
0. NA. Coded 4, 5, or 0 in col. 56.

59   *Opponents' Position—His Issue*

Qs. 7–9.   "What do you think of the position of the opposing parties on this issue? Why do you think they have taken that position? How much room for compromise is there between their position and your own on this issue?" How open is the respondent to compromise on this issue? Use code as a continuum.
1. Very open.
2. Basically open, though closed to some opponents on some aspects of the problem.
3. Pro-con. Open to some opponents, closed to others. No clear predominance.
4. Basically closed, though open to some opponents on some aspects of the problem.
5. Very closed.
0. NA.

60   *What is Suggested Issue*

Q. 10.   "Another problem recently discussed here is _____." What is the specific issue suggested and actually discussed?
1. Economic planning (*programmazione*).
2. Poverty.
3. Crime.
4. Transport.

MAC———— 8. Other.
0. NA.

The following 19 columns deal with the substantive analysis of the four suggested issues. After coding column 60, go directly to the codes dealing

Column
Number   *Code*

60   with whichever substantive issue was discussed, using the guide given
Cont.   immediately below. All the columns dealing with the substance of the
            issues not discussed should be coded "0," with one exception: in a few
            interviews more than one of the suggested issues was discussed; e.g. at the
            end of the interview, poverty may have been discussed, even though the
            primary suggested issue was another. In this case code this subsidiary
            discussion in the appropriate columns below, e.g. cols. 62–71. This should
            not affect the coding of col. 60 above.

            Guide to substantive codes: economic planning: col. 61; poverty: cols.
            62–71; crime: cols. 72–76; urban transport: cols. 77–80.

61   *Attitude to Planning*

            Q. 10.   What does he think should be the role of the government in the
            national economy and in particular in economic planning *(programma-
            zione)*? This code represents a continuum of increasing government in-
            volvement, not a set of discrete categories. Each category implicitly in-
            cludes all the forms of more limited involvement mentioned in previous
            categories, together with the kind of involvement specifically characteristic
            of that category. Thus, a person who mentioned indicative planning and
            government incentives, but also mentioned government ownership of
            major sectors of the economy should fall into category "6." Code the
            general thrust of the entire answer, and use the code as a continuum.

            1.   None. A free enterprise economy with no government planning,
                 controls, or intervention.
            2.   Voluntary master plan or guidelines for future development, to-
                 gether with (possibly) planning and coordination of the govern-
                 ment's budget. With this minimal intervention, he argues for a
                 free enterprise economy.
            3.   Government incentives and encouragement for private enterprise
                 to follow the governmental plan (perhaps regional development)
                 and very limited public enterprise. Emphasis still on private enter-
                 prise economy.
            4.   Some direct public intervention and investment, as well as in-
                 dicative planning and incentives. In any consultation with labor
                 and management, government is one among equals.
            5.   Fairly large sector of direct public control, especially through
                 public ownership, along with any earlier forms of intervention.
                 In any consultation with labor and management, government
                 clearly has upper hand.
            6.   Direct governmental or public control of the major sectors of the
                 economy, expecially over investment decisions, along with any
                 earlier forms of intervention. Some limited room left for private
                 enterprise and market forces.
            7.   Full governmental control of the economy. No private enterprise
                 or market forces.

Column
Number   *Code*

61
Cont.

MAC———— 8.   Some other view of the proper role of the government in the economy outside the present frame of reference.

0.   NA.

62–63,   *Causes of Poverty*

64–65,   Q. 10.   "What are the sources of this problem of poverty?" Code up to
66–67   3 mentions.

Individual-Personal Factors

11.   Stupidity; lack of ability; incompetence.
12.   Laziness.
13.   Problem families; incompetent parents.
14.   Large families.
15.   Apathy; indifference.

MAC————18.   Other.

Historical Factors

21.   Late, slow, low economic development.
22.   Regional backwardness, lack of regional development.

MAC————28.   Other.

Natural Factors

31.   Poor land.
32.   No natural resources.
33.   Climate.

MAC————38.   Other.

"Objective" Social Factors Affecting Particular Groups

41.   Wage structure; lower-paid workers.
42.   Agricultural backwardness.
43.   Sectoral imbalance.
44.   Lack of education.
45.   Older people.
46.   Poor or inadequate housing.
47.   Unemployment.

MAC———— 48.   Other.

General Social Factors

51.   Exploitation.
52.   Capitalism.
53.   Socioeconomic structure; pattern of ownership, etc.
54.   Wrong sense of values.
55.   Maldistribution of income.

MAC————58.   Other

Governmental Policies

Column
Number   *Code*

62–67   61.   Governmental policies in general.
Cont.   62.   Welfare statism; uncontrolled welfare benefits.
               63.   Inflation; overspending.
               64.   Inadequate social welfare benefits.
               65.   War; other foreign policies.
               66.   Administrative problems with welfare programs.
MAC————68.   Other.

       Miscellaneous

MAC————88.   Other causes not falling under above headings.
               99.   None. No causes of poverty. Refuses to agree poverty is a prob-
                      lem; *not* inconsistent with other mentions.
               00.   NA. No further mentions.

68–69,   *Cures of Poverty*
70–71   Q. 10. "What can be done about this problem of poverty?" Code up to
                      2 mentions.

       Economic Development

               11.   General economic development; raise general standard of living.
               12.   Economic planning; *programmazione*.
               13.   Regional development.
               14.   More jobs.
               15.   Industrialization.
MAC————18.   Other.

       Type of Economic System

               21.   Socialism; develop and encourage public enterprise.
               25.   Capitalism; develop and encourage private enterprise.
MAC————28.   Other.

       Specific Economic Reforms

               31.   Reform the wage structure; incomes policy.
               35.   Agrarian reform.
MAC————38.   Other.

       Social Policies

               41.   Raise social welfare benefits.
               43.   Social workers' assistance, e.g. in home management.
               45.   Make social welfare benefits more selective.
               47.   More and better housing.
MAC————48.   Other.

       Fiscal Policy

               51.   Tax reform and income redistribution.
MAC————58.   Other.

       Education

               61.   More and better education.

Column
Number   *Code*
68–71
Cont.
MAC——— 68.   Other.
               Individual Improvement
               71.   Individual moral or spiritual improvement.
MAC———78.   Other.
               Miscellaneous
MAC———88.   Other policies not falling under above headings.
               99.   Nothing can be done. No particular policy. Time alone.
               00.   NA; no further mention.
72, 73,   *Causes of Crime*
74   Q. 10.   "What are the sources of this problem of crime?" Code up to 3
               mentions.
               1.   Breakdown of discipline, morality, authority, religion; reduced
                     police powers.
               2.   Public scandals; corruption in high places.
               3.   Commercialism; advertising; consumer society; materialism.
               4.   Social change: urbanization; industrialization; social mobility.
               5.   Social injustice; poverty; unemployment.
               6.   Regional traditions.
               7.   Too much money; affluence.
               8.   Family breakdown.
MAC——— 9.   Other.
               0.   NA. No further mentions.
75, 76   *Cures for Crime*
               Q. 10.   "What can be done about this problem of crime?" Code up to
               two mentions.
               1.   Moral improvement; sense of purpose; individual responsibility;
                     moral training; family training.
               2.   Good examples set by leaders; end corruption in high places.
               3.   General social reform.
               4.   Education; child development; youth programs.
               5.   Full employment; jobs.
               6.   Stiffer penalties; stricter enforcement.
               7.   Improved police techniques; crime prevention programs; re-
                     form of administration of justice.
MAC——— 8.   Other.
               9.   Don't know. Would ask sociologist; study facts; do more re-
                     search.
               0.   NA. No further mentions.
77, 78   *Causes of Urban Transport Problem*
               Q. 10.   "What are the sources of this problem of urban transport?" Code
               up to two mentions.

Column
Number   *Code*

77–78   1.   Motorization, as a social process.
Cont.   2.   Unplanned growth of cities.
               3.   Heritage of past; old cities.
               4.   The motorist; mania for car-buying. (This category as distinct
                     from "1," involves blaming individuals.)
               5.   Governmental policies imposed by private interests (e.g. au-
                     tomobile manufacturers).
               6.   Difficulties of public transport (costs, etc.).
               7.   Not enough money spent.
MAC————— 8.   Other.
               0.   NA. No further mentions.

79–80   *Cures of Urban Transport Problem*

           Q. 10.   "What can be done about this problem of urban transport?" Code
           up to two mentions.
               1.   Tighter control over the use of cars. Ban cars, etc.
               2.   Public transport developed, made more attractive.
               3.   Coordination, integration, planning of transport system.
               4.   Urban planning.
               5.   Pricing systems; taxes on car use.
               6.   Technical traffic or automotive innovations.
               7.   Individual discipline; exhortations to individuals.
MAC————— 8.   Other.
               0.   NA. No further mentions.

Column	
Number	*Code*
01–02	*Study Number* (33)
03–04	*Deck Number* (02)
05	*Country*

        1.   Britain
        2.   Italy

06–08   *Respondent Number*

09   *Questionnaire Version*

Repeat code given in deck 01, column 09.

10   *What is Suggested Issue*

Q. 10. What is the specific issue suggested for discussion and actually discussed?

        1.   Economic planning *(programmazione)*.
        2.   Poverty.
        3.   Crime.
        4.   Transport.
MAC———— 8.   Other.
        0.   NA; Inap.

11   *Generalizer-Particularizer—Suggested Issue*

See deck 01, column 34 for code.

12   *Historical Context—Suggested Issue*

See deck 01, column 35 for code.

13   *Moralizer—Suggested Issue*

See deck 01, column 36 for code.

14   *Utopias—Suggested Issue*

See deck 01, column 37 for code.

15   *Nature of Solution—Suggested Issue*

See deck 01, column 38 for code.

16   *Reference to Ideology—Suggested Issue*

See deck 01, column 39 for code.

17, 18   *Which Ideology—Suggested Issue*

See deck 01, columns 40 and 41 for code.

Column Number	Code
19	*Deductive-Inductive Thinking—Suggested Issue* See deck 01, column 42 for code.
20	*Reference to Group Benefits—Suggested Issue* See deck 01, column 43 for code.
21–22, 23–24, 25–26, 27–28	*What Groups Mentioned—Suggested Issue* See deck 01, columns 44–51 for code.
29	*Acceptability—Suggested Issue* See deck 01, column 52 for code.
30	*Practicality—Suggested Issue* See deck 01, column 53 for code.
31	*Cost—Suggested Issue* See deck 01, column 54 for code.
32	*Tradition—Suggested Issue* See deck 01, column 55 for code.
33	*Conflict of Interest—Suggested Issue* See deck 01, column 56 for code.
34	*Zero-Sum Conflict—Suggested Issue* See deck 01, column 57 for code.
35	*Conflict Resolution—Suggested Issue* See deck 01, column 58 for code.

36   *Suggested Issue Depends on Party*

Q. 11.   "Does the resolution of this problem depend on which party is in power?"

1. Yes, a great deal, and my party would do better.
3. Yes, somewhat and my party would do better.
5. Not much; none.
7. My party might not do better.

MAC———— 8. Other.

0. NA.

37   *Use of "Democracy" in Discussing His Issue*

Qs. 5–9.   How often does the word "democracy" or cognates appear in the discussion of "his" issue?

Code actual number from 0–7.

MAC———— 8. 8 times or more. (MAC for 9 mentions or more)

9. NA

38   *Use of "Democracy" in Discussing Suggested Issue*

Qs. 10–11.   How often does the word "democracy" or cognates appear in the discussion of the "suggested" issue? Use code given for col. 37.

Column
Number   *Code*

39   *Mode of Change Preferred*

Qs. 5–11.   Code on the basis of the entire discussion of issues up to this
point. What is the respondent's apparently preferred mode for political
and social change?
1.   Revolution.
2.   Radical change. (Government makes important changes).
3.   Planned evolution. (Government actively guides natural forces).
4.   Spontaneous evolution. (Government passive; natural social
     forces primary mechanism for change).
5.   No change desired.
0.   NA.

40   *Consultation*

Q. 12.   "If you had the power to take this decision, would you consult
with the various groups involved or do what you think best?"
1.   Definitely consult.
3.   Pro-con. Consult, but go ahead.
5.   Definitely go right ahead.
0.   NA.

41   *Feasibility Question—Where Asked*

Q. 13.   "Are there ever situations in which what's politically feasible has
to take precedence over what's ideally desirable?" *Where* in the interview
was this question asked?
1.   At this point, i.e. immediately after the discussion of issues.
2.   At the end of the interview, i.e. immediately after the questions
     on conflict, cooperation, and compromise (Questions 30–41).
3.   Elsewhere in the interview.
0.   NA. *Not Asked*

42   *Feasibility vs. Desirability*

Q. 13.   What is the respondent's opinion about political feasibility
versus ideal desirability? Use as a continuum.
1.   Political feasibility should never take precedence.
2.   Political feasibility must sometimes take precedence, but this is
     to be regretted; negative aspects emphasized.
3.   Political feasibility may take precedence, but only as a step
     toward the ideal, or with ideals firmly in mind; both positive
     and negative aspects of this are discussed.
4.   Political feasibility should often take precedence; this is not to be
     regretted; positive aspects emphasized.
0.   NA. Coded 0 in col. 41.

43, 44,   *Who Has the Power?*

45   Q. 14.   "In general, who really has the most influence on the outcome of
issues like these we've been discussing?" Code up to 3 mentions, in order
of prominence.

Column
Number   *Code*

45   1.   The Government; the Cabinet; ministers.
Cont.   2.   The party organizations.
            3.   Interest groups in general (*sindacati*) ; pressure groups.
            4.   Economic interests; big business; the monopolies; capitalists.
            5.   The Civil Service; the bureaucracy.
            6.   Parliament.
            7.   The public; the electorate.
            8.   Conservative forces or parties.
MAC————   9.   Other.
            0.   NA.

46   *Power of Government*

            Q. 14. "What is the importance/power of the Government (or Cabinet
            or executive)?" N.B. This question may not have been asked if the answer
            was volunteered. Code only if answer explicitly given. Use code as con-
            tinuum.

            1.   Very important. (Either most important actor mentioned or
                 superlatives used)
            2.   Quite important.
            3.   Some importance. Pro-con.
            4.   Unimportant.
            5.   Very unimportant; no real power.
            0.   NA.

47   *Power of Parliament*

            Q. 14. "What is the importance/power of Parliament and Members of
            Parliament?" Code according to instructions given for col. 46 above.

48   *Power of Bureaucracy*

            Q. 14. "What is the importance/power of the higher-level Civil Service?"
            Code according to instructions given for col. 46 above.

49   *Power of Interest Groups*

            Q. 14. "What is the power/importance of private groups and organiza-
            tions, such as unions or business organizations?" Code according to in-
            structions given for col. 46 above.

50   *Power of Parties*

            Q. 14. "What is the importance/power of the party organizations?"
            Code according to instructions given for col. 46 above.

51   *Power of the Opposition*

            Q. 14. "What is the importance/power of the Opposition(s)?" Code
            according to the instructions given for col. 46 above.

52–53,   *Changes in Power-Pattern*
54–55,   Q. 15. "Do you think there should be any important changes in this
56–57,   pattern of power?" Code any important changes mentioned, *either* in
58–59   response to this question *or* in the earlier discussions of the pattern of

Column
Number   *Code*

52–59   power in response to question 14, if it is clear that changes are proposed.
Cont.   Code up to four mentions, in order of importance where some indication
             is available, in order of mention otherwise.

             Executive-Cabinet

             11.   Technical reorganization of the executive/cabinet (for greater
                    efficiency).
             13.   Increase power of Minister with respect to Civil Servants.
             15.   Increase power or discretion of executive.
             17.   General reform to reduce the power of the executive.
MAC————18.   Other.

             Parliament

             21.   Technical reorganization of Parliament (for greater efficiency).
             22.   General parliamentary reform to increase the importance of
                    Parliament and/or the MP.
             23.   Specialist parliamentary committees.
             24.   More autonomy for MP from party directives; more "free votes."
             25.   More support and staff facilities for MP.
             27.   Increase the power/influence of Opposition.
MAC————28.   Other.

             Parties

             31.   Technical reorganization of the parties (for greater efficiency).
             32.   General reform to reduce the power of the parties.
             33.   Democratize parties.
             34.   Party realignment.
MAC————35.   Change in partisan balance of forces.
             36.   Fewer parties.
             37.   General reform to increase the power of the parties.
MAC————38.   Other.

             Interest Groups

             41.   Technical reorganization of interest groups (for greater effi-
                    ciency).
             42.   Reforms to reduce the influence of all interest groups.
             43.   Reforms to reduce the influence of trade unions.
             44.   Reforms to reduce the influence of business groups.
             45.   More cooperative, effective consultation between interest
                    groups and government.
             46.   Reforms to increase the influence of interest groups in general.
             47.   Reforms to increase the influence of *un-organized* interests.
MAC————48.   Other.

             Bureaucracy

             51.   Technical reorganization of the bureaucracy (for greater effi-
                    ciency).

Column
Number   *Code*

52–59   52.   General reform to reduce the autonomy/influence of the bureau-
Cont.   cracy.
             53.   Introduction of "outsiders" into the bureaucracy.
             54.   Less clientelism or patronage or subjugation of bureaucracy to
                   parties.
             57.   General reform to increase the importance/power of the bureau-
                   cracy.
MAC———58.   Other.

Popular Participation and Decentralization

             61.   Technical changes in the role of the public (for greater efficiency).
             62.   General increase in the power of the people.
             63.   General decentralization of power.
             64.   Strengthening of local government.
             65.   Establishment and/or strengthening of regional government.
             66.   Less secrecy in government—more public awareness of politics
                   and power structure.
             67.   Reform to reduce the influence of the public.
MAC———68.   Other.

Miscellaneous

             85.   *General* improvements in political institutions.
MAC———88.   Other changes not included under general headings above.
             99.   No changes proposed, although the question was asked. Not
                   inconsistent with further codes.
             00.   **NA**

60   *Extent of Changes in Power-Pattern*

             Qs. 14–15.   What is the extent of any changes proposed in the existing
             pattern of power? Code this for all respondents asked Q. 14. Use this code
             as a continuum, not a set of discrete categories.
             1.   Revolutionary (in effect, if not method) changes in the pattern
                  of power.
             2.   Changes involving an important shift in the balance of power
                  relations.
             3.   Changes involving marginal shifts in the balance of power re-
                  lations.
             4.   Technical organizational reforms designed primarily to increase
                  efficiency. No indication of changes in power relations.
             5.   No changes desired.
             0.   NA.

61   *Role of Public—Question Asked*

             Q. 16.   "What do you think is the ideal role of the public in politics?"
             N.B. Code only if asked and answered in this form. Code highest alterna-
             tive possible.

Column
Number   *Code*

61   1.   Voting; choosing leaders.
Cont.   2.   Interest and attention to politics.
               3.   Complaining to leaders; making views known to leaders.
               4.   More active involvement (unspecified).
               5.   Participation in parties or other organizations.
               6.   Direct involvement in government and decision making.
               7.   Active involvement for qualified minority only.
MAC———   8.   Other.
               0.   NA.

62   *More Participation*

               Q. 16.   "Do you think there should be more popular participation in
               politics and government?"
               1.   Yes. This is volunteered or clear from prior answers without the
                     above question being specifically asked.
               3.   Yes. When specifically asked.
               4.   No, except at local level.
               5.   No.
               7.   You can't/won't get more participation.
               0.   NA.

63   *Kind of Greater Participation*

               Q. 16.   If the respondent thinks more participation is desirable, what
               form should it take? Code highest alternative.
               1.   More voting.
               2.   Greater interest and attention to politics.
               3.   More communication to leaders.
               4.   More active involvement in unspecified ways.
               5.   More active participation in parties or other organizations.
               6.   More direct participation in government and decision making.
MAC———   7.   Other.
               8.   More participation *only* at local level.
               9.   Don't know how.
               0.   NA.

64–65,   *Essentials of Democracy*
66–67,
68–69,   Qs. 17–19, esp. Q. 17.   "What are the essentials of a democracy? What
70–71,   are the disadvantages of a democracy? How could this country be more
72–73   democratic?" Code up to five mentions.

               Government by the People
               11.   Government by the people in general; rule of the people; popular
                     power; control by the people. [N.B. This category has a low
                     priority; that is, more specific categories (e.g. categories 12–17)
                     should be used in preference when possible.]
               12.   Popular interest in and awareness of politics.

Column
Number   *Code*

64–73   13.   Responsibility or answerability of the government (or the re-
Cont.   presentative) to the people; government by consent; government
                      based on electoral mandate.

                14.   A dialogue between the government and the people, with both
                      government and people taking an active role in the discussion.

                15.   Popular participation: an active role of the people; popular
                      involvement in decision making; direct democracy.

                16.   Decentralized government; government close to the people.

                17.   Decisions taken in public; no secrecy; public informed about
                      policy; publicity and public debate.

MAC————18.   Other aspects of government by the people.

                   Equality and Social Democracy

                21.   Equality in general.

                22.   Political equality; one man, one vote.

                23.   Equality of opportunity; each person has the opportunity to
                      develop himself as far as possible.

                24.   Just standard of living; freedom from want; social and economic
                      security for all.

                25.   Classless society; less social distance; fewer rich and poor; less
                      social privilege.

                26.   Equality of respect; dignity for all.

                27.   Social ownership/control over the economy; industrial demo-
                      cracy.

MAC————28.   Other aspects of equality and social democracy.

                   Liberty

                31.   Liberty, freedom in general.

                32.   Political or civic liberties in general.

                33.   Freedom of expression (speech, press, etc.)

                34.   Minority rights; consideration of the minority.

                35.   Limited government; dispersion of power; no arbitrary govern-
                      mental power; checks and balances.

                36.   Laissez-faire, socially and economically. Freedom from govern-
                      ment interference in socio-economic affairs.

                37.   Religious liberty; able to practice beliefs.

MAC————38.   Other aspects of liberty.

                   Governmental Institutions and Procedures

                41.   Elections; the vote (N.B. One man, one vote is to be coded under
                      political equality, code "22" above.).

                42.   Majority rule.

                43.   Representative or parliamentary government in general.

                44.   Parliamentary power; parliamentary or legislative control over
                      the executive.

                45.   Administrative due process; possibility of appeal against execu-
                      tive power.

Column	
Number	*Code*

66–73	46.	Constitutionalism; monarchy; hereditary chamber, etc.
Cont.	47.	Rule of law; legal rights; legal incorruptibility; fair legal system.
MAC——48.		Other aspects of governmental institutions and procedures.

Political Competition and Choice

	51.	The possibility of changing the government; an alternative government; non-self-perpetuating government; the minority can become majority.
	52.	Party competition; more than one party; electoral choice.
	54.	Strong, critical opposition.
	55.	Possibility of removing individual executive or representative disapproved by electorate.
	56.	Elected oligarchy; elite competition.
MAC——58.		Other aspects of political competition.

Social Conditions

	61.	Pluralism: a variety of private associations and institutions.
	62.	Consultation by the government with groups and organizations in society.
	64.	Parties as centers of participation and/or channels for expressing popular will.
	65.	Discussion; cooperative communication.
	67.	Pluralism of the press and communications.
MAC——68.		Other aspects of social conditions.

Characteristics of citizens; Morality

	71.	Mature, educated, intelligent, thoughtful citizens.
	72.	Liberty, not license; freedom to do what is right; individual self-control.
	73.	Assumption of responsibility and duties.
	74.	Action in interest of collectivity, not of individuals.
	75.	Reciprocal respect and tolerance.
MAC——78.		Other characteristics of citizens.

Miscellaneous

	81.	Strong, stable, effective, disciplined government.
MAC——88.		Other responses not included under general headings above.
	00.	NA; No further mentions.

| 74–75 | *Rejected Essentials of Democracy* |

Qs. 17–19, esp. Q. 17. Are any characteristics explicitly rejected as not being characteristic of "real" or "true" democracy? Use code outline given for cols. 64–73.

| 76 | *Focus of "Democracy"* |

Qs. 17–19, esp. Q. 17. What is the general focus of his conception of democracy? Use this code as a continuum.

Column Number	Code	
76 Cont.	1.	Wholly instrumental. An exclusive emphasis on democratic methods and institutions.
	2.	Generally instrumental. General emphasis on methods and institutions, but some mention of values and ideals.
	3.	Mixed. Instrumental and normative elements equally important.
	4.	Generally normative. General emphasis on values and ideals, but some mention of methods and institutions.
	5.	Wholly normative. An exclusive emphasis on democratic ideals and values.
	0.	NA.

Column	
Number	*Code*

01–02   *Study Number* (33)

03–04   *Deck Number* (03)

05   *Country*

    1.   Britain

    2.   Italy

06–08   *Respondent Number*

09   *Questionnaire Version*

Repeat code given in deck 01, column 09.

10   *Classical Model of Democracy*

Qs. 17–19, esp. Q. 17.   How prominent is the classical model of democracy, with emphasis on *direct* popular participation and control?

    1.   This is central to his discussion.

    3.   This model appears in his discussion, but is not central.

    5.   Does not appear.

    0.   NA.

11   *Schumpeterian Model of Democracy*

Qs. 17–19, esp. Q. 17.   How prominent is the Schumpeterian model of democracy, with emphasis on competition between several teams of leaders?

Scale as in col. 10.

12   *Liberal Model of Democracy*

Qs. 17–19, esp. Q. 17.   How prominent is the liberal model of democracy, with emphasis on parliament, political liberties and the rule of law?

Scale as in col. 10.

13   *"Social" Model of Democracy*

Qs. 17–19, esp. Q. 17.   How prominent is the "social" model of democracy, with emphasis on social or economic equality and security?

Scale as in col. 10.

Note: Codes of "21" and "23" in the "essentials of democracy" master code, by themselves, justify only a "3" in this column; a code of "22," by itself, justifies only a "5"; codes of "24" to "28" may justify a "1."

14   *Sympathy to Democracy*

Column
Number   *Code*

14   Qs. 17–19.   Is there any indication that he is not wholly sympathetic to
Cont.   "democracy?"
    1.   Yes, seems strongly opposed to "democracy."
    2.   Yes, seems partly opposed to "democracy."
    3.   Approves *his* notion of "democracy," but defines it quite idio-
       syncratically.
    5.   No evidence of lack of sympathy with democracy.
    0.   NA.

15   *Role of Public—Overall Rating*
    Qs. 16–19.   What is his view of the ideal role of the public in politics?
    Note: Code for all respondents asked about democracy. Code from entire
    discussion of democracy and popular participation. Code highest alter-
    native which realistically represents the respondent's view.
    1.   Voting; choosing leaders.
    2.   Interest and attention to politics.
    3.   Complaining to leaders; making views known to leaders.
    4.   More active involvement (unspecified).
    5.   Participation in parties and other organizations.
    6.   Direct involvement in government.
    8.   Favors quite active involvement for some qualified minority;
       favors minimal involvement for the rest of the public.
    9.   More *passive* role; favors *less* involved public.
    0.   NA.

16   *More Democracy?*
    Q. 19.   "Is there some way this country should be more democratic than
    it is now?" How ready is the respondent to support more democratization
    of the country? Use this code as a continuum, not a set of discrete cate-
    gories.
    1.   Demands major change. This is evident from his discussion of
       the meaning of "democracy."
    2.   Ready for important changes. This is evident from his answer
       to Q. 19.
    3.   Ready for modest, but not radical changes.
    4.   Believes that there are no important improvements to be made.
    5.   Somewhat opposed to normal notion of democracy, but proposes
       some changes to improve system.
    6.   There is some evidence that he believes the system is too demo-
       cratic already.
    0.   NA.

17–18,   *How More Democratic*
19–20,   Q. 19.   "How could this country become more democratic?"
21–22   Note: If the respondent has mentioned elsewhere in the interview ways
    in which this country could be more democratic, code these earlier re-
    sponses here as well. This could have arisen:

Column	
Number	*Code*

17–22
Cont.

1. in mentioning "essentials" of democracy which he claims this country does not, but should meet.
2. by referring in his answer to Q. 19 ("How more democratic?") to earlier answers, e.g. in response to Q. 15 (Changes in Pattern of Power). Do *not* code earlier answers of this sort *unless* they are explicitly referred to at this point (Q. 19) in the interview.
3. by *explicitly* justifying, earlier in the interview, some proposed change by reference to the need to improve democracy in this country.

Code up to 3 mentions.

The People and Their Role in Government

11. More popular participation in government or decision making. (N.B. "more voting" alone is coded "19").
12. More popular interest and awareness of politics; informed public; more publicity; less secrecy.
13. Initiative and referendum.
14. Recall.
15. Greater popular control over representatives; more responsive government.
16. More participation in parties, trade unions, etc.
17. More participation in local government.
MAC————18. Other improvements in the role of the people.
19. More voting.

Socioeconomic Reforms

21. General socioeconomic reform; "implementing the Constitution" (when used in broad sense to refer to socioeconomic matters).
22. Abolish the power of monopolies, other privileged groups; make private power more accountable.
23. Public ownership and control of the economy.
24. Educational reform. More and more democratic educational system.
25. Abolish poverty. Freedom from want. Fairer distribution of income; more/better social welfare programs.
26. Jobs; full employment.
27. Workers' control; industrial democracy.
MAC————28. Other socioeconomic reforms.
29. More equality of respect; less class snobbery.

Liberty

31. More liberty in general.
32. More political and civic freedom.
34. More rule of law; administrative redress.
36. Less governmental interference in socioeconomic affairs.
MAC————38. Other.

Governmental Institutions and Procedures

17–22	41.	General improvements in the functioning of government.
Cont.	42.	Devolution; decentralization; regional government.
	43.	More power and influence of Parliament and Members of Parliament; improvements in functioning of Parliament.
	44.	More autonomy of parliamentarians from party controls.
	45.	More elective control of local government and administrative boards; improvements in functioning of local government.
	46.	More democratic electoral system; primary elections; more frequent elections; other electoral changes.
	47.	Reform House of Lords.
MAC———	48.	Other changes in government institutions and procedures.

Partisan Political Changes

	51.	General changes in the partisan system and relations among the parties.
	52.	Increase in power of working class parties.
	53.	Abolishment or limitation of power of the PCI.
	54.	Abolishment or limitation of power of the DC.
	56.	Greater chance for parties alternating in power; greater fluidity in voting.
MAC———	58.	Other partisan, political changes.

Social Conditions

	61.	More pluralism; more "associationism."
	67.	More press pluralism; press less dependent on wealth.
MAC———	68.	Other changes in social conditions.

Moral—Psychological Changes

	71.	More capable, responsible, mature citizens.
	72.	Less corruption; more honesty.
	73.	More respect for authority.
	74.	Less selfishness and more concern for interests of others.
MAC———	78.	Other improvements in individual responsibility or capability.
	88.	Other changes not included under general headings above.
	00.	NA. No further mentions.

23		*Disadvantages of Democracy*

Q. 18.   "What are the disadvantages of a democracy?"
1.   Slowness; inefficiency.
2.   Short-run interests put before long-run interests of the community; unpopular policies dropped.
3.   Need to please special interests; greed (possibly greed of electorate).
4.   Irresponsibility; anarchy; instability; government by committee instead of one person.
5.   Need to oversimplify complex issues; irrationality and ignorance of public.

Column
Number   *Code*

23   6. Apathy.
Cont.   7. Party discipline; influence of parties; *partitocrazia*.
MAC——— 8. Other disadvantages.
                9. *No* disadvantages.
                0. NA.

24–25   *Recall of Name*

Q. 20. "What proportion of your constituents would remember your name?" Code actual percentage, *except*
                01. None.
                97. "Most."
                98. "99%" or "all."
                99. Don't know.
                00. NA.

26   *Attitude to Political System*

Qs. 14–19.   Code on basis of the entire discussion of pattern of power and essentials of democracy. What is the respondent's attitude to the existing political order? (Acceptance or rejection of system depends on the respondent's self-defined position.)
                1. Passionate, total rejection—destruction proposed.
                2. Rejected as a system, but ameliorative reforms proposed.
                3. Accepted as a system, but ameliorative reforms proposed.
                4. Accepted with little inclination for change.
                5. Passionate affirmation of existing system; strong resistance to change.
                0. NA.

27, 28, 29 *Party Differences*

Q. 21. "What are the most important differences between the major parties?" In what terms does he describe the interparty differences? Code up to three modes of description. Where there is some indication of relative importance of the various modes, code according to importance; otherwise according to order of mention.
                1. Ideological: refers explicitly to commitment to particular ideologies, philosophies, or doctrines (e.g. socialism; Catholicism).
                2. Programmatic: refers to socio-political stance (e.g. reformist; "left-right") or socio-political attitudes.
                3. Policies: refers to differences on particular, fairly narrow issues (e.g. Common Market, social security).
                4. Historical: traces historical origins.
                5. Representative: refers to classes or groups represented by or composing parties (e.g. working class).
                6. Capability: refers to ability of leaders, unity of party, "common sense" of party members; openmindedness; adaptability.

Column *Number*	*Code*

7. Stylistic-normative: ideological/principled/doctrinaire vs. pragmatic/opportunist/practical, etc.

8. Commitment to democracy.

MAC———— 9. Other differences.

0. NA.

30   *Abstract Framework for Parties*

Q. 21. Does the respondent have a general theory of history, society and/or politics which he uses to explain the differences among the parties? Use this code as a continuum.

1. Yes. Uses highly abstract general theory as main basis for classifying parties; his classification scheme links politics to a more general theory of society and/or history.

2. Yes. Uses explicit classification scheme which is "expandable"—i.e. could easily accommodate additional "new" parties.

3. Yes. Elements of such a theory, but primarily "static" (i.e. terms —e.g., 'conservative'—used primarily as synonyms for party names, without sense of abstract, expandable scheme).

4. Elements of an abstract theory appear, but use is only implicit.

5. No. Classification of parties done in fairly concrete terms, without use of theoretical abstractions.

0. NA

31   *Extent of Party Differences*

Q. 21 and Q. 22: "All in all, do you think there is a great deal of difference between the parties, some difference, or not much difference?" (Consider the parties *he* defines as "major" parties.) Code on the basis of the description of the differences between the parties, as well as of this specific question. Use this code as a continuum.

1. Very great differences—virtually nothing in common.

2. Very great differences, except for limited group which is closer.

3. Important differences.

4. Important differences, except for limited group which is closer.

5. Marginal, but significant differences, except for limited group which is much farther away.

6. Marginal, but significant differences.

7. Not much difference; no difference—except for limited group which is much father away.

8. Not much difference; no difference.

0. NA.

32   *Extent of Party Differences—Changes*

Q. 23. "Are the differences greater or smaller today than 15 years ago?" If the answer to this question is explicitly given, code it even if this question itself was not explicitly asked.

Column
Number   *Code*

32   1.   Greater.
Cont.   3.   About the same.
                5.   Smaller.
                0.   NA.

33   *Real vs. Perceived Differences*

Qs. 21–23.   Does he make any reference to whether party differences are greater or smaller than "most people think" or "appears on the sur-face?"

                1.   Yes. Actually differences are *greater* than people think.
                5.   Yes. Actually differences are *smaller* than people think.
                0.   NA. No such reference.

34   *Other Parties Endanger Country*

Q. 26.   "Would the policies and activities of a [opposing party] Government ever seriously endanger the country's welfare?" Code only if question actually asked.

                1.   Yes, definitely.
                3.   Yes, but only unintentionally or marginally.
                5.   No.
                0.   NA.

35, 36   *Others' Leaders—Descriptive Mode*

Q. 24.   "What kind of men are the leaders of the other parties?" In what terms does he describe the leaders of the other main parties? Code according to importance when some indication is available; otherwise, code according to mention. Ignore evaluative overtones for this code. Code up to 2 modes of description.

                1.   Ideological: refers to commitment to particular ideology, philosophy, or doctrine.
                2.   Policy: refers to policy or programmatic positions.
                3.   Social Background: refers to occupational, educational, other social background factors.
                4.   Capability: refers to intelligence, common sense, general leadership or executive ability.
                5.   Personality-stylistic: (e.g. doctrinaire, relaxed, etc.)
                6.   Moral-ethical: (e.g. dishonest, demagogues, opportunists).
                7.   Political experience and/or professional commitment to politics.
MAC———— 8.   Other.
                0.   NA.

37   *Others' Leaders—Evaluation*

Q. 24.   To what extent are the leaders of the other party(s) rejected? Use this code as a continuum.

                1.   Basic moral rejection.
                3.   Political rejection (or partial or implicit moral rejection).

Column
Number   *Code*

37   5.   No rejection. Description objective or neutral.
Cont.   0.   NA.

38   *Area of Agreement*

Qs. 21, 22, and Q. 25:   "How much of their program could you personally support?" or "which of the parties do you feel closest to . . . farthest from?" How large is the area of possible agreement or collaboration with partisan opponents? Use this code as a continuum.

1.   Can agree with virtually no opponents on virtually no issues.
2.   Can agree with few opponents on few issues.
3.   Can agree with some opponents on some issues.
4.   Can agree with many opponents on many issues.
5.   Can agree with very many opponents on very many issues.
0.   NA.

39   *Trust Opponents—Question Asked*

Q. 27.   "To what extent can you trust and rely on members of other parties?" What is his personal orientation toward opponents, when dealing with political subjects? Code only if Q. 27 explicitly asked.

1.   Total distrust and rejection.
2.   General distrust and rejection (exceptions made).
3.   Pro-con; noncommital.
4.   General trust, though with reservations.
5.   Trust and acceptance without reservations.
7.   Personal relations are acceptable, but this is politically irrelevant, because party constraints supervene.
8.   Can trust opponents in nonpublic context, but in public they become less trustworthy and reliable.
0.   NA.

40   *Trust Opponents—General Rating*

Qs. 21–27.   Considering the tone of his entire discussion of interparty differences and relations, what is his personal orientation to opponents? Use code as continuum.

1.   Total distrust and rejection.
2.   General distrust and rejection (exceptions made).
3.   Pro-con; noncommital.
4.   General trust and acceptance, though with reservations.
5.   Trust and acceptance without reservations.
0.   NA

41   *Bipartisan Cooperation*

Q. 28.   "Have you ever considered it possible and desirable to cooperate politically with members of other parties?" How often does he (claim to) cooperate *in fact* with opponents? Use this code whenever possible as a continuum.

Column
Number   *Code*
41   1.   Never
Cont.   2.   Infrequently; or only on insignificant issues.
             3.   Often, but only on insignificant issues; occasionally on signi-
                  ficant issues but only with certain groups.
             4.   Occasionally on significant issues; often on significant issues
                  but only with certain groups.
             5.   Often on significant issues.
             0.   NA.

42   *Bipartisan Friendship*

             Q. 29. "Do you have any close friends in other parties?"
             1.   Yes. definitely.
             3.   Yes, but not *close*.
             5.   No.
             0.   NA.

43   *Evil Motives Attributed*

             Qs. 21–29.   How prominently are evil or insidious motives ascribed
             to opposing parties or politicians? Code primarily on the basis of the
             discussion of party differences and relations; striking examples elsewhere in
             the interview are relevant, however. Use code as continuum.
             1.   Frequently. This is a central element of his discussion of parties.
             2.   Occasionally.
             3.   Seldom or only vaguely.
             4.   Never.
             0.   NA.

44   *Version of Conflict Questions*

             Qs. 30 or 36.   With which of the following questions does this section of
             the interview open?
             1.   "What is the most important conflict or controversy you can
                  remember?"
             2.   "Some people say there is always conflict among groups in so-
                  ciety; others say these groups have a great deal in common. What
                  do you think?"
             3.   Some other opening question.
             0.   NA.

45   *Conflict vs. Common Interests*

             Q. 36.   "Some people say there is always conflict among groups in society;
             others say these groups have a great deal in common. What do you think?"
             Use code as a continuum.
             1.   Consensus is by far more typical.
             2.   Consensus basically more typical, though there are some con-
                  flicts.
             3.   Pro-con. Both common; neither clearly more typical.
             4.   Conflict basically typical, but there are some shared interests.

Column
Number   *Code*

45   5.   Conflict is by far more typical.
Cont.   0.   NA.

46   *Class Conflict*

Q. 39. "Do you think that there must be conflict among social classes or can they get along together without conflict?" This question may have been answered explicitly without having been asked explicitly. Use code as continuum.

     1.   Class harmony universally true; no real conflicts of interest.
     2.   Class harmony typical, though there are some conflicts.
     3.   Pro-con.
     4.   Class conflict typical, though there are some common interests.
     5.   Class conflict clear; no common interests.
     0.   NA.

47   *Conflicts Irreconcilable*

Q. 40. "Are conflicts like these generally irreconcilable or not?" If this question was not explicitly asked, do not code unless explicitly answered anyway. Use code as continuum.

     1.   Yes, they are definitely irreconcilable.
     2.   Yes, they are usually irreconcilable.
     3.   Pro-con.
     4.   No. They are usually reconcilable.
     5.   No. They are definitely reconcilable.
     0.   NA.

48   *Conflict vs. Cooperation—Changes*

Qs. 35 or 41. "Has the balance between conflict and cooperation changed much in the last 15 years?"

     1.   Yes. Amount of conflict has increased.
     3.   Pro-con. No change.
     5.   Yes. Amount of cooperation has increased.
     0.   NA.

49–50   *Most Important Controversy*

Q. 30. "What is the most important controversy or conflict you can remember?" Code the first one mentioned.

Italian foreign problems

     11.   NATO Pact; *Patto atlantico.*
MAC———18.   Other Italian foreign policy problems.

Italian Constitutional Problems

     21.   Change from monarchy to republic.
     22.   Majoritarian electoral law; *legge truffa.*
     23.   Implementing the Constitution.
     24.   Tambroni government.
     25.   Law establishing the regional governments.
MAC———28.   Other Italian institutional problems.

Column
Number   *Code*
49–50   Italian Partisan Political Problems
Cont.
      31.   Formation of the *centro-sinistra.*
      32.   Trade union unity.
      33.   Election of Saragat.
      34.   Antifascism after 1943.
      35.   Anti-Stalinist struggle within PCI.
MAC————38.   Other Italian partisan political problems.

Italian Domestic Problems
      41.   General social philosophy.
      42.   Education; *la scuola.*
      43.   *Riforma fondiario;* land reform.
      44.   Divorce law
      45.   *Diritto di famiglia* [family law].
      46.   Church-State.
MAC————48.   Other Italian domestic problems.

British Foreign Problems.
      51.   Suez.
      52.   The Common Market; "Europe."
      53.   Pre-World War II diplomacy; Munich.
      54.   Defense policy.
      55.   German rearmament.
      56.   Rhodesia.
      57.   Imperial status (pre- and post-WW II).
MAC————58.   Other British foreign problems.

British Institutional or Partisan Political Problems
      61.   Bevanite disputes within Labour Party.
      62.   Profumo case.
MAC————68.   Other British institutional or partisan problems.

British Domestic Problems
      71.   General social philosophy (free enterprise vs. socialism).
      72.   Nationalization of the steel industry.
      73.   Nationalization of other industries; nationalization battles in general.
      74.   National Health Service.
      75.   Selwin Lloyd's "pay pause."
      76.   General Strike of 1926.
      77.   Resale Price Maintenance.
MAC————78.   Other British domestic problems.
      88.   Any controversies not included in general headings above.
      99.   Don't know. Question asked, but not answered.
      00.   NA.

51   *Mentions Intra-Party Dispute*
      Q. 30.   Does the respondent mention an intraparty or cross-party dispute in reply to this question?

Column
Number   *Code*

51   1.   Yes.
Cont.   3.   He begins by asking whether interviewer wants intraparty disputes.
         5.   No.
         7.   Before he answers the question, the interviewer phrases the question so as to exclude intraparty or cross-party disputes.
         0.   NA.

52   *Compromiser*

Qs. 31–32. "Would you generally [N.B., not just in this particular case] be inclined to stick to your guns or to look for a compromise?" Use code as a continuum.
         1.   Definitely would look for compromise.
         2.   Leans to compromise.
         3.   Pro-con. It depends. (No indication of propensity.)
         4.   Leans to sticking to guns.
         5.   Definitely would stick to guns.
         0.   NA.

53   *Conflicts vs. Collaboration*

Q. 34. "Which is more typical of your experience: conflicts like these or collaboration on some common purpose?" Use code as continuum.
         1.   Definitely collaboration more typical.
         2.   Usually collaboration, though conflicts not rare.
         3.   Pro-con. It depends.
         4.   Usually conflict, though collaboration not rare.
         5.   Definitely conflict more typical.
         0.   NA.

54   *Conflict vs. Consensus—General View*

Qs. 30–41. Considering his entire discussion of conflict and cooperation in this section of the interview, how prominent is conflict of interest in his view of politics? Use code as a continuum, not a set of discrete categories.
         1.   He sees virtually no real conflict of interest in politics.
         2.   He sees some conflict of interest, but conflict is generally deemphasized and clearly overshadowed by cooperation.
         3.   Pro-con. He sees both conflict of interest and areas of cooperation. These seem equally important.
         4.   Conflict of interest is more typical of politics as he sees it. This conflict is, however, limited and reconcilable, so that cooperation is possible.
         5.   Conflict of interest is dominant of his view and difficult to reconcile, but it is possible to reach a modus vivendi.
         6.   Conflict of interest is dominant of his view and is irreconcilable. Cooperation is rarely, if ever, possible.
         0.   NA.

Column
Number   *Code*

55   *Actual Versus Necessary Conflict*

Qs. 30–41.   To what extent does the respondent distinguish between the actual amount of conflict presently characteristic of society and politics in his country and the amount of conflict of interest which is in principle logically necessary? That is, to what extent does he assert that there is presently more conflict than there need be, that some of the present "conflictful behavior" is not based on real conflict of interest, but is artificial or unnecessary?

1.   Makes this distinction explicitly. There is much more conflict than there need be.
2.   Makes this distinction explicitly. There is some more.
3.   Makes this distinction implicitly. There is much more conflict than there need be.
4.   Makes this distinction implicitly. There is some more.
5.   Does not make this distinction.
0.   NA.

56–57,   *Leadership Traits*
58–59,
60–61,   Qs. 46–47.   "How would you describe the job of a party leader? What
62–63,   personal qualities must he have?" Read this entire section on leadership
64–65,   before coding the following items. What attributes (or tasks or traits)
66–67   does he stress for a party leader? Code up to six mentions, according to
             the following comprehensive code. Where there is some indication of the
             relative importance the respondent attributes to the various traits, code
             in order of importance. Where there is no such indication, code in order
             of mention.

Policy-Making
11.   Develops policies and programs.
12.   Makes decisions; decision-making capacity; personal involvement in decision-making.
13.   Develops general, "grand" strategy for party.
15.   Gathers, interprets, and expresses popular needs and desires.
17.   Capacity for synthesis—putting various problems together, ordering priorities; a generalist.

MAC————18.   Other.

Intellectual Tasks and Qualities
21.   General intellectual qualities; intelligence; imagination; ability.
22.   Clear ideas; knowledge of problems; (emphasis on *knowledge*).
23.   Practicality; common sense; wisdom; judgment.
24.   Understanding of contemporary society and/or politics; interpretation or vision of society and politics.
25.   Knows, develops, and applies party ideology, doctrine, or philosophy.
26.   General cultural preparation.
27.   Sense or knowledge of history; takes long view; has vision.

Column
Number   Code
56–67
Cont.
MAC————28.   Other.

Commitment to Party

31.   Loyalty or commitment to party's traditions and/or principles.
32.   Long experience in the party.
33.   Respects, defends, executes policies determined by party.
34.   Interprets and expresses general will of party.

MAC————38.   Other

Moral Qualities and Character

41.   Physical and mental stamina and toughness.
42.   Courage; willingness to take unwelcome decisions; firmness, ruthlessness.
43.   Personal integrity; honesty; sincerity.
44.   Passion and self-sacrifice; commitment to ideals; moral conviction.
45.   Patience; calm; equilibrium; detachment.
46.   Responsibleness; seriousness; prudence.
47.   Modesty; sense of own limitations.

MAC————48.   Other.

Public Stature and Charismatic Qualities

51.   General charisma; magnetism; personal dominance; prestige.
52.   Inspires respect and confidence in party supporters and colleagues.
53.   Inspires respect and confidence in the nation as a whole.
54.   Close personal ties with "the people," the masses, the common people; "a man of the people."
55.   Ability to communicate; good on TV or public platform.
56.   "Teacher of nation;" leads public opinion.
57.   Good family background.

MAC————58.   Other.

Organizational Tasks and Qualities

61.   General organizing or administrative ability.
62.   Keeps party organization in good shape.
63.   Maintains good set of expert advisers.
64.   Maintains good team of lieutenants; delegates authority well.
65.   Deals with (or good at) tactical political questions: alliances, day-to-day maneuvers, etc.
66.   Wins. (elections, etc.)
67.   Keeps in touch with supporters and members.

MAC————68.   Other.

Sociability and Conciliatory Tasks and Qualities

71.   Friendly; personable: good mixer; sense of humor; tactful; understands people (on personal basis); openness.

Column
Number   *Code*

56–67   72.   Loyal; fair; just.
Cont.   73.   Good working relations with colleagues and supporters.
               74.   Persuasive; establishes consensus around him.
               75.   Sensitive to party feelings; "political sixth sense."
               76.   Unites, welds together, synthesizes party. *No* reference specifically to intraparty differences or factions. Reference is to programmatic unity.
               77.   Unites, welds together, synthesizes party. Respondent makes specific reference to differing opinions or factions within party. Reference is to programmatic unity.
MAC———78.   Other.
               79.   Organizes and runs party democratically (not autocratically).
               Miscellaneous
               81.   Seeks national interest above sectional interest.
MAC———88.   Other tasks or qualities not included under general headings given above.
               99.   Don't know.
               00.   NA. No further mentions.

68   *Problem-Solving Traits*

               Qs. 46–47.   Does he mention policy-making, problem-solving, or decision-making attributes?
               1.   Yes, prominently.
               3.   Yes, but only vaguely or in passing.
               5.   No.
               0.   NA.

69   *Intellectual Traits*

               Qs. 46–47.   Does he mention intellectual or ideological or cultural attributes? (Note: Codes 21, 22, or 23 in comprehensive leadership code above justify only a '3' rating here.
               Scale as in col. 68.

70   *Moral-Character Traits*

               Qs. 46–47.   Does he mention moral or character attributes? Note: Codes 41 and 45 in the comprehensive leadership code above justify only a '3' rating here.
               Scale as in col. 68.

71   *Public Stature Traits*

               Qs. 46–47.   Does he mention charismatic or public stature attributes? Note: Codes 54 and 55 in the comprehensive leadership code above justify only a '3' rating here.
               Scale as in col. 68.

72   *Organizational Traits*

               Qs. 46–47.   Does he mention technical, administrative, or organizational

Column
Number   Code

72   attributes? N.B. Certain responses coded '11' above (policy making), if
Cont.   phrased in terms of technique, could justify a '1' or '3' here. Responses
            dealing with public relations ('55' above) justify at least a '3' here.

            Scale as in col. 68.

73   *Conciliation Traits*

            Qs. 46–47. Does he mention conciliation attributes? Note: Codes of 71,
            72, or 73 in the comprehensive leadership code above justify no more than
            a '3' rating here.

            Scale as in col. 68.

74   *Party Loyalty Traits*

            Qs. 46–47. Does he mention party loyalty attributes? Note: A code of 31
            in the comprehensive leadership code justifies a '1' here. Codes of 32, 25,
            75, 76, or 77 could justify a '1' or '3' here, if reference is made to party
            loyalty. Note that this item refers to a characteristic of the party *leader;*
            ignore references to a need for loyalty from his supporters.

            Scale as in col. 68.

75   *Leader-Follower Relations*

            Qs. 48–49. "What are the obligations and responsibilities of the leader to
            his supporters? What are the obligations and responsibilities of the sup-
            porters to the party leader?" Code if explicitly answered. In the re-
            spondent's discussion of these questions, is his emphasis on the obligations
            of supporters to the leader or on the obligations of the leader to the sup-
            porters? Is the emphasis on communication and demands flowing upward
            to the leader from the followers or downward from the leader to the fol-
            lowers? Use this code as a continuum.

            1.   Great emphasis on obligations of supporters to leader, on need
                 for absolute loyalty; no mention of constraints on leader.
            2.   Primary emphasis on obligations of supporters to leader, but
                 some statement of obligations of leader to consider desires of
                 followers.
            3.   Pro-con. Equal emphasis on obligations of leaders and followers.
            4.   Primary emphasis on leader's obligation to followers, to consider
                 their desires and carry out their wishes. Leader allowed some
                 latitude for free action, however, and followers supposed to give
                 (conditional) loyalty.
            5.   Heavy emphasis on obligation of leader to followers and their
                 right to control him. Leader merely an agent of the party. Follow-
                 ers have no obligation of loyalty if they disagree with the
                 leader.
            0.   NA.

76   *Political Liberties*

            Q. 50. "Some people say that certain organizations engage in unfair
            or illegitimate or dangerous tactics. . . . Do you think there should be

Column
Number   *Code*

76   more controls over such activity?" What is his general orientation to
Cont.   controls over radical or subversive political activity? Use this code as a
             continuum, not a set of discrete categories.

1.   He is quite willing to impose stringent and far-reaching con-
     trols.
2.   He is willing to consider some limits on such activity. There is
     no reference to the need to protect political freedom.
3.   Pro-con. He refers to the need to protect political freedom, but
     also refers to certain definite limits which should be imposed.
4.   He is generally opposed to limits, though certain minor excep-
     tions are made. Reference to political liberties may be made.
5.   No limits on such activity proposed, but no reference is made to
     the need to protect political liberties.
6.   He is opposed to any limits on such activity, and refers to the
     need to protect political liberties.
8.   No discussion of controls on political liberties.
0.   NA.

77   *Rejection of Future Question*

Q. 42.   "How would the society you'd like to see for your children differ from that of today?" To what extent does he object to or refuse to
answer this question, for example on the ground that it is difficult, or
impossible, or unhelpful to discuss the future?

1.   Clearly objects.
3.   Weakly or vaguely objects.
5.   No objection.
0.   NA.

N.B. Substantive codes for this question begin in Deck 04, column 10–21.

Column Number	Code
01–02	*Study Number* (33)
03–04	*Deck Number* (04)
05	*Country*

    1.   Britain
    2.   Italy

06–08	*Respondent Number*
09	*Questionnaire Version*

Repeat code given in deck 01, column 09.

10–11,	*Desires for the Future*
12–13,	Qs. 42–43. "How would the society you'd like to see for your children
14–15,	differ from that of today? What practical changes would be necessary to
16–17,	reach that sort of society?" Code up to six mentions.
18–19,	
20–21	

Political-Governmental Changes

11. Democracy.
12. Parliamentary democracy; plural party system; effective two-party system.
13. Decentralization and devolution.
14. Increased popular political participation and involvement.
15. Freedom of political expression and association.
16. Greater equality of influence; limit power of the powerful.
17. More modern, efficient, reformed state and governmental structures.

MAC————18. Other.

Social Justice and Equality

21. Greater social justice, fairness, equality in general; economic democracy.
22. Socialist society; end or limitation of capitalist system.
23. *Equality* of opportunity; emphasis on equal chances. (N.B. Where "equality of opportunity" emphasis falls on opportunity for advancement without hindrance, response should be coded '33' below.) Each person can develop own talents and personality.

291

Column
Number   *Code*

10–21   24.   Less social privilege; fewer extremes of wealth; less exploitation.
Cont.   25.   Less snobbery; more equality of respect; dignity.
              26.   Fewer territorial and sectoral inequalities.
              27.   Social welfare, social security, social assistance programs for the
                    weak or unfortunate.
MAC————28.   Other.

              Liberty

              31.   Greater liberty, freedom in general.
              32.   Capitalist economic system; private enterprise.
              33.   Opportunity for advancement; no restrictions on individual
                    achievement and acquisitions; reduce taxes.
              34.   Individual self-sufficiency and responsibility.
              35.   Freedom of choice.
              36.   Pluralism; wide variety of social associations allowed and
                    encouraged.
              37.   Rule of law; less arbitrary government interference; fairer legal
                    system.
MAC————38.   Other.

              Morality

              41.   Less moral laxity; less crime, pornography, etc.; more discipline.
              42.   Greater religious faith; personal creed.
              43.   Better family relations; protect the family.
              44.   Less materialism; more spiritual and moral concern.
              45.   Sense of purpose; national goals.
              46.   More mature, responsible citizens, cognizant of obligations to
                    the collectivity, putting public interest before private interest.
              47.   More tolerant, humanist society; less restrictive, clerical, paro-
                    chial society.
MAC————48.   Other.

              Material-physical welfare

              51.   Higher standard of living; economic progress; more wealth.
              52.   Technological advancement; greater socioeconomic efficiency.
              53.   More jobs; full employment; good working conditions.
              54.   Less (or absence of) poverty; higher salaries.
              55.   Better pensions; care for elderly.
              56.   Better health care.
              57.   Better housing; fewer slums.
MAC———— 58.   Other.

              Knowledge-culture

              61.   General intellectual improvement.
              62.   More and better education.
              63.   More and better cultural opportunities and culture.

Column
Number   *Code*

10–21   64.   More leisure time; fewer working hours.
Cont.   65.   Openness to new ideas.
MAC————68.   Other.

Security-safety-sense of community

71.   Security; *la certezza del domani;* tranquillity; stability.
73.   Sense of community, cooperativeness, fraternity.
74.   More compassionate, charitable, loving, kindly society; less acquistive, competitive, selfish society.
75.   Greater consensus and reciprocal understanding.
76.   Greater social participation.
77.   Retention of national heritage and traditions.

MAC————78.   Other.

Miscellaneous

81.   Vibrant, resilient, adventurous, conflictful society full of ferment.
82.   Western (or Anglo-Saxon) society.
83.   City planning; urban development.
84.   Husbanding national resources; economizing on national expenditures.
85.   Solving population problems.
86.   Dealing with immigration problems.

MAC————88.   Other changes not included in general headings given above.
00.   NA; no further mentions.

22   *Image of Future—Generalizer-Particularizer*

See Deck 01, column 34 for code.

23   *Change Desired for Future*

Qs. 42–43.   How much change does he desire for the future? Use this code as a continuum.
1.   Major changes in the structure of society, revolutionary in effect, if not method.
2.   Important changes.
3.   Minor changes.
4.   No change.
0.   NA.

24.   *Optimism*

Q. 44.   "How much progress toward such a society is realistically likely? Are you basically optimistic or pessimistic?"
1.   Optimistic.
3.   Pro-con; neutral.
5.   Pessimistic.
0.   NA.

25   *Growth vs. Welfare*

Q. 45. "If you had to make a choice, would you opt for faster economic
growth or more equal distribution of wealth and income?"
    1. Definitely faster growth.
    2. Probably faster growth [or growth to get equality].
    3. Pro-con.
    4. Probably equal distribution.
    5. Definitely equal distribution.
    0. NA.

NOTE: The following items are to be coded on the basis of the *entire*
        interview.

26   *Dichotomous Thinking*

To what extent does this respondent display a dichotomous view of reality:
society-and-politics is a frontal struggle between two hostile forces, one
wholly good, one wholly evil, without possibility of mediation?
    1. Very frequently. This view prevades his discussion.
    3. Occasionally.
    5. Almost never.
    0. NA.

27   *Left-Right Spectrum*

Where does this respondent stand on a left-right dimension? Code as a
continuum.
    1. For much more state involvement and/or social provision.
    2. For some more state involvement and/or social provision.
    3. For the present balance.
    4. For some more free enterprise and/or individual initiative.
    5. For much more free enterprise and/or individual initiative.
    0. NA.

28   *Legalist Role*

In terms of his focus of attention and role perceptions (i.e. "my job is to
. . . ") to what extent is this respondent a "legalist," focusing on legal and
legislative processes?
    1. Very much.
    3. Somewhat.
    5. Very little.
    0. NA.

29   *Tribune Role*

In terms of his focus of attention and role perceptions, to what extent is
this respondent a "tribune," focusing on protesting injustice and fighting
for the interests of a social group, class, or cause?
Scale as in col. 28.

Column
Number   *Code*

30   *Technician Role*

In terms of his focus of attention and role perceptions, to what extent is this respondent a "technician-inventor," focusing on solving technical policy-problems?

Scale as in col. 28.

31   *Broker Role*

In terms of his focus of attention and role perceptions, to what extent is this respondent a "political broker," focusing on resolving social and political conflicts?

Scale as in col. 28.

32   *Ombudsman Role*

In terms of his focus of attention and role perceptions, to what extent is this respondent an "ombudsman," focusing on protecting and defending the interests of individual constituents?

Scale as in col. 28.

33   *Trustee Role*

In terms of his focus of attention and role perceptions, to what extent is this respondent a "trustee," focusing on defending the national interest?

Scale as in col. 28.

34   *Bystander Role*

In terms of his focus of attention and role perceptions, to what extent is this respondent a "bystander," focusing on observing the political drama around him?

Scale as in col. 28.

35   *"Advertiser" Role*

In terms of his focus of attention and role perceptions, to what extent is this respondent an "advertiser," focusing on social prestige or political advancement?

Scale as in col. 28.

36   *Leadership-Public Gap*

Does he ever refer in the course of the interview to some gulf or gap or alienation between political leaders or governmental institutions and the public?
    1.   Yes, explicitly.
    3.   Yes, but only vaguely or in passing.
    5.   No.
    0.   NA.

37   *"Ideology" Reaction*

What is his orientation to the term "ideology" or cognates, such as "ideological?"
    1.   Term is used and favorably evaluated.

Column
Number   *Code*

37   3.   Term is used and neutrally evaluated; no clear evaluation.
Cont.   5.   Term is used and negatively evaluated.
              9.   Term is not used.
              0.   NA.

38   *Cynicism*

              Does he ever refer in the course of the interview to some disparity which
              he alleges or implies to exist between the words of (some) politicians and
              their actions or true intentions?
              1.   Yes, clearly and explicitly.
              3.   Yes, but only vaguely or in passing.
              5.   No.
              0.   NA.

39   *Tolerance of Ideas*

              How reluctant is he to entertain opinions contrary to his own? How tol-
              erant is he of opposing opinions? (Do *not* consider in this code his re-
              sponse to Q. 50, on political liberties.)
              1.   Very intolerant; very reluctant to entertain different ideas.
              3.   Somewhat intolerant; generally, but not always rejects op-
                   posing ideas.
              5.   Tolerant; not reluctant to consider opposing ideas.
              0.   NA.

40   *Party Orthodoxy*

              What is the apparent relationship between his ideas and those of others
              in his party?
              1.   Differs explicitly (at least once) from others in his party.
              5.   Claims identity of views with the other members of his party at
                   least once. [*Not* when asked about party position.]
              8.   Does *both* at least once.
              0.   NA.

41   *Cabalism*

              How prominent are cabalistic interpretations of politics in this interview?
              (A cabal is a small, well-defined group of people who control all important
              social and political decisions in their own interests.)
              1.   Very prominent. This theme pervades many discussions in the
                   interview.
              3.   Somewhat prominent. This theme appears occasionally in the
                   interview.
              5.   Absent. This theme does not appear in the interview.
              0.   NA.

42   *Attitude to Social System*

              What is this respondent's general attitude to the existing socioeconomic
              order?

Column
Number   Code

42   1.   Passionate, total rejection—destruction proposed.
Cont.   2.   Rejected, but ameliorative reforms proposed.
           3.   Accepted, but ameliorative reforms proposed.
           4.   Accepted; no important reforms proposed.
           5.   Passionate affirmation of existing order or demands movement
                to preexisting order.
           0.   NA.

43   *Conceptual Scheme*

           Does this respondent thave a single, simplified conceptual explanatory
           schema which he applies to all discussion of political issues? Do all
           his discussions of politics revert to a single, fairly coherent set of concepts?
           Use as a continuum.
           1.   Yes, definitely.
           2.   [Intermediate high].
           3.   Yes, frequently. Many, though not all discussions are phrased
                in terms of such a schema, but it is not tightly integrated and
                highly simplified.
           4.   [Intermediate low].
           5.   No. Issues and topics discussed in a variety of frameworks. No
                single theme dominates discussion.
           0.   NA.

44   *Interviewer*

           Who was the interviewer for this respondent?
           1.   Putnam.
           2.   Poulter.
           3.   Mastropaolo.

45   *Where Interviewed*

           Where did the bulk of the interview take place?
           1.   A public room at the Parliament.
           2.   A private room at the Parliament.
           3.   His office.
           4.   His home.
           5.   His hotel.
           6.   A restaurant.
           7.   Parliamentary party headquarters.
           8.   Constituency headquarters.
           0.   NA.

46   *When Interviewed*

           What was the month of the interview (of the first meeting, if more than
           one)?
           1.   February 1967.
           2.   March 1967.

Column Number	Code

46 Cont.	3. April 1967.
	4. May 1967.
	5. October 1967.
	6. November 1967.
	7. December 1967.
	8. January 1968.
	9. February 1968.
	0. March 1968.

47–48   What day of the month did the (first) interview occur on? Code actual date.

49   *Frankness*

How frank was the respondent?

1. Very frank and open.
2. Basically frank.
3. Pro-con.
4. Basically reserved.
5. Very reserved and closed.
0. NA.

50–51   *Party Membership*

What party is he a member of?

11. Labour
12. Liberal
13. Conservative
21. PCI
22. PSIUP
23. PSI
24. PSDI
25. PRI
26. DC
27. PLI
28. PDIUM
29. MSI
30. Rightist independent
31. SVP (Alto Adige)

52   *Simplified Party Membership*

1. Labour
2. Conservative
3. PCI
4. PSIUP
5. PSI-PSDI
6. DC
7. PLI

Column
Number   *Code*

52   8.   Other Italian Right: MSI; PDIUM; independent
Cont.   9.   Other (British Liberal; PRI; SVP)

53–54   *Length of Interview*

How long is the transcript? Code actual number of pages, rounded to the nearest whole page.

55   *Coder*

Who was the auxiliary coder?

1.   Giacomo Costa
2.   Peter DiLorenzi
3.   Hugh Grambau
4.   Sally Rentschler

56–58   *Rank Order of Interview in Coding Process.*

Code the position of this interview in the coding process; e.g. if it was the first done, code "001."

Column
Number   *Code*

01–02   *Study Number* (33)

03–04   *Deck Number* (05)

05   *Country*
             1.   Britain
             2.   Italy

06–08   *Respondent Number*

09–10   *Number of Questionnaire Items Answered*

Code actual number of items completed on the written questionnaire. If questionnaire was not filled out, code "00" here and code "0" in columns 11–40 of this deck.

11   Most politicians can be trusted to do what they think is best for the country.
             1.   Agree strongly
             3.   Agree
             7.   Disagree
             9.   Disagree strongly
             0.   NA

12   Certain people are better qualified to run this country, because of their traditions and family background.
             Scale as in col. 11.

13   To compromise with our political opponents is dangerous because it usually leads to the betrayal of our own side.
             Scale as in col. 11.

14   Any government that wants to help the poor people will have to take something away from the rich in order to do it.
             Scale as in col. 11.

15   I don't mind a politician's methods if he manages to get the right things done.
             Scale as in col. 11.

16   Groups of citizens have a perfect right to lobby for legislation which would benefit them personally.
             Scale as in col. 11.

Column Number	Code
17	A few strong leaders would do more for this country than all the laws and talk.
	Scale as in col. 11.
18	Those who get ahead usually get ahead at the expense of others.
	Scale as in col. 11.
19	No one is going to care much what happens to you when you get right down to it.
	Scale as in col. 11.
20	It is only when a person devotes himself to an ideal or cause that life becomes meaningful.
	Scale as in col. 11.
21	People ought to be allowed to vote even if they cannot do so intelligently.
	Scale as in col. 11.
22	The ends and the objectives of political ideology are much more important than the manner and the methods used to attain them.
	Scale as in col. 11.
23	Unless there is freedom for many points of view to be presented there is little chance that the truth can ever be known.
	Scale as in col. 11.
24	A group which tolerates too much difference of opinion among its own members cannot exist for very long.
	Scale as in col. 11.
25	Few people really know what is in their own best interest in the long run.
	Scale as in col. 11.
26	It's no use giving some children an expensive education because they're just not able to benefit from it.
	Scale as in col. 11.
27	In this complicated world the only way we can know what is going on is to rely on leaders or experts who can be trusted.
	Scale as in col. 11.
28	Of all the different philosophies which exist in the world, there is only one which is true.
	Scale as in col. 11.
29	Every citizen should have an equal chance to enfluence government policy.
	Scale as in col. 11.
30	Pressure groups and special interests, like trade unions, commercial associations, professional organizations, and so on, hamper the proper working of government.
	Scale as in col. 11.

Column	
Number	*Code*

31   If you don't watch yourself, people will take advantage of you.

Scale as in col. 11.

32   Generally speaking, in political controversies extreme positions should be avoided, for the proper approach usually lies somewhere in the middle.

Scale as in col. 11.

33   The best advice on a proposed policy usually comes from the interests directly affected.

Scale as in col. 11.

34   People who go into public office usually think of the good of the people more than of their own.

Scale as in col. 11.

35   When an individual or group gains, it usually means that another individual or group loses.

Scale as in col. 11.

36   To bring about great changes for the benefit of mankind often requires cruelty and even ruthlessness.

Scale as in col. 11.

37   There are a number of people I have come to hate because of the things they stand for or believe in.

Scale as in col. 11.

38   It will always be necessary to have a few strong, able people actually running everything.

Scale as in col. 11.

39   Politics is "the art of the possible" and political leaders should not worry about grand plans and distant ideals.

Scale as in col. 11.

40   Does he object to the questionnaire item about "politics is the art of the possible" (column 39) on the grounds that the two clauses are not incompatible?

        1.   Yes.
        5.   No.
        0.   NA; Inap.

Index

Acquiescence response set, 24, 199*n*
Adams, John Clarke, 211*n*
Adelson, Joseph, 134*n*, 142*n*
Adorno, T. W., 24*n*
Age: impact on attitudes, 64, 66–68, 140–41, 180–81, 192, 238; and egalitarianism, 220–25. *See also* Generations, political; Life cycle
Alienation, political, 52*n*, 194, 278, 296–97; and questionnaire response, 20; and ideological style, 50–52. *See also* Political institutions, evaluations of
Almond, Gabriel, 2*n*, 84*n*, 97*n*, 156*n*, 231, 235*n*
Anderson, C. A., 138*n*
Anton, Thomas J., 76*n*
Apter, David E., 33*n*, 78*n*, 81*n*
Aristotle, 27*n*, 93, 161
Aron, Raymond, 33*n*
Aronson, Elliot, 69*n*
Asch, Solomon, 126
Authoritarian democracy. *See* Democracy, conceptions of: authoritarian
Authoritarianism, 56, 71. *See also* Dogmatism
Authority, attitudes toward. *See* Equality, political; Leader-follower relations; Participation, political
Axelrod, Robert, 95, 96

Bagehot, Walter, 85, 148*n*
Barber, James David, 3*n*
Barile, Paolo, 211*n*
Barker, Anthony, 191*n*
Barnes, Samuel H., 31*n*, 45*n*, 49*n*, 79*n*, 135*n*, 138*n*, 235*n*
Beardsley, Monroe C., 82*n*
Beer, Samuel H., 121*n*, 164, 165*n*, 215
Behavior, 2–3; and attitudes, 22*n*, 25–27
Bell, Daniel, 33*n*, 211*n*
Bell, Wendell, 3*n*
Beller, D. C., 75*n*
Bentham, Jeremy, 162

Bergmann, Gustav, 32*n*
Beveridge, William H. (Lord), 143
Birch, A. H., 163, 165, 233
Blackmer, Donald L. M., 217*n*
Blalock, Hubert M., Jr., 133*n*
Blau, Peter, 138*n*
Bosanquet, Bernard, 95
Bottomore, T. B., 1*n*
Braibanti, Ralph, 32*n*
Braybrooke, David, 76*n*
Britain: conduct of study in, 8, 18; compared with Italy, 9, 78–88 passim, 137–40, 146–49, 182–95 passim, 198–203, 208–12, 227–29, 239; history, 9, 87, 139, 142–45, 164–65; economic growth and stability, 9, 137–39, 142–45; contemporary politics, 9–10; sample, 12–18; political recruitment in, 13–14, 221–22; dimensions of political style, 44; age, ISI and IPH in, 65–68; partisan hostility in, 67–68, 87; policy making in, 77, 151; education and political advancement, 80*n*; legal tradition, 81; political development in, 83, 231; attitudes toward class conflict, 103–04; latent issue conflict in, 112; views on poverty, 113; age and attitude to social conflict in, 140–41; social conflict in, 142–45; attitudes toward democracy, 166–68, 171, 180–81, 182–95 passim; attitude toward parliamentary reform, 190–92; attitudes toward equality, 198, 200, 202, 215, 227–29; support for political liberty, 209–12 227–29; age and egalitarianism in, 221–22, 224–25; uses of democratic concepts in, 230–31, 233
Buck, Philip W., 13*n*
Budge, Ian, 160*n*
Bureaucracy, 12, 13, 116, 191 194,
Burke, Edmund, 94
Burks, R. V., 32*n*
Butler, David, 65*n*, 131*n*, 138*n*, 151*n*

Cabinet, 13. *See also* Government

Yale Studies in Political Science